Understanding Arabs: A Contemporary Guide to Modern Society

Sixth Edition Praise:

"This book is so much more than an academic work on Arabs and their culture. Dr. Nydell brings her professional experiences in academics, language, culture, business and diplomacy together in this 6th Edition to the benefit of her readers who travel, vacation or do business in the Arab world. The revisions in this edition add additional clarity to recent events in the Middle East and enhance the book's ability to prepare readers for their travels or business. I continue to recommend Understanding Arabs to my students, colleagues and my clients who need to understand the nuances of travel in that part of the world."

—F. Rusty Capps, Former FBI Supervisory Special Agent, Adjunct Professor at Radford University and President, CT/CI Training Partners LLC, Lexington, Virginia

Praise for the Fifth Edition:

"Margaret Nydell blends her informed understanding of Arab history and contemporary politics with deep and thoughtful insight into Arab culture and psychology. Many authors know much about the former, and a few know much about the latter, but only *Understanding Arabs* conveys a deep understanding of the synergies of both. This is essential reading for those working in—or with—Arab countries, or seeking to understand Arab society."

—Lawrence R. Velte Associate Professor of Near East South Asia Center for Strategic Studies, National Defense University, and Associate, Washington Center for Protocol, Inc.

"This book is a must-read for anyone wanting to comprehend the Middle East. The writing is fluid, full of examples, and updated to include the Arab Spring. Dr. Nydell, a world renowned linguist with decades of practical experience in the field, is an authoritative voice. She provides profound insights into Arabs' perceptions underlying political events, and our interactions with each other."

—Elizabeth McKune, Executive Director, Sultan Qaboos Cultural Center, and Former US Ambassador to the State of Qatar

"For her understanding of the Arab mind, her expertise in teaching, and her skill in crafting this book, Dr. Nydell is truly a national treasure. *Understanding Arabs* should be required reading for any professional or policy maker who is involved in any way with working with Arabs or on matters impacting the Middle East."

—F.L. Rusty Capps, Former FBI Supervisory Special Agent, and President of Counterterrorism, Counterintelligence Training Partners LLC.

"This is an important and fascinating book, especially for Americans in the crucial time in U.S.-Arab relations. Dr. Nydell presents a timely, lucid, and engaging guide to the values and cultures of the Arab world, based on her many years of working and living there, and on her training as a professional linguist. This candid and wonderfully readable book captures the contrasts and the characteristics of this great civilization and brings them vividly to life for a Western audience."

—Karin Ryding, PhD, Sultan Qaboos bin Said Professor of Arabic, and Chair of the Department of Arabic Language, Georgetown University

"Still the only volume of its kind. This timely and needed volume supports serious-minded efforts to learn, understand, and communicate with Arabs and Muslims. Nydell combines her many years of experience living in the region with her special linguistic expertise to offer today's students insights they are obliged to critically consider before study or research abroad. The accessible presentation succeeds in humanizing as it reveals both the difficult issues and the abiding values that govern peoples' experiences. Nydell reminds us that in the Middle East and North Africa there will be much more to grasp as continued rapid change alters those lives daily."

— Terrence M. Potter, Visiting Associate Professor, Georgetown University

"The fifth edition of *Understanding Arabs* is a great introduction to the Arab world for both the general public and college students who wish to expand their knowledge of the region. Nydell's book is of tremendous use in the classroom, as it engages the cultural, linguistic, religious and political diversity of the Arab peoples and the Arab lands."

—Douja Mariem Mamelouk, Assistant Professor, French and Arabic Literatures, University of Tennessee, Knoxville.

UNDERSTANDING
ARABS

SIXTH EDITION

A Contemporary Guide to Arab Society

MARGARET K. NYDELL

INTERCULTURAL PRESS

an imprint of Nicholas Brealey Publishing

BOSTON • LONDON

This new and updated sixth edition first published in 2018 by Intercultural Press
An imprint of Nicholas Brealey Publishing. An imprint of John Murray Press

An Hachette UK company

23   4   5   6   7   8   9   10

A CIP catalogue record for this title is available from the British Library

Library of Congress Cataloging-in-Publication Data

Names: Nydell, Margaret K. (Margaret Kleffner), author.Title: Understanding Arabs : a
contemporary guide to Arab society / Margaret K. Nydell.Description: Sixth edition. |
Boston, MA : Nicholas Brealey Publishing, 2017. | Includes bibliographical references
and index. Identifiers: LCCN 2017044925 (print) | LCCN 2017048704 (ebook) | ISBN
9781473690899 (ebook) | ISBN 9781473690905 (library ebook) | ISBN 9781473669970
| ISBN 9781473669970(pbk.) | ISBN 9780983955818(ebook)Subjects: LCSH: Arabs.
Classification: LCC DS36.77 (ebook) | LCC DS36.77 .N93 2017 (print) | DDC
909/.04927--dc23LC record available at https://lccn.loc.gov/2017044925

ISBN 978-1-47366-997-0
US eBook ISBN 978-1-47369-089-9
UK eBook ISBN 978-1-47369-091-2

Printed and bound in the United States of America

John Murray Press policy is to use papers that are natural, renewable, and recyclable
products and made from wood grown in sustainable forests. The logging and
manufacturing processes are expected to conform to the environmental regulations of
the country of origin.

John Murray Press Ltd   Nicholas Brealey Publishing
Carmelite House   Hachette Book Group
50 Victoria Embankment   53 State Street
London EC4Y 0DZ   Boston, MA 02109, USA
Tel: 020 3122 6000   Tel: (617) 263-1834

www.nicholasbrealey.com

CONTENTS

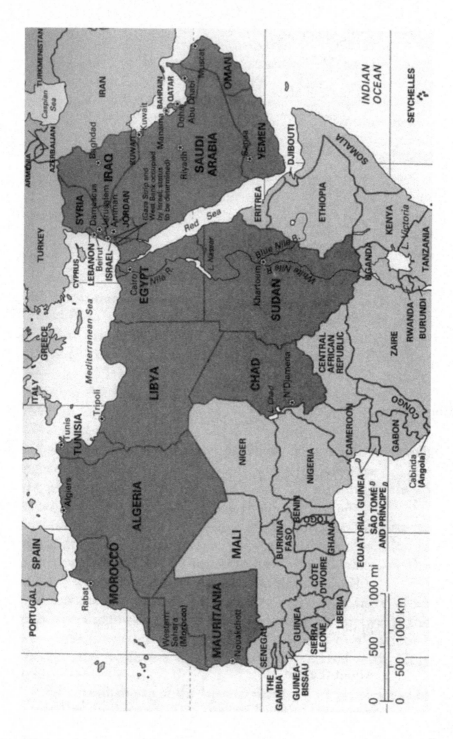

✹ ✹ ✹ ✹ ✹ ✹ ✹ ✹ ✹ ✹ ✹ ✹ ✹ ✹ ✹ ✹ ✹ ✹ ✹ ✹

PREFACE

I wrote the first edition of *Understanding Arabs* in the 1980s to provide background and context for increasing cultural awareness between Westerners (Americans and Europeans) and Arabs. Since then, the world has been bombarded with conflicting images of Arab culture, from terrorist acts to freedom demonstrations and Arabs who are distressed about the actions of their extremist counterparts, knowing that such terrorism reflects on all of them.

This is a handbook. It is not an academic text. It is intended to be read easily and quickly by people who are not specialists in the Middle East. In order to understand modern Arabs, we look at thought patterns, social relationships, and ways of life of urban Arabs in the twenty-first century. The majority of today's Arabs, the people we are likely to encounter in the media or in person, are mostly middle class (or slightly above or below), not exotic Bedouins from the desert. It is time to get away from "the Bedouin ethos."* When you picture an Arab in your mind, think of an accountant or a computer programmer who lives in a high-rise building.

We have seen the Arab Spring, civil wars, and the return of authoritarian governments. It is no wonder that Westerners don't know what to believe when it comes to the Arabs. These contradictory images involve one of the most ancient, complex, and often misunderstood cultures in the world.

---

* The Bedouin ethos was the basis for the code of chivalry brought to Europe in Crusader and post-Crusader times. It is no more relevant to the lives of modern Arabs than the Christian code of chivalry is to the lives of modern Westerners. Modern Arab society is not tied to the Bedouin ethos.

It is essential that we look at Arabs realistically as they are *today*, and not attempt to describe and explain them in terms of Middle East history that goes back centuries. Too often ancient and medieval history are cited, but they cannot be used to provide reasons for the present-day nature of Arab society—there have been too many changes, especially in the last one hundred years, approximately since the end of World War I. We do not need to refer here to pre-Islamic Arabia, the Muslim conquests, the eleventh-century Assassins, the twelfth- and thirteenth-century Golden Age, the harems, the House of War, and the like. This information is interesting but not very relevant.

Arabs are 420+ million people *in some eighteen countries who speak the Arabic language.* The term *Arab* does *not* mean that they have the same ethnic (Arabian) origin (consider blond Syrians and dark Sudanese and everything in between). Rather, *Arab* is a *cultural and political* term, and Arabs are not all alike—they speak different dialects of the language (which was foreign to most of them before the Islamic conquest) and there are many regional differences in customs and appearance. Contrary to widespread belief, not all Arabs are Muslim. About 5 percent of the Arabs are Christian, mainly in Lebanon, Egypt, Jordan, and Syria. Muslims are spread throughout the world, and only 20 percent of all Muslims are Arab.

Other prominent countries in the Middle East are not Arab: the Iranians, Afghanis, Pakistanis, and Kurds are not Semitic; they are of Indo-European (Aryan) origin. Turks are originally of Mongolian origin. The languages of these countries are still in use and did not give way to Arabic, despite the people adopting the Arabic alphabet in some cases and using Arabic religious expressions. Arabs who visit these countries need interpreters or use English.

Most of us are aware of the degree to which different national and cultural groups stereotype each other, at a distance or in person-to-person relations. When Westerners and Arabs interact, especially if neither understands the other, they often come away with impressions that are *mutually negative.*

Similarly, the Israeli-Palestinian conflict is about Israelis and Palestinians of today, who are not the same people referred to in the Bible as Hebrews and Ishmaelites (Arabians). Many Israelis are of European and other non-Semitic origins, and their culture is completely Westernized.

The Palestinians are *Arabs* but not *Arabians* from the Arabian Peninsula.*
They are descended from indigenous populations such as Canaanites,
Moabites, and Jebusites. The current conflict is political, a clash over land,
and has its origins entirely in the twentieth century.

The conflict is *not* religious; Islam is far closer to Judaism than is
Christianity. Muslims accept all of the Jewish prophets and many of their
religious practices. Muslims have no historical grievance against Jews
(a motivating factor among Christians) and did not engage in periodic
persecutions as happened in Europe, causing many Jews to flee south.
However, after eighty years of bitter conflict and sixty years of military
occupation, the religion of Judaism and the political ideology of Zionism
have become mixed, by both sides.† Still, I have never heard an Arab or
a Muslim say anything about the Jewish faith (how could they? Islam is
based on Judaism) or the Jewish people *except in the context of Israel and
its policies.*

The shared Judaic origins of Islam and Christianity have often been
overshadowed by the historical conflicts between the two religions—"the
Crusader mentality" and "the clash of civilizations." Both religions have
a concept of Holy War—Crusade and Jihad. Conflicts have accentuated
the differences and polarized the West and the Middle East, obscuring
the shared beliefs of the three interrelated monotheistic faiths: Judaism,
Christianity, and Islam.

A word about the title: *Arab* is a very general term, something like
the word *European*. People in these groups have much in common, but
there are distinct regional differences. The term *Arab* is useful, though,

---

* The distinction between Arabs and Arabians is crucial and often blurred for political purposes. Confusing these groups leads to statements like "Jews . . . were settled in
the country a thousand years before the coming of the Arabs [Arabians] in A.D. 634."[1]
Columnist Charles Krauthammer misspoke when he wrote: "Israel was the ancestral
homesite of the first two Jewish commonwealths for a thousand years—long before Arabs
[before the Arabian armies of the seventh century, but not the indigenous people], long
before Islam, long before the Holocaust."[2] The reader can appreciate how explosive this
simple factor is.

† A reporter asked several Israelis why they thought the Palestinians hated them. The
more educated the Israeli was, the more likely the answer was because of the history of
how Israel was established and how it continues to rule. The less educated the respondent, the more likely the answer was that "they hate us simply because we are Jews."[3]

in contexts such as the Arab world, pan-Arabism, and the Arab League. *Arab* refers not to ethnicity, but to *all Arabic-speaking people* regardless of origin or ethnicity. They use this term constantly.

The Arab region has always been in the news because of the strategic location of the region, linking Europe, Africa, and Asia. Oil resources in many countries have led to their geopolitical prominence. Now Arabs are in the news because of the civil war in Syria; widespread violence in Iraq, Yemen, Libya, and South Sudan; and the rise of terrorist groups such as Al-Qaeda and the Islamic State (IS).* But on the positive side there are the people who, in many countries, impressed the world during the Arab Spring with their calls for democratic rule and freedom to determine their governments. They were the ordinary common people, many age thirty or under, and it indicates their aspirations for the future.

✤ THE ARAB SPRING

The year 2011 opened with stunning news from the Middle East: the overthrows of the governments of Tunisia and Egypt—Tunisia in a month and Egypt after seventeen days. Such uprisings were unprecedented. New ways of thinking were spread and facilitated through electronic social media such as Facebook and Twitter. Wael Ghoneim, who instigated the Egyptian opposition, said, "The revolution started on Facebook." It would have occurred anyway, as previous revolutions have, but not as quickly and not with such a large number of organized protesters.

Demonstrations throughout the region seemingly occurred all at once, despite brutal government reprisals; repression had led to a social and political problem waiting to boil over. This was a watershed event, and under the superficial stability reimposed by governments it will never be the same.

The first uprising was in Tunisia, spurred by a seemingly routine (but highly significant) event. A poor street vendor was abused by a police officer and, in his despair, set himself on fire in front of a police station.

---

* There is confusion about the name ISIS or ISIL, the Islamic State in Iraq, and "Sham," the Levantine area; it is a matter of translation of this term as "Syria" or "Levant." Probably the best term is simply the Islamic State, or IS.

This shocked people and pushed them to indignant action, with very fast results: the president, Ben Ali, departed the country in just a month.

In Egypt, a long-standing resistance had been forming too, enabled by communication through Facebook in particular. Action was initiated after a young man was beaten to death by police. Again, it was one symbolic action that brought forth the latent outrage. Egyptians massed in a downtown square every day and relentlessly called for an end to the Mubarak regime until they had success.

Now it remains for both Tunisia and Egypt to work out their future governing systems. Tunisia is in fact making progress toward democracy, whereas in Egypt the government is run by a former military officer who took over after the elected Muslim Brotherhood government was removed by popular acclaim. The situation there is still developing, but it appears that the new regime is more repressive than Mubarak's regime ever was.

Resistance and demands for political and economic reform (not necessarily democracy) caught on virtually everywhere in the Arab world. The ideas took on a depth and momentum that propelled the demonstrators to face violence and overcome fear of their despotic regimes.

Results have certainly been mixed, and rarely can it be said that there is success and stability. In fact, in many countries the situation is so bad that some observers are describing the emergent authoritarianism and extremism as the Arab Winter. Today Iraq, Syria, Libya, Yemen, and South Sudan are among the most high-risk nations in the world.[4] Iraq has been in dire straits since the U.S. invasion of 2002, and recently taking back Mosul from the IS produced another one million refugees.[5] Syria is in the midst of an ever-worsening civil war, and in Libya there is a power vacuum, with no authority in full control and the IS controlling several cities. Yemen has been in a full-fledged civil war since 2014, and the government has moved to Aden because the Houthi (Shia) rebels have occupied the capital city of Sana. Civilian deaths are increasing, and there is a food and shelter crisis. A mass famine has set in, in both Yemen and in South Sudan, where the people have been driven from their homes and are desperate just to survive.

In Morocco, Algeria, and Jordan, demands by demonstrators led to reforms and promises of more to come. In all countries, there is a tension between people who want secular democracy (or something close to it) and those who want Islamist parties (or at least a prominent role for Islam). In all the Arab countries, the people are demanding economic and political reform.

❧ TERRORISM

Currently the dominant stories coming out of the Middle East deal with terrorism in one form or another. Terrorism has been part of local conflicts and civil wars, and it occurs regularly in Arab and Muslim countries, where thousands have been killed.

Of more concern to us here, though, is terrorism directed at Western targets, as a protest of political and economic policies and acts, American especially. In the U.S., the events of 9/11, the worst terrorist act in American history, changed the public mindset and gave rise to worsening anti-Muslim sentiment. In parts of Europe, this sentiment is even stronger because of terrorism there and because Muslims constitute a greater percentage of those societies (they are about 1 percent in the U.S.).

We all remember where we were when we heard the news of September 11, 2001. The shock and anger are still there and still underlie attitudes toward Arabs and Muslims nearly twenty years later. I was near the Pentagon strike. In the late morning of September 11, after the attacks, I walked from the Georgetown University campus in Washington, D.C., and crossed the Key Bridge into Virginia. I found many buildings evacuated, public transportation stopped, and all roads going past the Pentagon blocked off. I finally found a taxi, and the driver assured me that he would help me get home to Crystal City by skirting around the Pentagon area and going far into the Virginia suburbs. He did so, using small residential streets, until I was close enough to walk home. It took over an hour. He was Pakistani and, of course, Muslim. He was near tears (I was crying openly). He did not want to take any money. He said he was going to do this all day as a public service. I gave him money anyway and told him that if he didn't want to take it, he could donate it to charity.

The terrorist attacks on the World Trade Center and the Pentagon on September 11 left Americans and millions of others around the world bewildered as well as shocked and angry. Who could have done such a thing? As the smoke cleared, a Saudi Arab, Osama bin Laden, was identified as the chief perpetrator, commanding a network called

Al-Qaeda (pronounced al-KAH-e-da), which was previously unknown to the general public. Its known members and accomplices were mostly Arabs and all Muslims.

The shock of 9/11 brought all Americans together in a moment of clarity—we are one nation, one world. I hope this clarity will persist and will encourage us to seek greater understanding of other cultures while also dealing with threats to security. America is part of the world. We must not isolate ourselves. We are all one family now. We are all in it together. We need solutions.

People all over the world asked why. Why the United States? Why the attacks in Europe in subsequent years? What motivates these acts? The media, impelled as always to provide instant answers, came up with a variety of theories of varying degrees of merit. Some of them were based on popular misconceptions about Muslims, notably:

- This is a religion- and culture-based clash—the "clash of civilizations" theory. Extremist groups like Al-Qaeda and others, are characterized as representative of the thinking of the majority of Muslims.
- The attackers (and others who "hate America") are envious of the American way of life. They want to change American values and eliminate American freedoms.
- These particular attackers were motivated by visions of rewards in paradise because for them this was a jihad (a so-called Holy War) against infidels.

All of these explanations are incorrect. They confuse the motives of this particular terrorist group with the prevailing discontent in the Islamic world. But the Al-Qaeda group did not come out of nothing; it is an aberrant, cult-like faction that grew out of the Middle East milieu.* This and

---

* Al-Qaeda arose from a puritanical version of Islam, Wahhabism (also called Salafism), which is followed officially only in Saudi Arabia. It is also the prevailing interpretation of Islam among the Taliban in Afghanistan. This version of Islam forbids, for example, theaters and churches. It forbids the marking of graves. No alcohol or pork products may be imported. Publications are censored. Government-appointed officials enforce the law that requires all commercial establishments to close during prayer time. Wahhabis require women to cover their faces. This puritanical Islam is not practiced elsewhere. The Islamic State (IS) builds on Wahhabism and is also an apocalyptic group, aspiring

other terrorist acts are rooted in *political* grievances, expressing anger at American actions and policies through terrorist violence.

Statements such as "They hate American freedom" and "They want to destroy America" do not satisfy for long—they are impossibly vague. As time passes, we have identified reasons that make more sense. We must dig deeper, because unless the terrorists are all crazy or all evil, there must be better reasons. If the statements above were true, they would lead us to despair, then to defiance, and ultimately back to despair. There would be no solution.

Resentments against the United States have grown out of a context with which few Americans are familiar. The resentments are not primarily against American wealth and power as such. Rather, many people in the Middle East are profoundly angry at how they *perceive* America using its wealth and power when dealing with other countries and regions. This is a part of history about which few Americans are informed.

Perceptions become realities to people who hold them, and people who lack cross-cultural experience can easily misunderstand the attitudes and behaviors they confront. Americans, for example, are notoriously ill-informed about the Middle East. In turn, the average Middle Eastern individual actually knows very little about Western (American and European) societies and generalizes from television and films. Each side has misconceptions about the other. We do not yet know each other well. It is just a matter of time and the resentment and fear will calm down.

Language is a huge barrier. If we accept the premise that all people express themselves more accurately and candidly in their own language, then we should be skeptical about statements being reported from conversations with foreigners, filtered through English or other languages. Unfortunately, too many of our Middle East experts and reporters do not speak the local languages (imagine an expert on the U.S. who did not speak English). Thus, they have severely limited access to information, they do not read the local press or watch television news, and they may gravitate toward people with whom they can communicate easily, people who sometimes misrepresent the thinking of the general populace.

---

to establish a caliphate and bring on the "end times," the end of the world after battles between Muslims and infidels. This shows their degree of extremism.

There are many arguments that can be made on both sides, but one thing is certain: the language barrier accounts for much of the misunderstanding. In the forty years I have been listening to political discussions in Arabic, among Arabs who were talking to one another and not to me, I have never heard resentment expressed about anything American except for foreign policy. Middle Easterners in general care only about American activities that negatively affect their own lives. Consider the explanations offered by the terrorist leaders and others we have associated with terrorist movements. We must not ignore what they are saying; we must try to understand their statements, recognizing that this does not require agreeing with them:

- Bin Laden, 2001: "They violate our land and occupy it and steal the Muslims' possessions, and when faced with resistance, they call it terrorism .... What America is tasting now is something insignificant compared with what we have tasted for scores of years. Our nation has been tasting this humiliation and this degradation for more than eighty years."*
- The late Muhammad Omar, leader of the Taliban: "America has created the evil that is attacking it . . . the United States should step back and review its policy."
- A spokesman, Muslim Brotherhood (Egypt): "We want to understand, are the Americans in favor of human rights and freedom? Or is that the privilege of some people and not others?"
- Ayatollah Sayyed Ali Khamanei, religious leader in Iran: "We are neither with you nor with the terrorists .... They (America) expect the entire world to help them because their interests demand it. Do they ever care about others' interests? These are the characteristics that make America so hated in the world."
- A spokesman for the Islamic State: "Just as your missiles continue to strike our people, our knife will continue to strike the necks of your people. It is you who started the transgression against us."

None of these statements expresses threats that any group or faction is setting out to conquer the United States, force it to change its society,

---

* Few Americans can hear this and know what happened in the 1920s. (See Chapter 12.)

or impose its own ways of thinking. As far as I know, there have been no such statements. The September 2001 attacks were not aimed at targets like the Statue of Liberty, a cathedral, or a packed baseball stadium, but at structures that symbolize U.S. economic and military power.

How do Americans respond to this kind of criticism? Righteous indignation is natural but not very productive over time. We need to examine the anti-American statements and try to understand the context out of which they come. It is not appeasement to search for knowledge we do not currently have. How can terrorist acts be prevented from happening again if the *real reasons* for the acts are left undiscovered—or worse, ignored? In my opinion one of the most tragic aspects of this trauma has been that thousands of victims and families are left damaged or bereaved, and they do not know why this happened to them. Perhaps this book can help.

Understanding Arabs was first written before the problem of world terrorism assumed its present proportions. It is primarily a guide for Westerners, particularly Americans. To make the book more relevant to the current situation and to broaden the intended audience, I offer here some salient points that I believe must be considered as the world's people decide how as nations they will cope with this emergent terrorist threat. My purpose is to list what I believe to be objective facts rather than to interject recommendations or to suggest specific solutions.

- ❧ Mainstream Muslims do not approve of terrorist acts. In fact, they are horrified. The decision to engage in terrorism is the response of fanatic, misguided cult-mentality groups. Terrorism is not jihad and is in no way supported by the doctrines of the Islamic religion, which has always placed emphasis on human relationships and social justice. (There is much material on this topic, some of it available on the Internet.)
- ❧ Al-Qaeda group members in the 9/11 incident, and some perpetrators of other terrorist acts, disguised themselves as immigrants to the U.S., thus taking advantage of the good reputation Middle Eastern immigrants have earned. As a group, the immigrants to the U.S. are known to be industrious and family-centered. The terrorists betrayed these people. They posed as immigrants who wanted to share in the bounties of the

West, but from the very beginning they had an entirely different agenda.

⚜ Mainstream Muslims do not want to change Western (or other non-Muslim) cultures. Many Muslims do not want some Western values to enter their own societies, but providing their own lives are not affected, Muslims (and Middle Easterners in general) are not concerned with how Westerners and others structure their own lives. The vast majority do not resent Western prosperity and freedom; in fact, millions of them immigrate to the West because they admire many of the social values and want to participate in Western society. They want their children to grow up free and with the possibility of prosperity.

⚜ We must not allow a cult or extremist subgroup to represent an entire religion. The bombing of abortion clinics is not justified by mainstream Christian faith. Sectarian violence in Ireland does not represent mainstream Protestantism or Catholicism. The Muslim terrorist groups can be quite accurately equated with the Ku Klux Klan in America and its relation to mainstream Christianity. The KKK and white supremacist groups oppose non-Christians and engage in violence in the name of Christianity, and ordinary (mainstream) Christians can't really do much about it.

⚜ Muslims, Arabs, and other Middle Easterners do not blame Americans as individuals. Their assumption, right or wrong, is that the people of the United States cannot be held personally responsible because they are generally unaware of their government's activities. Americans are known in other nations as being uninformed about their country's foreign policies. (Less obvious to Middle Easterners is the fact that many Americans, at least prior to 9/11, also didn't care.) Unlike the terrorists' sympathizers, most Middle Easterners have genuinely grieved for innocent lives lost in any violent warlike act. They are like people everywhere.

⚜ The 9/11 attack was not a real jihad. The term *jihad*, as used in mainstream Islam, is misunderstood. Its primary meaning is not "Holy War," although that has become its meaning in Western

languages.* Most pertinent here, a true fighting jihad must be
a response to an overt attack or threat made by non-Muslims
toward the Muslim community. *Muslims may not initiate
a jihad.* The terrorists have interpreted Western, and most
recently American, political and military power in the Middle
East as an attack on their people.

❖   The terrorists are trying to promote enmity between Islam and
Christianity. They are misusing the term *jihad* just as they mis-
use terms like *Crusade, infidel* and *unbeliever.* The term *jihad*
has become politicized and is constantly being invoked and
misused for *political purposes.* During the war between Iraq and
Iran, for example, each declared a jihad against the other.

❖   The Qur'an and other Muslim sacred scriptures, like those of
other religions, are long, complex, and open to wide-ranging
interpretations. Emphasis on details such as presumed rewards
in paradise for people who die in a jihad are, frankly, irrelevant
and insulting to most educated Muslims. Muslims are not religiously motivated in any way to harm or kill non-Muslims. As
with any body of sacred scripture, a selective choice of quotes
can "prove" anything, including completely opposite ideas.

❖   Focusing on Islamic terrorists is too narrow a goal. It will not
end the threat. These terrorists are short-term enemies, current
targets against whom the United States now wages war. But
even if the groups are eliminated, *the root causes of resentment
will continue to exist.* The U.S. must reverse the negative perceptions about itself, and this cannot be done by force. No security
is effective enough to prevent an attack by a person who is willing to commit suicide. Long-term strategic thinking is needed.

Sweeping statements that are frightening but do not suggest a remedy
are not a solution. What use are statements such as "All humanity is at
risk," and "You will never take down this great nation," and "What the
United States has done to attract violent attacks is to be strong, wealthy,
and successful"? If Americans blindly declare that the terrorists hate them

---

* *Jihad* means "effort" and it refers to the effort one must make to live according to
God's design. It can also be used casually, as in, "I had to work overtime today, it was
really a jihad."

for their freedom and successes, where does it lead? It does not help in framing an appropriate response. If the United States and the Western world continue to ignore accusations, especially those they do not fully understand, they do so at their own peril. What brings forth statements that America is "morally corrupt and hypocritical"? Why is America accused of "supporting state-sponsored terrorism"? Why is there cheering when someone says, "Americans never see the blood"? These are the types of statements that must be thoughtfully considered if there is to be any hope of a just and lasting peace.

❧ FILLING A GAP

We must not confuse Arabs with Muslims. There are eighteen Arab countries referred to here (it is a matter of definition; there are twenty-two members of the Arab League).* There currently about 425 million Arabs in the world, 5 percent of whom are Christians or practice other religions. Owing primarily to immigration, Islam will become the second-largest religion in the U.S. by 2040, and is already the second-largest in much of Europe.[5]

Understanding Arabs deals with the Arab countries in the Middle East and North Africa. It does not include the primarily Muslim but non-Arab populations in Turkey (where the people speak a language of Mongolian origin) or the Middle Eastern countries in which people speak Aryan languages, which are part of the Indo-European language family: Iran (Persia), Afghanistan, Pakistan, and the Kurds. In contrast, most Arabs are Semitic in their ethnic origin; in Africa, many are Berber and indigenous Egyptian, but they are partly Semitic. Semitic people originated in the Arabian Peninsula and include the Hebrews† and many Ethiopians.

Foreigners find very little material available to help them understand modern Arab society. Not much has been written on the subject of current cultural and social practices, either in Arabic or in Western languages. A great deal of the material that exists is forty years old or

---

* Other countries sometimes listed include Mauritania, Chad, Somalia, Djibouti, and the Comoros islands.
† This is the origin of the term anti-Semitic.

more and appears dated to anyone who is familiar with Arab society today.* Some observations made two or three decades ago are no longer applicable. Many foreign writers and reporters have very limited contact with ordinary Arab people, often only government and military officials, intellectuals, the media, and people who speak English. In recent years, changes in education, housing, health, technology, and the media (especially the Internet) have had a marked effect on attitudes and customs; this is well illustrated by the sudden appearance of uprisings and political opposition during the Arab Spring.

The most serious deficiency in research about Arab society is the lack of attention given to the large majority of urban, educated (often Western-educated) Arabs. Researchers, especially anthropologists, have mainly focused on village life and nomadic groups and on the study of traditional, sometimes quaint, social patterns. Interesting as these studies are, they offer little directly applicable information for Westerners who will, for the most part, encounter Arabs who are well educated, well traveled, and sophisticated. Keep in mind that the large majority of the people (more than 95 percent) are never mentioned in the news, because they are getting on with their lives and do not engage in newsworthy activities.

This book is an attempt to fill that gap. It focuses on the middle and upper classes—businesspeople, bureaucrats, managers, scientists, professors, military officers, lawyers, banking officials, and intellectuals—the way they interact with foreigners and with each other. At the same time, many traditions and customs still affect the Arabs' way of life, including their goals, values, and codes of accepted behavior. The many similarities among social groups and among the various Arab countries still outweigh the differences, so valid generalizations are possible. Any significant differences among groups will be pointed out.†

---

* The well-known book *The Arab Mind* by Raphael Patai[6] was based on his residence in Jerusalem in the 1930s and 1940s, and his acquaintances during that era, many of whom were Bedouin or uneducated. He lived in the U.S. after 1947 and was a "frequent visitor" to the Jerusalem area. The book was outdated when it was published in 1973. It has continued to be published, most recently in 2007, essentially unchanged. It is heavily based on the Bedouin ethos, and much other information is inaccurate, even outlandish. It should be read, if at all, with skepticism.

† The term *Arab* is so broadly used that many people wrongly assume that they are all one block of people. It is confusing, for example, to read about the "Janjaweed Arab militias" in South Sudan. They are called Arabs because they share the language and religion (in

Scholars have varying opinions about the sociological effort to characterize groups of people as the same, different, ahead, or behind. Multiculturalists say that all cultural practices are equally valid, so attempts at comparisons can be a form of racism. Other scholars are quick to criticize certain cultures and quick to draw their own conclusions, especially when compared to, in this case, the West. We hear of "cultural stagnation" and "cultural failure" and the justifications for creating such (insulting) labels—it's amazing how Western observers, from historians to reporters to government officials, are never lacking in confidence when it comes to explaining what Arabs think.

These opinions are often based on erudite references to events back through several centuries, and they come to sweeping conclusions such as, "The fury of the Arab world is that it isn't really about us. It's about their own internal demons . . . . They prefer to blame others, to sleep-walk through history . . . . The truth is that Arabs have a deep inferiority complex. They're afraid that they really might not be able to build a successful modern state, to say nothing of a postmodern, information-based society."[7] My goal, in contrast, is to present what most Arabs believe and leave it at that.

I hope that this book will help alleviate stereotyping in two ways:

1. By explaining some of the behavioral characteristics of the Arabs in terms of cultural background, thereby deepening the reader's understanding and helping to avoid negative interpretations, and
2. By serving as a guide to cross-cultural interaction with Arabs, which will help Westerners avoid inadvertent insults and errors of etiquette, and help them make a favorable impression.

Westerners who interact with Arabs should be aware of the particular characteristics of Arab etiquette and patterns of behavior and thought, since the differences may be quite subtle and, initially, hard to identify. It is easy to be lulled into the security of assuming that the superficial similarities of appearance, dress, and lifestyle among educated Arabs mean that they are "just like us." One is more likely to remain alert for

---

contrast to most people in South Sudan), but they have no other similarities, ethnically or culturally, with Arabs of the Middle East.

different social proprieties when seated in a tent or a village house; it is not so easy to remember the differences when seated in a conference room or the living room of a modern Arab home, surrounded by Western-style furnishings and English-speaking Arabs.

Any attempt to describe the motives and values of an entire people is challenging. On the one hand, it leads to generalizations that are not true in all cases, and on the other, it necessarily involves the observer's perspectives and interpretations and leads to emphasizing some traits over others. I will try to present a balanced view, one that is generally descriptive of Arabs throughout the entire cultural area of the Arab world. Most of the material in this book, including anecdotes (I have many) comes from my own personal experiences and from interviews with others. These interviews have taken place in virtually all of the Arab countries—in North Africa, the Levant, the Fertile Crescent, and the Arabian Peninsula.

College students return from a stay in the Arab world enthusiastic, even effusive, in their praise of the Arab people they have met, and they are often anxious to find a way to go back. "They are so friendly . . . they were so nice to me . . . everyone was helpful . . . people in public would say, 'Welcome' in English . . . I loved sitting in a café playing backgammon with Syrians and Iraqis"—not what we would expect based on media images.

There are many delightful surprises that await foreigners as they come to know more: the hospitality, the wonderful food, the kindness to children and elderly people, the large and loving families. But this is not a book for tourist agencies. We also need to look at the problem areas, as many of them as possible, in order for this book to be helpful. Many factors can lead to mistaken interpretations, on both sides, and perhaps lead to serious errors in judgment.

The Arabs have been subjected to so much direct or indirect criticism by the West that they are very sensitive to a Westerner's statements about them (they hear the title of this book and are afraid to open it). I am trying to be straightforward, especially when contrasting Arab and Western cultural behavior. Value judgments do not belong here; there is no assumption that one cultural approach is somehow *better* than another. They both work just fine for the people who practice them, and neither side would want to change.

❄ LOOKING TO THE FUTURE

There is hope for the future, there really is. Not soon, but when Al-Qaeda and the Islamic State are no longer significant and jihadi groups lose support (the anarchists didn't survive because they lost, or never had, community support), we will see again that Arabs as a whole like America and Americans, and Westerners in general. They are invariably nice to Western tourists, and many aspire to emigrate to the U.S., Canada, Australia, and Europe. Everyone wants to learn English. They admire our free societies and want better economic opportunities. And in the Arab world itself, change will inevitably continue, driven by the political aspirations of the younger generation.

In the West and in the Arab world, we sometimes read outrageous statements made about each other's culture, invariably made by ignorant people or those with a political or religious agenda (Westerners are immoral, Muslims cannot go to Heaven). Unfortunately, this nonsense is newsworthy, especially on the Internet. It does a lot of damage, because many people assume that such characterizations are being expressed by everyone in the other culture.

But this is balanced by the great mass of ordinary, well-intentioned people who are open to new ideas. After interacting with Arabs in the Middle East for many years, I have seen the goodwill and curiosity of those I meet. On the whole, they are nice people, in many ways not all that different from us.

An Arab saying is "Seek knowledge" (*Utlub al-'ilm*) and another is "Kindness is a mark of faith" (*Al-hanan 'allamat al-iman*). May we learn to understand and be good to each other.

Note: Arabic words may be written in English in their conventional spelling, or spelled in a way that is closer to the actual Arabic pronunciation. Both ways are fine; it depends on your purpose. We see variant spellings: *Moslem/Muslim, Mohammed/Muhammad, Koran/Qur'an*, and names with *Abdel/Abdul*. You will also see the prefix *al-* (or *el-, il-, ul-*), which means *the* and is often included in names.

Finally, the word *Shiite* in English was coined so we could add *-s* and make it look like an English plural. In Arabic, the singular is *Shii* and the plural is *Shia*. *Shia* is the term used in this book.

Introduction:
Patterns of
Change

A rab society has been subjected to enormous pressures from the out-side world, particularly since the Second World War. Social change is evident everywhere because the effects of economic modernization and political experimentation have been felt in all areas of life. Even for nomads and residents of remote villages, the traditional way of life is disappearing.

❀ Modernization

Most social change has come through the adoption of Western technology, consumer products, healthcare systems, financial structures, educational concepts, and political ideas. These changes, necessarily, are controversial but inevitable and are present to varying degrees in all Arab countries.

Arab nations have experienced an influx of foreign advisers, managers, businesspeople, teachers, engineers, healthcare and military personnel, diplomats, politicians, and tourists. Through personal contact and increased media exposure, Arabs have learned how outsiders live. Thousands of Arab students have been educated in the West and have returned with changed habits and attitudes. The spread of the Internet has had a major impact as well.

Tens of thousands of Westerners live, or have lived, in the Arab world, and most of them love the experience. Many stay on for years and have a wide circle of Arab friends. They comment that human relations seem deeper, and friendships or even business transactions feel more personal and meaningful than in Western societies.

Arab governments are building schools, hospitals, housing units, airports, and industrial complexes so fast that entire cities and towns change their appearance in a few years. It is easy to feel lost in some Arab cities if you have been away only a year or two. Modern hotels are found in any large city. The streets and roads are jammed with cars, and the telephone, fax, and Internet services are often overtaxed. Imported consumer products are abundant in most Arab countries, ranging from white wedding dresses to goods in supermarkets. While these are surface changes, they also symbolize deeper shifts in values.

Overall rates of literacy have skyrocketed since the 1960s. In 1980, an Arab fund was created for eliminating illiteracy.[1] In the past forty years, the number of educated people more than doubled in some countries and increased ten times or more in others. Literacy in the Arab countries is an average of 78 percent,[2] and literacy in the states of the Arabian Peninsula rose from less than 10 percent to above 90 percent today. Literacy rates are higher in urban areas, and much higher among youth than older citizens—90 percent on average for males and 81 percent for females; this gender disparity is most prominent in Morocco, Egypt, Sudan, and Yemen.[3] The only country where literacy has declined is Iraq, with 86 percent (it once had one of the highest rates).

Education at the university level is rising even faster, sometimes doubling or tripling in one or two decades.

PERCENTAGE ENROLLED IN UNIVERSITY EDUCATION[4]

	1980	2001	2012–2014
Jordan	13	31	58
Saudi Arabia	7	22	61
Tunisia	5	23	35
Oman	0	7	29
Lebanon	28 (1985)	45	43

Arab women are becoming more educated and active professionally. In 1973 only 7 percent of women were employed in the workforce.[5] Currently the average is 30 percent. Arab women are aware that this percentage is still well below the worldwide rate. The industrial world, by comparison, averages from 40 to 50 percent female employment.

As more women enter the workforce, they will constitute a large, well-educated, and largely untapped resource, which will greatly strengthen the societies of the region.

❋ ❋

Percentage of Women in the Workforce (Economically Active) 2016[6]

Qatar	53
UAE	47
Kuwait	45
Bahrain	42
Oman	32
Tunisia	26
Egypt	25
Lebanon	25
Morocco	25
Saudi Arabia	22
Algeria	16
Jordan	16

Improved healthcare is changing the quality and length of life. The vast number of new hospitals, clinics, and medical graduates has completely transformed the quality of life. Life expectancy has increased dramatically.

❋ ❋

Life Expectancy[7]

	1955	2015
Morocco	43	76.1
Egypt	42	73.7
Kuwait	55	77.8
Saudi Arabia	34	75

This increased longevity is reflected in population statistics. Since the 1950s, the average rate of population growth has ranged between 2.5 and 3 percent, as high as anywhere in the world. In the four years between 1986 and 1990, the overall Arab population grew 5 to 7 percent (8 percent in the UAE and 10 percent in Oman); now, it has leveled out to 2.3 percent. Rising education and the availability of contraception account for the lowering of the birthrate.

The Muslim world is facing the fastest demographic or population decline ever recorded in history. Muslim birthrates are converging on Europe's catastrophically low fertility.[8]

Arabic is the sixth most-spoken language in the world and it is one of the official languages at the U.N. The word "Arab" means "nomad," because it originated from nomadic tribes in the desert regions of the Arabian Peninsula. Some 60 percent of the population is under 25 years old, making this one of the most youthful regions in the world, with a median age of 22 years compared to a global average of 28. More than 30 percent are between the ages of 15 and 29—roughly 300 million people.[9] The World Bank has estimated that the region will need 100 million more jobs by 2025.[10]

All over the Arab world, the population has been shifting from farms and villages to large urban areas, most dramatically during the period from the end of the Second World War to 1980. The magnitude of urbanization is illustrated by comparing the rates in recent years. Some countries are among the most urbanized in the world.

❂ ❂

PERCENTAGE URBANIZED[11]

	1970	1995	2015
Saudi Arabia	49	83	83
Jordan	51	71	84
Tunisia	43	62	67
UAE	57	84	85

Throughout the Arab world, 85 to 90 percent of the land is uninhabitable desert.

Urbanization brings its own problems. Except in the Gulf countries, governments face housing shortages, overuse of municipal services

(Amman, Jordan, has water only a few hours per day; public transportation is almost impossible in Cairo; everywhere traffic is far more than the roads were designed for), and overburdened social services, from schools to healthcare centers to job centers. In the poorer countries, unauthorized housing proliferates (notably Casablanca, Algiers, Cairo); in fact, 20 percent of Cairo's population live in illegal housing. And occasional political crises contribute to problems—at the end of 1990, after the invasion of Kuwait, 4 to 5 million people left the Gulf region.[12] Every year, it seems more refugees are created from Iraq, Syria, Yemen, Sudan, and Libya.

Internet access and usage illustrate the current situation well. In poorer countries, fewer than 30 percent have access; in the rich countries, it is used by 70 to 90 percent, with highs of 90 percent in Bahrain, 91 percent in the UAE, and 94 percent in Qatar.[13] This compares to 88.5 percent in the U.S. (2016) and 80 to 90 percent in the developed world.[14]

Some of the other major social changes and trends in the Arab world include the following:

- Family planning is promoted and increasingly practiced in most Arab countries, and it is accepted as permissible by most Islamic jurists.
- People have far more exposure to newspapers, television, radio, computers, and the Internet.
- Entertainment outside the home and family is more and more popular.
- More people travel, work, and study abroad.
- Parents are finding that they have less control over the children's choice of career and lifestyle.
- More people are working for large, impersonal organizations and industries.
- International trade is booming.
- Political awareness and participation have greatly increased.
- Educational and professional opportunities for women have changed family life.

❈ THE ARAB HUMAN DEVELOPMENT REPORTS

The publication of the *Arab Human Development Report* in 2002 was the first of its kind, a major event in Arab self-appraisal. It was written by a group of Arab intellectuals from the 22 countries in the Arab League and funded by the Arab Fund for Economic and Social Development, which is part of the United Nations. The report was notable for its frankness in pointing out the region's lack of freedom, economic development, and achievements in science and technology,* as well as gender inequality and the high rate of illiteracy. The report has been updated every year since then. The report stated, "There is a serious failing in the Arab world, and this is located specifically in the political sphere."[15] It called for greater political freedom, a sharing of absolute ruling power, and a curtailment of corruption. It also urged complete acceptance of "liberal democratic ideals."

There have been annual editions every year since then, each year centering on a different topic. Examples include: 2002, Building a Knowledge Society (literacy, Internet, technology, science); 2003, Creating Opportunities for Future Generations; and 2009, Empowerment of Arab Women.

The first report also mentioned that the Arab world has lost 25 percent of its university graduates to emigration because of poor economic conditions, and 15,000 medical doctors emigrated between 1998 and 2000 (no later numbers available). Economic conditions are poor in many countries, and the "brain drain" to Europe, America, Australia, and the Arabian Gulf is very real.

❀ THE EFFECTS OF CHANGE

The disruptive effects of the sudden introduction of foreign practices and concepts in traditional societies are well known. The social strains among groups of people who represent different levels of education and exposure to Western ideas can be intense, with mutual frustrations existing to a degree that can hardly be imagined by Westerners.

Both modernist and traditionalist ways of thinking are present at the same time in modern Arab society, forming a dualism. Modern science and technology are taught side by side with traditional law and religious subjects.

---

* It is refreshing to see a frank analysis of the current situation without reference to the glories of the Golden Age of Islamic civilization in medieval times. It is important to acknowledge these contributions, but it is also time to move on.

Arabs, particularly the younger generation, are *very attracted to* and *appreciative of* American culture and its products, including entertainment, music, clothing, and liberal ideals such as freedom and equal opportunity. The generation gap is very painful for some communities and families—some of the younger people are liberal and influenced by the West, while others have become more conservative and religious. All this affects family decisions—a Westernized Arab once equated the feelings of an Arab father whose son refuses to accept the family's choice of a bride with the feelings of a Western father who discovers that his son is on drugs.

A common theme of Arab writers and journalists is the necessity for scrutinizing Western innovations, adopting those aspects that are beneficial to their societies (for example, scientific and technical knowledge) and rejecting those that are harmful (such as lessening concern for family cohesion or social morality).

Arabs have been concerned that Westernization is often a part of modernization. They want to modernize, but not at the expense of certain traditions. It is a mistake to assume that Arabs aspire to create societies identical to Western models. Many Americans, in particular, find it surprising that most foreigners are not all that interested in the ways Americans do things, in personal life or in society. Arabs often disapprove of what they hear about American or European social problems and moral standards (understood correctly or not), but they have no interest in changing the Western way of life. They just don't want it imposed on them.

The issue for Arabs is how they will be able to adopt Western technology without adopting the Western values and social practices that go with it, and thereby retain their cherished traditional values. Their ideal society would retain its Islamic character, relying on Islamic values while undertaking reform. Most Arabs do not want an Iranian-style theocracy or a completely Western-style democracy. The large majority both reject the militants and have serious reservations about the West—they want a "soft revolution" within their own context.

❋ THE MUSLIM VIEW

Interpretations of Islamic practices vary widely. Many of the customs that distinguish Middle Eastern countries stem from *local cultural practices* (family relationships, women's role in society, people's manner of dress, child-rearing practices, female circumcision*), *not religion*. Because Sunni Islam has no organized hierarchy and no central authority, decisions by religious scholars often vary as well.

Most educated people want to "renew" Islam in order to face the new conditions of modern life. But this is more easily said than done, particularly in face of the recent emphasis on traditional Islam.

All over the Arab world and the entire Middle East, religious studies have increased in universities, as has the publication of religious tracts, and more religious orations are heard in public. This has been going on for a long time—the number of religious broadcasts and Islamic newspapers and books tripled in the 1980s alone.[16] There has also been a steady increase in Islamic-oriented organizations, laws, social welfare services, educational institutes, youth centers, publishers, and even Islamic banks. Many tradition-oriented Muslims have entered politics. A more visible Islamic dimension has become a part of everyday life.

The resurgence of conservative religion further supports the views of the traditionalists, who oppose any reinterpretations of Islam, and this group contains many government authorities, military officers, teachers, journalists, and intellectuals. *But traditionalists are not fundamentalists* if we use the term *fundamentalist* to mean "militant Islamist." Traditionalists want to maintain cultural and religious authenticity; they are exactly like traditionalists in other religions. The Muslim traditionalist view is that while Islam must accommodate modernity, modernity must also accommodate Islam.[17]

Since the 1960s, it was assumed that the Arab world was becoming more like the West politically, either socialist or democratic. There was a

---

* Female genital mutilation (FGM) is controversial. The practice is supported by traditional beliefs. In some communities, it is valued as a rite of passage to womanhood. FGM is rooted in culture, and many believe it is done for religious reasons, but it has not been confined to a particular culture or religion. It is not required in Islam, and is often discouraged; it was not mentioned in the Qur'an or the Sunnah. (FGM National Clinical Group)

FGM can be dated back at least 2,000 years. It is believed that it was practiced in ancient Egypt as a sign of distinction among the aristocracy. The practice evolved from the earliest times in primitive communities that wished to establish control over the sexual behavior of women.

FGM has been illegal in Egypt since 2008, and is also illegal in 23 other African countries.

predominant secular-nationalist vision. But by the 1980s, discourse was being shaped and dominated by the emergence of political Islam, and the "secular radicalism" was replaced with governing models that accommodate religion and, in many cases, preserve traditional monarchies.[18]

Muslims are determined to deal with change their own way. They believe they can contribute to the changing world and to a possible new global order. While the West excels at progress through the development of technology, Islam can provide a humanizing factor: morality. The goal is a universally *moral and materially advanced* global world order. Many non-Westerners believe that the Western exercise of world power lacks a strong underpinning of morality that leads to preferences for their own interests, without consideration of whether the policies are right or wrong for all people.

Benazir Bhutto once characterized two groups of Muslims—reactionary and progressive:[19]

> I would describe Islam in two main categories: reactionary Islam and progressive Islam. We can have a reactionary interpretation of Islam, which upholds the status quo, or we can have a progressive interpretation of Islam, which tries to move with a changing world.

Islamic societies will change, but they will always reflect diverse influences, lifestyles, and ideologies.

❊ ISLAMIC EDUCATION

There has long been discussion about how Islamic education could or should differ from Western education, and this subject is often mentioned in the media. Of particular concern is how science and technology relate to traditional Islamic values and ways of looking at the world, and how these can be retained. Many Muslim commentators believe that Western education relies too exclusively on process, without the spiritual dimension. They contend that the search for knowledge about the world constantly changes, but values do not change.

Many Muslims believe that textbooks should be prepared so that they reflect the Islamic outlook even as they present pertinent modern theories and discoveries. One educator, for example, suggested that in the natural sciences, the word "nature" could be replaced with "God" so that it is clear that God is the source of natural growth and development, the properties of chemicals, the laws of physics and astronomy, and the like. Historical events are to be evaluated not for military or political significance but by their success in furthering the spiritual aims of humanity; for example, an agnostic society that amassed a great empire would not be judged as successful.[20]

It seems to me that evangelical Christians would find very little to differ with in the above statement.

The relationship between Islam and science is uncertain and attracts many opinions. Some assert that "Islamic science" does not exist, saying that Islam does not encourage free, creative inquiry, while others are confident that the two can be reconciled.[21] Some Muslims find Western science lacking in that it asks "what" and "how" but not "why," the last bringing in a religious/philosophical dimension.

Muslim intellectuals are actively seeking Islamic alternatives for their societies. In many countries, young people belong to informal groups in which the role and contributions of Islam to modern society are avidly discussed.

❄ FACING THE FUTURE

Outside pressure toward change is glaringly visible in the Arab countries' architecture and city planning. Skyscrapers and air conditioning have replaced thick-walled traditional houses that were designed to condition the air themselves by means of a wind tower. Many crowded "old city" districts, with twisted lanes and jumbled markets and houses, have been destroyed; those that are left are in stark contrast with the newer parts of cities, built with wide streets on a city-block plan. Unfortunately, modern housing often does not address the needs of families and communities: There is no daily gathering place for women or separate living and entertainment areas for men and women. In most Arab cities, it is difficult nowadays for members of an extended family to find housing in one place or even in one area.

Many young people agonize about their identity (family? nation? Arab region? religious group or secular?) and what constitutes appropriate lifestyle choices, a dilemma that is simply unknown among Westerners.

Balancing between the modern and the authentic traditional way of life in their own personal lives is a concern among Arabs at all levels in society.

Westerners may perceive a dual personality present in many educated Arabs, who have the ability to synthesize two diverse ways of thinking and appreciate both. Few of us in the West have to contend with a dualism of this kind.

It is clear that a great deal of confusion and upheaval is still to be experienced. Consider the questions that modernity raises in the mind of an Arab: How do you compare the relative value of a communications satellite with the wisdom of a village elder? What good is a son who is a computer expert but lacks filial respect? How do you cope with a highly-educated daughter who announces that she never intends to marry?

This is the context in which Westerners encounter Arabs today. This is the background for Arabs' choices and aspirations.

✵ ✵ ✵ ✵ ✵ ✵ ✵ ✵ ✵ ✵ ✵ ✵ ✵ ✵ ✵ ✵ ✵ ✵ ✵

CHAPTER 1

BELIEFS AND VALUES

When we set ourselves the task of coming to a better understanding of groups of people and their culture, it is useful to begin by identifying their most basic beliefs and values. These beliefs and values determine our outlook on life and govern our social behavior. We have to make broad generalizations in order to compare groups of people—in this case, Arabs and Westerners. Bear in mind that this generalizing can never apply to all individuals in a group; the differences among Arabs of the eighteen nations described here are numerous, although all have an Arab identity.

Westerners tend to believe, for instance, that the individual is the focal point of social existence, that laws apply equally to everyone, that people have a right to certain kinds of privacy, and that the environment can be controlled by humans through technological means. These beliefs have a strong influence on what Westerners think about the world around them and how they behave toward each other.

Arabs characteristically believe that many, if not most, things in life are controlled, ultimately, by fate rather than by humans, that everyone wants and loves children, that wisdom increases with age, and the inherent personalities of men and women are vastly different. These beliefs play a powerful role in determining the nature of Arab culture.

One might wonder whether there is, in fact, such a thing as Arab culture, given the diversity and spread of the Arab region. Looking at a map, one realizes how much is encompassed in the phrase "the Arab world." The Arab countries cover a vast territory, almost all of it desert or wilderness; if the uninhabitable land were removed, the Arab world would be *very small* for its 425 million people. Much of the inhabited land is along coasts and rivers. Sudan is larger than Western Europe, yet its population was 42 million in 2017 (as compared with 192 million in Western Europe); Saudi Arabia is bigger than Texas and Alaska combined, yet had only 31 million people in 2017. Egypt, with 94.5 million people in 2017, is 95 percent desert.* One writer has stated, "A true map of the Arab world would show it as an archipelago: a scattering of fertile islands through a void of sand and sea. The Arabic word for desert is *sahara* and it both divides and joins."[3]

The differences among Arabs in various regions are immediately obvious—they have different foods, manner of dress, housing, decorative arts, and architectural styles. The political diversity is also notable; governmental systems include monarchies, military governments, "socialist republics," and the faint possibility of some kind of participatory democracies.

Despite the differences, Arabs are more homogeneous than Westerners in their outlook on life. All Arabs share basic beliefs and values that cross national and class boundaries. Social attitudes have remained relatively constant because Arab society is conservative and demands conformity from its members. Arab beliefs are influenced by Islam, even if they are not Muslims (many family and social practices are cultural, some are pre-Islamic); child-rearing practices are nearly identical; and the family structure is essentially the same. Arabs have not been as mobile as people in the West, and they have a high regard for tradition. Some features shared by all Arab groups are: the role of the family, class structure, religious and political behavior, standards of social morality, the presence of change, and the impact of economic development on people's lives.[4]

Initially, foreigners may feel that Arabs are difficult to understand, or that sometimes their behavior patterns are not what was expected (Arabs feel the same about Westerners). In fact, though, their behavior is very comprehensible, even predictable. For the most part it conforms to certain patterns that make Arabs consistent in their reactions to other people.

---

* Like many Arab countries, Egypt is large; statistics on population density reflect that. In terms of total area, Egypt's population density is 200 persons per square mile.[1] If considering only the habitable area, it is 3,820 persons per square mile.[2]

It is important for a foreigner to be aware of these cultural patterns, to distinguish them from individual traits. By becoming aware of patterns, one can achieve a better understanding of what to expect and thereby cope more easily. The following lists of Arab values, religious attitudes, and self-perceptions are central to the Arab culture and will be examined in detail in subsequent chapters.

Basic Arab Values

- One should always behave in a way that will create a good impression on others.
- A person's dignity, honor, and reputation are of paramount importance, and no effort should be spared to protect them. Honor (or shame) is often viewed as collective, pertaining to the entire family or group.
- Loyalty to one's family takes precedence over personal preferences.
- Social class and family background are the major determining factors of personal status, followed by individual character and achievement.
- Conservative social morality standards should be maintained, through laws if necessary.

Basic Arab Religious Attitudes

- Everyone believes in God, acknowledges His power, and has a religious affiliation.
- Humans cannot control events; some things depend on God's will, that is, fate.
- Piety is one of the most admirable characteristics in a person.
- There should be no separation between church and state; religion should be taught in schools and promoted by governments (this is the Islamic view, not necessarily shared by Arab Christians).
- Established religious beliefs and practices are sacrosanct. Liberal interpretations or indiscriminate imitations of Western culture

can lead to social disorder, lower moral standards, and a weakening of traditional family ties, so they must be rejected.*

Basic Arab Self-Perceptions

❀ Arabs are generous, humanitarian, polite, and loyal. Arabs see
these traits as characteristic of themselves and as distinguishing
them from some other groups.

❀ Arabs have a rich cultural heritage, as illustrated by their contributions in medieval times to religion, philosophy, literature,
medicine, architecture, art, mathematics, and the natural sciences (some of which were made by non-Arabs living within the
Islamic empire). Most of these outstanding accomplishments
are largely unknown and unappreciated in the West.

❀ Although there are many differences among Arab countries,
the Arabs are a clearly defined cultural group and perceive
themselves to be members of the Arab Nation (*al-Umma
al-'Arabiyya*).

❀ Arabs see themselves as having been victimized and exploited
by the West. For them, the experience of the Palestinians represents the most painful and obvious example, although recent
suffering by Iraqi and Syrian civilians is now a close second.
They believe that Arabs are misunderstood and wrongly characterized by most Westerners; many people in the West are anti-
Arab and anti-Muslim. Most Westerners do not distinguish
between Arabs and Muslims.

---

* Often cited are the West's tolerance of youthful rebellion, alcohol, drugs, pornography, homosexuality, unchaperoned dating, and the rate of illegitimate births (currently
43 percent in the U.S.).[5] In America, half a million children are in foster care. Surveys
indicate that the dominant perception in Arab and Muslim countries is that religion
and family are not very important in Western societies. Arabs value social morality far
more than individual choice.

CHAPTER 2

FRIENDS AND STRANGERS

Relationships are very personalized in the Arab culture. Friendships start and develop quickly. But the Arab concept of friendship, with its rights and duties, is quite different from that in the West.

❋ THE CONCEPT OF FRIENDSHIP

Westerners, especially Americans, usually think of a friend as someone whose company they enjoy. A friend can be asked for a favor or for help if necessary, but it is considered poor form to cultivate a friendship primarily for what can be gained from that person or from his or her position. Among Arabs, also, a friend is someone whose company one enjoys. *However, equally important to the relationship is the duty of a friend to give help and do favors to the best of one's ability.*

Differences in expectations can lead to misunderstandings and, for both parties, a feeling of being let down. The Westerner feels set up to do favors, and the Arab concludes that no Westerner can be a true friend. To avoid such feelings, we must bear in mind what is meant by both sides when one person calls another "friend."

❋ RECIPROCAL FAVORS

For an Arab, good manners require that one never openly refuse a request from a friend. This does not mean that the favor must be done, but rather that the response must not be stated as a direct "no." If a friend asks you for a favor, do it if you can—this keeps the friendship flourishing. If it is unreasonable, illegal, or too difficult, the correct form is to listen carefully and suggest that while you are doubtful about the outcome, you will at least try to help. Later, you express your regrets and offer instead to do something else in the future. In this way, you have not openly refused a favor (as if you didn't care) and your face-to-face encounters have remained pleasant.

I once talked to an Egyptian university student who told me that he was very disappointed in his American professor. The professor had gratefully accepted many favors while he was getting settled in Egypt, including assistance in finding a maid and buying furniture. When the Egyptian asked him to use his influence in helping him obtain a graduate fellowship in the United States, the professor told him that there was no point in trying because his grades were not high enough to be competitive. The Egyptian took this as a personal affront and felt bitter that the professor did not care about him enough to help him work toward a better future. The more appropriate response by the professor would have been to make helpful gestures; for example, helping the student obtain information about fellowships, assisting him with applications, and offering encouragement—even if he was not optimistic about the outcome.

In Western culture, actions are far more important and more valued than words. In the Arab culture, *an oral promise has its own value* as a response. If an action does not follow, the other person cannot be held entirely responsible for a failure because it is assumed that he or she at least tried.

If you fail to carry out a request, you will notice that no matter how hopeful your Arab friend was that you would succeed, he or she will probably accept your regrets graciously without asking precisely why the favor could not be done (which could embarrass you and possibly force you to admit a failure). You should be willing to show the same forbearance and understanding in inquiring about one of your requests. Noncommittal answers probably mean there is no hope. This is one of the most frustrating cultural patterns Westerners confront in the Arab world. You must learn to work with this idea rather than fighting against it.

When Arabs say "yes" to your request, they are not necessarily certain that the action will or can be carried out. Etiquette demands that your request have a positive response. The result is a separate matter. A positive response to a request is a declaration of intention and an expression of goodwill—no more than that. *Yes* should not always be taken literally. You will hear phrases such as *Inshallah* (If God wills) used in connection with promised actions. This is called for culturally, and it sometimes results in lending a further degree of uncertainty to the situation.

It is more polite on both sides to express goodwill rather than to criticize a person's ideas or refuse a request bluntly. Arabs are responding to a different culturally defined concept of politeness; it does not mean that they are "lying" or that they are not dependable. This is a subtle point, and it depends on the situation.*

Sometimes an Arab asks another person for something and then adds the phrase, "Do this for my sake." This phrasing sounds odd to a foreigner, especially if the people involved do not know each other well, because it appears to imply a very close friendship. In fact, the expression means that the person requesting the action is acknowledging that he will consider himself indebted to return the favor in the future. "For my sake" is very effective in Arab culture when added to a request.

An Arab expects loyalty from anyone who is considered a friend. The friend is therefore not justified in becoming indignant when asked for favors, once it is understood from the beginning that giving and receiving favors is an inherent part of the relationship. Arabs will not form or perpetuate a friendship unless they also like and respect you; their friendship is not as calculated or self-serving as it may appear. The practice of cultivating a person only in order to use him or her is no more acceptable among Arabs than it is among Westerners.

❋ INTRODUCTIONS

Arabs quickly determine another person's social status and connections when they meet. They will, in addition, normally give more information about themselves than Westerners will. They may indulge in a little (or a lot of) self-praise and praise of their relatives and family, and they may

---

* This is from a recording made of a Qatari woman's speech: "There is no polite flattery or indirectness—I liked this in Europe. They tell the truth when they talk. If someone likes something, he tells you *yes*. If he doesn't like it, he says *no*. I might get irritated, but it's the truth."[1]

present a detailed account of their social connections. When Westerners meet someone for the first time, they tend to confine personal information to generalities about their education, profession, spouse and children, and interests.

To Arabs, information about the extended family and social connections is important, possibly even more important than the information about themselves. Family information and social connections are also what they want from you. They may find your response so inadequate that they wonder if you are hiding something, while your impression is that much of what they say is too detailed and largely irrelevant. Both parties give the information they think the other wants to know.

Your Arab friends' discourse about their influence network is not bragging, and it is not irrelevant. This information may turn out to be highly useful if you are ever in need of high-level personal contacts, and you should appreciate the offer of potential assistance from insiders in the community. Listen to what they have to say.

❋ VISITING PATTERNS

Arabs feel that good friends should see each other often, at least every few days if possible, and they offer many invitations to each other. Westerners who have Arab friends sometimes feel overwhelmed by the frequent contact and wonder if they will ever have any privacy. There is no concept of privacy among Arabs. In translation, the Arabic word that comes closest to *privacy* means "loneliness."

A British resident in Beirut once complained that he and his wife had almost no time to be alone—Arab friends and neighbors kept dropping in unexpectedly and often stayed late. He said, "I have one friend who telephoned and said, 'I haven't seen you anywhere. Where have you been for the last three days?'"

By far the most popular form of entertainment in the Arab world is conversation (although television and the Internet are making inroads). Arabs enjoy long discussions over shared meals or many cups of coffee or tea. You will be expected to reciprocate invitations, although you do not have to keep pace precisely with the number you receive. If you plead for privacy or become too slack in socializing, people will wonder if they have offended you, if you don't like them, or if you are sick. You can say that you have been very busy, but resorting to this too often without sufficient explanation may be taken as an affront. "Perhaps," your friends may think, "you are just too busy for us."

I once experienced a classic example of the Arab (and especially Egyptian) love of companionship in Cairo. After about three hours at a party where I was surrounded by loud music and louder voices, I stepped onto the balcony for a moment of quiet and fresh air. One of the women noticed and followed immediately, asking, "Is anything wrong? Are you angry at someone?"

An Arab American was quoted as saying:

> In the United States . . . you can have more personal space. I guess
> this is about the best way to put it. You have privacy when you want
> privacy. And in Arab society they don't really understand the idea
> that you want to be alone. That means that you're mad, you're angry
> at something, or you're upset and you should have somebody with
> you.[2]

People want to be surrounded by others when they are sick in the hospital or in a state of mourning, times when a Westerner might prefer to be alone. All hospital rooms have facilities for relatives, and a patient cannot possibly keep them out, even if he or she wants to. Arabs feel terribly lonely in a new place where they don't know anyone; a comfortable security has been lost. This is a description of an Arab woman who had just arrived in England, written by her daughter:

> She hated the cold weather and the rain, and she complained she
> could scarcely keep the house warm. She was lonely and longed for
> company. In the Arab world, you were never alone for a moment.
> Your neighbors or friends were always there to call on every day and,
> in any case, there was the family around you at all times.[3]

If you are not willing to increase the frequency or intensity of your personal contacts, you may hurt your friends' feelings and damage relationships. Ritual and essentially meaningless expressions used in Western greetings and leave-taking, such as "We've got to get together sometime," may well be taken literally, and you have approximately a one-week grace period in which to follow up with an invitation before your sincerity is questioned.

Some Westerners, as they learn about the intricate and time-consuming relationships that develop among friends, decide they would rather keep acquaintances at a distance. If you accept no favors, you will eventually be asked for none, and you will have much more time to yourself, but you will soon find that you have no Arab friends. Arab friends are generous with their time and efforts to help you, they are willing to inconvenience themselves for you, and they are concerned about your welfare. They will go to great lengths to be loyal and dependable. If you spend much time in an Arab country, it would be a great personal loss if you develop no Arab friendships.

❀ BUSINESS FRIENDSHIPS

In business relationships, personal contacts are much valued and quickly established. Arabs do not fit easily into impersonal roles, such as the "business colleague" role (with no private socializing offered or expected) or the "supervisor/employee" roles (where there may be cordial relations during work hours but where personal concerns are not discussed). For Arabs, all acquaintances are potentially friends.

A good personal relationship is the most important single factor in doing business successfully with Arabs. A little light conversation before beginning a business discussion can be extremely effective in setting the right tone. Usually Arabs set aside a few minutes at the beginning of a meeting to inquire about each other's health and recent activities. If you are paying a business call on an Arab, it is best to let your host guide the conversation in this regard—if he is in a hurry, he may bring up the matter of business almost immediately; if not, you can tell by a lull in the conversational amenities when it is time to bring up the purpose of your visit. If an Arab is paying a call on you, don't be in such a rush to discuss business that you appear brusque.

The manager of the sales office of a British industrial equipment firm based in Kuwait told me about his initial inability to select effective salesmen. He learned that the best salesmen were not necessarily the most knowledgeable, eager, or efficient but were instead those who were relaxed, personable, and patient enough to establish friendly personal relations with their clients.

You will find it useful to become widely acquainted in business circles, and if you learn to mix business with pleasure, you will soon see how the latter helps the former proceed. *In the end, personal contacts lead to more efficiency than following rules and regulations.* This is proven over and over again, when a quick telephone call to the right person cuts through lengthy procedures and seemingly insurmountable obstacles.

❈ OFFICE RELATIONS

When Westerners work with the same people every day in an office, they sometimes become too casual about greetings. Arabs are conscientious about greeting everyone they see with "Good morning" or "Good afternoon" if it is the first encounter of the day, and they will go out of their way to say "Welcome back" when you return after an absence. Some Westerners omit greetings altogether, especially if they are distracted or hurried, and Arab co-workers invariably take notice. They usually understand and are not personally offended, but they interpret it as a lack of good manners. They are simply more formal; it is a matter of *adab*, good manners. One always takes time for social formalities.

An American nurse at a hospital in Taif, Saudi Arabia, had an enlightening experience on one occasion when she telephoned her Saudi supervisor to report arrangements for an emergency drill. She was enumerating the steps being taken when the Saudi said, "That's fine, but just a moment—first of all, how are you today?"

If you bring food or snacks into the office, it is a good idea to bring enough to share with everyone. Arabs place great value on hospitality and would be surprised if you ate or drank alone, without at least making an offer to share. The offer is ritual, and if it is obviously your lunch or just enough food for yourself, it is usually politely refused; it depends on the situation.

Remember to inquire about business colleagues and co-workers if they have been sick, and ask about their personal concerns from time to time. Arabs do mention what is happening in their lives, usually good things like impending trips, weddings, and graduations. You do not need to devote much time to this; it is the gesture that counts.

In Arab offices supervisors and managers are expected to give praise to their employees from time to time, to reassure them that their work is noticed and appreciated. Direct praise, such as, "You are an excellent employee and a real asset to this office," may be a little embarrassing to a Westerner, but Arabs give it frequently. You may hear, "I think you are a wonderful person, and I am so glad you are my friend," or, "You are so intelligent and knowledgeable; I really admire you." Statements like these are meant sincerely and are very common.

I was once visiting an American engineering office in Riyadh and fell into conversation with a Jordanian translator. I asked him how he liked his work. He answered in Arabic so that the Americans would not understand, "I've been working here for four years. I like it fine, but I wish they would tell me when my work is good, not just when they find something wrong." Some Westerners assume that employees know they are appreciated simply because they are kept on the job, whereas Arab employees (and friends, for that matter) expect and want praise when they feel they have earned it. Even when a Westerner does offer praise, it may be insufficient in quantity or quality for the Arab counterpart.

❦ CRITICISM

Arab employees usually feel that criticism of their work, if it is phrased too bluntly, is a personal insult. A foreign supervisor is well advised to take care when giving criticism. It should be indirect and include praise of any good points first, accompanied by assurances of high regard for the individual. To preserve the person's dignity, avoid criticism in front of others, and consider using an intermediary (see below for further discussion of intermediaries). The concept of constructive criticism truly cannot be translated into Arabic—forthright criticism is almost always taken as personal and destructive.

The need for care in criticism is well illustrated by an incident that occurred in an office in Amman. An American supervisor was discussing a draft report at some length with his Jordanian employee. He asked him to rewrite more than half of it, adding, "You must have entirely misunderstood what I wanted." The Jordanian was deeply hurt and said to one of the other employees, "I wonder why he doesn't like me." A far better approach would have been, "You are doing excellent work here, and this is a good report. We need to revise some things, however; let's look at this again and work through it together, so we can make it even better."

I remember overhearing a dramatic confrontation in an office in Tunis, when an American supervisor reprimanded a Tunisian employee because he continually arrived late. This was done in front of other employees, some of whom were his subordinates. The Tunisian flared up in anger and responded, "I am from a good family! I know myself and my position in society!" Clearly, he felt that his honor had been threatened and was not at all concerned with addressing the issue at hand.

❧ INTERMEDIARIES

The designation of one person to act as an intermediary between two other people is very common in Arab society. Personal influence is helpful in getting decisions made and things done, so people often ask someone with influence to represent them (in Arabic this process is called *wasta*).

If you are a manager, you may find that some employees prefer to deal with you through another person, especially if that person knows you well. An intermediary may serve as a representative of someone with a request or as a negotiator between two parties in a dispute.

Mediation or representation through a third party also saves face in the event that a request is not granted, and it gives the petitioner confidence that maximum influence has been brought to bear. You may want to initiate this yourself if an unpleasant confrontation with someone appears necessary. But because you, as an outsider, could easily make a mistake in selecting an intermediary, it is best to consult with other Arab employees (of a higher rank than the person with whom you have a conflict).

Foreign companies have local employees on their staff who maintain liaison with government offices and help obtain permits and clearances. The better acquainted the employee is with government officials, the faster the work will be done and the better the service will be. Arab "government relations" employees are indispensable; no foreigner could hope to be as effective with highly placed officials.

You will observe the wide use of intermediaries in Arab political disputes. Mediators who try to intervene when a political problem arises (the recent clashes between revolutionaries and leaders comes to mind) may be able to establish personal contact and influence that makes consensus possible. Their success depends on the quality of the personal relationship that is established. If mediators are recognized by both parties as being honorable and trustworthy, they have already come part of the way in solving the problem. That is why some negotiators and diplomats are more effective than others: Personalities and perceptions, not issues, may determine their relative success.

❧ PRIVATE AND PUBLIC MANNERS

In the Arab way of thinking, people are clearly divided into friends and strangers. The manners required when dealing with these two groups are quite different. With friends and personal acquaintances, it is essential to be polite, honest, generous, and helpful at all times. When dealing with strangers, "public manners" are applied and do not call for the same kind of considerateness.

It is accepted practice for many people to do such things as crowd into lines, push, drive aggressively, and overcharge tourists. If you are a stranger to the person or persons you are dealing with, then they will respond to you as they do to any stranger. Resenting this public behavior will not help you function better in Arab societies, and judging individuals as ill-mannered because of it will inhibit the development of needed relationships.

All over the Arab world people drive fast, cross lanes without looking, turn corners from the wrong lane, and honk their horns impatiently. Yet, if you catch a driver's eye or ask his or her permission, the driver will graciously motion for you to pull ahead or will give you the right-of-way.

While shopping in a tourist shop in Damascus, I watched a busload of tourists buy items at extremely high prices. When they were gone, I chatted with the shopkeeper for a few minutes and then bought some things. After I had left, a small boy came running after me—the shop owner had sent him to return a few more pennies in change.

Whenever I am in a crowded airport line, I try to make light conversation with the people around me. Never has anyone with whom I talked tried to push in front of me; in fact, they often motion for me to precede them.

Personal contact makes all the difference. If you feel jostled while you are waiting in line, the gentle announcement of "I was here first" or "Please wait in line" (along with a smile, if you can possibly manage it) will usually produce an apology, and the person will at least stand behind you, if not others. Keep calm, avoid scenes, and remember that none of the behavior is directed at you personally.

❀ ❀ ❀ ❀ ❀ ❀ ❀ ❀ ❀ ❀ ❀ ❀ ❀ ❀ ❀ ❀ ❀ ❀ ❀

CHAPTER 3

Emotion and Logic

How people deal with emotion or what value they place on objective versus subjective behavior is culturally conditioned. *While objectivity is given considerable emphasis in Western culture, the opposite is true in Arab culture.* But whatever you encounter, there are always reasons; no behavior is random.

❋ Objectivity and Subjectivity

Westerners are taught that objectivity, the examination of facts in a logical way without the intrusion of emotional bias, is the mature and constructive approach to human affairs. One of the results of this belief is that in Western culture, subjectivity—a willingness to allow personal feelings and emotions to influence one's view of events—represents immaturity. Arabs believe differently. They place a high value on the display of emotion, sometimes to the embarrassment or discomfort of foreigners. It is not uncommon to hear Westerners label this behavior as immature, imposing their own values on what they have observed.

A British office manager in Saudi Arabia once described to me his problems with a Palestinian employee: "He is too sensitive, too emotional about everything," he said. "The first thing he should do is grow up." While Westerners label Arabs as too emotional, Arabs may find Westerners cold and inscrutable.

Arabs consciously reserve the right to look at the world in a subjective way, particularly if a more objective assessment of a situation would bring to mind a painful truth. There is nothing to gain, for example, by pointing out Israel's achievements in land reclamation or comparing the quality of some Arab-made consumer items with imported ones. Such comments will generally not lead to a substantive discussion of how Arabs could benefit by imitating others; more likely, Arab listeners will become angry and defensive, insisting that the situation is not as you describe it and bringing up issues such as Israeli occupation of Arab lands or the moral deterioration of technological societies. They would have to do this, because you have offended their pride and failed to observe polite conventions (*adab*).

❋ FATALISM

Fatalism, or a belief that people are powerless to control events, is part of traditional Arab culture. It has been overemphasized by Westerners, however, and is far more prevalent among traditional, uneducated Arabs than it is among the educated elite today. Nevertheless, it still needs to be considered, since it is often encountered in one form or another.

For Arabs, fatalism is based on the belief that God has direct and ultimate control of all that happens. If something goes wrong, people can absolve themselves of blame or can justify doing nothing to make improvements or changes by assigning the cause to God's will. Indeed, too much self-confidence about controlling events is considered a sign of arrogance tinged with blasphemy. The legacy of fatalism in Arab thought is most apparent in the ritual phrase *Inshallah*, noted in Chapter 2.

Western thought has essentially rejected fatalism. Although God is believed by many Westerners to intervene in human affairs, Greek logic, the humanism of the Enlightenment, and cause-and-effect empiricism have inclined the West to view humans as having the ability to control their environment and destiny.

❋ WHAT IS REALITY?

Reality is what you perceive—if you believe something exists, it is real to you. If you select or rearrange facts and if you repeat these to yourself often enough, they eventually become your reality.

The difference between Westerners and Arabs arises not from the fact that this selection takes place, but from the manner in which each makes the selection. Arabs are more likely to allow subjective perceptions to determine what is real and to direct their actions. This is a common source of frustration for Westerners, who often fail to understand why people in the Middle East act as they do. This is not to say that Arabs cannot be objective—they can. But there is often a difference in outward behavior.

If Arabs find that something threatens their personal dignity, they may be obliged to deny it, even in the face of facts to the contrary. A Westerner can point out flaws in their arguments, but that is not the point. If they do not want to accept the facts, they will reject them and proceed according to their own views of the situation. Arabs will rarely admit to errors openly if doing so will cause them to lose face. *To Arabs, honor is more important than facts.*

Any Arab would understand what is happening, and would never suggest that the other person is lying ("lying" is a common Western accusation). Nor would he insist on proving the facts and thus humiliate the other person.

An American woman in Tunis realized, when she was packing to leave, that some of her clothes and a suitcase were missing. She confronted the maid, who insisted that she had no idea where they could be. When the American found some of her clothes under a mattress, she called the company's security officer. They went to the maid's house and found more missing items. The maid was adamant that she could not account for the items being in her home. The security officer said that he felt the matter should not be reported to the police (who would have been brutal); the maid's humiliation in front of her neighbors was sufficient punishment.

An American diplomat recounted an incident he had observed in Jerusalem. An Israeli entered a small Arab-owned cafe and asked for some watermelon, pointing at it and using the Hebrew word. The Arab proprietor responded that it should be called by the Arabic name, but the Israeli insisted on the Hebrew name. The Arab took offense at this point. He paused, shrugged, and instead of serving his customer, said, "There isn't any!"

At a conference held to discuss Arab and American cultures, Dr. Laura Nader related this incident:

The mistake people in one culture often make in dealing with another culture is to transfer their functions to the other culture's functions. A political scientist, for example, went to the Middle East to do some research one summer and to analyze Egyptian newspapers. When he came back, he said to me, "But they are all just full of emotions. There is no data in these newspapers." I said, "What makes you think there should be?"[1]

Another way of influencing the perception of reality is by the choice of descriptive words and names. The Arabs are very careful in naming or referring to places, people, or events; slogans and labels are popular and provide an insight into how things are viewed. The Arabs realize that *names have a powerful effect on perception.*

There is a big psychological gap between opposing labels like "Palestine/Israel," "the West Bank/Judea and Samaria," and "freedom fighters ('hero martyrs' if they are killed)/ terrorists." Even the establishment of Israel has its own name, the Catastrophe, as in "ten years after the Catastrophe . . . ."

Be conscious of names and labels—they matter a great deal to the users.* If you attend carefully to what you hear in conversations with Arabs and what is written in their newspapers, you will note how precisely they select descriptive words and phrases. You may find yourself being corrected by Arab acquaintances ("It is the Arabian Gulf, not the Persian Gulf," for example), and you will soon learn which terms are acceptable and which are not.

❋ THE HUMAN DIMENSION

Arabs look at life in a personalized way. They are concerned about people and feelings and place emphasis on human factors when they make decisions and analyze events. They feel that Westerners are too prone to look at events in an abstract or theoretical way and that most Westerners lack sensitivity toward people.

---

* They matter in America, too. The Department of Homeland Security sounds much better than "The Department of Defense Against Terrorism." Depending on region, Americans say "the Civil War" or "The War Between the States."

In the Arab world, a manager or official is always willing to reconsider a decision, regulation, or problem in view of someone's personal situation. Any regulation can be modified or avoided by someone who is sufficiently persuasive, particularly if the request is justified on the grounds of unusual personal need. This is unlike most Western societies, which emphasize the equal application of laws to all citizens. *In the Arab culture, people are more important than rules.*

T. E. Lawrence stated it succinctly: "Arabs believe in persons, not in institutions."[2] They have a long tradition of personal appeal to authorities for exceptions to rules. This is commonly seen when they attempt to obtain special permits, exemptions from fees, acceptance into a school when preconditions are not met, or employment when qualifications are inadequate. They do not accept predetermined standards if these standards are a personal inconvenience.

Arabs place great value on personal interviews and on giving people the opportunity to state their case. They are not comfortable filling out forms or dealing with an organization impersonally. They want to know the name of the top person who makes the final decision and are always confident that the rejection of a request may be reversed if top-level personal contact can be made. Frequently, that is exactly what happens.

❀ PERSUASION

Arabs and Westerners place a different value on certain types of statements, which may lead to decreased effectiveness on both sides when they negotiate with each other. Arabs respond much more readily to personalized arguments than to attempts to impose "logical" conclusions. When you are trying to make a persuasive case in your discussions with Arabs, you will find it helpful to supplement your arguments with personal comments. You can refer to your friendship with each other or emphasize the effect approval or disapproval of the action will have on other people.

In the Middle East, negotiation and persuasion have been developed into a fine art. Participants in negotiations enjoy long, spirited discussions and are usually not in any hurry to conclude them. Speakers feel free to add to their points of argument by demonstrating their verbal cleverness, using their personal charm, applying personal pressure, and engaging in personal appeals for consideration of their point of view.

The display of emotion also plays its part; indeed, one of the most commonly misunderstood aspects of Arab communication involves their "display" of anger. Arabs are not usually as angry as they appear to be. Raising the voice, repeating points, even pounding the table for emphasis may sound angry, but in the speaker's mind, they merely indicate sincerity. A Westerner overhearing such a conversation (especially if it is in Arabic) may wrongly conclude that an argument is taking place. *Emotion connotes deep and sincere concern for the substance of the discussion.*

Foreigners often miss the emotional dimension in their cross-cultural transactions with Arabs. A British businessman once found that he and his wife were denied reservations on a plane because the Arab ticketing official took offense at the manner in which he was addressed. The fact that seats were available was not an effective counterargument. But when the Arab official noticed that the businessman's wife had begun to cry, he gave way and provided them with seats.

Arabs usually include human elements in their arguments. In arguing the Palestine issue, for instance, they have often placed the greatest emphasis on the suffering of individuals rather than on points of law or a recital of historical events. This is beginning to change, however, with a growing awareness of how to relate effectively to the way Westerners think and argue. The use of stark facts may be mentioned, especially among educated people (often preceded by "excuse me, but . . . .)"

CHAPTER 4

GETTING PERSONAL

The concept of what constitutes personal behavior or a personal question is culturally determined, and there are marked differences between Westerners and Arabs. This is a subject that is rarely discussed openly, since how one defines what is personal or private seems so natural to each group. On the whole, Westerners feel that Arabs become too personal, too soon.

❋ PERSONAL QUESTIONS

Arabs like to discuss money and may ask what you paid for things or about your salary (this is more common among less Westernized people). If you don't wish to give out the information, consider responding without answering. You can speak about money in general—how hard it is to stay ahead, high prices, inflation. After a few minutes of this, the listener will realize that you do not intend to give a substantive answer. This is the way Arabs would respond if they were asked a question they did not really want to answer.

If you are unmarried or you are married and childless, or have no sons, some Arabs may openly ask why. They consider it unusual for an adult to be unmarried, since marriage is arranged for most people by their families and, in any event, is expected of everyone. People want children, especially sons, to enhance their prestige and assure them of care in their old age.

Unmarried people may well find themselves subjected to well-intentioned matchmaking efforts on the part of Arab friends. If you wish to avoid being "matched," you may have to resort to making up a fictitious long-distance romance! You might say, "I am engaged and we're working out the plans. I hope it won't be long now." Statements such as, "I'm not married because I haven't found the right person yet" or, "I don't want to get married" make little sense to many Arabs.

When you explain why you don't have children, or more children, don't say, "We don't want any more children," (impossible to believe) or, "We can't afford more" (also doubtful). A more acceptable answer is, "We would like to have (more) children, and if God wills, we will have."

Questions that Arabs consider too personal are those pertaining to women in the family (if asked by a man). It is best to talk about "the family," not a person's wife, sister, or grown daughter.

❈ SENSITIVE SUBJECTS

There are two subjects that Arabs favor in social conversation with foreigners—religion and politics—and both can be sensitive.

Muslims enjoy discussing religion with non-Muslim Westerners because of their curiosity about Western religious beliefs and because they feel motivated to share information about Islam with friends as a favor to them. They are secure in their belief about the completeness of Islam, since it is accepted as the third and final refinement of the two previously revealed religions, Judaism and Christianity. They like to teach about Islam, which eventually leads to the question: Why don't you consider conversion? A Westerner may feel uncomfortable and wonder how to give a gracious refusal. The simplest, most gracious and most acceptable answer is to state that you appreciate the information and respect Islam as a religion but that you cannot consider conversion because it would offend your family. Another option is to assure people that you are a serious, committed Christian (if this is the case). There is a widespread perception that most Westerners are not religious; if you are, people will be very impressed.

Arabs like to talk politics with Westerners and readily bring up controversial issues like the Palestine issue, the Iraq wars, and the legacies of colonialism and imperialism. Yet they are not prepared for frank statements of disagreement with their positions on these questions or even inadvertent comments that sound negative toward their point of view or supportive of the opposing side of the argument. The safest response, if you cannot agree fully, is to confine yourself to platitudes and wait for the subject to change, expressing your concerns for the victims of war and your hope for a lasting peace. *A frank, two-sided discussion is usually not constructive if the subject is an emotional one,* and you may find that Arabs remember only the statements you made in support of the other side.

You will be able to tell when you have brought up a sensitive subject by the way your Arab friend evades a direct answer to your questions or comments. If you receive evasive answers, don't press further; there is a reason why the person does not want to pursue the subject.

It is useful to introduce other topics into the conversation if you can, to change the subject. These are suggested topics that most people love to discuss:

- The Golden Age of the Arabs and their contributions in the Middle Ages
- The culturally required traits of an "ideal person"
- The experience of making the Hajj (pilgrimage)
- The person's extended family
- The Arabic language, its literature, and poetry (whether you are interested or not)

SOCIAL DISTANCE

Arab and Western cultures differ in the amount of touching they feel comfortable with in interpersonal relations and in the physical distance they maintain when conversing. These norms are largely unconscious, so both Arabs and Westerners may feel uncomfortable without knowing exactly why.

In general, Arabs tend to stand and sit closer and to touch other people (of the same sex) more than Westerners do. It is common to see two men or two women holding hands as they walk down a street, which is simply a sign of friendship. You must be prepared for the possibility that an Arab will take your hand, especially when crossing the street. After shaking hands in greeting, Arabs may continue to hold your hand while talking—if the conversation is expected to be brief. They will then shake it again when saying goodbye. Kissing on both cheeks is a common form of greeting (again, only with members of the same sex),* as is embracing. It is also common to touch someone repeatedly during a conversation, often to emphasize a point. Children, especially if they are blond, should be prepared to have their heads rubbed by well-meaning adults.

Arab culture does not have the same concept of public and private space as do Western cultures. Westerners, in a sense, carry a little bubble of private space around with them. Arabs, on the other hand, are not uncomfortable when they are close to or touching strangers. (This is not the case in the Arabian Peninsula and the Gulf, where people are less effusive and more formal. Touching other people is not common and can even be offensive.)

Westerners are accustomed to standing in an elevator in such a way that maximum space is maintained between people. In the Arab world, it is common for a person to board an elevator and stand close beside you rather than moving to the opposite corner. When an Arab boards a bus or selects a seat on a bench, he often sits beside someone rather than going to an empty seat or leaving a space between himself and others. To give a typical example, this tendency was particularly annoying to an American who was standing on a street corner in Beirut waiting for a friend. He had a good view of the intersecting streets until a Lebanese man came to the corner and, apparently also waiting for someone, stood directly in front of him.

When Arabs and Westerners are talking, they may both continually shift position, in a kind of unconscious dance, as the Arab approaches and the Westerner backs away, each trying to maintain a comfortable social distance. For Arabs, the space that is comfortable for ordinary social conversation is approximately the same as that which Westerners reserve for intimate conversation.

Anthropologist Edward T. Hall was the first to write about the concept of personal space in his classic book *The Hidden Dimension*, never since equaled:

> For the Arab, there is no such thing as an intrusion in public. Public means public . . . . In the Western world, the person is synonymous with an individual inside a skin. And in northern Europe generally,

---

* Unless the people are very Westernized, but this is rare.

the skin and even the clothes may be inviolate. You need permission to touch either if you are a stranger . . . . For the Arab, the location of the person in relation to the body is quite different. The person exists somewhere down inside the body . . . . Tucking the ego down inside the body shell not only would permit higher population densities but would explain why it is that Arab communications are stepped up as much as they are when compared to northern European communication patterns. Not only is the sheer noise level much higher, but the piercing look of the eyes, the touch of the hands, and the mutual bathing in the warm moist breath during conversation represent stepped-up sensory inputs to a level which many Europeans find unbearably intense.[1]

You do not have to adopt Arab touching patterns, of course; just be aware that they are different from your own and accept them as natural and normal.

❋ GESTURES

Arabs make liberal use of gestures when they talk, especially if they are enthusiastic about what they are saying. Hand and facial gestures are thus an important part of Arab communication. If you can recognize them, you will be able to get the full meaning of what is being said to you.

Listed here are some of the most common gestures used in Arab countries. There are variations among countries, but most are in wide use. Men use gestures more than women do, and less educated people use them more than the educated do. You should not try to use these gestures (foreigners often use gestures in the wrong place or situation), but you should learn to recognize them.

- ❋ Moving the head slightly back and raising the eyebrows = no. Moving the head back and the chin upward = no. Moving the chin back slightly and making a clicking sound with the tongue = no.
- ❋ After shaking hands, placing the right hand to the heart or chest = greeting someone with respect or sincerity.
- ❋ Holding the right hand out, palm downward, and moving it as if scooping something away from you = go away.

- Holding the right hand out, palm upward, and opening and closing it = come here.
- Holding the right hand out, palm upward, then closing the hand halfway and holding it = give it to me.
- Holding the right hand out, palm downward, and moving it up and down slowly = quiet down.
- Holding the right hand out, palm upward, and touching the thumb and tips of fingers together and moving the hand up and down slowly = calm down, be patient, slowly.
- Holding the right forefinger up and moving it from left to right quickly several times (the "windshield wiper") = no, never.
- Holding the right hand out, palm downward, then quickly twisting the hand to show the palm upward = what? why?

❖ NAMES

In many Western societies, one indication of the closeness of a personal relationship is the use of first names. In Arab society, the first name is used immediately, even if it is preceded by "Miss," "Mrs.," or "Mr." Arabs do not refer to people by their third, or "last," name. Arab names, for both men and women, consist of a first name (the person's own), the father's name, and the paternal grandfather's name, followed by a family name (in countries where family names are used). In other words, an Arab's name is simply a string of names listing ancestors on the father's side. A Western example might be John (given name) Robert (his father) William (his grandfather) Jones.

Because names reflect genealogy on the father's side, women have masculine names after their first name. Some people include *ibn/bin* (son of) or *bint* (daughter of) between the ancestral names. This practice is common in the Arabian Peninsula and can be seen in names like Abdel-Aziz ibn Saud (son of Saud), the founder of the Kingdom of Saudi Arabia, and Khalifa bin Zayed Al Nahyan, the ruler of the United Arab Emirates. If there is no hyphen, the word *Al* often means "family," as in Al Saud, translated as the House of Saud, and Al Nahyan, the Nahyan family. In North Africa, the words *Ben* or *Ould* are used to mean "son of"; *Bou* (father of) is also a common element of a family name. Examples are political figures, such as Abdelaziz Bouteflika, the president of Algeria;

Mohamed Ould Abdel Aziz, the president of Mauritania; and Zine Al-Abidine Ben Ali, the former president of Tunisia.

Because a person's first name is the only one that is really his or hers, Arabs use it from the moment they are introduced, including with a title. A Western man can expect to be called "Mr. Bill" or "Mr. John." If he is married, his wife would be called "Mrs. Mary," or possibly "Mrs. Bill." An unmarried woman would be "Miss Mary." First names are also used with titles such as "Doctor" and "Professor," as well as with military ranks.

A person may retain several names for legal purposes but omit them in daily use. A man named Ahmad Abdullah Ali Muhammad, for example, would be commonly known as Ahmad Abdullah; if he has a family or tribal name, let's say Al-Harithi, he would be known as Ahmad Abdullah Al-Harithi, or possibly Ahmad Al-Harithi. Similarly, a woman whose full name is Zeinab Abdullah Ali Muhammad Al-Harithi may be known as Zeinab Abdullah or Zeinab Al-Harithi. People are not always consistent when reciting their names on different occasions.*

When a genealogical name becomes too long (after four or five generations), some of the older names will be dropped. The only pattern that is really consistent is that the father's name will be retained along with the family name if there is one. It is entirely possible that full brothers and sisters may be registered with different combinations of names.

In Arabian Peninsula countries, the telephone books list people under their family names. In some Arab countries, however, the telephone book lists people under their first names, because the first name is the only one that can be depended on to be consistently present (and telephone books don't work well; they are rarely consulted). Some business organizations find it easier to keep payroll records by first name.

A family or tribal name identifies a large extended family or group whose members still consider themselves tied by bonds of kinship and honor. A family name may be geographical (Hijazi, "from Hijaz," Halaby, "from Aleppo"); denote an occupation (Haddad, "smith," Najjar,

---

* An article in the *Washington Post* on May 5, 2011, referring to Saddam Hussein was titled, "Hussein trial court to be disbanded." Arabs unused to the Western naming system would not understand who this referred to.[2] This is why you usually hear Arabs say his name as simply Saddam. In Egypt, the name of former president Mubarak was used by the West to the point that the Egyptians adopted it; in a face-to-face situation, he was called "President Hosni."

"carpenter"); be descriptive (Al-Ahmar, "red," Al-Taweel, "tall"); denote tribe (Al-Harithi, Quraishi); or sound like a personal name because it is the name of an ancestor (Abdel-Rahman, Ibrahim).

An Arab Muslim woman does not change her name after marriage, since she does not take her husband's genealogy. Arabs are very proud of their mother's family and want her to retain the name and refer to it. Only informally is a wife called "Mrs." with her husband's first or last name.

When people have children, an informal but very pleasing and polite way to address the parents is by the name of the oldest son or oldest child: *Abu* (father of) or *Umm* (mother of) the child; for example, Umm Ahmad (mother of Ahmad). These terms of address are considered respectful, and *Umm* is especially useful when talking to a woman because it provides a less personal way of addressing her.

Arabs do not name their sons after their father, but naming a child after his paternal grandfather is common. You will meet some men whose first and third names are the same.

Titles are used more widely in Arabic than in English. Anyone with an MD or PhD degree is addressed as "Dr." ("Duktor" for a man, "Duktora" for a woman). It is important to find out any titles a person may have; omitting the title will be noticed. "Sheikh" is a respectful title for a wealthy, influential, or elderly man. Government ministers are called *Ma'ali*, and senior officials are given the honorary title *Sa'ada* before their other titles and name.

Most Arab names have a meaning and can be clues to certain facts about a person. Many names indicate religion or country of origin. Because the exchange of personal information is so important, some people introduce themselves with various long combinations of names, especially if their first and last names are ambiguous (used by more than one group).

It is useful for foreigners to be able to place people, at least partially, upon hearing their names. Here are a few guidelines:

- If a name sounds Western (George, Antoine, Mary), it marks a Christian.
- If a name is that of a well-known figure in Islamic history (Muhammad, Bilal, Salah-Eddeen, Fatima, Ayesha), it marks a Muslim.

❀ Most hyphenated names using "Abdel-" are Muslim. The name means "Servant (Slave) of God," and the second part is one of the attributes of God (Abdullah, "Servant of God/Allah"; Abdel-Rahman, "Servant of the Merciful"; Abdel-Aziz, "Servant of the Powerful"). There are a few Christian names on this pattern (Abdel-Malak, "Servant of the Angel"; Abdel-Massih, "Servant of the Messiah"; Abdel-Qaddous, "Servant of the Most Holy") but over 90 percent of the time you can assume that a person with this type of name is Muslim. Of the ninety-nine attributes for God (the Knowing, the Compassionate, the Wise, the Generous, etc.), most are currently in use as names.

❀ Names containing the word *deen* (religion) are Muslim (Sharaf-Eddeen, "The Honor of Religion"; Badr-Eddeen, "The Moon of Religion"; Salah-Eddeen, "the Rightness of Religion").

❀ Many names are simply descriptive adjectives (Saeed, "happy"; Amin, "faithful"; Jameela, "beautiful"). Such descriptive names do not mark religion.

❀ Names that derive from both the Qur'an and the Bible (Ibrahim, "Abraham"; Sulaiman, "Solomon"; Daoud, "David"; Yousef, "Joseph") do not distinguish whether the person is Muslim, Christian, or Jewish. Issa (Eisa), "Jesus," is a common name among Muslims.

❄ ❄ ❄ ❄ ❄ ❄ ❄ ❄ ❄ ❄ ❄ ❄ ❄ ❄ ❄ ❄ ❄ ❄

CHAPTER 5

MEN AND WOMEN

Of great interest to Westerners is the relation between men and women in Arab society. There are misconceptions, too, depending on which stories one has heard.

In Arab society, the nature of interaction between men and women depends on the situation. Continual interaction is expected at work or in professional situations (although it remains reserved by Western standards, and in Saudi Arabia is actually restricted), but social interaction is very carefully controlled. The degree of control differs among Arab countries, depending on their relative conservatism, but nowhere is it as free and casual (chatting freely, laughing together, having lunch together) as in Western societies.

But don't generalize about the lives of women from examples in highly conservative cultures such as Saudi Arabia, Afghanistan, or Pakistan. Most women live in more liberal societies and have many personal choices.

❄ SOCIAL INTERACTION

The maintenance of family honor is one of the highest values in Arab society. Many Westerners fail to understand that because misbehavior by women is believed to do more damage to family honor than misbehavior by men, clearly defined patterns of behavior have been developed to protect women (in the traditional view) and help them avoid situations that may give rise to false impressions or unfounded gossip. Women interact freely only with other women and close male relatives.

Arab men and women are careful about appearances when they meet. They avoid situations where they would be alone together, even for a short time. It is improper to be in a room together with the door closed, to go out on a date as a couple, or to travel together (unless in a group), even on a short daytime trip. Guarding a woman's image is neither a personal nor a family choice; it is imposed by the culture, just as chaperones were once required in Western society. The point is not the woman's character, or what did or did not happen—the point is how it looks.

Shared activities take place with other people present. At mixed social events, women are accompanied by their husbands or male relatives. In Saudi Arabia (only), "religious police" may question couples who are at a restaurant or in a car together and ask for proof that they are married.

Foreigners must be aware of the restrictions that pertain to contact between Arab men and women and then consider their own appearance in front of others. *Arabs quickly gain a negative impression if you behave with too much (presumed) familiarity toward a person of the opposite sex.* They will interpret your behavior on their own terms and may conclude that you are a person of low moral standards. If an embarrassing incident involves a Western man and an Arab woman, they may feel that the Westerner insulted the woman's honor, thereby threatening the honor of her family.

A Western man can feel free to greet an Arab woman at a social gathering (though it is not a common practice in Saudi Arabia), but their subsequent discussion should include other people rather than just the two of them. A married Western woman may greet and visit with Arab men, provided she is accompanied by her husband (in the same room). If a woman is unmarried or if her husband is not present, she should be more reserved.

In many Arab countries, men and women separate into their own conversation groups shortly after arrival at a social gathering; this depends on the customs of a given area. In Saudi Arabia, women are often excluded from social gatherings altogether, or they may be more restricted in their behavior when they are included (they usually sit separately). It is important to point out that social separation is not practiced merely because it is required by custom; it is often preferred by both men and women because they feel more comfortable. Westerners can expect to spend much of their social time in all-male or all-female groups.

Western men and women should also give thought to their appearance in front of others when they interact among themselves. Behavior such as overly enthusiastic greetings, animated and joking conversations, and casual invitations to go somewhere are easily misinterpreted by Arabs and reinforce their stereotype of Westerners.

❈ DISPLAYING INTIMACY

The public display of intimacy between men and women is strictly forbidden by the Arab social code, including holding hands, linking arms, or any gesture of affection such as kissing or prolonged touching. Such actions, even between husband and wife, are highly embarrassing to Arab observers.

A public display of intimacy is a particularly serious offense in Saudi Arabia, and incidents of problems and misunderstandings are frequent. One such incident occurred when an American woman was observed getting into a car with an American man, sliding over to his side, and kissing him on the cheek. A captain of the Saudi National Guard, who happened to see this, demanded proof that they were married. They were, but not to each other. The woman was deported, and the man, who compounded his problem by being argumentative, was sent to jail. Even behavior such as holding hands (especially among young people) is still viewed by most people everywhere with disapproval.

❈ THE STATUS OF WOMEN

The degree to which women have been integrated into the workforce and circulate freely in public varies among the Arab countries. In Morocco, Tunisia, Egypt, Lebanon, Syria, Jordan, and Iraq, educated women have been active at all levels of society. Women have been heads of state in four non-Arab Islamic countries: Pakistan, Bangladesh, Indonesia, and Turkey.

In the Arabian Gulf states, fewer women have jobs outside the home (few need the income), but there is a huge push from those governments to encourage women's education and participation in the workplace to lessen dependence on foreigners. Saudi Arabia is a special case—women are becoming well educated, but few are present in the workplace. Those who do work are mainly in the professions, in all-female environments;

an exception is made for the medical professions. All Arab governments now support efforts to increase women's educational opportunities.

In domestic law, Arab women have traditionally not fared so well. Weighing Islamic law (*Sharia*) against current Western criteria of what constitutes women's equality has become very controversial, and an impassioned discussion of this issue is ongoing virtually everywhere and in the media. Traditional Islamic law restricts the rights of women, and this seems to many people to be seriously outdated. The various points of view rest on interpretations of the Qur'an, which, like any holy book, can be obscure and unclear. Like the Bible, the Qur'an is a product of its times and does not reflect modern concepts on issues such as slavery and women's rights.

Morocco and Tunisia have been outstanding in efforts to blend Sharia law with women's rights. There is a Muslim organization in Europe, LibForAll Foundation, which promotes moderate interpretations of Sharia throughout the Islamic world. Dr. Abu Zayd at the foundation has asserted that the Qur'an need not be interpreted literally; when interpreted "sensibly in context," it carries a strong message of social justice and women's rights.[1] There is a project to retranslate the Qur'an in light of modern academic scholarship, which is yielding interpretations in keeping with "the ethics of the modern age" and fighting against cultural practices that are justified as religious.[2] Fierce opposition can be expected, but more discussion and many adjustments are coming. It will not be the same everywhere because Muslim societies are so culturally, socially, ethnically, and, to an extent, religiously diverse.

Many of the orthodox Islamic scholars insist on medieval understanding of the text as final and irrevocable, whereas modern scholars, of no less intellectual integrity and knowledge, insist that there can be multiple understandings of holy text. This debate between orthodox and modern scholars has been going on practically in every Islamic country.

Feminism in the Middle East is not the same as in the West. Muslim women do not expect an all-at-once liberation from traditional and social gender roles. They are working *within* religious values, picking their battles, and taking it step by step.

Westerners have an exaggerated image about the status of women in Arab countries, having heard so many lurid stories in the news. A kind of folk knowledge has grown up—the image of Muslim women as oppressed, servile, and without rights. Much information about Arab women, in print and online, is very dated; anything over five years old should be viewed with skepticism and checked. Some stories have dealt with unusual, news-worthy events, and many are based on the worst possible examples—the Taliban in Afghanistan, the Wahhabis in Saudi Arabia, the strict rules in post-revolutionary Iran. It is natural to generalize from certain incidents and arrive at a distorted view of this issue, whereas most Muslim women are in fact happy in their lives, all the while working to make them better. Dramatic and even horrific events are more interesting and gain wide currency, but they are not as common as news stories make them seem.

Governments are easing up on some rules. Even in Saudi Arabia, 18 women were elected to positions in municipal governments in 2015, in the first elections open to women voters. Most countries are considering improvement of personal-status laws to give women more rights in matters of divorce and custody.

In 2006, a Gallup poll asked whether the respondents agreed that women should have leadership roles. The responses in favor were 74 percent in Morocco, 55 percent in Jordan, 92 percent in Lebanon, and 54 percent in Egypt. Only Saudi Arabia was below the halfway mark, at 40 percent.*,3 It is certainly time for another poll.

Arab first ladies have been active in promoting women's rights for years. Six international Arab Women's Conferences have been held, from 2002 to the most recent in 2016, where many prominent women called for greater awareness and efforts to protect women's rights. Many smaller organizations exist, such as the Egyptian Centre for Women's Rights, the General Union of Syrian Women, the Libyan Women's Platform for Peace, and the Organization of Women's Freedom in Iraq. These alliances are breaking taboos and getting feminist issues on the political agenda. The fourth Arab Women in Leadership and Business Summit is scheduled for April 2018 in Dubai.

Certainly things could be better, and women constantly confront obstacles. After the 2011 revolution in Tunisia, only two women were included in the transitional government. In Egypt, no women at all

---

* The non-Arab countries included were Turkey, 96 percent, and Pakistan, 58 percent.

participated in revamping the constitution. This makes women worry that conservatives may try to repeal or reinterpret progressive family laws.[4]

More and more women are assuming leadership roles in education, banking, finance, science, and medicine. When you visit offices and companies, the increase in women's participation is obvious in virtually all Arab countries.

The Internet and expanded media communications are facilitating regionwide contacts and making both men and women open to new ideas. Impediments are political and traditional, *not religious*. Because the laws are subject to change (forward or backward), the role of women in Arab society and in Islam is by no means static or fixed.

❀ WOMEN'S RIGHT TO VOTE

In all Arab countries women now have the right to vote. Below is a summary of the current situation.

DATE WOMEN FIRST GIVEN THE VOTE

Iraq	1948
Syria	1949/1953
Lebanon	1952
Egypt	1956
Tunisia	1957/1959
Algeria	1962
Morocco	1963
Libya	1964
Sudan	1964
Jordan	1974
Yemen	1993
Oman	1994
Qatar	1998/2003
Bahrain	2001/2002
Kuwait	2005
UAE	2015
Saudi Arabia	2015

❁ WOMEN IN GOVERNMENT POSITIONS

Arab women are increasingly represented at various levels of their governments. Women serve in the cabinets of most countries, except the most conservative. Women are generally well represented in parliaments, where most countries have a quota. Women's share of seats in parliament increased to an average of 18.1 percent in 2016, maintaining steady progress over the past decade.

❁ ❁

PERCENT AND NUMBER OF WOMEN IN ARAB PARLIAMENTS[6]

Country	Year	% in parliament	# in parliament
Algeria	2017	25.8%	119
Tunisia	2014	31.3%	68
Sudan	2015	30.5%	130
South Sudan	2016	28.5%	109
Iraq	2014	25.3%	83
Morocco	2016	20.5%	81
UAE	2011	20%	8
Saudi Arabia	2016	19.9%	30
Libya	2014	16%	30
Jordan	2016	15.4%	20
Egypt	2015	14.9%	89
Syria	2016	13.2%	33
Bahrain	2014	7.5%	3
Kuwait	2016	3.1%	2
Lebanon	2009	3.1%	4
Oman	2015	1.2%	1
Qatar		0	0
Yemen		0	0

In the Arab states, women's representation in senior executive posts reached 9.7 percent in 2017, from 9.5 percent in 2015. Tunisia's rate of women's representation rose significantly from 10.5 percent in 2015 to 23.1 percent in 2017. The UAE increased women's presence in government to 26.7 percent; these are the only two countries in the region to surpass 20 percent.[7]

❀ WOMEN'S POWER IN THE FAMILY

In traditional Arab society, men and women have well-defined spheres of activity and decision making. Do not assume that because Arab women are not highly visible in public, their influence is similarly restricted in private life.

Inside the family, women have a good deal of power. They usually have the decisive voice in matters relating to household expenditures, the upbringing and education of children, and sometimes the arrangement of marriages. Men are responsible for providing the family's material welfare; even if a woman has her own money, she need not contribute to family expenses. Many women do have their own money, and many own property. Islamic law states clearly that they retain sole control of their money and inheritance after marriage.

The older a woman becomes, the more status and power she accrues. Men owe great respect to their mothers all their lives and must make every effort to obey their mother's wishes, including her whims. All older women in the family are treated with deference, but the mother of sons gains even more status.

❀ THE HEADSCARF AND THE VEIL

The wearing of the hijab (the headscarf) is, of course, controversial (covering the hair should not be referred to as "veiling," since that requires that the face be covered). Everyone who visits the Arab world on a regular basis can't help but notice that the number of women wearing the hijab has increased enormously in the past twenty years. It began with the Islamic revival in the 1980s and 1990s and has gradually and steadily spread throughout society.

Most Westerners see the hijab as a symbol of women's oppression, but not all Muslims agree. It may only be a sign that the wearer is conservative, with no political significance attached. Some say that it can have political significance; it depends on the wearer. A woman is (theoretically) making a free choice, since the hijab *is not required by the Islamic religion*. However, there is growing social pressure from family or friends to wear the head covering. On the other hand, some families are distressed that their daughters are doing so.

Some observers believe that the voluntary wearing of headscarves is a manifestation, in a person or in the whole society, of a growing sense of Muslim identity. Women often say that by masking their sexuality, they are far freer in their movements in society—the headscarf deters unwelcome attention from men because they see it and respect it. Many women wear headscarves that are chic, expensive, and highly decorated.

The situation differs widely among countries and regions. Tunisia forbade head covering in 2006 and permitted it after the revolution in 2011. Turkey forbade head covering in 1980 and strengthened the law in 1997, but after an Islamic government was elected, it is permitted.

The full-face veil is banned in Syria, but not the hijab, which is in fairly wide use. Syria's current government is secular, and this practice could change. In Jordan, about half of the women wear a hijab, but a face veil is rare. The hijab is seen in Lebanon, though at a much lower rate than in other Arab countries. In Gaza, Hamas enforces the hijab.

In Egypt, the hijab is widespread, worn by about 80 percent of the women. It is not encouraged by the current government, nor is it forbidden. In some cases, the hijab has been seen as a political symbol, but many Egyptian women use the hijab for social acceptance among peers and as a fashion statement. A small number of women wear a face veil (the niqab) as well; in 2009, scholars at the Azhar University* stated that *full veiling of the face is not required under Islam*: "It is a custom and not a form of worship."[8] There was a ban against the veil on college campuses during examinations, but after protests, the bans were lifted in both Egypt and Syria.

In Morocco, the hijab is not encouraged, and is generally frowned upon by the urban middle and upper classes. It is not traditional, and its use is often viewed as a borrowed religious or political symbol. It is more common in the north and in the workers' class; in one French-owned factory, more than 95 percent of the women cover their hair, compared with only 20 percent ten years earlier.[9]

Women in the conservative countries of the Arabian Peninsula all cover their hair, and most wear a face veil in public, although not

---

* The Azhar is as close as Sunni Islam comes to having a central authority; it is recognized as the premier religious center.

necessarily indoors. The veil is more strictly required in Saudi Arabia than elsewhere.

In any case, many Muslim women feel that Westerners are too concerned with the way they dress, which is superficial, compared with other issues they face. Many feminists defend their conservative dress in terms of nationalism, anti-imperialism, or as a matter of personal faith.

The Qur'an itself says nothing explicit about veiling or, for that matter, secluding women from men in a separate part of the house. These were later developments and did not become widespread in the Islamic empire until three or four generations after the death of Muhammad. The custom of veiling and secluding women came into the Muslim world from Persia and Byzantium, where women had long been secluded.*[11]

The Qur'an is far more protective of women's rights and status than is the case with more recent social practices. It contains only three verses referring to women's modesty, none of which mentions hair.[12] Here are the two most cited (the third refers to the Prophet's wives, who generally conversed with people from behind a curtain):

> O Prophet, tell the wives and daughters that they should cast their outer garments over their persons when abroad, that is the most convenient, that they should be known and not molested. (33:59)

> Say to the believing men that they should lower their gaze and guard their modesty . . . . And say to the believing women that they should lower their gaze and guard their modesty; that they should not display their beauty and ornaments except what must appear thereof; that they should draw their veils over their bosoms and not display their beauty except to their husbands, their fathers . . . . (it goes on to list male relatives, small children, etc.) (24:30–31)

While some Arab Muslim women see the hijab as a religious, cultural, or political statement, other women strongly disagree and disapprove. When in the West, some women continue to wear a hijab, and others don't. It is certainly not required.

---

* Certainly, there were restrictions on women in the West. "In the Middle Ages the position was reversed: Then the Muslims were horrified to see the way Western Christians treated their women in the Crusader states, and Christian scholars denounced Islam for giving too much power to menials like slaves and women."[10]

In a 2013 poll, people were asked if a woman should be allowed to decide if she wears a hijab. Over half said "yes" in Tunisia, Morocco, Lebanon, and Palestine. Fewer than half agreed in Egypt, Jordan, and Iraq.[13]

Arab women generally wear clothing that is at least knee-length, with sleeves that cover at least half of their arms. The practice of wearing more conservative, floor-length, long-sleeved clothing is increasing, not decreasing (as it once was), even in modern cities like Cairo and Amman.

❈ POLYGAMY

The issue of polygamy in the Arab world is overemphasized in the West, where many people think it is a common practice and is widely condoned. In fact, though, polygamy is allowed only under certain conditions in most Arab countries and is outlawed altogether in others. About 1 or 2 percent of married men have more than one wife. Because laws are more traditional in the Arabian Peninsula, and men have more money, polygamy is more common there. In other places, polygamy is conditional—the man must prove he can support all wives separately and equally, or a judge's permission may be required based on unusual conditions (if the wife is childless, for example), or the first wife must be informed and can obtain a divorce if she disapproves.

Many secular elements in governments disapprove of polygamy, as do the middle and upper classes in non-peninsular countries. There is considerable variation among countries because it is a controversial issue. Nowadays hardly anyone can afford the cost of maintaining more than one family, so polygamy is practiced only by the very rich or by villagers and peasants who need help with labor and do not incur large expenses.

Polygamy was sanctioned in the seventh century, after a series of battles in which many men were killed and many widows and orphans were left behind. The following verse from the Qur'an refers to the aftermath of these battles:

> If you fear that you will not act justly towards the orphans, marry such women as seem good to you, two, three, four; but if you fear that you will not be able to deal justly (with them), then only one, or what your right hands own. That will be more suitable to prevent you from doing injustice. (4:3)

Most modern commentators take this verse to mean that polygamy is restricted to certain circumstances and monogamy is encouraged. "What your right hands own" refers to slaves or captives, common in the seventh century. The Qur'an continues:

> You will not be able to be fair and just between your wives, even if it is your ardent desire. (4:129)

This is, at best, ambiguous, and it is easy to see how the verses could have multiple interpretations.

It is unfortunate that we see so many references in Western magazines and newspapers to polygamy, making it look commonplace.* Most mainstream Muslims realize that it has outlived its time and purpose. Polygamy was decreasing markedly for years, although with the recent rise of religious conservatism, we may see it increase once again. It is no surprise that Osama bin Laden, who was wealthy and deeply conservative, is said to have married 11 to 16 women, although only four at a time.

Polygamy is permitted in Saudi Arabia, Kuwait, the UAE, Libya, Jordan, Morocco, Lebanon, and Egypt. It is conditionally permitted in Iraq, Syria, and Algeria and outlawed in Tunisia.[15]

❈ TRADITIONAL GENDER ROLES

Westerners hear and read about events involving certain Muslim women and perceive them as typical of the subjugation of women in Islamic

---

* A case in point is Bernard Lewis' article, "Targeted by a History of Hatred: the United States is now the unquestioned leader of the free world, also known as infidels," which appeared in *the Washington Post* on September 10, 2002, during the first Gulf War.[14] The subject was his explanation of Muslims (referring to all of them) hating the United States and hating the West for centuries. It goes on to state that hatred has been growing, and "one reason for the contempt with which they regard us" is due to "what they perceive as the rampant immorality and degeneracy of the American way" (the reference to "they" is unclear). Then polygamy is mentioned as a factor to explain contempt toward Christianity and, more generally, toward the West. There follows a quote from "a recent Arabic newspaper article in defense of polygamy." The quote is explicit, detailed, and to Western ears offensive, yet the source is left vague and the author gives the impression that polygamy is part of the modern Arab way of life, when 98 percent of Arab men are monogamous and most would not even consider polygamy. I mention this because I think that making these statements without any qualifications reinforces stereotypes about Middle Eastern Arabs and Muslims and may strengthen a negative image.

society as a whole. Some of this is a valid criticism and many people in the West and the Middle East believe that legal redress is urgently needed. Nevertheless, even if we Westerners disagree with the status quo, we must at least try to *understand* the traditional view and not be too quick to judge and condemn motives and cultural practices, many of which are *not* related to religion.

Unlike Western assumptions about Arab society, *tradition-oriented* Arab men and women do not view social customs and restrictions as repressive but as *an appropriate acknowledgment of the nature of women.* They do not see this as cruel, nor do they despise women. They sincerely see the restrictions as providing protection for women so that they need not be subjected to the stress, competition, temptations, and possible indignities found in outside society—but this is a very conservative view. Most Arab women, even now, feel satisfied that the present social system provides them with security, protection, and respect.

Middle East gender roles have traditionally been governed by a patriarchal kinship system that had already existed in the regions to which Islam spread. Many of the variations in the status of women are due to local traditions (such as covering the entire face). Men are expected to provide for their families; women, to bear and raise children; children, to honor and respect their parents and grow up to fulfill adult roles (which include marriage).[16] It is important for an outsider to keep these points of view in mind when analyzing and discussing the status of Arab women. A woman who was elected to Iraq's National Assembly stated, "To tell you the truth, I am not a feminist. I don't want to commit the same mistakes Western women have committed. I like that family should be the major principle for women here."[17]

❀ WESTERN WOMEN

Western women find that they do not quite fit into Arab society; they are not accorded the full rights of men but they are not considered bound by all the restrictions of Arab women, either.

Western women are expected to behave with propriety, but they are not required to be as conservative as Arab women in dress or in public behavior. They need not veil in Saudi Arabia, for example. But they are expected to dress conservatively, preferably in loose clothing. They may go shopping, attend public activities, or travel alone. The respectability of a Western woman will be judged by *the way she is groomed and dressed.*

Arabs accept professional Western women and admire them for their accomplishments. Well-educated women find that their opinions are taken seriously, and they are often invited to all-male professional gatherings. Women have had great success as diplomats in the region. When a woman has a work-related reason to call on someone or to be present at any event, she is usually welcomed, and men are comfortable with her presence.

CHAPTER 6

SOCIAL FORMALITIES AND ETIQUETTE

Social formalities and rules of etiquette are extremely important in Arab society. *Good manners constitute the most salient factor in evaluating a person's character.*

❋ HOSPITALITY

Arabs (and all Middle Easterners) are generous in the hospitality they offer to friends and strangers alike, and they admire and value the same in others. *Generosity to guests is essential for a good reputation.* It is a serious insult to characterize someone as stingy or inhospitable.

Arabs assume the role of host or hostess whenever the situation calls for it—in their office, home, or shop. Sometimes people say, "Welcome to my country" (in English) when they see a foreigner on the street or in a shop, thus assuming the role of host to a guest. Arabs are always willing to help a foreigner, again, because they take on the role of host. If you ask directions, some people may insist on accompanying you to your destination. One American tourist reported that when she and her husband were visiting Egypt, people sometimes took their hands to help crossing the street amid harrowing traffic.[1]

A guest in someone's home or in the workplace never stays long without being offered something to drink, and it is assumed that the guest will accept and drink at least a small quantity as an expression of friendship or esteem. When you are served a beverage, accept and hold the cup or glass with your right hand.

No matter how much coffee or tea you have had elsewhere, never decline this offer (some shops and offices have employees whose sole duty is to serve beverages to guests). You will notice that while a Westerner would likely ask guests, "Would you care for coffee or tea?" using an intonation pattern that suggests that the guest may or may not want any, a Middle Easterner would ask, "What would you like, coffee or tea?" simply giving the guests a choice. If someone comes to a home or place of business while food is being served, the people eating always offer to share the food. Usually an unexpected guest declines, but the gesture must be made.

The phrases *Ahlan wa Sahlan* or *Marhaba* (Welcome) are used when a guest arrives, and they are repeated several times during a visit. A guest is often given a seat of honor (this is particularly common as a gesture to a foreigner), and solicitous inquiries are made about the guest's comfort during the visit. Sometimes you may feel uncomfortable because you are getting so much attention.

Regardless of pressing circumstances, an Arab would never consider refusing entrance to a guest, even if he or she is unexpected and the visit inconvenient. The only excusable circumstance would be if a woman (or women) were at home alone when a man dropped by—then it would be the visitor who would refuse to enter, even if his prospective host were expected back very soon.

Arabs are proud of their tradition of hospitality and have many anecdotes illustrating it. A favorite is the story of the Bedouin who killed his last camel (or sheep) to feed his guest. The word for "generous, hospitable" in Arabic is *kareem*, and this concept is so highly valued that its meanings extend to "distinguished, noble-minded, noble-hearted, honorable, respectable" (there are 25 meanings in the dictionary).

In turn, Arabs expect to be received with hospitality when they are guests, and your personal image and status will be affected by people's perceptions of your hospitality.

The most important components of hospitality are welcoming a guest (including using the word *Welcome*), offering the guest a seat (in many Arab homes, there is a special room set aside for receiving guests, called the "salon"), and offering something to drink. As a host, stay with your guests as much as possible, excusing yourself for brief absences from the room only as necessary. This is a description of Arab hospitality written by an Arab woman:

> For Arabs, hospitality is at the heart of who we are. How well one treats his guests is a direct measurement of what kind of a person she or he is. Hospitality is among the most highly admired of virtues. Indeed, families judge themselves and each other according to the amount of generosity they bestow upon their guests when they enter-tain. Whether one's guests are relatives, friends, neighbors, or relative strangers, they are welcomed into the home and to the dinner table with much the same kindness and generosity.[2]

A guest does not see the rest of the house and meets only the family members who are presented. Privacy *within* a family is not valued, but privacy from *the outside* is essential. Most houses are behind high walls.

Hospitality extends to the public sphere, too. In Tunis, Cairo, Beirut, and Amman I have asked for directions and been escorted to my destination, though in each instance it was a long walk and considerable inconvenience for my guide. When thanking someone for such a favor, you will hear the response, "No thanks are needed for a duty." No task is too burdensome for a hospitable host.

❀ TIME AND APPOINTMENTS

Among Arabs, time is not as fixed and rigidly segmented as it tends to be among Westerners. It flows from past to present to future, and Arabs flow with it. Social occasions and appointments need not have fixed beginnings or endings. Arabs are thus much more relaxed about the timing of events than they are about other aspects of their lives. Nevertheless, these attitudes are beginning to change as people respond to the demands of economic and technological development and modernization.

Some Arabs are careful to arrive on time (and impatient with those who do not), and some are habitually late, especially for social events. Given these attitudes, a person who arrives late and has kept you waiting may not realize that you have been inconvenienced and expect an apology.

Frequently, an Arab shopkeeper or someone in a service trade fails to have something finished by a promised time. This also pertains to public services (such as getting a gas line repaired), personal services, bus and train departures, customer services (where standing in long lines can be expected), and bureaucratic procedures. Be flexible; everyone expects delays. You will appear unreasonably impatient and demanding if you insist on having things finished at a precise time.

If you invite people for dinner or a social event, do not expect all your guests to arrive at the specified time. A dinner should be served rather late, and plans should always be flexible enough to accommodate latecomers.

The Arabic word (and sentence) *Ma'alish* represents an entire way of looking at life and its frustrations. It means "never mind," or, "it doesn't matter," or, "excuse me—it's not that serious." You will hear this said frequently when someone has had a delay, a disappointment, or an unfortunate experience. Rather than give in to pointless anger, Arabs often react to impersonally caused adversity with resignation and, to some extent, an acceptance of their fate.

❊ DISCUSSING BUSINESS

Arabs mistrust people who do not appear to be sincere or who fail to demonstrate an interest in them personally or in their country. They also don't like to be hurried or to feel they are being pressured into a business agreement. If they like you, they will agree to work out an arrangement or a compromise; if they do not like you, they will probably stop listening. *Arabs evaluate the source of a statement or proposal as much as the content.*

Initial reactions by your Arab counterparts to your suggestions, ideas, and proposals can be quite misleading if taken at face value. Arabs are not likely to criticize openly but are more likely to hint that changes are needed or to give more subtle indications that the proposal is unacceptable—by inaction, for instance. They may promise to be in touch but fail to do so (which is more polite than a refusal), or they might offer a radical counterproposal that may constitute a position from which compromise is expected.

Don't take flattery and praise too seriously. It will more likely be adherence to good manners than an indicator of potential success in the business transaction. Some decisions simply require consultation with superiors (if you are not dealing with the top person). A noncommittal reaction to a proposal does not mean it has been rejected, nor does it guarantee ultimate acceptance. Only time will tell the outcome, with success dependent, more often than not, on patience and the cultivation of good personal relations.

Despite the frustration you may feel from delays, *if you press for a specific time by which you want a decision, you may actually harm your chances of success.* Your counterpart may perceive it as an insult, especially if the person is a high-ranking manager or executive.

The vice president of an American engineering company was meeting with a high-level Saudi official in the Ministry of Planning in Riyadh. The company's local representative had been trying for several weeks to obtain approval for one of the company's proposals. The vice president decided at the meeting to request that the ministry give them a definite answer during the week he was to be in town. The Saudi looked surprised and appeared irritated, then answered that he could not guarantee action within that time. The proposal was never approved.

If a decision is coming slowly, it may mean that the proposal needs to be reassessed. Do not expect to conclude all your business at once, especially if several decisions are required. Patience and repeated visits are called for. Arabs have plenty of time, and they see little need to accommodate foreigners who are in a hurry and trying to pressure them.

❈ SHARING MEALS

Arabs enjoy inviting guests to their home for meals; a foreigner will probably be a guest at meals many times. Sharing food together provides an Arab host and hostess with a perfect opportunity to display their generosity and demonstrate their personal regard for you.

It is not an Arab custom to send written invitations or to request confirmation of acceptance. Invitations are usually verbal and often spontaneous.

If it is your first invitation, check with others for the time meals are usually served and for the time you are expected to arrive. Westerners often arrive too early and assume the meal will be served earlier than is customary. In most Arab countries (but not all), a large midday meal is served between 2 and 3 p.m., and a supper (with guests) is served about 10 or 11 p.m. Guests should arrive about two hours before the meal, since most of the conversation takes place before the meal, not after it. If the dinner is formal and official, you may be expected to arrive at the specified time, and you can expect the meal to end within an hour or two.

Arabs serve a great quantity of food when they entertain—indeed, they are famous for their munificence and very proud of it. They do not try to calculate the amount of food actually needed; on the contrary, the intention is to present abundant food, which displays generosity. (The leftover food does not go to waste; it is consumed by the family or by servants for several days afterward.)

Most foreigners who have experienced Arab meals have their favorite hospitality stories. For example, I was told about a banquet once given by a wealthy merchant in Qatar who was known for his largesse. After several courses, the guests were served an entire sheep—one per person!

You can expect to be offered second and third helpings of food, and you should make the gesture of accepting at least once. Encouraging guests to eat is part of an Arab host's duty and is required for good manners. This encouragement to eat more is called *uzooma* in Arabic, and the more traditional the host, the more insistently it is done. Guests often begin with a ritual refusal and allow themselves to be won over by the host's insistence. You will hear, for example,

"No, thanks."

"Oh, but you must!"

"No, I really couldn't!"

"You don't like the food!"

"Oh, but I do!"

"Well then, have some more!"

Water is often not served until after a meal is finished; some people consider it unhealthy to eat and drink at the same time. In any case, Arab food is rarely "hot," although it may be highly seasoned.

A guest is expected to express admiration and gratitude for the food. Because you are trying to be polite, you will probably overeat. Many people eat sparingly on the day they are invited out to dinner because they know how much food will be served that evening.

When you have eaten enough, you may refuse more by saying, *Alham-dulillah* (Thanks be to God). When the meal is over and you are about to leave the table, it is customary to say, *Dayman* (Always) or *Sufra dayma* (May your table always be thus) to the host and hostess. The most common responses are *Ti'eesh* (May you live) and *Bil hana wa shifa* (To your happiness and health).

After a meal, tea or coffee will be served, usually presweetened. Conversation continues for a while longer, perhaps an hour, and then guests prepare to leave. In some countries, bringing a tray of ice water around is a sign that dinner is over and guests are free to leave. In the Arabian Peninsula countries, incense or cologne may be passed around just before the guests depart. When guests announce their intention to leave, the host and hostess usually exclaim, "Stay a while—it's still early!" This offer is ritual; you may stay a few more minutes, but the expression need not be taken literally, and it does not mean that you will give offense by leaving. Generally, you can follow the example of other guests, except that many Arabs prefer to stay out very late, so you may be the first to leave. In most Arab countries, you do not have to stay after midnight.

When you are invited to a meal, it is appropriate, although not required, to bring a small gift—flowers, candy, or cakes are the most common. You will see elaborately wrapped gifts of sweets displayed in stores; they are intended for hospitality gifts.

If you invite Arabs to your home, consider adopting some of their meal-time customs. It will improve their impression of you. In the countries of the Arabian Peninsula, women rarely go out socially in mixed company. When you invite a man and his wife to your home, the wife may not appear. It depends largely on whether the couple is accustomed to socializing with foreigners and on who else will be there. It is considerate, when a man is inviting a couple, to say, "My wife invites your wife," and to volunteer information about who else is invited. This helps the husband decide whether he wishes his wife to meet the other guests, and it assures him that other women will be present. Don't be surprised if some guests do not come, or if someone arrives with a friend or two.

Always serve plenty of food, with two or three main meat dishes; otherwise you may give the impression of being stingy. I once heard an Egyptian describe a dinner at an American's home where the guests were served one large steak apiece. "They counted the steaks, and they even counted the potatoes," he said. "We were served baked potatoes—one per person!"

If you serve buffet-style rather than a sit-down dinner with courses, your eating schedule will be more flexible and the visual impression of the amount of food served will be enhanced. Give thought to your menu, considering which foods are eaten locally and which are not. Serve foods in simple, recognizable form, so guests won't wonder what they are eating in a foreigner's home. Arabs usually do not care for sweetened meats or for sweet salads with the main meal.

Muslims are forbidden to eat pork. Some foreigners serve pork (as one of the choices at a buffet) and label it; this is not advisable, since it can be disconcerting to Muslim guests, who may wonder if the pork has touched any of the rest of the food.

The consumption of alcohol is forbidden for Muslims. Do not use it in your cooking unless you either label or mention it. If you cook with wine or other alcohol, you will limit the dishes available to your Muslim guests—it does not matter that the alcohol may have evaporated during cooking. If you wish to serve wine or alcoholic beverages, have non-alcoholic drinks available too.

Be sure to offer your guests second and third helpings of food. Although you don't have to insist vigorously, you should make the gesture. Serve coffee and tea at the end of a meal.

❊ SMOKING

A majority of Arab adults smoke, although women seldom smoke in public. Smoking is considered an integral part of adult behavior and constitutes, to some extent, the expression of an individual's "coming of age." Arab men, in particular, view smoking as a right, not a privilege. Do not be surprised if you see people disregarding "no smoking" signs in airplanes, waiting rooms, or elevators.

Arabs are rarely aware that smoking may be offensive to some Westerners. You can ask someone to refrain from smoking by explaining that it bothers you, but he may light up again after a few minutes. If you press the point too strongly, you will appear unreasonable. If possible, have a place available where people are welcome to smoke; it will help them relax.

There are nascent anti-smoking campaigns, just getting started.

❋ RULES OF ETIQUETTE

Listed below are some of the basic rules of etiquette in Arab culture:

- ❋ It is important to sit properly. Slouching, draping the legs over the arm of a chair, or otherwise sitting carelessly when talking with someone communicates a lack of respect for that person. Legs are never crossed on top of a desk or table when talking with someone.
- ❋ When standing and talking with someone, it is considered disrespectful to lean against the wall or keep one's hands in one's pockets.
- ❋ Sitting in a manner that allows the sole of one's shoe to face another person is an insult. But they know that many foreigners are not aware of this, and it is not as serious as you may have been told.
- ❋ In many countries and homes, a guest removes his or her shoes at the door. You can tell if this is required by watching others and by noting whether there is a pile of shoes at the door. This is especially common in the Arabian Peninsula, which is one reason that slip-on sandals are usually worn. Removing your shoes is a sign of respect; it is always required in a mosque.
- ❋ Failure to shake hands when meeting or bidding someone goodbye is considered rude. When a Western man is introduced to an Arab woman, it is the woman's choice whether to shake hands or not; she should be allowed to make the first move. (Pious Muslims may decline to shake hands with a woman; this is not an insult.)
- ❋ Casual dress at social events, many of which call for rather formal dress (a suit and tie for men; a dress, high heels, and jewelry for women) may be taken as a lack of respect for the hosts or the occasion. There are, of course, some occasions for which casual dress is appropriate. Notice how others are dressed.

- One who lights a cigarette in a group must be prepared to offer cigarettes to everyone.
- Men stand when a woman enters a room; everyone stands when new guests arrive at a social gathering and when an elderly or high-ranking person enters or leaves.
- Men allow women to precede them through doorways, and men offer their seats to women if no others are available.
- It is customary to usher elderly people to the front of any line or to offer to stand in their place. Elderly people should be greeted first.
- When saying goodbye to guests, a gracious host accompanies them to the outer gate, or to their car, or at least as far as the elevator in a high-rise building.
- If a guest admires something small and portable, an Arab may insist that it be taken as a gift. Guests need to be careful about expressing admiration for small, expensive items.
- In many countries, gifts are given and accepted with both hands and are not opened in the presence of the donor.
- In some social situations, especially in public places or when very traditional Arabs are present, it may be considered inappropriate for women to smoke or to drink alcoholic beverages. Don't be the first to do it.
- When eating with Arabs, especially when taking food from communal dishes, guests should not use the left hand (it is considered unclean). This is overemphasized by Westerners, though; it does not pertain if you have your own plate and are eating with a knife and fork.
- At a restaurant, Arabs will almost always insist on paying, especially if there are not many people in the party or if it is a business-related occasion. Giving in graciously after a ritual offer and then returning the favor later is an appropriate response.
- Arabs have definite ideas about what constitutes proper masculine and feminine behavior and appearance. They do not approve of long hair on men or mannish dress and comportment by women.
- Family disagreements and disputes in front of others or within hearing of others are avoided.

- ❈ People should not be photographed without their permission.
- ❈ Staring at other people is not usually considered rude or an invasion of privacy by Arabs (especially when the object is a fascinating foreigner). Moving away is the best defense.
- ❈ When eating out with a large group of people where everyone is paying his or her own share, it is best to let one person pay and be reimbursed later. Arabs find the public calculation of a restaurant bill embarrassing.
- ❈ During Ramadan, when you are with people who are fasting, it is polite to refrain from eating or drinking in front of them. Even if they insist, you can say that you choose this out of respect for them.
- ❈ Most Arabs do not like to touch or be in the presence of household animals, especially dogs. Pets should be kept out of sight when Arab guests are present.

It is impossible, of course, to learn all the rules of a foreign culture. The safest course of action is to imitate. In a social situation, *never be the first one to do anything!* In some situations, such as in the presence of royalty, it is incorrect to cross your legs; in some situations, in the presence of royalty or a high-ranking older man, for instance, it is incorrect to smoke. You learn this by observing.

✲ ✲ ✲ ✲ ✲ ✲ ✲ ✲ ✲ ✲ ✲ ✲ ✲ ✲ ✲ ✲ ✲ ✲ ✲

CHAPTER 7

THE SOCIAL STRUCTURE

A rab society is structured into social classes, and individuals inherit the social class of their family. The governments of Libya and the former South Yemen (Aden) have experimented with classless societies, but this has not affected basic attitudes.

✸ SOCIAL CLASSES

In most Arab countries, there are three social classes. The upper class includes royalty (in some countries), large and influential families, and some wealthy people, depending on their family background. The middle class is composed of professionals, government employees, military officers, and moderately prosperous merchants and landowners. Peasant farmers and the urban and village poor make up the lower class. Bedouins, of whom about 10 percent are nomadic, do not really fit into any of these classes; they are mostly independent of society and are admired for their preservation of Arab traditions. Bedouins live in Libya, Egypt (Sinai), Lebanon, Jordan, Syria, Iraq, and throughout the Arabian Peninsula.

The relative degree of privilege among the classes and the differences in their attitude and way of life vary from country to country. Some countries are wealthy and underpopulated, with a large privileged class; others are poor and overpopulated, with a high percentage of peasants and manual laborers.

There is usually very little tension between social classes. Arabs accept the social class into which they were born, and there is relatively little effort on the part of individuals to rise from one class to another. In any case, it would be difficult for a person to change social class, since it is determined almost entirely by family origin. One can improve one's status through professional position and power, educational attainment, or acquired wealth, but the person's origins will be remembered. A family of the lower class could not really expect social acceptance in the upper class for two or three generations. Similarly, an upper-class family that squandered its wealth or influence would not be relegated to lower-class status for some time.

Foreign residents of Arab countries automatically accrue most of the status and privileges of the upper class. This is due to their professional standing, their level of education, and their income.

❈ IMAGE AND UPPER-CLASS BEHAVIOR

Certain kinds of behavior are expected of people in the upper class who wish to maintain their status and good public image. Some activities are not acceptable in public and, if seen, cause shock and surprise.

If you know the basic norms of upper-class behavior, you will be free to decide the extent to which you are willing to conform. While you risk giving a negative impression by breaking a rule, doing so will not necessarily be offensive. You may simply be viewed as eccentric or as having poor judgment.

No upper-class person engages in manual labor in front of others. Arabs are surprised when they see Westerners washing their cars or sweeping the sidewalk. While upper-class Arabs may do some menial chores inside their homes, they do not do them in public or in front of others.

A white-collar or desk job in an office is much desired by Arabs because of the status it confers. There is an enormous difference between working with one's hands and working as a clerk. Arabs who have white-collar jobs will resent being asked to do something they consider beneath their status. If, in an office situation, your requests are not being carried out, you may find that you have been asking a person to do something that is demeaning or threatening to his or her dignity. And not wishing to offend you, the employee would be hesitant to tell you.

An Egyptian interpreter in an American-managed hospital once told me that she was insulted when a Western doctor asked her to bring him a glass of water. She felt that her dignity had been threatened and that she had been treated like the "tea boy" who took orders for drinks.

Manual work is acceptable if it can be classified as a hobby—for example, sewing, painting, or craftwork. Refinishing furniture might get by as a hobby (though it would probably raise eyebrows), but repairing cars is out. If you decide to paint the exterior of your house or to refinish the floors yourself, expect to be the object of conversation.

Upper-class Arabs are careful about their dress and appearance whenever they are in public, because the way a person dresses indicates his or her wealth and social standing. Arab children are often dressed in expensive clothes, and women wear a lot of jewelry, especially gold. The men are partial to expensive watches, cuff links, pens, and cigarette lighters. Looking their best and dressing well are essential to Arabs' self-respect, and they are surprised when they see well-to-do foreigners wearing casual or old clothes (faded jeans, a tattered T-shirt). Why would a person dress poorly when he or she can afford better?

Usually upper-class Arabs do not socialize with people from other classes, at least not in each other's homes. They may enjoy cordial relations with the corner grocer and newsstand vendor, but, like most Westerners, they would not suggest a dinner or an evening's entertainment together. (A possible exception is a big occasion like a wedding.)

When you plan social events, do not mix people from different social classes. You can invite anyone from any class to your home, and the gesture will be much appreciated, but to invite a company director and your local baker at the same time would embarrass both parties.

❈ DEALING WITH SERVICE PEOPLE

Westerners living in an Arab country usually have one or more household servants. You may feel free to establish a personal relationship with your household help; they appreciate the kindness and consideration they have come to expect from Westerners—"Please" and "Thank you" are never out of place. You may, in fact, work right alongside your servant, but you will notice that the relationship changes if Arab guests are present. The servant will then want to do all the work alone so as not to tarnish your social image. If a glass of water is spilled, for example, you should call the servant to clean up, rather than be seen doing it yourself. Inviting your servant to join you and your guests at tea or at a meal would be inappropriate and embarrassing to everyone.

Servants expect you to assume some responsibility for them; you may, for example, be asked to pay medical expenses and to help financially in family emergencies. Give at least something as a token of concern, then ask around to find out how much is reasonable for the situation. If you feel that the expense is too high for you to cover completely, you can offer to lend the money and deduct it from the person's salary over a period of time. Be generous with surplus food and with household items or clothing you no longer need, and remember that extra money is expected on holidays. All this is in keeping with the cultural and religious requirement to be generous with charity.

Make the acquaintance of shopkeepers, doormen, and errand boys. Such acquaintances are best made by exchanging a few words of Arabic and showing them that you like and respect them.

If you become friendly with people who have relatively little money, limit the frequency of your social visits. They may be obliged to spend more than they can afford to receive you properly, and the problem is far too embarrassing to discuss or admit. It is enjoyable to visit villages or the home of a taxi driver or shopkeeper, but if you plan to make it a habit, bring gifts with you or find other ways to compensate your hosts.

CHAPTER 8

THE ROLE OF THE FAMILY

Arab society is built around the extended family. Individuals feel a strong affiliation with all their relatives—aunts, uncles, and cousins—not just with their immediate family. The degree to which all blood relationships are encompassed by a family unit varies among families, but most Arabs have over a hundred "fairly close" relatives.

FAMILY LOYALTY AND OBLIGATIONS

Family loyalty and obligations take precedence over loyalty to friends or the demands of a job. Relatives are expected to help each other, including giving financial assistance if necessary. Family affiliation provides security and assures a person that he or she will never be entirely without resources, emotional or material. Only the most rash or foolhardy person would risk being censured or disowned by his or her family. Family support is indispensable in an unpredictable world; the family is a person's ultimate refuge.

Members of a family are expected to support each other in disputes with outsiders. Regardless of personal antipathy between relatives, they must defend each other's honor, counter criticism, and display group cohesion, if only for the sake of appearances. Internal family disputes rarely get to the point of open, public conflict.

Membership in a well-known or influential family ensures social acceptance and is often crucial in obtaining a good education, finding a good job, or succeeding in business. Arabs are very proud of their family connections and lineage.

The reputation of any member of a family group reflects on all the other members. One person's indiscreet behavior or poor judgment can damage his or her relatives' pride, social influence, and marriage opportunities. For this reason, family honor is the greatest source of pressure on an individual to conform to accepted behavior patterns, and one is constantly reminded of his or her responsibility for upholding that honor.

The family is the foundation of Middle Eastern society, and family security is essential. The peace and security offered by a stable family unit is greatly valued and seen as essential for the spiritual growth of its members. A harmonious social order is created by the existence of close extended families. Strong families create strong communities and underpin social order.

An employer must be understanding if an employee is late or absent because of family obligations. *It is unreasonable to expect an Arab employee to give priority to the demands of a job if they conflict with family duties.*

❈ RELATIONS AMONG FAMILY MEMBERS

An Arab man is recognized as the head of his immediate family, and his role and influence are overt. His wife also has a clearly defined sphere of influence, but it exists largely behind the scenes. Although an Arab woman is careful to show deference to her husband in public, she may not always accord him the same in private.

In matters where opinions among family members differ, much consultation and negotiation take place before decisions are made. If a compromise cannot be reached, however, the husband, father, or older men in the family prevail.

Status in a family increases as a person grows older, and most families have patriarchs or matriarchs whose opinions are given considerable weight in family matters. Children are taught profound respect for adults, a pattern that is pervasive in Arab society at all ages. It is common, for example, for adults to refrain from smoking in front of their parents or older relatives.

Responsibility for other members of the family rests heavily on older men in the extended family and on older sons in the immediate family. Children are their parents' "social security," and grown sons, in particular, are responsible for the support of their parents. In the absence of the father, brothers are responsible for their unmarried sisters.

Members of a family are very dependent on each other emotionally, and these ties continue throughout life. Some people feel closer to their brothers and sisters and confide in them more than they do their spouses. A directive written for social workers in the Muslim Arab world stated:

> A family's involvement in individual helping may be considerable, and could make the social worker's task more complex. In Muslim Arab communities, many are raised to consider the family unit as a continual source of support. Extended family members may be highly valued as well. They may be expected to be involved and may be consulted in times of crisis. When a family member experiences a problem, the person's restoration may be of concern to many other members . . . although Muslim Arab peoples may value privacy and guard it vehemently, their personal privacy within the family is virtually nonexistent. Decisions regarding healthcare are made by the family group and are not the responsibility of the individual.[1]

In the UAE, a conference was held called, "Role of the Family and Welfare of the Elderly," in which the ruler's wife stated:

> We believe our sons and daughters are responsible toward God and our nation for their parents when they grow old. We believe that undertaking this responsibility is one of the essential anchors of our society. . . . We have noticed, regretfully, some family members who do not care for the elderly. These contravene our values and traditions. We hope this seminar will help in fighting these trends and suggest necessary legislation to punish those who are responsible for contravening our values and traditions.[2]

In the traditional Arab family, the roles of the mother and the father are quite different as they relate to their children. The mother is seen as a source of emotional support and steadfast loving-kindness. She is patient, forgiving, and prone to indulge and spoil her children, especially her sons.

The father, while seen as a source of love, may display affection less overtly; he is also the source of authority and punishment. Some Arab fathers feel that their status in the family is best maintained by cultivating awe and even a degree of fear in other members of the family, but this is quite rare.

In most Arab families, the parents maintain very close contact with their own parents and with their brothers and sisters. For this reason, Arab children grow up experiencing constant interaction with older relatives, including their grandparents, who often live in the same home. This contributes to the passing on of social values from one generation to another, as the influence of the older relatives is continually present. Relatively few Arab teenagers and young adults rebel against family values and desires, certainly not to the extent common in Western societies. Even people who affect modern tastes in dress, reading material, and entertainment subscribe to the prevailing social values and expect their own family lives to be very similar to that of their parents. Many Arab extended families living in the West gather together every weekend if possible.

❀ MARRIAGE

Most Arabs still prefer family-arranged marriages. Though marriage customs are changing in some modern circles, couples still seek family approval of the person they have chosen. This is essential as an act of respect toward their parents, and people rarely marry in defiance of their families.

Many Arabs feel that because marriage is such a major decision, it is considered prudent to leave it to the family's discretion rather than to choose someone solely on the basis of emotion or ideas of romance. In almost all Arab countries and social groups, however, the prospective bride and bridegroom have the opportunity to meet and become acquainted—and to accept or reject a proposal of marriage. The degree to which the individuals are consulted will vary according to how traditional or modern the family is.

Among Muslim Arabs, especially in rural and traditional communities and in the Arabian Peninsula, the preferred pattern of marriage is to a first or second cousin. In fact, marriage to relatives is on the rise. On average, about one-third of all marriages are between cousins or someone in the same kin group (the global average is about 20 percent).[3] In the

Arabian Peninsula, though, estimates vary between 20 and 50 percent. Genetic problems occur in about 10 percent of these marriages.[4] Globally, Middle East countries rank high in percentage of birth defects.*

There are good reasons for this marriage pattern. Since an important part of a marriage arrangement is the investigation into the social and financial standing of the proposed candidates, it is reassuring to marry someone whose background, character, and financial position are well known. Marrying within the family is the principal means of reinforcing kinship solidarity (this is one reason many Arabs do not give their first loyalty to their nation and remain kin- and clan-oriented; even heads of state often place other loyalties ahead of national interests). Marrying a cousin acts as a protection for the wife, who already has good relations with her in-laws and can win their support in time of need. Daughters who marry relatives will be better able to care for elderly parents who are kin to the husband. If the bride is outside the family, potentially her husband may develop more solidarity with her family and lessen his loyalty to his own. Marriage to a cousin also ensures that money, in the form of a dowry or inheritance, stays within the family.

In contrast to Western couples, Arab couples do not usually enter marriage with idealistic or exaggerated romantic expectations. True, they are seeking companionship and love, but equally important, they want financial security, the social status of being married, and children. These goals are realistic and are usually attained. Arab marriages are, overall, very stable and characterized by mutual respect. Having a happy family life is considered a paramount goal in the Arab world.

❈ DIVORCE

Most Arab Christians belong to denominations that do not permit divorce. Among Muslims, divorce is permitted and regulated by religious law (in some countries, civil law also plays a part). Divorce is common enough that it does not carry a social stigma for the individuals involved, and people who have been divorced are eligible for remarriage.

---

* Defects per 1,000 births are 82 in Sudan and 81 in Saudi Arabia, and are in the 70s in Palestine, the UAE, Iraq, and Kuwait. The world average is around 50; Western nations have percentages in the 30s and 40s.[5]

Although a Muslim may divorce his wife if he wishes, he risks severe damage to his social image if he is arbitrary or hasty about his decision. The process in traditional Islam is quite simple: He merely recites the formula for divorce ("I divorce you") in front of witnesses. If he says the formula once or twice, the couple can still be reconciled; if he repeats it a third time, it is binding. Almost every Middle Eastern country has modified this and now requires court proceedings, stipulating the wife's rights to alimony and child support. A woman has more difficulty in initiating divorce proceedings, but usually she is successful on grounds of childlessness, desertion, or nonsupport. A woman must go through court proceedings in order to divorce her husband. In Jordan, Syria, and Morocco, she may write into her marriage contract the right to initiate divorce. Such protections are increasing.

When a Muslim woman is divorced, her husband must pay a divorce settlement, which is included in every marriage contract and is usually a very large sum of money. In addition, she is entitled to financial support for herself for at least three months (a waiting period to determine that she is not pregnant) and more if she needs it, as well as support for her minor children when they are in her custody. Additional conditions can be written into a marriage contract.

A few Arab countries follow Islamic law entirely in matters of divorce, but most have supplemented it. Laws pertaining to divorce have been widely discussed, and changes are constantly being proposed. For example, the custody of children is theoretically determined by Islamic law. They are to stay with their mothers to a certain age (approximately seven years for boys and nine years for girls, although it differs slightly among countries), and then they may go to their fathers. This shift is not always automatic, however, and may be ruled upon by a court or religious judge, according to the circumstances of the case.

❖ CHILD-REARING PRACTICES

Arabs dearly love children, and both men and women express that love openly. Arab children grow up surrounded by adoring relatives who share in child rearing by feeding, caring for, and even disciplining each other's children. Because so many people have cared for them and served as authority figures, and because the practice is so universal, Arabs are remarkably homogeneous in their experience of childhood. Arab children learn the same values in much the same way; their upbringing is not as arbitrarily dependent on the approach of their particular parents as it is in Western societies.

In traditional Arab culture, there has always been a marked preference for boys over girls because men contribute more to the family's influence in the community. Arab children are provided different role models for personality development. Boys are expected to be aggressive and decisive; girls are expected to be more passive. This attitude toward boys and girls is starting to change now that women are being educated and becoming wage earners. Many Arab couples practice birth control and limit the size of their families to two or three children, even if they are all girls.

Some educated or liberal-thinking Arabs find the pressure from the family to conform to rigid social standards to be oppressive. Much of what has been written about Arab character and personality development in childhood is negative, particularly statements made by Arabs themselves. Clearly many Arabs feel resentful of the requirements imposed by their families and society, and they believe that conformity leads to the development of undesirable personal traits.

Most Arabs feel that while their childhood was, in many ways, a time of stringent training, it was also a time of indulgence and openly expressed love, especially from their mothers. Failure to conform is punished, but methods of discipline are usually not harsh.

In Arab culture, the most important requirement for a "good" child is respectful behavior in front of adults. Unlike Westerners, all adults may share in correcting a child, because parents know that all adults have the same values. Children grow up without confusion about social requirements. Children must greet adults with a handshake, stay to converse for a few minutes if asked, and refrain from interrupting or talking back. Children often help to serve guests, and they learn the requirements of hospitality early. Westerners who want their children to make a good impression on Arab guests might wish to keep these customs in mind.

Among Arabs it is an extremely important responsibility to bring children up so that they will reflect well on the family. It is an insult to accuse someone of not being well-raised (this is said in a well-known phrase when angry). Children's character and success in life reflect directly on their parents—Arabs tend to give parents much of the credit for their children's successes and much of the blame for their failures. Parents readily make sacrifices for their children's welfare, and they expect these efforts to be acknowledged and their parental influence to continue throughout the child's lifetime.

Many Western parents begin training their children at an early age to become independent and learn responsibility. They give the children token jobs and regular allowance money and frequently encourage them to make their own decisions. This training helps children avoid being dependent on their parents after they have reached adulthood.

Arab parents, on the other hand, welcome their children's dependence. Mothers, especially, try to keep their children tied to them emotionally. Young people continue to live at home until they are married. It is customary for the parents of a newly married couple to furnish the couple's home entirely and to continue to help them financially. In many cases, extended families live together.

❀ TALKING ABOUT YOUR FAMILY

Given this emphasis on family background and honor, you may want to carefully consider the impression you will make when giving information to Arabs about your family relationships. Saying the wrong thing can affect your image and status.

Arabs are very surprised if someone talks about poverty and disadvantages experienced in early life. Rather than admiring one's success in overcoming such circumstances, they wonder why anyone would admit to humble origins when it need not be known.

If your father held a low-status job; if you have relatives—especially female relatives—who have disgraced the family; or if you have elderly relatives in a nursing home (which Arabs find shocking), there is nothing to be gained by talking about it. If you dislike your parents or any close relatives, keep your thoughts to yourself. On the other hand, if you are from a prominent family or are related to a well-known person, letting people know this information can work to your advantage.

In sum, if you do not have positive things to say about your family, things that will incline Arabs toward admiration, it is best to avoid the subject.

✸ ✸ ✸ ✸ ✸ ✸ ✸ ✸ ✸ ✸ ✸ ✸ ✸ ✸ ✸ ✸ ✸ ✸ ✸

CHAPTER 9

RELIGION AND SOCIETY

Arabs identify strongly with their religious groups, whether they are Muslim or Christian and whether they participate in religious observances or not*. A foreigner must be aware of the pervasive role of religion in Arab life to avoid causing offense by injudicious statements or actions.

✸ RELIGIOUS AFFILIATION

Religious affiliation is essential for every person in Arab society. There is no place for an atheist or an agnostic. If you have no religious affiliation or are an atheist, this should not be mentioned. Shock and amazement would be the reaction of most Arabs, along with a loss of respect for you. Arabs place great value on piety and respect anyone who sincerely practices his or her religion, no matter what that religion is.

✸ RELIGIOUS PRACTICES

An Arab's religion affects his or her whole way of life on a daily basis. Religion is taught in the schools, the language is full of religious expressions, and people practice their religion openly, expressing it in numerous ways: religious names, decorations on cars and in homes, and jewelry in the form of gold crosses, miniature Qur'ans, or pendants inscribed with Qur'anic verses.

---

* They also admire Jews who sincerely practice their religion, although there is often an underlying association of Judaism with Zionism.

The Qur'an provides an all-encompassing code of interpersonal relations, beyond ethical teachings and exhortations to faith. Much of the Qur'an was revealed when the Prophet Muhammad was administering a community, so it deals with forming a just society, government, economic principles, laws, and conducting business. It is a religious text and a legal code, all in one.

Muslims say the Qur'anic formula, "In the name of God, the Merciful, the Compassionate" (*Bismillah ar-Rahman ar-Raheem*), whenever they are setting out on a trip, about to undertake a dangerous task, or beginning a speech. This formula, sometimes called the Invocation, is printed at the top of business letterheads and included in the beginning of reports and personal letters—it even appears on business receipts.

Islam does not permit pictures or statues in a place of worship (the same as in Judaism). For this reason, artistic decoration has taken the form of elaborate calligraphy and geometric "arabesque" patterns. Depictions of the Prophet Muhammad are rare, but some occur in some miniature paintings, especially Persian and Mogul art from several centuries ago. Not all Muslims are upset by this; it depends on their interpretations of verses.

For both Muslims and Christians, marriage and divorce are controlled by religious law. In some countries, there is no such thing as a civil marriage; it must be performed by a religious official. For Muslims, inheritance is also controlled by religious law, and in conservative countries religious law partially determines methods of criminal punishment.

The practice of "Islamic banking" is gaining in popularity. The Islamic religion forbids lending money at a fixed rate of interest, viewing it as unfair and exploitative. Islamic banks, therefore, place investors' money in "shared risk" partnership accounts, with rates of return varying according to profits (or losses) on investments.

Marriage across religious lines is rare, although the Islamic religion permits a Muslim man to marry a Jewish or Christian woman without requiring that his wife convert. A Muslim woman, however, must marry a Muslim man; in this way, the children are assured of being Muslim (children are considered to have the religion of their father). Tunisia ended this rule in 2017, the only Muslim country to do so.

Never make critical remarks about any religious practice. *In Arab culture, all religions and their practices are treated with respect.* If you are a Christian foreigner and ask Christian Arabs about accompanying them to church services, they will be very pleased. Non-Muslims do not normally attend Islamic religious services, however, and you should not enter a mosque until you have checked whether it is permitted, which varies from country to country and even from mosque to mosque.

❈ THE RELIGION OF ISLAM

To understand Arab culture, it is essential that you become familiar with Islamic history and doctrine. If you do, you will gain insights that few Westerners have, and your efforts will be greatly appreciated.

The Islamic religion had its origin in northern Arabia in the seventh century A.D. The doctrines of Islam are based on revelations from God to His last prophet, Muhammad, over a period of twenty-two years. The revelations were preserved and incorporated into the holy book of the Muslims, the Qur'an, which means "the Recitation."

The God Muslims worship is the same God Jews and Christians worship (*Allah* is simply the Arabic word for *God*; Arab Christians pray to *Allah*). Islam is defined as a return to the faith of Abraham, the prophet and monotheist who made a covenant with God.

The word *Islam* means "submission" (to the will of God), and the term *Muslim* (also spelled "Moslem," which is more familiar to Westerners but not as close to the Arabic pronunciation) refers to a *person* who practices Islam, "one who submits." The doctrines of the Islamic religion are viewed as a summation and completion of previous revelations to Jewish and Christian prophets. Islam shares many doctrines with Judaism and Christianity, and Jews and Christians are known as "People of the Book" (the Scriptures), which gives them a special status.

Shortly after the advent of Islam, the Arabians began an energetic conquest of surrounding territory and eventually expanded their empire from Spain to India in about 100 years. The widespread conversion to Islam by the people in the Middle East and North Africa accounts for the fact that today over 90 percent of the Arabs (Arabic speakers) are Muslims.

The basic tenets of the Islamic faith are known as "the Five Pillars," the primary obligations for Muslims:

1. *Reciting the Declaration of Faith ("There is no God but God and Muhammad is the Messenger [Prophet] of God").* The recitation of this declaration with sincere intent in front of two male Muslim witnesses is sufficient for a person to become a Muslim. There are no sacraments.

   Arabs, Muslims and Christians alike, intersperse their ordinary conversations with references to the will of God (see "Social Greetings" in the Appendix). To make a good impression, you are advised to do the same. The constant use of Arabic religious expressions acts as a formal acknowledgment of the importance of religious faith in Arab society.

2. *Praying five times daily.* The five prayers are said at dawn, noon, afternoon, sunset, and night, and their times differ slightly every day. Muslims are reminded to pray through a prayer call broadcast from the minaret of a mosque. A Muslim prays facing in the direction of the Kaaba in Mecca. The weekly communal prayer service is the noon prayer in the mosque on Fridays, generally attended by men (women may go but it is not as common, nor is it expected). The Friday prayer also includes a sermon.

   Prayer is regulated by ritual washing beforehand and a predetermined number of prostrations and recitations, depending on the time of day. The prayer ritual includes standing, bowing, touching the forehead to the floor (which is covered with a prayer mat, rug, or other clean surface), sitting back, and holding the hands in a cupped position, all while reciting sacred verses. Muslims may pray in a mosque, in their home or office, or in public places. Avoid staring at, walking in front of, or interrupting a person during prayer.

   The Call to Prayer, broadcast five times a day, contains the following phrases, the repetition of which varies slightly depending on the time of day:

   God is Great.
   I testify that there is no God but God.
   I testify that Muhammad is God's messenger.
   Come to prayer.
   Come to success.
   God is great.
   There is no God but God.

If you learn the Call in Arabic, it will add to your pleasure in hearing it (many Westerners become so accustomed to
the Call that they miss it when they leave). The first statement,
Allahu Akbar (God is Great), is much used in Islam in other contexts as well. It is exclaimed at times of joy, admiration, births or
deaths, and distress, and is most commonly known in the West as a
battle cry.

3. *Giving alms (charity) to the needy.* Muslims are required to give as
Zakat (a religious offering) 2.5 percent of their net annual income
(after basic family expenses) for the welfare of the community in
general and for the poor in particular. Some people assess themselves annually and give the money to a government or community
entity; others distribute charity throughout the year.

If you are asked for alms by a beggar, it is best to give a token
amount. Even if you give nothing, avoid saying "no," which is very
rude. Instead, say *Allah ya'teek* (God give you); at least you have
given the person a blessing. There is a very strong emphasis on
charity in Islam; it is hugely important. Muslims see Islam as the
religion of social justice.

4. *Fasting during the month of Ramadan.* Ramadan is the ninth month
of the Islamic lunar calendar year (which is 11 days short of 365,
so religious holidays move forward every year). During Ramadan,
Muslims do not eat, drink, or smoke between sunrise and sunset. The purpose of fasting is to experience hunger and depriva-
tion and to perform an act of self-discipline, humility, and faith.
The Ramadan fast is not required of persons whose health may be
endangered, and travelers are also excused; however, anyone who
is excused must make up the missed fast days later when health
and circumstances permit. Ramadan brings with it a holiday atmo-
sphere. Work hours are shortened, shops change their opening and
closing times, and most activities take place in the early morning or
late at night. People gather with family and friends to break the fast
at elaborate meals every evening. This meal is called the *Iftar*—by
all means go if you are invited.

Be considerate of people who are fasting during Ramadan by
refraining from eating, drinking, or smoking in public places during the fasting hours. To express good wishes to someone before or

during Ramadan, you say *Ramadan Kareem* or *Ramadan Mubarak* (Blessed Ramadan), to which the response is usually *Allahu Akram* (God is more gracious).

5. *Performing a pilgrimage to Mecca at least once during one's lifetime if finances and health permit.* The Hajj is the peak religious experience for many Muslims. In the twelfth month of the Islamic year, Muslims from all over the world gather in Saudi Arabia to perform several separate activities, which are carried out at different sites in the Mecca and Medina area over a period of six days. The Hajj commemorates events in the life of the patriarch Abraham.

   Pilgrims, men and women, wear white garments to symbolize their state of purity and their equality in the sight of God (and women may *not* cover their face). At the end of the Hajj period is a holiday during which all families who can afford it sacrifice a sheep (or other animal) and, after taking enough for one meal, share the rest of it with the poor. The sacrifice relates to Abraham's test of faith—he was willing to sacrifice his son but was instructed to sacrifice a ram instead. Sharing on this holiday is such an important gesture that each year many governments send surplus sacrificial meat to refugees and to the poor in low-income Muslim countries around the world.

   When someone is departing for the pilgrimage, the appropriate blessing is *Hajj Mabroor* (Reverent Pilgrimage). When someone returns, offer congratulations and add the title *Hajj* (*Hajja* for a woman) to the person's name (except in Saudi Arabia, where the title is not used).

The Qur'an contains doctrines that guide Muslims to correct behavior so that they will find salvation on the Day of Judgment, narrative stories illustrating God's benevolence and power, and social regulations for the Muslim community. It is the single most important guiding force for Muslims and touches on virtually every aspect of their lives. It is supplemented by the *Hadith*, "Traditions of the Prophet," which are collections of sayings and decisions that the prophet was reported to have made, many gathered together in the 9th century. Because the Hadith are so variable and some are of arguable authenticity, many differences of opinion exist as to their validity.

The Hadith Project has been undertaken in Turkey to re-evaluate Hadith, some of which are controversial, unsubstantiated, or invented to manipulate society.[1] It is one of several investigations into Islam's role in the 21st century. It is in Turkey where there is the most interest in reconsidering Sharia law. The process of "modernizing" Islam has accelerated since the 1980s, although this has lessened after the Erdoğan presidency, which is turning Turkey away from the secularism that characterized it for decades. Religious scholars have said, "We are not reforming Islam, we are reforming ourselves, our own way of religiosity."[2] This is not supported by conservatives in the Islamic world, who follow ancient, traditional interpretations.

The Sunni and Shia have different sets of Hadith. There is also the Sunnah, more accounts of the prophet's practices, especially how to deal with friends, family, and government. Some of the practices predate Islam, and some are based on local customs.

✻ SUNNI AND SHIA

Most of the Muslim Arabs are *Sunni* (also called "orthodox"), and they constitute 90 percent of Muslims. Ten percent are *Shia* and are found in large numbers in Lebanon, Iraq, and the Arabian Gulf. Iran, the most important Shia country, is not Arab. The separation of the Muslims into two groups stems from a dispute over the proper succession of authority (the "caliphate") after the death of the Prophet Muhammad. Sunnis and Shia differ today in terms of their religious practices and emphases on certain doctrines, but both groups recognize each other as Muslims.

✻ THE SHARIA, ISLAMIC LAW

About 90 percent of Islam's *Sharia* law comes from the Hadith.[3] The most infamous rules in the Sharia (the lower status of non-Muslims, seclusion of women, the ban on fine arts, and many violent punishments for sinful behavior) come from *the Hadith*, *not* the Qur'an.[4] This means that rules are open to discussion and amendment.[5] Sunni jurists also use analogy and consensus when interpreting and applying Islamic law.

The application of Islamic law differs by country and local interpretations of the Sharia. Some countries (Saudi Arabia, Yemen, Kuwait, Bahrain, the UAE, Sudan), follow it almost exclusively in domestic and criminal law, but most countries have modified or supplemented it. In many countries, the legal system is secular, and Muslims can choose to bring familial and financial disputes to Sharia courts.

Islamic jurists are faced with new issues on which there has not been final agreement or consistency. Birth control, for instance, which is permitted in most Islamic countries, is openly promoted by some and discouraged by others. In Pakistan and Bangladesh (Muslim, non-Arab countries), for example, birth control is a social taboo based on the local interpretation of religious principles. There have been Islamic conferences where issues such as population control, abortion, women's dress, capital punishment, nuclear and biological warfare, terrorism, human rights, and societal pluralism are discussed. Among the Sunnis, however, there is no binding central authority to enforce agreed-upon decisions.

The Sharia can be narrowly interpreted by fundamentalists as requiring Muslims to live the way they lived 1,300 years ago, or, by most, as simply the law which Muslims follow, but which does not have a specific format and shifts over time. There are instances in the West of Muslims requesting female police officers cover their hair when entering a mosque, women-only hours be established at swimming pools, and the option of Islamic banking (without predetermined interest) be available. But some Westerners see any instance of requests for Sharia compliance as threatening; a pamphlet at a Tea Party gathering in Florida in August 2010 stated, "Why do Muslims want to take over the world and place us under Sharia law?"[6]

❋ THE QUR'AN AND THE BIBLE

Much of the content of the Qur'an is similar (though not identical) to the teachings and stories found in the Old and New Testaments of the Bible. Islamic doctrine accepts the previous revelations to biblical prophets as valid, but states, as the Bible does, that the people continually strayed from these teachings.* Correct guidance had to be repeated through

---

* As an aside, it is interesting to note that although Islam is associated with violence in the thinking of Westerners, the Qur'an contains less violence than the Bible, both Old and New Testament.[7]

different prophets, one after the other. By the seventh century, doctrines and practices again had to be corrected through the divine revelations to Muhammad, who is known as the last, or "seal," of the prophets.

The Qur'an is divided into 114 chapters, arranged in order of length, longest to shortest (with a few exceptions). The chapters are not in chronological order, although the reader can identify whether a chapter was revealed in Mecca (earlier) or Medina (later). Each chapter is made up of verses. If you decide to read the Qur'an in translation, it is a good idea to obtain a list of the chapters in chronological order and read through them in that order so that the development of thought and teachings becomes clear.*

Most of the chapters of the Qur'an are in cadenced, rhymed verse, while some (particularly the later legalistic ones) are in prose. The sustained rhythm of the recited Qur'an, combined with the beauty of the content, account for its great esthetic and poetic effect when heard in Arabic. The Qur'an is considered the epitome of Arabic writing style, and when it is recited aloud, it can move listeners to tears. The elegance and beauty of the Qur'an are taken as proof of its divine origin—no human being could expect to produce anything so magnificent.

The three most often cited characteristics of the Qur'an are these: It is inimitable, it is eternal (it always existed but was not manifested until the seventh century), and it is Arabic (the Arabic version is the Word of God, so translations of the Qur'an into other languages are not used for prayer). Verses from the Qur'an are much used for decoration, usually the same ones over and over, so learning to identify part of the verse can lead to deciphering the whole thing.

It is common for Muslims to memorize the Qur'an, or large portions of it; a person who can recite the Qur'an is called a Hafiz. Reading and reciting the Qur'an was once the traditional form of education, and often the only education many people received. In most Arab schools today, memorization of Qur'anic passages is included in the curriculum (for Muslim students).

The Qur'an and the Bible have much in common:

---

* A list of the Qur'an's chapters in chronological order may be found in Richard Bell's *Introduction to the Qur'an* (1953). It is also available on the Internet.

- The necessity of faith
- Reward for good actions and punishment for evil actions on the Day of Judgment
- The concepts of heaven (paradise) and hell
- The existence of angels who communicate between God and man
- The existence of Satan (*Shaytan* in Arabic)
- The recognition of numerous prophets*
- The prohibition of the consumption of pork and the flesh of animals not slaughtered in a ritual manner, which is very similar to kosher dietary laws in the Old Testament
- The teaching that Jesus was born of a virgin; Mary is called "Miriam" in Arabic (the theme is the same, although details differ)
- The teaching that Jesus worked miracles, including curing the sick and raising the dead

There are some notable differences between the Qur'an and the Bible as well:

- Islam does not recognize the concept of intercession between God and man; all prayers must be made to God directly. Jesus is recognized as one of the most important prophets, but the Christian concept of his intercession for man's sins is not accepted.
- Islam teaches that Jesus was not crucified; instead, a person made to look like him was miraculously substituted in his place on the cross. God would not allow such an event to happen to one of His prophets.
- Islam does not accept the doctrine of Jesus' resurrection and divinity.
- Islam is uncompromisingly monotheistic and rejects the Christian concept of the Trinity.

---

* The Qur'an recognizes eighteen Old Testament figures as prophets (among them Adam, Noah, Abraham, Ishmael, Isaac, Jacob, Moses, Joseph, Job) and three New Testament figures (Zachariah, John the Baptist, and Jesus), and it mentions four Arabian prophets who do not appear in the Bible. Of all these prophets, five are considered the most important. In order of chronology, these are Noah, Abraham, Moses, Jesus, and Muhammad.

Some of the biblical stories that are retold in the Qur'an (in a shortened version) include the following:

- The story of the Creation
- The story of Adam and Eve
- The story of Cain and Abel
- The story of Noah and the flood
- The story of the covenant of Abraham and his willingness to sacrifice his son as an act of faith*
- The story of Lot and the destruction of the evil cities
- The story of Joseph (told in much detail)
- The story of David and Goliath
- The story of Solomon and the Queen of Sheba
- The story of the afflictions of Job
- The story of the birth of Jesus†

Muslims feel an affinity with the Jewish and Christian religions and find it unfortunate that so few Westerners understand how similar the Islamic religion is to their own. Islam is a continuation of the other two religions, and Muslims view it as the completed true faith.

❧ PASSAGES FROM THE QUR'AN

Selected passages from the Qur'an are presented here to give the reader an idea of the tone and content of the book (from *The Koran Interpreted*, A. J. Arberry, 1955). Titles of chapters refer to key words in that chapter, not to content.

Chapter 1: *The Opening*

In the name of God, the Merciful, the Compassionate.
Praise belongs to God, the Lord of all Being

---

* Islam holds that Abraham was ordered to sacrifice Ishmael, whereas the Bible states that it was Isaac. Abraham is recognized as the ancestor of the Arabs through Ishmael.
† In the Qur'anic version, Jesus was born at the foot of a palm tree in the desert and saved his unmarried mother from scorn when, as an infant, he spoke up in her defense and declared himself a prophet, saying, "Peace be upon me, the day I was born, and the day I die, and the day I am raised up alive" (referring to his resurrection on the Day of Judgment). This is a miracle of Jesus not recorded in the Bible.

the All-merciful, the All-compassionate
the Master of the Day of Judgment.
Thee only we serve; to Thee alone we pray for help.
Guide us in the Straight Path,
the path of those whom Thou has blessed,
not of those against whom Thou art wrathful,
nor of those who are astray.

Chapter 5: The Table

(Verse 3)
Today the unbelievers have despaired of
your religion; therefore fear them not,
but fear you Me.
Today I have perfected your religion
for you, and I have completed My blessing
upon you, and I have approved Islam
for your religion.

(Verse 120)
To God belongs the kingdom of the heavens
And the earth, and all that is in them,
and He is powerful over everything.

Chapter 93: The Forenoon

(This chapter begins with an oath, which is common in the Qur'an.)

In the name of God, the Merciful, the Compassionate.
By the white forenoon and the brooding night!
Thy Lord has neither forsaken thee nor hates thee
and the Last [life] shall better for thee than the First.
Thy Lord shall give thee, and thou shalt be satisfied.
Did He not find thee an orphan, and shelter thee?
Did He not find thee erring, and guide thee?
Did He not find thee needy, and suffice thee?
As for the orphan, do not oppress him,
and as for the beggar, scold him not;
and as for thy Lord's blessing, declare it.

＊ ＊ ＊ ＊ ＊ ＊ ＊ ＊ ＊ ＊ ＊ ＊ ＊ ＊ ＊ ＊ ＊ ＊ ＊

CHAPTER 10

COMMUNICATING
WITH ARABS

This chapter is about the Arabic language and how speech is used in the Arab culture. Though you may never learn Arabic, you will need to know something about the language and how it is used. Arabic is the native language of 400 million to 425 million people and the official language of some twenty countries. In 1973, it was named the fourth official language of the United Nations (there are now six), and it is the fifth most widely spoken language in the world.* Arabic originated in the Arabian Peninsula as one of the northern Semitic languages. The only other Semitic languages still in wide use today are Hebrew (revived as a spoken language only a century ago) and Amharic (Ethiopian), which is from the southern Semitic branch. There are still a few speakers of the other northern Semitic languages (Aramaic, Syriac, and Chaldean) in Lebanon, Syria, and Iraq.

Many English words have come from Arabic, the most easily recognizable being those that begin with *al* (the Arabic word for "the"), such as *algebra, alchemy, alcove, alcohol,* and *alkali.* Many pertain to mathematics and the sciences; medieval European scholars drew heavily on Arabic source materials in these fields. Other Arabic words include *cipher, algorithm* and *almanac.* Some foods that originated in the East brought their

---

* The ranking of the top ten languages is: Mandarin Chinese, Spanish, English, Hindi-Urdu, Arabic, Bengali, Portuguese, Russian, Japanese, Punjabi.

Arabic names west with them, such as *coffee, sherbet, sesame, apricot, ginger, saffron,* and *carob.**

❈ VARIETIES OF ARABIC

Spoken Arabic in all its forms is very different from written Arabic. The written version is Classical Arabic, the language that was in use in the seventh century A.D. in the Hejaz area of Arabia. It is this rich, poetic language of the Qur'an that has persisted as the written language of all Arabic-speaking peoples since that time. Classical Arabic, which has evolved into Modern Standard Arabic to accommodate new words and usages, is sacred to Muslims. It is esthetically pleasing and far more grammatically complex than the spoken (or colloquial) dialects.

The spoken languages are "Formal Spoken Arabic," a classicized style of speech comprehensible to all educated Arabs, and colloquial (ordinary spoken) Arabic, which includes many dialects and subdialects. Although some of them differ from each other as, or more than Spanish does from Italian or the Scandinavian languages do from each other, they are all recognized as Arabic. When Arabic spread throughout the Middle East and North Africa with the Arabian conquests, it mixed with and assimilated local languages, spawning the dialects that are spoken today.

An overview of Arabic language usage reveals the following:

Classical/Modern Standard Arabic: Classical Arabic is used in the Qur'an; Modern Standard Arabic is almost the same, used for all writing and for formal discussions, speeches, and news broadcasts but not for ordinary conversation. It is based on Classical Arabic, and is the same in all Arab countries, except for occasional variations in regional or specialized vocabulary.† This is taught far more than the dialects in Western schools and universities. It is the only kind of Arabic taught in the Middle East.

Colloquial Arabic (dialects). Colloquial Arabic is used for everyday spoken communication but not for writing, except sometimes in

---

* For more examples, see the *Mawrid* dictionary[1] 101–112, or Al-bab.com, which lists some 200 words.

† Classical and Modern Standard Arabic differ, but differences are technical.

very informal correspondence, in film or play scripts, or as slang in cartoons and the like.

Formal Spoken Arabic. Formal Spoken Arabic (Educated Spoken Arabic) is improvised, consisting principally of Standard Arabic terminology within the structure of the local dialect; it is used by educated people when they converse with Arabs whose dialect is very different from their own. It is an acquired skill, with no hard-and-fast rules.

❄ THE SUPERIORITY OF ARABIC

It is not an exaggeration to say that *Arabs are passionately in love with their language.* Just speaking and hearing it can be a moving experience. Arabs are secure in the knowledge that their language is superior to all others. This attitude about one's own language is held by many people in the world, but in the case of the Arabs, they can point to several factors as proof of their assertion.

Most importantly, when the Qur'an was revealed directly from God, Arabic was the medium chosen for His message; its use was not an accident. Arabic is also extremely difficult to master, and it is complex grammatically; this is viewed as another sign of superiority. Because its structure lends itself to rhythm and rhyme, Arabic is pleasing to listen to when recited aloud. Finally, it has an unusually large vocabulary, and its grammar allows for the easy coining of new words, so that borrowing from other languages is less common in Arabic than in many other languages. In other words, Arabic is richer than other languages, or so it is argued.

While most Westerners feel an affection for their native language, the pride and love Arabs feel for Arabic are much more intense. The Arabic language is their greatest cultural treasure and achievement, an art form that unfortunately cannot be accessed or appreciated by outsiders.

Arabic, if spoken or written in an ornate and semi-poetic style, casts a spell. Hearing the words and phrases used skillfully is an esthetic, poetic experience, and people respond as much or more to the style as to the content. A talented orator can wield power in this subtle way. Beautiful Arabic conjures up images of once-memorized Qur'an passages or bits of poetry, and it can be just as intricate orally as the most complex Arabic calligraphy designs are visually. Arabs love poetry, which in ancient times was the nomadic Arabs' chief means of artistic expression and still has a powerful place in their culture.*

❊ THE PRESTIGE OF CLASSICAL ARABIC

The reverence for Arabic pertains only to Classical/Standard Arabic, which is what Arabs mean by the phrase "the Arabic language." This was illustrated by the comment of an Egyptian village headman who once explained to me why he considered the village school to be important. "For one thing," he said, "that's where the children go to learn Arabic."

To the contrary, Arabic dialects have no prestige. Some people go so far as to suggest that they have "no grammar" and are not worthy of serious study. The dialects differ from each other, but now they are on the way to becoming more mutually intelligible and less of a block to communication. Satellite television has exposed everyone to other dialects, through programs from other countries and through frequent news interviews, often among people of mixed nationalities. Even speech from distant areas is commonly heard now. Committees of scholars have coined new words and tried to impose conventional usages to partially replace the dialects, but they have had no more success than language regulatory groups in other countries.

A good command of Standard Arabic is highly admired in the Arab culture because it is difficult to attain. Few people other than scholars and specialists in Arabic have enough confidence to speak extemporaneously in Standard Arabic or to defend their written style. In Arabic, the written language is called "The Most Eloquent Language."

---

* Most Westerners are not particularly sensitive toward poetry. But the power of poetry in Arab culture is well described by Saudi statesman and author Ghazi Algosaibi: "Arabic poetry was born in an environment which knew no other form of literature or fine art. Unlike numerous other civilizations which were fascinated by singing, dancing, acting, painting, sculpture, and music, pre-Islamic Arabs knew no medium of artistic expression other than poetry. To the Arabs, poetry, regardless of its political and social role, represented what the other fine arts combined stood for in other cultures. This perhaps explains the special position poetry occupied in the minds and souls of the Arabs."[2]

To become truly literate in Arabic requires more years of study than are required for English literacy. The student must learn new words in Standard Arabic (more than 50 percent of the words are different from the local dialect in some countries) and a whole new grammar, including case endings and new verb forms. A significant part of the literacy problem in the Arab world stems from the difficulty of Standard Arabic. Even people who have had five or six years of schooling are still considered functionally illiterate (unable to use the language for anything more than rudimentary needs, such as signing one's name or reading signs).

On the other hand, the written language is not entirely a foreign language to illiterates or even to preschool children. They hear it passively on a constant basis, in news broadcasts, in speeches and formal discussions, on *Sesame Street* and in children's books and recordings.

From time to time Arab scholars have suggested that Standard Arabic be replaced by written dialects to facilitate education and literacy. This idea has been repeatedly and emphatically denounced by the large majority of Arabs and has almost no chance of acceptance in the foreseeable future. The most serious objection is that Classical Arabic is the language of the Qur'an. Another argument is that if it were supplanted by the dialects, the entire body of Arabic literature and poetry would become inaccessible, and the language would lose much of its beauty. There has also been some talk of simplifying the language, but this is not popular either.

There is a political argument for Standard Arabic—it is a cultural force that unites all Arabs. To discard it, many fear, would lead to a linguistic fragmentation that would exacerbate the tendencies toward political and psychological fragmentation already present. As one language expert said, "The Arabic language becomes instrumental in preserving our cultural hemisphere and protecting our heritage, religion, and values."[3]

❋ ELOQUENCE OF SPEECH

Eloquence is emphasized and admired in the Arab world far more than in the West, which accounts for the flowery prose in Arabic, both in written and spoken form. *Instead of viewing rhetoric in a disparaging way, as Westerners often do, Arabs admire it.* The ability to speak eloquently is a sign of education and refinement.

Foreign observers frequently comment on long-winded political speeches and the repetition of phrases and themes in Arabic, failing to understand that the speaker's style of delivery and command of the language often appeal to the listeners as much as does the message itself. Exaggerations, threats, promises, and nationalistic slogans are meant more for momentary effect than as statements of policy or belief, yet foreigners too often take them literally, especially when encountered in the cold light of a foreign language translation. *In the Arab world, how you say something is as important as what you have to say.*

Eloquence is a clue to the popular appeal of some nationalistic leaders whose words are far more compelling than their deeds. Much of the personal charisma attributed to them is due in large part to their ability to speak in well-phrased, rhetorical Arabic. Repetition of refrains is common, as is exaggeration, which sometimes expresses wish fulfillment and provides a satisfying substitution of words for action.

Arabs devote considerable effort to using their language creatively and effectively. This is from a Christmas card I received in English from an Iraqi refugee, who had interviewed for a teaching position:

> When fate bestows on a person, lost in a distant land, a drop of tenderness, a bouquet of love, that person's health and trust in others is restored.
>
> I found in you true brotherhood, when you planted in my heart, which beats and which is not able to be still in its anxieties and its yearnings, that tenderness.
>
> Perhaps I will meet you some day in my beautiful Baghdad in order to return to you some of the kindness which you have shown me.
>
> May this Christmas be the right occasion to realize our shared dream to build a world driven by friendship, love, and peace, so that the people of the earth will be blessed with justice, democracy, and the solidarity of mankind.

Leslie J. McLoughlin, a British specialist in Arabic, has written:

> Westerners are not in everyday speech given, as Arabs are, to quoting poetry, ancient proverbs, and extracts from holy books. Nor are they wont to exchange fulsome greetings . . . . Perhaps the greatest difference between the Levantine approach to language and that of

Westerners is that Levantines, like most Arabs, take pleasure in using language for its own sake. The sahra (or evening entertainment) may well take the form of talk alone, but talk of a kind forgotten in the West except in isolated communities such as Irish villages or Swiss mountain communities—talk not merely comical, tragic, historical, pastoral, etc., but talk ranging over poetry, storytelling, anecdotes, jokes, word games, singing and acting.[4]

When the American television show *The Apprentice* was copied in the Arab world, it was felt too harsh to say to someone, "You're fired!" Instead, the candidates were refused with "God be good to you."[5] Any listener understood the message from the context. There are several expressions of goodwill that are used to mask a different or negative meaning.

❋ SPEECH MANNERISMS

Making yourself completely understood by another person is a difficult task under the best of circumstances. It is more difficult still if you each have dramatically different ways of expressing yourself. Such is the problem between Westerners and Arabs, which often results in misunderstanding, leaving both parties feeling bewildered or deceived.

Arabs talk a lot, repeat themselves, shout when excited, and make extensive use of gestures. They punctuate their conversations with oaths (such as "I swear by God") to emphasize what they say, and they exaggerate for effect. Foreigners sometimes wonder if they are involved in a discussion or an argument.

If you speak softly and make your statements only once, Arabs may wonder if you really mean what you are saying. People will ask, "Do you really mean that?" or, "Is that true?" It's not that they do not believe you, but they need repetition and a few emphatic "yeses" to be reassured.

Arabs have a great tolerance for noise and interference during discussions; often several people speak at once (each trying to outshout the other), interspersing their statements with gestures, all the while being coached by bystanders. Businessmen interrupt meetings to greet callers, answer the telephone, and sign papers brought in by clerks. A foreigner may feel that he or she can be heard only by insisting on the precondition of being allowed to speak without interruption. *Loudness of speech is mainly for dramatic effect and in most cases should not be taken as an indication of aggression or insistence on the part of the speaker.*

In a taxi in Cairo once, my driver was shouting and complaining and gesticulating wildly to other drivers as he worked his way through the crowded streets. Amid all this action, he turned around, laughed, and winked. "You know," he said, "sometimes I really enjoy this!"

Some situations absolutely demand emotion and drama. In Baghdad, I was in a taxi when it was hit from the rear. Both drivers leapt out of their cars and began shouting at each other. After waiting ten minutes, while a crowd gathered, I decided to pay the fare and leave. I pushed through the crowd and got the driver's attention. He broke off the argument, politely told me that there was nothing to pay, and then resumed arguing at full voice.

Loud and boisterous behavior does have limits, however. It is more frequent, of course, among people of approximately the same age and social status who know each other well. It occurs mostly in social situations, less often in business meetings, and is not acceptable when dealing with elders or social superiors, in which case polite deference is required. Bedouins and the Arabs of Saudi Arabia and the Gulf tend to be more reserved and soft-spoken, at least in more or less formal discussions. In fact, *in almost every respect, protocol is stricter in the Arabian Peninsula than elsewhere in the Arab world.*

❀ PLEASANT AND INDIRECT RESPONSES

In general, Arab speech is rich in color and emotion. It is vibrant, and not tied down to sterile logic. Arab culture values hospitality and goodwill over precision and directness in conversation.

If you ask for directions, you will almost always get a response, even if the person is not sure. It is more important to make a token effort of helpfulness (even if the information is wrong) than to refuse the request (the person didn't misguide you, he helped). If bad news is imminent, it may be considered more polite to engage in circumlocution rather than going directly to the brutal truth. Indirect speech is also called for when making a request of a prominent or elderly person; it is a sign of deference.

❀ THE POWER OF WORDS

To the Arab way of thinking (consciously or subconsciously), words have power; they can, to some extent, affect subsequent events. Arab conversation is peppered with blessings, which are like little prayers for good fortune, intended to keep things going well. *Swearing and use of curses and obscenities are very offensive to Arabs.* If words have power and can affect events, it is feared that curses may bring misfortune just by being uttered. There is no point in provoking fate.

The liberal use of blessings also demonstrates that the speaker holds no envy toward a person or object; in other words, that he or she does not cast an "evil eye" toward something. Belief in the evil eye (often just called "the eye") is common, and it is feared or acknowledged to some extent by most Arabs, although less so by the better educated. It is widely believed that a person or object can be harmed if viewed (even unconsciously) with envy—with an evil eye. The harm may be prevented, however, by offering blessings or statements of goodwill. We teach students of Arabic a large number of what we call "benedictions." Learning them is not enough; one must also remember to use them.

Foreigners who do not know about the evil eye may be suspected of giving it. When a friend buys a new car, don't express envy. Instead, say, "May you always drive it safely." When someone moves to a new house, say, "May you always live here happily." When meeting someone's children, say, "May they always be healthy," or, "May God keep them for you." All these are translations of much-used Arabic expressions. Westerners must learn to use benedictions as a new speech habit. Omitting benedictions can be seen as rude.

❀ EUPHEMISMS

Arabs are uncomfortable discussing illness, disaster, or death. This trait illustrates how the power of words affects Arab speech and behavior. *A careless reference to bad events can lead to misfortune or make a bad situation worse.* Arabs avoid such references as much as possible, and use euphemisms instead.

Euphemisms serve as substitutes, and a foreigner needs to learn the code in order to understand what is really being said. For example, instead of saying that someone is sick, Arabs may describe a person as "a little tired." They avoid saying a word like *cancer*, saying instead, "He has it," or, "She has the disease," and often wait until the illness is over before telling others about it, even relatives. Arabs do not speak easily about death and sometimes avoid telling others about a death for some time; even then they will phrase it euphemistically.

Some years back I was visiting the owner of an Egyptian country estate when two men came in supporting a third man who had collapsed in the field. The landlord quickly telephoned the local health unit. He got through just as the man slipped from his chair and appeared to be having a heart attack. "Ambulance!" he screamed. "Send me an ambulance! I have a man here who's . . . a little tired!"

These are social manners—in technical situations, of course, where specificity is required (doctor to patient, commander to soldier), explicit language is used, not courtesies.

These substitutions, blessings, and benedictions mean that Arabic is a "high-context" language—one must know the context to fully understand.

❖ THE WRITTEN WORD

Arabs have considerable respect for the written as well as the spoken word. Some very pious people feel that anything written in Arabic should be burned when no longer needed (such as newspapers) or at least not left on the street to be walked on or used to wrap things, because the name of God probably appears somewhere. Decorations using Arabic calligraphy, Qur'anic quotations, and the name *Allah* are never used on floors (unlike crosses in floors of churches, especially in Europe). They are often seen, however, in framed pictures or painted on walls. If you buy something decorated with Arabic calligraphy, ask what it means; you could offend Arabs by the careless handling of an item decorated with a religious quotation.

If you own an Arabic Qur'an, you must handle it with respect. It should be placed flat on a table or in its own area on a shelf, not wedged in with many other books. Best of all, keep it in a velvet box or display it on an X-shaped wooden stand (both are made for this purpose). Under no circumstances should anything (an ashtray, another book) be placed on top of the Qur'an.

Written blessings and Qur'anic verses are effective in assuring safety and preventing the evil eye, so they are seen all over the Arab world. Blessings are posted on cars and trucks and engraved on jewelry. You will see religious phrases in combination with the color blue, drawings of eyes, or pictures of open palms, all of which appear as amulets against the evil eye.

❀ PROVERBS

Arabs use proverbs far more than Westerners do, and they have hundreds. Many are in the forms of rhymes or couplets. A person's knowledge of proverbs and when to use them enhances his or her image by demonstrating wisdom and insight.

Here is a selection of proverbs that help illuminate the Arab outlook on life. Proverbs frequently refer to family and relatives, poverty and social inequality, fate and luck.

- Support your brother, whether he is the tyrant or the tyrannized.
- The knife of the family does not cut.
  (If you are harmed by a relative, don't take offense.)
- You are like a tree, giving your shade to the outside.
  (You should give more attention to your own family.)
- One hand alone does not clap.
  (Cooperation is essential.)
- The hand of God is with the group.
  (There is strength in unity.)
- The young goose is a good swimmer.
  (Like father, like son.)
- Older than you by a day, wiser than you by a year.
  (Respect older people and their advice.)
- The eye cannot rise above the eyebrow.
  (Be satisfied with your station in life.)
- The world is changeable, one day honey and the next day onions.
  (This rhymes in Arabic.)
- Every sun has to set.
  (Fame and fortune may be fleeting.)

- ❈ Seven trades but no luck. (This rhymes in Arabic.)
  (Even if a person is qualified, because of bad luck he may not find work.)
- ❈ It's all fate and chance.
- ❈ Your tongue is like a horse—if you take care of it, it takes care of you; if you treat it badly, it treats you badly.
- ❈ The dogs may bark but the caravan moves on.
  (A person should rise above petty criticism.)
- ❈ Patience is beautiful.
- ❈ The slave does the thinking and the lord carries it out.
  (Man proposes and God disposes.)
- ❈ Bounties are from God.

And finally, my very favorite:

- ❈ The monkey in the eyes of his mother is a gazelle.

CHAPTER 11

ISLAMIC FUNDAMENTALISM (ISLAMISM)

Islamic fundamentalism is a political and social issue, not part of the mainstream Islamic religion. For this reason, it is considered here rather than in the chapter describing Islam.

❋ DEFINITIONS AND NUMBERS

The efforts to understand evolving Islamic thought have been completely overwhelmed by the (notorious) emergence of fundamentalism. (More accurate terms are *Islamism, militant Islam, political Islam,* and the latest term, *Jihadism.* However, *fundamentalism* has caught on and is the most common word to designate extremist Islamic thought.)*

One problem with using *fundamentalism* in this way is that genuine Muslim fundamentalism refers to the same principles as in other religions: returning to original sacred writings and applying these to social issues in the present. The word *fundamentalist* in Arabic derives from the word "roots." About 10 percent of the Muslims describe themselves as true

---

* There are also the Salafists, who are an even more ascetic fringe group, with a cult-like character.

fundamentalists (religious conservatives, *not* extremist Islamists). I will use the term *Islamism** to refer to extreme militant Islam.

This chapter is intended as a description of militant Islamism in the Middle East and in the West (the United States and Europe). Exploring the various ramifications of the Islamist phenomenon is the goal here.

Extremists exist in every religion. There is no reasoning with people *who know exactly what God wants*. All society can do is to try to control them.

Militant Muslim groups who espouse violence cannot represent even 1 percent of Muslims in the United States (that would be 50,000) or in the world (that would be 15 million). If it was even 1 percent we would be overrun with wild-eyed fanatics. Islamists who resort to violence add up to *less than* one-tenth of 1 percent; we have only to consider numbers.†
But terrorists do act, they engage in violence, and they are certainly getting most of the publicity.

We need to step back for a moment from the television images—chanting mobs, bombings of innocent people, and violent killings. It is simply common sense to realize that *these groups cannot possibly represent Arab or Muslim societies and people as a whole*. There are 1.8 billion Muslims in the world, 600 million people in North Africa and the greater Middle East (including non-Arabs), and 380 million Arab Muslims. The vast majority of these people have no interest whatever in jihad and militancy.

Some estimates claim that as many as 10 to 15 percent of the Muslims are fundamentalists (presumably meaning militant, not necessarily violent, Islamists). Author Daniel Pipes claims that the Islamist element includes some 100 million to 150 million adherents worldwide, his estimate based on "election data, survey research, anecdotal evidence, and the opinions of informed observers," with no sources cited. It is not clear if he means sympathizers or activists, nor is it clear what they are

---

* Islamism is an important technical term. President Trump misspoke badly when he addressed Arab heads of state in Saudi Arabia. He referred to "Islamic extremism," when it was planned that he would say "Islamist extremism."
† The U.S. and other countries have been arresting terrorists worldwide since 2001. The largest number ever detained at Guantanamo was around 650. This is assuming that the identification of these terrorists is related to militant Islam. The definition of *terrorist* is itself unclear; there are many national groups, such as the Chechens, who are not counted here.

adhering to. He also states (without sources), "Reliable statistics on opinion in the Muslim world do not exist [??],* but my sense is that one half of the world's Muslims—or some 500 million persons—sympathize more with Osama bin Laden and the Taliban than with the United States. That such a vast multitude hates the United States is sobering indeed."[1]

I daresay that more than half of the people in the entire *world*, Buddhists, Hindus, Chinese, and others, sympathize more with Osama bin Laden's anti-U.S. *grievances* than with U.S. *foreign policy* (which is not the same as "hating the United States.")† When making such grand claims, it is important to clarify the wording carefully unless the purpose is to scare people.

One U.S. congressman claimed that 85 percent of the mosques in the U.S. have extremist leadership.[2] The author of a 2002 book *American Jihad: The Terrorists Living Among Us*,[3] claims that "fundamentalists" control 80 percent of the mosques, his reason being that many mosques are funded at least partially with Saudi money. The same author had stated in 1995 that Islam "sanctions genocide, planned genocide, as part of its religious doctrine."[4]

Unqualified statements like these are alarmist. They fan hysteria and they libel the entire Muslim community. When such comments are repeated in the media, most ordinary readers assume that such statements are true of *all* Muslims, or if they don't know the difference, "all those Arabs," unless the Islamist context is repeatedly made very clear and the difference explained. Islamists have created their own definition of *infidels* and *jihad*, which are totally unorthodox.

Ordinary Muslims do not go around referring to Christians and Jews as infidels or unbelievers. They would no more do this than Westerners would use similar (embarrassing, degrading) Crusade-era terms about them. In 45 years, I have never heard this term used by ordinary Muslims to refer to Westerners or their society and institutions, not once. When some Western scholars insist on using terms like *infidel* or *unbeliever*

---

* There are numerous excellent polls taken every year, all over the Middle East and the Muslim world.

† Bin Laden's statements bear this out. He repeatedly mentioned policy issues (Palestine, Iraq, sanctions), not religious differences or a desire to destroy the American way of life. It is probable that these terrorists would take action even if there were *no* religious differences.

(they are not quoting, they are just being emphatic),* it is insulting to ordinary Muslims because, again, politicians and the media rarely emphasize that such terms are used *only* by Islamists, who also refer to *mainstream Muslims*, anyone who disagrees with them, as unbelievers. Westerners rightly take offense when characterized as infidels, so it is essential that they understand the source of such labels.

Muslims all over the world just want to get on with their lives, get an education, find a job, raise their children, and participate in family and community life. They are not inscrutable. They are not mysterious or exotic. They are ordinary people with *no interest* in harming non-Muslims or interfering with their way of life. That Muslims have normal human priorities is so obvious that it should not need to be stated.

As for Islamists, however, criticism is justified and should not be euphemized if statements are the truth. Islamist militants advocate violence, deny rights to women, and oppose individual freedom. They do not deserve to be protected by a regard for political correctness. *They are doing devastating harm to everyone*, including Arabs and Muslims, whom they have killed by the thousands.

Every society has deviant groups. We as Westerners understand the reasoning and motives of such groups in our own society. Some scholars have compared extremist Islamists to the Ku Klux Klan in the U.S., which is Christian but definitely not mainstream (it has 5,000 to 8,000 members today).[5] I think a better analogy is the white Aryan groups, because they are more active and they, too, are committed Christians with grievances. The American terrorists had their own reasons to justify bombing the federal building in Oklahoma City (1995) or the killing of nine people in an African-American church (2015).

The number of hate groups in the U.S. jumped from 497 in 1999 to 917 in 2017, almost double.[6] At the site of the Southern Poverty Law Center, you can see a "Hate Map" of the U.S. showing where the hate groups are located, and what type they are. There are neo-Nazis, racist skinhead groups, antigovernment groups, and "patriot" separatists.

---

* Examples: "The Western world, or as they would put it, the infidel countries"; "They had dealt with one of the infidel superpowers"; "We infidels are the only hope for Islam"; "... showing a lack of gratitude or total indifference when we infidels come to their rescue"; " ... repeated commands for Muslims not to befriend infidels/unbelievers (all non-Muslims)."

Anti-Muslim hate groups increased from 5 in 2010 to 101 in 2017, which is only seven years.[7] The nature of hate groups is changing—there are fewer symbols and costumes in the "alternative right," and more think tanks and nonprofits. It is a "rebranding for public relations purposes."[8] Many groups operate mainly on the Internet until they can take action in the real world.

There are two important factors in the case of Islamism that explain why it is growing so quickly. They come from circumstances often experienced by extremist groups in the U.S. and other societies:

1. Their numbers will continue to grow rapidly because they act on perceived grievances *that are constantly being reinforced.*
2. There are many Muslims, especially the young, who feel lost, hopeless, alienated, and uncertain of their future. They need support from a group and a sense of purpose. They are idealists. They have a sense of moral outrage. They fervently believe the doctrine they are being taught. They accept martyrdom as a kind of self-sacrifice,* and once they belong, it is shameful to turn back, so leaders can send them into battle.†[11]

It is understandable that Islamists receive a disproportionate amount of attention in the media. To uninformed Westerners, such extremists appear to be numerous, but to the thousands of Westerners who visit or live in Muslim countries, these groups are no more a factor in life than are the fringe groups in this country.

Here is an analogy. All Westerners readily understand the grievances of anti-abortion groups. Some agree and some disagree, some even join rallies, but this does not mean that these supporters are galvanized to condone or participate in violent acts. Understanding motivations, even

---

* "They are not misfits, criminally insane, or professional losers. Typically . . . they are deeply integrated into social networks and emotionally attached to their national communities."[9]

† Another factor is occupation by American troops. "Suicide terrorists are twenty times more likely to come from Muslim countries with American military presence for combat operations [or Israeli, seen as an American surrogate]" "Religion matters, but mainly in the context of national resistance to foreign occupation."[10]

sympathizing with them, must not be confused with a willingness to support violence.

❊ JIHAD

Jihad is used here to mean "Holy War," which is how the term is used by Islamic militants and the Western media (only). In this sense, *jihad* is the same concept as *crusade*, that is, fighting in the name of a religion.

A more accurate interpretation of jihad refers to the effort that a Muslim makes to live and structure his or her personal life, and the wider society, on Islamic principles, a much more benign meaning. Anyone who combats temptations to live a righteous life can identify with this.

The concept of jihad has undergone changes over time. The Hadith, which were collected 150 years after the Prophet Muhammad's death, were all about fighting, and the original idea of internal struggle almost disappeared.[12] Over the next 400 to 500 years, when Islamic law was being codified, the notion of jihad as fighting came to dominate. And it changed again in the 19th and 20th centuries. Jihad has become a wide-ranging cluster of ideas.[13]

Islamic historian Reza Aslan has stated, "These groups, in many ways, represent a wholly new sect that has arisen out of Islam. One in which all the multiplicity [and] diversity of Islamic thought, and the pillars upon which this faith and practice have rested for 14 centuries, [have] been diluted into this one single notion—jihad and nothing else."[14]

In January 2002, in the wake of the September 11 attack, at a conference of the Muslim World League, scholars defined *terrorism* and *jihad*. *Terrorism* is defined as "an unlawful action, acts of aggression against individuals, groups or states [or] against human beings, including attacks on their religion, life, intellect, property or honor."[15] Terrorism, then, is any violence or threat designed to terrorize people or endanger their lives or security. *Jihad* is "self-defense, meant for upholding right, ending injustice, ensuring peace and security, and establishing mercy."

Muslims cannot *initiate* an attack and call it a jihad—a jihad *must be called in self-defense only*. Extremists have decided that because the West continues to oppress them, they are justified in a "self-defensive" jihad.

Jihad is not a central prop of Islam, despite the Western perspective. But it was and remains a duty for Muslims to commit themselves to a struggle on all fronts—moral, spiritual, and political—to create a just and decent society.[16] This doctrine is, however, open to distortion.

❋ ISLAMISTS AND MUSLIM SOCIETY

Islamists do not recognize any interpretations of the Qur'an made by Islamic jurists over the centuries;* they want to "sweep away the cobwebs." They want to go back to a seventh-century "pure" society as they understand it, with no regard for the realities of the modern world. Some people agree with these unfounded interpretations; most people are dismayed. Many people attend mosques where they hear Islamists preach, but they are not necessarily Islamists themselves, or terrorists. The next steps to extremist action are built on a *deviant* interpretation of religious doctrines. Those who commit to extremist groups belong to a *cult*.

Much has been written by Muslims about the Islamists and their ideology. The ideology is anti-intellectual and reactive, nihilistic and lacking faith in all political systems, in history, and in past social developments.[18] Islamists demonize not just the West, but mainstream Islamic culture and philosophy as well. As one scholar put it, "There is no vision of economic, social, or foreign policy, or a legislature, just the caliph, territory, and Islamic law."[19] They don't know what a state would look like (Muhammad did not create a state; he created a community of believers). They believe a fantasy, based on a false reading of human nature and how the world works.

---

* A good example is a verse often quoted in the Western press and by extremists, "Kill them [infidels] wherever you find them." (2:191) The context of this revelation was the twelve-year persecution of the nascent Muslim community by enemies who were intent on eradicating it, and it was directed toward the Arabian pagans. This verse in no way refers to noncombatant non-Muslims today.[17]
The Prophet Muhammad himself sent a letter to the monks in St. Catherine's Monastery in Sinai, which is still preserved, assuring them that they would be protected by the Muslims. Muhammad also intentionally shielded Christian Ethiopia from conquest. When Caliph Omar entered Jerusalem, he issued an edict that all Christian lives and property would be safe, and he allowed the Jews to return (they had been expelled by the Byzantines). One wonders how Islamic zealots accommodate such precedents. They also have to account for this verse in the Qur'an: "Those who believe, and those who follow the Jewish scriptures, and the Christians and the Sabaens [Ethiopians], any who believe in God and the Last Day and work righteousness shall have their reward with their Lord." (2:62)

The Islamists' message is first and foremost directed at other Muslims, who have fallen away from God, and they can be sacrificed if they do not accept it. Islamist leaders *presume to judge who is or is not a good Muslim*.

It has become quite clear that people do not join the Islamists simply because of poverty or oppression, or for religious reasons. They join because they are in search of purpose, excitement, or status. Ideology is less important than group dynamics and filling psychological and emotional needs;[20] the ideology tends to be acquired later. About one-fourth who join have criminal backgrounds; they constituted 22 percent of those who were linked to Islamic State plots in the West between July 2014 and August 2015.[21,*]

Converts to Islam are over-represented among terrorists. Reasons for this include:

1. They know little about Islam and are susceptible to propaganda, and often they have no one else to consult.
2. They want to prove themselves, demonstrate their loyalty, and show that they belong.
3. They have something to prove, so are more likely to show their loyalty through extreme actions.

In 2015, 81 U.S. residents linked to Islamist terrorism were identified; this compares with a total of 28 in 2014 and 22 in 2013. Average ages were 27, 24, and 28. In 2015, twenty of them, or one quarter, were converts to Islam, seven were women, and twelve had a prior criminal record.[22]

Because these groups resemble cults, there has been considerable effort to "de-program" members. It is a battle of ideas, using theological ammunition.[23] Programs for this type of education were begun in Yemen and have been tried in Indonesia, Saudi Arabia, Egypt, Singapore, Iraq, the U.S., and Britain.[24] Committed Muslims can work effectively with Muslim terrorists. Using violence to overcome violence does not work, and military force makes it worse. In fact, there seems to be success in more than half of the cases where counseling is used, after which the individuals renounce violence.[25]

---

* Eric Hoffer, in his seminal 1951 book, *The True Believer*, addressed this issue. He said that mass movements can provide a "refuge from a guilty conscience." High-risk, high-intensity activism can provide criminals or ex-criminals with a supportive community of fellow outsiders, a positive identity, and the promise of cleansing away past sins.

Many Muslims have found themselves torn between two quite different worldviews. Most seek a synthesis. But others, usually poorly educated, commit totally to groups who tell them what to believe. The leaders of these groups are better educated and have a political-power agenda.[26]

Islamist groups can also gain followers through extensive charity work, not just ideology. They provide social services that local governments cannot or will not undertake, notably in Egypt, Lebanon, Morocco, Tunisia, Algeria, and Yemen. (Helping the poor is considered an Islamic obligation on the part of the ruling power.) Many organizations, such as the Muslim Brotherhood, have schools, training centers, clinics, dental services, pharmacies, job centers, food banks, welfare agencies, and scholarships.[27] They are well organized and well financed, and have created an institutional structure which is parallel to the state.[28] Some of these charities do not have an overt association with their original sponsor, because the governments disapprove. It is significant that Hezbollah, which now controls the Lebanese government, has a hospital, schools, discount pharmacies, groceries, and an orphanage, and is open about it.[29] It benefits an estimated 250,000 Lebanese and is the country's second-largest employer.

Some of these groups' interpretations of specific Islamic doctrines are bizarre indeed. Because suicide has *never* been condoned in Islam (the incidence of suicide in Muslim societies is lower than that of any other regional or religious group),[30] suicide has to be classified as "jihad martyrdom" to gain any acceptance at all. A prominent writer said of Islamists, "The truth is that nothing is further from true Islam than this extremist and unilateral approach, because Islam . . . requires its adherents to accommodate other cultures and integrate them into Islam's great civilization."[31]

It is also time to put the "72 virgins" to rest; this is a quaint, lurid, provocative interpretation of an obscure passage in the Qur'an, avidly seized upon by Westerners who find it amusing and use it repeatedly to ridicule Islamic belief. Typical is an article in the *Washington Post* that opened, "He was promised a straight shot to Heaven and 72 maidens to wait on him once he got there, but Hoshir Sabir Hasan was not ready to die."[32] A brochure from the Institute of Islamic Education states, "The promise of '70 or 72 virgins' is fiction written by some anti-Islam bigots."[33] This belief is to mainstream Muslims as the belief that we will one day be issued wings and a harp, and walk on clouds, is to mainstream Christians.* I have never seen the "72 virgins" refuted in the Western media.

❀ MAINSTREAM MUSLIMS

Moderate Muslims are aware that *mainstream Islam is also a target of the extremists*. They issue news releases, hold conferences, and publicize their repudiation of Islamist violence, but usually they get little or no news coverage, at least in the West.

Muslim authors have written extensively (some will be quoted here), trying to disassociate mainstream Islam from the outrageous statements made by Islamists that invariably get into the Western press. The idea is to reclaim Islamic heritage and promote an "Islamic renewal," a diffuse but growing social, political, and intellectual movement whose goal is a profound reform of Muslim societies.[35] They recognize that throughout time, Muslims have had to revise or bypass Islamic law and some ancient practices to adapt their states and societies to changing realities (this is the centuries-old concept of *Ijtihad*). Outside the Islamic framework, there is much less chance of substantive reform in the Middle East. Independent, moderate Muslim thinkers and leaders are confronting violence, oppression, and intolerance *in the name of Islam*.[36]

A well-known spokesman for moderate Islam is Tariq Ramadan, a Swiss-born Islamic specialist who has written and spoken extensively. He believes in reinterpreting Islam, tailoring it to specific circumstances, and advocates creating a "Western Islam" in the U.S. and Europe, taking into account cultural differences. There is a difference between religion and citizenship; Muslims should participate and contribute to their community wherever they are.[37] Because of an isolationist tendency, Muslims

---

* "[The] first proponents [of this imagery] had nothing to do with the anti-Islamic myth that martyrs are motivated by the hope of being greeted by dozens of virgins waiting in heaven. It began with Hindu Tamils in Sri Lanka . . . [and] when it spread to Palestine over the past decade, it was an act of last-resort desperation by frustrated people . . . . Al-Qaeda has merely taken [up] an old technique."[34]

These are the relevant verses: "Facing each other on thrones, round which will be passed to them a cup from a clear-flowing fountain . . . and beside them will be chaste women, their glances, with big eyes . . . ." (37:44–48) This is very brief and vague, and it has given rise to many commentaries over the centuries. The Islamist interpretation is based on commentaries.

have been poor at representing their image, but many are quietly and successfully integrating with the West.[38]

There are several new "evangelical," wildly popular spokesmen for moderate Islam. Their televised sermons are watched by millions, and they reach an audience through writings, the Internet, CDs, tapes, and social media. Most prominent among them is Amr Khaled, an Egyptian who advocates a blend of conservative Islamic belief with what is compatible with Western culture, regardless of where one lives (he is called "the world's most famous televangelist," and came in at No. 13 in *Time's* 2007 list of the world's 100 most influential people).[39] Amr Khaled emphasizes first putting one's own life in order, succeeding at studies and in adult life, and finding ways to contribute—teaching illiterates, distributing food and clothing, fixing potholes, volunteering—activities that instill a sense of purpose and are part of everyday religion.[40] An example of this was seen when young people periodically picked up trash at Tahrir Square during the Egyptian demonstrations. He appeals to the upper middle class, those truly capable of changing the Islamic world. He blends Islam with feel-good optimism; one can enjoy the world and still be religious and have a "purpose-driven" life. Muslims in the West should not just take from the host country, but participate. Like evangelical Christian preachers, he blends self-help with management-training jargon and religion, a new phenomenon in the Muslim world. After the Danish-cartoon controversy, Khaled organized a conference to talk to young Europeans about Islam, press freedom, and tolerance.[41]

Other influential televangelists, with essentially the same message, include Ahmed Al Shugairi of Saudi Arabia, who advocates equality for women and speaks against sectarianism. He has stated, "Islam is an excellent product that needs better packaging."[42] He sees the Qur'an as a modern ethical guidebook, not a harsh set of medieval rules. Moez Masoud, Khaled al Gendy, and dozens of others are speaking out.[43,44]

The Middle East had about 600 satellite channels in 2012, and about 24 broadcast only religious content. Many other stations have increased their religious programming. Religious programs have different purposes—to fight terrorist ideology, adapt religious practices to modernity, generate dialogue among Muslims, or focus on religious education. Much of the battle over defining Islam in a new political era is being waged on television screens.[45] It is now the primary news medium.

Satellite television disseminates news, documentaries, and talk shows in every country, available for people in other countries to tune in. This affects trends in Islam as well as other topics. Islam is not static; it is constantly being discussed, from women's rights to family dynamics. Discussions about sex, marriage, divorce, religion, and terrorism can be viewed on the same channel. Satellite TV is reinforcing the commonality among Arabs from Marrakesh into Beirut.

The older generation are not as likely to become activists in adapting Islam. It is for the younger generation to work at changing Islam's image. They are opening economic and political systems that had been tightly closed. The nonprofit organization Free Muslims Coalition Against Terrorism was created "to eliminate broad-based support for Islamic extremism and terrorism and to strengthen democratic institutions in the Middle East."[46] In U.S. Muslim communities, people have been invited to send anonymous reports of any Muslim individuals or groups that "advocate Muslim extremist ideology, engage in apologetic support for terrorist organizations, or advocate jihad."[47]

Muslims have been alarmed, embarrassed, and often incredulous at what is happening. They know that Islamism is causing a crisis in the image of their religion that needs to be addressed, and soon. Sunni Muslims do not have a central authority to make and enforce decisions to combat extremism—they must do it themselves as groups and communities. The moderates are fighting back and the tide is turning.

Muslims have been taking action against extremism:

- French Muslims came together and condemned the attacks in Paris in 2015.
- Tunisian hotel employees formed a human shield to protect tourists in 2015.
- More than 100 imams (mosque leaders) in the UK made a video against the Islamic State in 2014.
- Muslims around the world protested IS savagery by flooding social media with the image "Not in My Name" in 2014.
- Mosques all over the Western world opened their doors and invited members of the local communities, some sharing an Iftar (Ramadan) meal. We can expect to see more of this in the future.

CHAPTER 12

ANTI-AMERICANISM

A guidebook about Arabs cannot ignore the growing sentiment of anti-Americanism* (and anti-European sentiment) among Middle Eastern Arabs and Muslims today. It is an important trend, it is increasing, and we need to know why. Here are the results of recent polls.

The 2016 Arab Opinion Index, conducted by the Arab Center for Research and Policy Studies (an independent research institute that examines the key issues affecting the Arab world, governments, and communities) in Doha, Qatar, found that among foreign powers, only Israel was perceived to be a bigger threat to the Arab region than the U.S. U.S. foreign policy in the Middle East remained unpopular across the board, with 80 percent of respondents reporting negative views of U.S. actions in Palestine, and more than 70 percent reporting negative perceptions of U.S. involvement in Iraq, Yemen, and Libya.[1]

The Index, the largest of its kind in the world, surveyed people in Algeria, Egypt, Iraq, Jordan, Kuwait, Lebanon, Mauritania, Morocco, Palestine, Saudi Arabia, Sudan, and Tunisia. There were 18,310 respondents (50 percent men and 50 percent women).

A Pew poll in 2017 about America's global image included three Arab countries. The percentage which was favorable toward the U.S. was: Jordan, 15 percent; Tunisia, 27 percent; and Lebanon, 34 percent.[2]

Reasons given for these feelings include a perception that the U.S. acts unilaterally, as well as opposition to the war on terror, including drones,

---

* "America" refers to the United States in this book because this term is used in the media and also in the Middle East.

torture, and fears of America as a military threat—in other words, political policy.

In other questions, democracy was widely seen as the best form of government, by more than 70 percent of the Arabs. The people clearly value freedom of religion, free speech, and competitive elections. Some prioritize a good economy over democracy.

In July 2011, a poll was taken by the Arab American Institute in Morocco, Egypt, Lebanon, Jordan, Saudi Arabia, and the UAE. The reputation of the U.S. had fallen to a record low, mainly because of "U.S. interference in the Arab world," which ranked as high in the respondents' concerns as the continuing occupation of Palestinian lands.[3] It found that U.S. favorable ratings across the Arab world had plummeted, and the U.S. and Israel are still considered, by far, to be the two greatest threats to peace. But there is substantial affection for U.S. culture and "the American people" in these same countries.

Before we go further, it must be made clear that *Middle East Arabs and Muslims do not "hate" America*. Nor do they hate the American people. But they are *very angry* at America's government, and *very afraid* of it (many Arabs really do believe that America wants to take over the world, or at the very least, the Middle East). It is only the extremist fringe that hates America. I have never heard any ordinary Arab (unlike extremists) state that they hate America, nor have I heard such reports from others.

If the Arabs are *angry*, then there is hope. If we understand the reasons for their anger, we can address those reasons and not misdirect our efforts to bring about change. If they truly hated America and America's values, we would have a permanent breach, a real clash of civilizations, and that would be a hopeless situation, each side trying to eradicate the other. *It's not that bad.*

On both sides, anti-American and anti-Arab/Muslim sentiments are as much about *perceptions* as they are about *reality*—who and what people listen to and the conclusions they reach. Both sides generalize, and by now, each has a mostly negative, stereotypical image of the other. If people don't know a region or its inhabitants, they have to depend on the media to form their beliefs.

And there is a problem with the media in America. Even more than the Vietnam War, the wars in the Middle East have been censored, and

Americans do not see pictures of the dead, including civilians, or of American "atrocities."* Unlike the rest of the world, Americans do not see daily images of suffering Palestinians, Syrians, and Iraqis. It's not that other countries have news different from America—it's American news that is different.

Certainly, in the past many Americans truly did not understand how this all came about, although it has become clearer now to many people. In Saudi Arabia in 2017, President Trump's speech was reported by aide Elliott Abrams: "The speech, however, was deficient in an important respect." Abrams observed that "there was something missing, and that was an understanding of what produces extremism. [The terrorists] are coming from within the societies whose leaders he was addressing. He offered no explanation of what was producing this phenomenon."[4]

Much of what we read or hear is confusing, especially to people who don't know much about the Middle East. If, for example, any of the opinions you read here are difficult to understand, you can do several things:

1. Ask an Arab or a Muslim in your community for clarification (virtually everyone has Arabs and Muslims in their communities).
2. Talk to someone knowledgeable who has been in the region.
3. Look it up and read about it.

Most important is that you consider statements from all sources and then *make up your own mind* as to the nature of anti-Americanism.

Because we have already mentioned that most Arabs don't hate America but are very angry, let's begin right there. Statements about Arabs here refer to the *people*, not the elite or national leaders. Some of these statements go back years.

---

* For further information, see, for example, "U.S. Atrocities and War-Crimes Cover-Ups in Afghanistan," by Stephen Lendman, in *Global Research*, 14 November 2013. Or "United States Must Answer for War Crimes in the Middle East," by Alexander Kuznetsov, in *Online Journal*, Strategic Culture Foundation, 15 October 2016. There is much on this subject.

❋ REASONS FOR ARAB ANGER

Arab/Muslim and Some Western Views*

The terrorists who bombed the World Trade Center in 1993 sent a letter to the *New York Times*: "We declare our responsibility for the explosion on the mentioned building. This action was done in response for the American political, economic, and military support to Israel the state of terrorism and to the rest of the dictator countries in the region."

A Department of Defense study in 1997 concluded: "Historical data show a strong correlation between U.S. involvement in international situations and an increase in terrorist attacks against the United States."

Omar Al-Mateen, from the IS, killed in the Orlando, Florida, nightclub attack: "We hate you for your crimes against the Muslims; your drones and fighter jets bomb, kill, and maim our people around the world, and your puppets in the usurped lands of the Muslims oppress, torture, and wage war against anyone who calls to the truth."[5]

Osama bin Laden: "The events that affected my soul in a difficult way started in 1982 when America permitted the Israelis to invade Lebanon and the American Sixth Fleet helped them in that. And the whole world saw and heard but did not respond . . . . And as I looked at those demolished towers in Lebanon it entered my mind that we should punish the oppressors in kind and that we destroy towers in America in order that they taste some of what we tasted and so that they be deterred from killing our women and children."[6]

Steven Kull, political psychologist: "Large majorities in all the countries surveyed [in his own polls and focus groups in Muslim-majority countries, 2006–2010] said they believed it was a goal of the U.S. to maintain control of Middle Eastern oil. Many people also [said] that they believed the U.S. controlled even their own countries' elected officials . . . . And they frequently cited American support for Israel as an illustration of the fear that the U.S. dislikes Islam and maneuvers to dominate the region."[7]

Mohammad Sidique Khan, London suicide bomber: "I am directly responsible for protecting and avenging my Muslim brothers and sisters.

---

* This can include non-Arab Middle Easterners and non-Muslim Arabs.

Until we feel security you will be our targets, and until you stop the bombing, gassing, imprisonment, and torture of my people we will not stop this fight."[8]

Since 1980, the United States has engaged in fifteen direct military operations in the Middle East, all of them directed against Muslims.[9,*] There were nine interventions in the Middle East from 2002 to 2014.[10] There were also non-military actions such as the imposition of punitive embargoes, threats through military build-up, policies in support of some states against others, support of selected opposition groups, and provision of weapons (sometimes secretly). These actions are seen by the local people as American interference in their region, and resentment has continued to build. It affects America's image. Here are some more quotes.

Journalist Joe Lauria: "Little of this long history of Western manipulation, deceit and brutality in the Middle East is known to Americans because U.S. media almost never invokes it to explain Arab and Iranian attitudes towards the West."[11]

Islam specialists John Esposito and Dalia Mogahed: "Not a single respondent who condoned the 9/11 attacks used the Qur'an as a justification. Instead, they relied on political rationalizations, calling the U.S. an imperialist power or accusing it of wanting to control the world."[12]

Author Sheldon Richman: "Americans do not like to hear it, but their government has behaved like an imperial power in the Middle East [for] more than fifty years."[13]

What the US tends to forget, or intentionally ignores, is that armed reactionary groups like the Islamic State are born out of the destabilization created by Western military intervention. Hostile anti-American resistance groups gain momentum, sympathy, and legitimacy from the actions carried out by Western forces.

---

* This can be viewed at the *Information Clearing House* website, "U.S. Intervention in the Middle East." Military aid to Muslim Bosnia, Kosovo, and Somalia does not counterbalance the "anti-Muslim" activities in the Middle East, and those people are not Arabs. The U.S. has carried out lethal drone attacks in many places in the Middle East, leading to widespread destruction and many civilian deaths. Drones have been used in seven countries: Afghanistan, Iraq, Libya, Pakistan, Somalia, Syria, and Yemen. (Ben Norton, "U.S. Dropped 26,171 Bombs on Seven Muslim-Majority Countries in 2016," *AlterNet*, 10 January 2017.)

This is finally becoming recognized by Western commentators, if not governments. In May 2017, the heading of a report about the terrorist bombing in Manchester, England, had this title: "The Manchester Bombing is Blowback from the West's Disastrous Interventions and Covert Proxy Wars."[14] In June 2017, an article was titled "What Theresa May Won't Talk about When She Talks about Terrorism" and concerned her mention of "values" and "democracy" and "evil ideology" rather than a suggestion of changing foreign policy in the Middle East.[15]

The Greater Middle East Proposal

Arab nervousness is not helped by knowledge of America and Israel's "Greater Middle East" or "New Middle East" proposal. This planning goes back to the Iraq war and pertains to a "military roadmap," creating an arc of instability, chaos, and violence extending from Lebanon, Palestine, and Syria to Iraq, the Arabian Gulf, Iran, and the borders of Afghanistan.[16] It is part of the neo-conservative belief that the U.S., Britain, and Israel should realign the whole Middle East, and during the unrest, "redraw the map of the Middle East in accordance with their geo-strategic needs and objectives." The plan was that the "neo-liberal globalizers and neo-conservatives, and ultimately the Bush Administration, would latch on to 'creative destruction' as a way of describing the process by which they hoped to create their new world orders."[17] It would also lead to controlling all the oil and natural gas in the Middle East.

This is, of course, controversial. Here is a negative description, assuming that it has begun:

> "America's 'Greater Middle East' strategy, which involves violently redrawing the political map of a vast region, has destroyed the states of Syria, Libya, Iraq, and Yemen, and has led to an unprecedented surge in terrorism, a tremendous loss of human life, and a large influx of refugees to Europe."[18]

"The 'war on terror' is part of efforts to violently break apart states that reject U.S.-Israeli hegemony in the region."[19] It is ideas like this, which may or may not be adopted, that frighten the Arabs and lead to their distrust of America.

❈ THE ARAB MEDIA

For all practical purposes, the Arab media is inaccessible to most Westerners—few can follow developments in the media. The Arab media both reflects and reinforces anti-American sentiment. Most Arabs do not believe that the U.S. sincerely promotes democracy; rather, it uses this as a pretext to invade and occupy for its own interests. Here are comments from Arab media:

> "America wants the current unipolar world to remain as it is . . . and is cunningly maneuvering to establish a new regional security system in the Middle East to ensure that its interests in the region are protected. It is purely nonsense for the U.S. to say that its objective is to make the region enjoy democracy and human rights. These are nothing but mere slogans in a political campaign that seeks to hide its true intentions." Rageb Al-Banna, *October.*[20]

> "If we consider the Cold War to be the third world war, the war on terror is the fourth. It is tied to economic globalization, a North vs. South war aimed at protecting and popularizing American public life, which is purely founded on consumerism . . . [It] dominates American culture, for everything can be sold and bought, including ethics and principles." Said Al-Lawandi, *The Greater Middle East: An American Conspiracy Against Arabs.*[21]

> "This [invasion of Iraq] is the stupidest and most recklessly undertaken war in modern times. It is all about imperial arrogance unschooled in worldliness, unfettered either by competence or experience, undeterred by history or human complexity, unrepentant in brutal violence and cruel electronic gadgetry . . . . But what is truly puzzling is that the regnant American ideology is still undergirded by the view that U.S. power is fundamentally benign and altruistic. E. W. Said, *Al Hayat.*[22]

One of the dangers for Americans in deciding about the Islamist threat is continuing to believe—at the urging of senior U.S. leaders—that Muslims hate and attack us for what we are and what we think, rather than what we do. Most Americans have had little interest in foreign policy in the past (compared with Europeans, for example). But this has to change. The United States' foreign policies now can have a direct effect on the American people's lives.

"But there is one thing we have not done that is crucial to our future; we still have not engaged in a true national dialogue about what our foreign policy should be and what constitutes our national interests and values. It is an issue of national security no less vital than protecting our ports or airlines. Throughout our history there has always been a kind of unspoken presumption that foreign policy was outside the purview of the people, that it needed to be in the hands of specialists and policy mandarins and that ordinary Americans were just not equipped to make decisions about such highfalutin matters. That is a mistake we can no longer afford. American citizens pay taxes to support our policies overseas and send their sons and daughters to fight for the nation, which means they should be damn well able to pass judgment on what our foreign policy ought to be."[23]

❖ Some American and European Views

They Hate Our Freedom, Values, Way of Life

Former U.S. president George W. Bush: "How do I respond when I see that in some Islamic countries there is vitriolic hatred for America?" asked George W. "I'll tell you how I respond: I'm amazed. I'm amazed that there's such misunderstanding of what our country is about that people would hate us. I am—like most Americans, I just can't believe it because I know how good we are."[24]

George W. Bush: "They hate what they see right here in this chamber: a democratically elected government. Their leaders are self-appointed. They hate our freedoms:* our freedom of religion, our freedom of speech, our freedom to vote and assemble and disagree with each other."[26]

Conservative political commentator Glenn Beck: "We were attacked by the enemies of freedom. We are a good and decent people and we are free."[27]

---

* Bin Laden responded to this in 2006, asking why, if this were true, had he not attacked freedom-loving Sweden?[25]

Former New York City mayor Rudolph Giuliani: "Their maniacal, violent, and perverted interpretation of their religion, in which they train their young people to be suicide bombers, and they train them to hate you and despise you, and they train them to hate your religion and to not allow you to have a religion of your own or anyone else. They hate us for the reasons that are best about us, because we have freedom of religion . . . freedom for women . . . elections . . . a free economy. Well, we're not giving that up, and you're not going to come and take it from us."[28]

"Terrorists hate us and not because of anything bad we have done; it has nothing to do with Israel and Palestine. They hate us for the freedoms we have and the freedoms we want to share with the world."[29]

Paul Goodman, member of Parliament: "Foreign policy is not the main driver of Islamist terror. They don't kill us because of what we do. They kill us because of who we are."[30]

Warren Rudman, U.S. senator, on suicide bombers: "Oh, I think they are essentially borderline insane. To do what they did? I think if we changed our foreign policy in many ways in the Middle East, it wouldn't make a damn bit of difference. These people hate our culture, they hate our religion, they hate our democracy. They hate us."[31]

They Don't Know Enough about Us

After 9/11, the American government undertook a new initiative—strengthening programs that present information about the country and its values (public diplomacy). This was predicated on the assumption that anti-Americanism can be lessened by presenting more accurate or detailed information. The Bush White House had a stated policy that "spreading the universal principle of human liberty" was the key to changing conditions that spawn terrorism.

The American government set up a radio station, Radio Sawa, which attracts young viewers to the music (which they have always liked), but which they switch away from when it comes to the news; and a television station, Al-Hurra, which has a very low watching public, 1 to 2 percent. There was also a glossy magazine called *Hi*, which was expensive and did not sell. The public diplomacy effort described Muslims' lives in America, but Muslims in the Middle East all have friends or relatives in America, so they don't need this information. In addition, it described American families and communities, but the Arabs already know that Americans are nice people. Other efforts focused on explaining the workings of democracy and elections in the U.S.; equality of opportunity; rewards based on merit; and sports, entertainment, and education. Nothing about policy.

Al-Hurra had many ups and downs, including being criticized when it interviewed and allowed critics of U.S. policy to speak, in an effort to be more free and credible. It tries for a diverse range of voices, but it is hard to please everyone, and some said it should talk less about politics and more about democracy.

Here are some comments:

> "Despite the ten billion dollars spent to advance U.S. strategic interests since 9/11, foreign public opinion data shows that negative views towards the United States persist."[32]

> "Efforts . . . to boost America's image among Arabs have been hampered because many Arabs strenuously object to U.S. foreign policies, particularly over the Israeli-Palestinian conflict and the Iraq war . . . . The State Department, which sponsors the $4.5 million annual publication and distribution of the Arabic-language magazine *Hi*, said it stopped the presses because it was unclear how widely it was read."[33]

> "Hurting more than helping is Al-Hurra, the official Arabic-language broadcasting outlet sponsored by the U.S. government . . . . There was broad agreement that Al-Hurra has been a very costly mistake."[34] Its news is not trusted. Its campaign after 9/11, called 'Shared Values,' received little attention; practical issues of policy overshadow values. But its newer daily 'news magazine' Al-Youm is more popular because it is seen as straightforward news without a slant."

Anti-Americanism is An Excuse

Author Tiffany Gabbay: "When the people's discontent boils over, rather than assume responsibility, political and religious leaders across the Middle East attempt to deflect blame, thereby pointing a finger at the West, to claim that America is the genesis for all of their country's societal ills."[35]

Author Armstrong Williams: "Often, the leaders of the Arab world capitalize on these feelings of anger and inferiority to distract citizens from their own failed rule. Economic stagnation is blamed on a nexus of crippling political decisions handed down by America. Citizens are told their way of life is under assault. The youth display their loyalty to the state by strapping bombs to their chest and blowing themselves up. So long as the citizens are kept riled up, they have little time to reflect on the mismanagement and oppression of their own leaders. Nor do they push for things like equality, democracy, market privatization or any number of policies that are badly needed."[36]

Author Barry Rubin: "The basic reason for the prevalence of Arab anti-Americanism, then, is that it has been such a useful tool for radical rulers, revolutionary movements, and even moderate regimes to build domestic support and pursue regional goals with no significant costs."[37]

We Share a Long History of Hatred

This simplistic reason has been given repeatedly—if there is blind hatred, then the attacks make sense. Except that when one actually talks to ordinary Arabs, they do not express hatred or use outdated terminology like "infidels."

Here are comments:

Historian Bernard Lewis: "This is no less than a clash of civilizations—the perhaps irrational but surely historic reactions of an ancient rival against our Judeo-Christian heritage . . . . The struggle between these rival systems has now lasted some fourteen centuries. What is truly evil and unacceptable is the domination of infidels over true believers."[38,*]

Bernard Lewis: "The motive, clearly, is hatred . . . the hatred has been growing steadily for many years . . . . It is difficult if not impossible to be strong and successful and to be loved by those who are neither the one or the other . . . . This feeling, with far deeper roots and greater intensity, affects attitudes in the Muslim world toward the Western world or, as they would put it, the infidel countries."[39,†]

---

* Millions of Middle Eastern Muslims migrate to Europe and America precisely because they want to live under a Western government.

† Many authors, as well as reporters in the media, wrongly depict the thinking of people in the modern Middle East. I select the writings of Bernard Lewis as an example because he is widely read and quoted. In all his writings, Dr. Lewis speaks in generalities, not distinguishing historical or extremist views from those of ordinary Arabs and Muslims of the twenty-first century. Repeating and emphasizing insulting remarks about Westerners will resonate with readers and become associated in their minds with Arabs and

Unfortunately, it is not clear who is being described. This is the view of hardcore Islamists, but it reads as if it refers to everyone caught up in "the roots of Muslim rage."

U.S. political scientist Samuel Huntington: "Conflict along the fault line between Western and Islamic civilizations has been going on for 1,300 years . . . . On both sides, the interaction between Islam and the West is seen as a clash of civilizations."[40] "A complex of factors has increased the conflict between Islam and the West in the late twentieth century . . . . Muslim population growth . . . the Islamic Resurgence . . . the West's simultaneous efforts to universalize its values and institutions, to maintain its military and economic superiority . . . and to intervene in conflicts in the Muslim world . . . the collapse of communism . . . increasing contact between . . . Muslims and Westerners."[41]

❊ ARAB/MUSLIM VIEWS ON AMERICAN CULTURE

Author Zeinab Salbi: "Most Muslims in the Middle East and North Africa admire and aspire to the essence of Western life: freedom of opportunity, freedom of expression and creativity, and the diversity of options available in life. Hollywood plays a major role in promoting this life, in which people have decent homes and jobs, cars, and nice clothes. On a daily basis, these aspirations are reflected not only in people's love of Western popular

---

Muslims, even if they are outdated by a thousand years. Dr. Lewis continually uses phrases like "the enemies of God," "the infidels of the West," and "the House of Islam and the House of Unbelief," which have nothing to do with how modern, educated people think (perhaps it helps to sell books). He writes that "America has become the archenemy, the incarnation of evil, the diabolic opponent of all that is good," which must be limited to extremists unless ordinary Arabs think that the Western way of life and government are evil too (they don't).

I cannot imagine why he would assure us that "studying under infidel teachers was inconceivable," when it is not explained and thousands of Muslims study in the West. He cannot be describing ordinary people, but the damage is done. Arabs and Muslims do not think this way. Language like this does not reflect what I have been hearing in the Arab world for many years.

Most Western readers simply want to understand 9/11, the Iraqi insurgency, the Syrian civil war, the uprisings, and the current political climate in the Middle East. They don't know what is historical, current, or extremist. Such careless writing does not clarify current issues for Western readers; on the contrary, it does incalculable damage.

movies and TV series, but also through the latest fashion . . . music, too, is a key cultural influence."[42]

Author C. J. Werleman: "When a Jordanian goes into a Starbucks in Amman, or a Saudi visits a Pizza Hut in Riyadh, it's not necessarily because the coffee or pizza are better than the local fare—often they are not. Arabs frequent these franchises because they think they are buying a piece of America and are part of a worldwide fascination with the way of life conveyed through these products."[43]

Author Khaled Dawood: "Although there is widespread animosity toward America across the Arab world—especially over U.S. policy toward Israel and the Palestinians—many Arabs embrace aspects of American life and American culture . . . . American music is popular. American food is popular. American clothes are popular. People still wear jeans with American flags on them. They wear baseball hats and they don't see any contradiction in that."[44]

❊ VIEWS ON WESTERN-STYLE DEMOCRACY

Lately, with freedom-and-democracy demonstrations in the news, most Westerners have come to realize that the Arabs love the concepts of freedom and democracy after all. Democracy has an overwhelmingly positive image throughout the world. This is constantly emphasized in the Arab world, in speech and in writing.

Report, 2015 Arab Opinion Index: "While some in the West have argued that Islam or Middle Eastern culture are incompatible with democracy, responses to the 2015 Arab Opinion Index reflect a different reality. 72 percent of the respondents favor democracy. 79 percent believe that democracy is the most appropriate system of government for their home countries. 55 percent would accept an electoral victory and rise to power of a political party which they disagreed with. 62 percent would accept an Islamist group if it had an electoral mandate."[45]

Author, Rami Khouri: "We desperately want change, reform, democracy, prosperity, and modernity, but few of us believe that this will come through the barrels of Western guns."[46]

Author, Bessma Momani: "Citing polls, 92 percent of Arab youth want democracy, and studies leave no doubt that they mean liberal democracy . . . . There is already a social and cultural revolution in the very thinking of the youth. [They] favor entrepreneurialism, political freedom, and cosmopolitanism . . . . They do not view opposing the state as being disloyal."[47]

Some Americans have stated their hope that if the Arabs can gain freedom, they will leave behind anti-American political grievances, and they will recognize that America just wants what is best for them. Asked how Middle East democracy would turn out for the United States, 65 percent of the Americans said it would be mostly positive. And in the "long run," 76 percent said that democratization would be mostly positive for the U.S.[48]

We read that Arabs will recognize that America is not after their oil—America just wants their freedom:

Political commentator Charles Krauthammer: "When millions of Iraqis risk their lives [to vote] and then dance with joy at having been initiated into the rituals of democracy, a fact has been created. And the old clichés that America went to Iraq for oil or hegemony begin to look hollow."[49]

We read that demonstrations for freedom have taken place because the U.S. led the way:

University Professor Fouad Ajami: "What we are witnessing in the Arab world is similar to the spring of the European peoples in 1848."[50] "Now the Arabs, grasping for a new world, and the Americans who have helped usher in this unprecedented moment, together ride this storm wave of freedom."[51]

But there are fears. It's not simple. Attaining a democracy is not easy, and it can still entail serious risks. We hear some hyperbole and wishful thinking:

Charles Krauthammer: "We are at the dawn of an Arab Spring—the first bloom of democracy in Iraq, Lebanon, Egypt, Palestine, and throughout the greater Middle East."[52]

Americans are thinking about democracy, and many Americans are analyzing our own democracy, what it is, what it means. For any democracy to work, it requires an *informed citizenry* (a reasonable level of literacy); *a trust in the opposition* (they will give up power if voted out); and a *national identity* that transcends allegiance based on kin, tribe, religion, or ethnic origin.

National identity is difficult in some parts of the Middle East because many national borders were drawn arbitrarily and incorrectly by England

and France after they seized control of the region following World War I, making nations out of people who would not have willingly been united, and cutting off others who belong. Middle Easterners found themselves defined for the first time by *geography*. Even now, we cannot consider the borders of the Middle East as fixed. When the current chaos settles, very likely borders will be adjusted.*

The Arabs want democracy as an ideal. It can work in some countries, but the conditions have not been met in others. Reforms such as pluralism, rule of law, and accountability will come at the expense of the entrenched elites in every country. The situation is too complicated to predict with assurance.

The call for democracy "has already been happening for many years through the work of indigenous reformers and democrats and activists. It is not the American policy of promoting freedom that is starting to show dividends . . . . What has happened is that the Americans are finally supporting the democrats rather than supporting the tyrants, as they did for the last fifty years."[54]

❊ ISLAM

Islam in particular elicits vitriolic attacks and impassioned defenses. These are a very few of the comments; for a bigger picture, you can easily find more on the subject. This is, of course, selective.

Anti-Islam Comments

You can be sure that comments of this type are widely disseminated in the Middle East.

Political scientist Samuel Huntington: "Some Westerners have argued that the West does not have problems with Islam but only with violent Islamic extremists . . . . Fourteen hundred years of history demonstrate otherwise . . . . The underlying problem for the West is not Islamic fundamentalism. It is Islam."[55]

Evangelist Franklin Graham: "I believe [Islam is] a very evil and wicked religion."[56] "In most Islamic countries, it is a crime to build a Christian

---

* In the words of former president Obama, "What we're seeing in the Middle East and parts of North Africa is an order that dates back to World War I starting to buckle."[53]

church . . . . Christians are not free to worship Jesus in most Muslim countries . . . .* The brutal, dehumanizing treatment of women by the Taliban
has been well documented . . . the abusive treatment of women in most
Islamic countries is nearly as draconian."[57]

Televangelist Pat Robertson: "These people are crazed fanatics, and I
want to say it now: I believe it's motivated by a demonic power, it is satanic
and it's time we recognize what we're dealing with."[58]

Politician, author, and activist Ayaan Hirsi Ali: "We thought that after
1945, the end of the Second World War, that there was this enormous
insight in the West; no more anti-Semitism. Never again . . . . But in
Europe anti-Semitism is back, and it's back because of Islam."[59]

Bill O'Reilly: "Teaching our enemy's religion is like teaching *Mein
Kampf.*"[60]

Defense-of-Islam Comments

"We consider the September 11 . . . criminal act as foreign to our honored
culture, our peaceful and tolerant faith, and our hospitable way of life.
Terrorism cannot be eradicated until the underlying causes are justly
addressed."[61]

"If Islam were really the caricature that it is often reduced to, then
how would it be so appealing as to become the world's fastest-growing
religion? . . . Because it also has admirable qualities that anyone who has
lived in the Muslim world observes: profound egalitarianism and lack of
hierarchy that confer dignity and self-respect among believers, greater
hospitality than in other societies, an institutionalized system of charity
to provide for the poor. Many West Africans, for example, see Christianity as hierarchical and flock to Islam, which they view as democratic
and inclusive."[62]

It is interesting that after the terrible genocide, Rwandans converted
to Islam in large numbers. Muslims now make up 14 percent of the 8.2
million people in Africa's most Catholic nation. "We have our own jihad,
and that is our war against ignorance . . . it is our struggle to heal," said
the head mufti of Rwanda.[63] Fundamentalists from outside tried to organize and were rejected. During the genocide, Muslims were among the

---

* Christianity is openly practiced in all Muslim countries except Saudi Arabia. There are
thousands of churches in Muslim countries.

few Rwandans who protected both neighbors and strangers; the churches were not safe.

❀ CONCLUSION

The subject of anti-Americanism clearly elicits wide-ranging and conflicting opinions, both in explaining its causes and advocating its remedies. The issue is growing increasingly politicized. Because much of the media blends entertainment with news, in many instances there is little incentive to present thoughtful analyses of events backed up by thorough fact-checking. The stakes are high; they couldn't be higher. Every American needs to be knowledgeable on this subject and develop his or her own convictions.

❋ ❋ ❋ ❋ ❋ ❋ ❋ ❋ ❋ ❋ ❋ ❋ ❋ ❋ ❋ ❋ ❋

CHAPTER 13

ARABS AND MUSLIMS IN THE WEST

There has been a sharp rise in both Arab and Muslim immigration to the West, which has affected the host countries and also the societies back home. The trend toward increased emigration (except from Saudi Arabia and the Gulf states) continues. Muslims and Arabs, however, are entirely different populations. Statistics for both of these groups are variable and estimates vary widely.

❋ ARABS IN THE UNITED STATES

There are about 3.5 million people of Arab origin in the United States. Arab/Middle East ancestry is not listed clearly on census forms (it may be mixed with Asian or African), but it is being considered for 2020. Of the Arabs in the U.S., more than half (possibly as many as 70 percent) are Christian. Christians, especially Lebanese and Syrians, got a head start; they began emigrating in the late 19th and early 20th centuries. Arabs who arrived after the 1960s are mostly Muslims. About 63 percent of all the Arab Americans were born in the U.S. The following is the breakdown of Arabs' countries of origin by percentage:

*Country of Origin for Arab Americans**

Lebanon	32%
Egypt	11%

---

* There has not been an official count, so these percentages are estimates from the Arab-American Institute.

Syria	10%
Palestine	5%
Morocco	5%
Iraq	4%
Jordan	4%
(Other)	29%

Arab Americans as a group are younger, more educated, more affluent, and more likely to own a business compared with Americans as a whole. Arab Americans with college degrees are 45 percent (compared to 27 percent in the U.S. population as a whole).[1] Nearly three-fourths work in professional, managerial, technical, and administrative jobs, and 82 percent are citizens.[2] Arab American women work outside the home at the rate of 45 to 60 percent (compared to 73 percent in the nation as a whole).[3] Very few Americans are aware of the contributions Arab Americans have made to the U.S., probably because Arabs are so few in number.

After September 11, 2001, 69 percent of the Arab Americans supported a war with countries that support and/or harbor terrorists.[4] They very quickly raised money to donate to the Red Cross and to the victims of the attack. Some notable donations were the following: the National Arab-American Medical Association, $100,000; the Arab Bankers' Association, $100,000; Arab-Americans in Dearborn, Michigan, $125,000; the Syrian-Lebanese Foundation, $20,000; and groups in Texas and Philadelphia, $20,000 and $15,000, respectively.[5] The Arab Americans also sponsored blood drives, rallies, and vigils all over the nation.

After Hurricane Katrina in 2005, Muslim groups made a $1 million donation to relief efforts and helped provide hot meals to those in shelters.[6,7] Five hundred Muslim volunteers established food and supply centers throughout the states affected by Hurricane Sandy[8] and set up a "Muslims for Japan" campaign to collect donations after the tsunami in 2011.[9] When Jewish cemeteries were desecrated in Chicago and Philadelphia, Muslim veterans volunteered to guard the areas. Muslims raised over $100,000 for them as well.[10]

❀ MUSLIMS IN THE UNITED STATES AND CANADA

The Muslim population in the United States has increased to roughly 5 million (estimates range from 2.5 million to 7 million). Islam is now the third most commonly practiced religion in America and projected to be the second largest by 2040.[11] More than half of the American Muslims live in California, New York, Michigan, Illinois, and New Jersey.[12] In 2015, there were about 3,200 mosques, large and small Islamic centers, and prayer locations. This compares, for example, to 11,000 places of worship for Jehovah's Witnesses.[13]

In Canada, there were between 750,000 and 1.2 million Muslims in 2015 (numbers vary widely), most of them living in Ontario, Quebec, and British Columbia.[14] Canadian Muslims are optimistic about their future, and 90 percent think that tolerance will improve under the Liberal government of Justin Trudeau.[15] In 2010, there were about 200 mosques and Islamic centers, and more can be expected as refugees continue to arrive.[16]

Among the Muslims in the United States, 63 percent are immigrants.[17] Muslims are diverse: Arabs constitute about 20 percent, one-third are of South Asian origin (India, Pakistan, Bangladesh), 30 percent are African Americans, and others are mainly African and East Asian. They are the only faith community in America without a majority race.[18] There are about 5,900 Muslims serving in the U.S. active and reserve military forces.[19]

American immigrants of Middle Eastern Muslim ancestry (not just Arabs) are more affluent, better educated, and more likely to be married and have children than the average citizen. Many are in professional, managerial, and technical fields, especially in information technology, education, medicine, law, and the corporate world.[20] In the U.S., 77 percent of the Muslims are active in organizations that help the poor, sick, elderly, and homeless (this is part of their religion); 69 percent are active in school and youth organizations; and 46 percent belong to a professional organization.[21] They favor tougher laws to prevent terrorism at a rate of 84 percent; a 2011 survey found that 86 percent of Muslims say that terrorist tactics are rarely or never justified (this is similar to other religious groups).[22]

Mosque attendance is not linked to radicalization. Muslims who regularly attend mosques are more likely to be engaged in solving community problems and be registered to vote (74 percent).

A Pew poll in 2007 showed that Muslims are decidedly mainstream, largely assimilated, happy with their lives, and moderate on political issues.[23] About 70 percent lean toward the Democratic Party and 11 percent toward the Republicans.[24]

The vast majority of American Muslims were appalled by terrorist attacks because all of them have a huge stake in the future welfare of America. It also leads to erosion of their civil liberties. Many believe that the mainstream Muslim majority in the U.S. has been silent about extremism and terrorism for too long (they have been afraid of law enforcement personnel and of reprisals if their identification became known), and they are actively working to bring attention to anything of this sort to government authorities.

It is not surprising that Muslim terrorism has been sensationalized by the media. A study in 2015 found that in media descriptions of domestic terrorists, 81 percent were identified as Muslims; the FBI found that in the same period, it was actually 6 percent.[25] Between 1970 and 2012, about 2.5 percent of terrorist attacks in the U.S. were carried out by Muslims (60 out of 2,400), although statistics vary.[26] As an aside, it can be pointed out that five of the last twelve Nobel Prize winners were Muslim—can we generalize from this? If all Muslims are terrorists, then are all Muslims also scientists?

Like other Americans, Muslims' safety and security depend on combating terrorism. And *every time a terrorist incident occurs, those most vulnerable to unfounded suspicion are the Arabs and Muslims living in the West.* In 2004, the American Muslim Group on Policy was formed to focus on ways that the Muslim community can provide assistance and help build trust and communication in the nation. About half of Americans say that they do not personally know a Muslim,[27] and most say they know little or nothing about Islam.

❀ REFUGEES

Between 9/11 and 2016, the U.S. had admitted 784,000 refugees (from many countries). *Not one has been involved in a terrorist incident.*[*,28] Because of the high numbers worldwide, Syrian refugees are the most discussed.

---

* Two Iraqi refugees were arrested on terrorist charges. They had not planned an attack on America, but aided Al-Qaeda at home in Iraq. The Tsarnaev brothers of the Boston Marathon incident were not counted as refugees because they came as children when their father applied for asylum.

More than 12 million Syrians have been displaced from their homes by civil war, of which 7.5 million have been displaced within Syria and about 4.5 million have fled abroad, mostly to neighboring countries.[29] There are more than three million Iraqis displaced within the country since the start of 2014 and nearly 220,000 are refugees in other countries.[30] The U.S. has a moral responsibility to help them as well because they were impoverished by U.S. sanctions for ten years, and then by changes of government, before their country was destroyed. America has taken very few so far, because of a fear of terrorism. Since 9/11, all Middle East immigrants have been viewed through this lens.

In fact, refugees go through an elaborate vetting procedure. After referral by an American embassy or the U.N. High Commissioner for Refugees, they are screened by the Department of State Resettlement Service Centers located all over the world. This is in addition to screenings by the National Counterterrorism Center and by intelligence agencies. The entire process can take up to three years.[31] Certainly if a potential terrorist were determined to enter America to do harm, there are easier and faster ways to do so.

Syrians have fared better than some other groups of refugees, integrating quickly and finding work. The majority of them are women and children.[32] They are welcomed and resettled by many private groups and government agencies. In fiscal year 2016, the U.S. admitted 12,500 Syrians;[33] Canada has resettled 30,000; and there are 1.1 million in Europe.[34] The plan had been to admit 10,000 Syrians in the next fiscal year (of the total 85,000 refugees). After Donald Trump was elected president, he changed the plan and banned Muslim refugees from seven countries, later amended to six. Courts have declared his move illegal.

❀ MUSLIMS IN EUROPE

Statistics for the number of Muslims in Europe are indefinite. Muslims come from numerous countries of origin, and Europe's secular governments tend to collect fewer religious statistics than the United States does; furthermore, many Muslims are in Europe illegally and are therefore not counted in official estimates. There are 44 million Muslims in Western and Eastern Europe, and Islam is the second most commonly practiced religion there. The approximate breakdown for Muslims in Western Europe is shown in the following chart.

Number of Muslims in Western Europe 2016[35]

Germany	4,120,000
France	3,570,000
U.K.	3,115,000
Italy	2,200,000
Spain	1,020,000
Netherlands	920,000
Belgium	630,000
Greece	520,000
Austria	475,000
Sweden	450,000
Switzerland	430,000
Denmark	226,000
Norway	144,000
Ireland	43,000
Finland	42,000
Portugal	22,000
Luxembourg	13,000
(Australia)	(476,000)[36]

Unlike the Muslims in the United States and Western Europe, Eastern European Muslims are mostly indigenous; their ancestors converted to Islam while the region was part of the Ottoman Empire. Shown here are the statistics for Muslims in Eastern Europe.

Number of Muslims in Eastern Europe, 2016[37]

Russia	16,400,000*
Albania	2,200,000
Kosovo	2,100,000
Bosnia	1,500,000
Bulgaria	1,000,000
Macedonia	700,000
Georgia	450,000

---

* Muslims constitute about 12 percent of Russia's population.

Ukraine	400,000
Serbia	280,000
Croatia	56,000
Slovenia	49,000
Hungary	25,000
Poland	20,000
Belarus	19,000
Moldova	15,000
Czech Republic	4,000
Slovakia	4,000

Mosques and Islamic Centers in Western Europe[38,39]

France	2,000
U.K.	1,600
Germany	1,000
Netherlands	500
Belgium	350
Italy	250
Spain	200

Athens had been the only European Union capital without an official mosque, but a project for a mosque was finally approved in mid-2016. Minarets were banned in 2009 in Switzerland,[40] and similar bans are proposed in the Netherlands and Italy. A province in Austria requires new buildings to "fit within the overall look and harmony of villages and towns," which effectively bans mosques and minarets.[41] Muslims would like to re-create the "old city" of Cordoba, Spain, once the heart of Anda-lucía, which would include the right to worship in a cathedral that had originally been a mosque.[42]

Mega-mosques are especially controversial in Europe. Mega-mosques exist in Rome (the largest in Europe) and Amsterdam, and one is approved in Ireland. Others have been proposed for London, Copenhagen, Marseille, Stockholm, Florence, and Barcelona (among others) but have been stymied or mired in local objections, being considered too intrusive. In most cases, these would be paid for by governments of Muslim countries, such as Turkey, Saudi Arabia, Iran, Qatar, and the UAE.

Because Muslim numbers in Europe are increasing—their numbers doubled in the past thirty years—the situation is troublesome to some, although for the most part, Muslims have not shown an inclination to organize along racial or religious lines (they are too diverse, even with respect to understanding of religion).[43] Muslims have been entering Europe at a rate of 1.6 million to 2 million per year,[44] and recently numbers are vastly increased—by at least a million last year—due to the influx of refugees. In 2013, Muslims constituted 25 percent of Rotterdam, Marseilles, Brussels, and Amsterdam; 20 percent of Stockholm; 15 percent of Paris; and 10 to 12 percent of London, Copenhagen, and Vienna.[45]

Muslims in Western Europe originate from both Arab and non-Arab countries. Those in the U.K. are primarily from South Asia, in France from North and West Africa, in Germany from Turkey, in Belgium from Morocco, and in the Netherlands from Morocco and Turkey. The mix is slightly different in every country. Europe is affected far more than the U.S. by destabilization in the Muslim world because it is closer and also easier for illegal migrants to enter.

There are crucial differences between the Muslim population in Europe and that in the United States:

* U.S. Muslims are well educated, and most are professional and fairly affluent. Muslims in Europe are often not well educated and constitute an underclass, working at menial jobs, and they are often marginalized.
* U.S. Muslims are viewed as potential citizens. In Europe, they are often seen as immigrants or "guest workers," even after two or more generations.
* U.S. Muslims are mostly married with children. Muslims in Europe are often unmarried and not as committed to their host country. Many Muslims in Europe initially planned to stay only temporarily, and later decided to remain.
* U.S. Muslims are more geographically spread out than in any single country in Europe.
* Unlike the U.S., these small, old countries have deep historical, cultural, religious, and linguistic traditions. It is harder to think of non-Europeans as "belonging."

⚜ While earlier immigrants assimilated quite well, younger Muslims in Europe appear to be less inclined to true assimilation. Without integration, polarization and ghettos can result.[46]

⚜ American Muslims feel welcomed and quickly adapt to American ways. Half of all Muslims display the U.S. flag at home, in their office, or on their car.[47]

Because the social status and living conditions of many Muslims in Europe are not good, in that they are not well assimilated, *when riots or disturbances happen in England or France, for example, it does not mean that there will be similar unrest in the United States.*

Europeans are more likely to view Muslims as a threat than is generally the case in the United States. Many of the Muslims in Europe came in the 1950s and 1960s, when there was a severe shortage of workers; most were from Turkey, Algeria, Morocco, Tunisia, and Pakistan. They stayed and later settled in with their families. Very quickly, their increasing numbers become a significant percentage of local populations, whereas in the U.S., Muslims are barely 1 percent, if that.

In November 2004, European leaders met at a summit conference to discuss the level of legal migrants needed to compensate for continuing domestic labor shortages and Europe's aging population. An EU report said that the working population in the 25-nation bloc would fall from 303 million to 297 million by 2020, and to 280 million by 2030.[48] In fact, however, Muslim birth rates have leveled off and European birth rates have increased, both unexpectedly. (The fertility rate in Britain rose from 1.6 to 1.9 in six years; it rose in France from 1.7 in 1993 to 2.1 in 2007, despite a steady fall in birth rates among women not born in France; and it jumped 8 percent in Sweden in 2004 and has remained level.)[49] In 2004, the EU expected its population to decline by 16 million by 2050; now it is projected to increase by 10 million by 2060, some due to a higher birth rate, some due to immigration.[50]

Muslims have increasing opportunities to acquire citizenship. Because the vast majority are not radicalized (as was once feared), this settling in and enfranchisement are already integrating many European Muslims into the mainstream and also have the potential to produce a moderate type of Euro-Islam.[51]

❀ THE IMAGE OF ARABS AND MUSLIMS

Both Arabs and Muslims have been portrayed in Western media and print (especially in cartoons) as excessively wealthy, irrational, sensuous, and violent, and "the men seem not to go very far without their scimitars."[52] They are seen as alien and therefore dangerous. If a person in the news is Muslim, this is mentioned, even if national origin is not. There is little counterbalancing information about ordinary people who live family- and work-oriented lives on a modest scale. The media concentrate on reporting sensational events, not typical life.

The phenomenon of Islamophobia has been present for many years. It is defined as "the exaggerated fear, hatred, and hostility toward Islam and Muslims that is perpetuated by negative stereotypes resulting in bias, discrimination, and the marginalization and exclusion of Muslims from social, political, and civic life."[53]

Image in America

Over thirty years ago one observer remarked, "The Arabs remain one of the few ethnic groups who can still be slandered with impunity in America."[54] Unfortunately, not only has there been no improvement, the situation has actually gotten worse, in both the quantity and the quality of remarks. Twenty years later there was an almost identical statement, "Arabs are the only really vicious stereotypes acceptable in Hollywood."[55] Hollywood has portrayed Arabs as everything from violent terrorists and criminals to evil viziers, decadent sheikhs, and smarmy buffoons; examples include the films *True Lies, Executive Decision, Delta Force,* and *Black Sunday.*[56] Such stereotypical images are numerous and well documented, as are caricatures, which would not be tolerated for other groups. These reinforce a fear present among Americans that *can only be diminished through information and contact with Arab and Muslim citizens.*

Ever since the attacks of September. 11, 2001, especially in the first year, Muslims (and their young children) have faced increased discrimination, threats, name-calling, violence, and vandalism (Sikhs have been targeted too). From September. 11 to December. 6, 2001, the U.S. Equal Employment Opportunity Commission received more than double the number of complaints of discrimination toward Muslims in the workplace compared with the previous year (166 vs. 64).[57] In 2000, the FBI reported

33 anti-Muslim hate crimes across the country; in the four months following September. 11, authorities investigated more than 250 incidents.[58] Between 2001 and 2011, there was a 163 percent rise in workplace complaints.[59] Muslims are 1 percent of the population and victims in 14 percent of religious discrimination cases. There was an eightfold increase in anti-Muslim sentiment between 2000 and 2014.[60] And since Donald Trump's election in late 2016, anti-Muslim hate groups had tripled by mid-2017. In 2016 alone, they increased from 34 to 101.[61]

In 2014, a Pew poll found that Americans hold a more negative view of Islam than other religions.[61] It was explained that "conservative and liberal experts said Americans' attitudes about Islam are fueled in part by political statements and media reports that focus almost solely on the actions of Muslim extremists." A Gallup poll in 2015 showed that 43 percent of Americans had some degree of prejudice against Muslims.[62] One in three Americans had heard prejudiced comments about Muslims lately, and one in four admitted to harboring some personal bias against Muslims. Pollster James Zogby said he was not surprised by the results. "The intensity [of anti-Muslim statements] has not abated and remains a vein that's very near the surface, ready to be tapped at any moment . . . . Radio commentators have been talking about it nonstop."[63]

In the recent presidential campaign, former president Obama and others were criticized for not using the term "Islamic terrorism." It is very broad, and it would be more accurate to say "Muslim extremist terrorism" or possibly "jihadi terrorism." In late 2016, three men were arrested in Kansas who planned to bomb a mosque and an apartment building where Somali Muslims lived.[64] Would it be fair to refer to this plan, or, for example, white-supremacist activities as "Christian terrorism?" In 2011, Anders Breivik, who killed 77 people in Norway to further his "pro-Christian Europe" agenda, was called a "Christian terrorist," and this was met by widespread outrage.

A U.S. congressman objected when a newly-elected Muslim congressman wanted to use the Qur'an to take the oath of office. The objection was ignored; there are several precedents of oaths taken on books other than the Bible. Congressman Virgil Goode Jr. (R-VA.) stated, "We need to end the diversity visas policy . . . (we need to) adopt the strict immigration policies that I believe are necessary to preserve the values and beliefs traditional to the United States of America."[65]

A conservative radio commentator was fired for describing Islam as a "terrorist organization."[66] A high school teacher was fired when she lashed out at a group of students for opening a commemorative speech on the 9/11 attacks with the greeting *Assalamu Alaykum*, Arabic for "Peace be with you."[67] A college student was detained at the Philadelphia airport because he was carrying Arabic flash cards to study for his language course. He was handcuffed and held for two hours and not told why he was detained. He later won damages of $25,000.[68] In 2016, a Muslim family was forced off a United flight[69] and a student speaking Arabic on a cell phone was removed from a Southwest flight.[70]

A teacher was fired in New York for allowing T-shirts that said "Intifada"—she explained that the word is seen by many Arabs as a valid term for popular resistance to oppression, and she had a strong record of interfaith activism.[71] In this regard, it was reported that "Daniel Pipes, a pro-Israel conservative who created Campus Watch, a website dedicated to exposing alleged bias in university Middle East studies programs, wrote in the *New York Sun* that the [proposed new Islamic] school would cause problems because 'learning Arabic in [and] of itself promotes an Islamic outlook.'"[72] This seems to indicate that Arabic should not be taught.

Muslim charities have had a difficult time. Under the USA Patriot Act, the government is authorized to close down a charity while an investigation is going on, without revealing evidence used to justify seizure of assets or designation as a terrorist entity. After 9/11, from 2001 until 2006, six American Muslim charities were closed in this fashion, although the government never found evidence against any employees or board members, or documented a trail to a terrorist organization. In desperation, a group of Muslims started a new charity to try to get money to Palestinian children. Some of them believe that this harassment was a charade to make the American people believe that the government was disrupting terrorist financing.[73]

A similar case took place in 2005, when the Senate Finance Committee had investigated two dozen Muslim charities, think tanks, and other organizations for two years and found nothing that required additional follow-up.[74] Currently, many organizations still continue to be investigated and many cases are under appeal. The organizations that are exonerated have had projects interrupted, even inside the U.S. This is a contentious issue.

There is often controversy surrounding the building of mosques in the U.S. The most famous instance recently has been the proposed Islamic and community center in New York City in 2010, which was opposed through blogs, demonstrations, meetings, and very harsh rhetoric and denounced by many politicians. After the election of 2010, it died down and the site is now planned for use as an apartment tower and a small Islamic museum.[75] In Tennessee, a mosque was opposed with a sign "Keep Tennessee Terror Free" and a billboard, "Defeat Universal Jihad Now." This left the congregation, which has been there thirty years, bewildered by the vitriol.[76] The Reverend. Pat Robertson said of it, "The next thing you know, they're going to be taking over the city council. They're going to have an ordinance that calls for public prayer five times a day."[77] There has also been opposition to Islamic schools in many states and communities, because they are said to "teach terrorism."

Congressman Peter King (R-NY) held hearings in 2011 to investigate "Muslim radicals" in ordinary communities. He stated that there are "too many mosques" in this country and most of them are extremist.[78] He asserted that Muslim community leaders have failed to cooperate with law enforcement (*in fact, Muslims are the largest source of tips to authorities tracking terror suspects*). In 2011, a series of well-attended forums were held on Capitol Hill prior to Rep. King's hearings on home-grown Islamic terrorism. A leader stated that the forums were a way to remind the congressman that "the community has been cooperating with law enforcement for a number of years."[79] Donald Trump also accused Muslims of not reporting terrorist sympathizers and said that he believes "Islam hates us."[80]

Unlike in Europe, mosques in the U.S. are usually paid for by local Muslim congregations, because they want to be independent of overseas influences and money. Mosques do what churches do—they hold worship services, have classes for adults and children, arrange charity, provide counseling, and participate in interfaith programs.[81]

An Interfaith Center in Richmond distributed small signs written in Arabic on buses and at colleges, aimed at dispelling some of the public's fears about the Muslim community when they see Arabic written; the signs merely said, "Paper or plastic?" Many Americans were indeed alarmed. Some viewers assumed that it must be sinister and at first many thought the FBI should be called in to investigate.[82] There have been incidents of complaints on airplanes when a passenger boarded carrying an Arabic periodical or speaking Arabic on the phone; the passengers said they are "not comfortable."

On the plus side (there is a plus side), Senator. Richard Durbin (D-IL.) held hearings in 2011 on violations of the civil rights of Muslims. The *New York Times* lauded these hearings, in light of "the steady stream of more than 800 cases of violence and discrimination suffered by American Muslims at the hands of know-nothing abusers."[83] More U.S. employers are taking steps to create "Muslim-friendly" workplaces.[84]

In Washington, D.C., the Kennedy Center organized a "Festival of Arab Culture" in 2009 to "provide a counterpoint to the reality of war and violence that many Americans associate with the region." The festival included film, visual arts, literature, poetry, music, and dance.[85]

Muslims believe firmly that much prejudice is based on a lack of unbiased information about them. Some mosques have open-house receptions, and there are community outreach activities all over the country. The Islamic Society of North America (ISNA) has an informative website.* The Islamic Networks Group maintains a nationwide speakers' bureau.

Image in Europe

In parts of Europe, Muslims have been subject to verbal and physical attacks as well as discrimination in employment, schools, and housing. European governments have dealt with the Muslim minorities in various ways—considering them as temporary residents, trying to assimilate them, and giving them citizenship while encouraging them to maintain their cultural identity. Several countries are building obstructions at their borders to stop the flow of refugees, especially in Eastern Europe. Some observers refer to "manufactured controversies" that lead to reducing Muslims to second-class citizens.[86]

A high point of European worry about terrorism occurred between 2004 and 2006, when bombs exploded in Madrid and London, a controversial film director was killed in Amsterdam, and angry demonstrations took place against the Danish publication of satirical cartoons about the

---

* At the ISNA conference in 2002, someone asked, "What should we do now that the first anniversary of 9/11 is coming up?" The response was, "Don't hide—invite your neighbors to dinner."

Prophet Muhammad. As it turned out, the situation calmed down after that.

Mass radicalism among Muslims has not taken place. A Gallup poll in 2007 showed that when asked if violent attacks on civilians could be justified, 82 percent of French Muslims and 91 percent of German Muslims said no. Devoutness had no effect on the responses. (By comparison, a Gallup poll in the U.S. in 2007 showed that 24 percent of randomly selected Americans said such attacks are sometimes or often justified.)[87]

The demographic scenario that increasing numbers of immigrants and decreasing numbers of native Europeans is a dangerous trend persists in the public mind. A report in 2009 stated, "Though a steady drumbeat of apocalyptic forecasts continues, such fears are beginning to look misplaced."[88] Some commentators are extreme and alarmist. We have heard from Dr. Bernard Lewis (American) that France would soon be "part of the Maghreb" (Arab North Africa), and that Europe would be Islamic by the end of this century. Commentator Daniel Pipes opined in lurid fashion that if non-Muslims flee Europe(?), "grand cathedrals will appear as vestiges of a prior civilization—at least until a Saudi-style regime transforms them into mosques or a Taliban-like regime blows them up."[89]

In 2009, a Europol report showed that more than 99 percent of terrorist attacks in Europe over the last three years were carried out by non-Muslims.[90] In terms of fear and trauma, however, Muslim terrorism is the most notable. Between 2010 and 2015, less than 2 percent of terrorist attacks in Europe were carried out by Muslims (the majority were by separatist groups).[91] For example, in 2013, of 152 terror attacks, only two were religiously motivated.

Professor. Ruth Wodak in the U.K. studies right-wing populist movements and has written a book, *The Politics of Fear*.[92] She states that such movements share

1. Nativist nationalism
2. Exclusionary ideologies
3. Anti-intellectualism
4. Historical revisionism

The leaders exploit insecurities of their followers and legitimize anxieties.

Fear is mixed with a clash of values. Secular France banned the hijab hair cover in schools (it also stopped the wearing of large crosses and the yarmulke), and a full cover over the face and body cannot be worn in public or when driving or at the beach. This ban on full cover is also the law in Belgium and in parts of Italy and Switzerland. It is being considered elsewhere. It is also enforced in law courts in Denmark, and in law courts, hospitals, government buildings, and some schools in the Netherlands.[93] Full cover is banned in Belgium and some parts of Spain.[94] Headscarves are banned from schools in several states in Germany.[95] Fully covered women have been refused access to buses in the U.K.[96] The headcover ban was ruled non-discriminatory in Austria.[97] Some people say that the hair cover, or full face cover, symbolizes the oppression of women (if so, it is cultural, *not Islamic*).* It is seen by others as an unfortunate "mark of separation." Bans may be argued as essential because the countries emphasize secularism. These issues have not arisen in the U.S., probably because of low numbers and because Muslims do not live together as a community in one place where it can become the norm.

It is noteworthy that many Muslim women in Europe and the Middle East welcome the bans on the veil; they see it as a strike against the conservative Muslim right wing. Full cover is only an *interpretation* of the Qur'an, and they believe they should support resistance to any such practices in the name of culture and religion.[98]

Full face cover can be a legitimate matter of a nation's security, however, and women in airports must show their faces under controlled private circumstances in Britain and elsewhere. Controversies like this have led to extreme right-wing political movements in nations such as France, Britain, and the Netherlands, that now speak against Islam in general, not just its people. One British journalist stated, "Anti-Muslim bigotry [is] the last socially-acceptable racism."[99] But it has been getting better. In 2016, only 29 percent of the people in France, the U.K., and Germany had a negative view of Muslims (in other words, the majority were positive),

---

* Ayaan Hirsi Ali, a Somali-origin former Dutch politician, has written extensively about her unhappy upbringing, blaming many cultural practices on Islam, confusing the two. She blames Islam for women's status in Somalia, and she even blames it for female circumcision, which was a Nile Valley practice centuries before Islam, and spread to parts of Africa (but not all of the Arab or Muslim world). It is outlawed in many Muslim countries. She speaks of brutality to women "in the name of Islam." In any case, she believes that Islam is incompatible with Western values, hence a "clash of civilizations." She now lives in the U.S.

while only 35 percent were negative in the Netherlands and Sweden. Fifty percent in Spain and 69 percent in Italy had a negative view.[100] A majority of respondents felt that refugees constitute a threat of terrorism and a burden on the social system.

There is a growth in right-wing, anti-immigrant (mainly anti-Muslim) political parties across Europe. Recent regional and parliamentary elections show the following:[101]

2014	Sweden, Sweden Democrats	13%
2015	France, National Front	27%*
2015	Italy, Northern League	20%
2015	Germany, Alternative for Germany	25%
2016	Austria, Freedom Party	49%
2016	Norway, Progress Party	31%
2016	Denmark, Danish People's Party	21%

Austria rejected a far-right candidate for president.[102] In the Netherlands, the Party for Freedom looked very strong but slipped and came in second place after the Liberal Party in the election of March 2017. The party has a de-Islamization platform, including closing mosques.[103]

All far-right parties in Europe had growing support between 2013 and 2016.[104] While undoubtedly an element of racism is present, the reason most voters gave for supporting right-wing parties was fear of terrorism, and the immigrants' reluctance to integrate and to adopt local customs.

In Britain, France, Denmark, and the Netherlands, there are training programs for imams who head up mosques and Islamic centers. To be acceptable to the government, they must show that they have had some training in Europe and that they understand local values.[105] Imams have been deported in the past. The Islamic Council stated that extremist clerics "tarnish the image of Islam."[106]

In 2009, President Sarkozy of France launched a debate on national identity.[107] The debate was thought to be unnecessary by 55 percent of the French, and 42 percent said that it went in the wrong direction, focusing on problems caused by Muslims and immigrants, rather than on what it

---

* In the French presidential elections of May 2017, the National Party candidate had 34 percent of the votes.

means to be French. Some accused the president of "Islamodiversion" to move attention away from economic problems, but it grew in popularity.

A Gallup poll in 2009 asked Muslims to rate their success in the West to date, with these results:[108]

	Thriving	Struggling	Suffering
German Muslims	47%	48%	5%
French Muslims	23%	69%	8%
British Muslims	7%	72%	21%

By contrast, Muslims in the U.S. report 56 percent thriving and 4 percent suffering.[109]

Unemployment rates among Muslims in Europe are in the 20 to 30 percent range, and can be 50 to 60 percent among youth.[110]

The Muslims in Europe will have to make more effort to assimilate in order to be successful as citizens. They must make concessions regarding clothing, equality of the sexes, freedom of speech and the press, and violence. Forming and maintaining "parallel societies" will not bring about the desired result.

❋ THE FUTURE OF ISLAM IN THE WEST

With moderate Muslims speaking out more and more, in the West and in the Middle East, it will lead to an improved, vibrant Muslim community everywhere. If people take to heart the advice to be loyal to both their faith and, if in the West, the country in which they live, this will gradually heal the bruised image that Islam has today. Scholar Tariq Ramadan* has stated, "Loyalty to one's faith and conscience requires firm and honest loyalty to one's country. Sharia [law] requires honest citizenship."[111] In his book *Western Muslims and the Future of Islam*, Ramadan stated:

> We are currently living through a veritable silent revolution in Muslim communities in the West: more and more young people and intellectuals are actively looking for a way to live in harmony with

---

* Tariq Ramadan is a prominent intellectual who was denied entry into the United States in July 2004 and September 2006. When Barack Obama became president, he was allowed in, as there was nothing against him in any records anywhere.

their faith while participating in the societies that are their societies, whether they like it or not. French, English, German, Canadian, and American Muslims, women as well as men, are constructing a "Muslim personality" that will soon surprise many of their fellow citizens. Far from media attention, going through the risks of a process of maturation that is necessarily slow, they are drawing the shape of European and American Islam: faithful to the principles of Islam, dressed in European and American cultures, and definitively rooted in Western societies. This grass-roots movement will soon exert considerable influence over worldwide Islam.[112]

Some neoconservative Americans have called for modernizing Islam to result in "an American Islam committed to American values." *It is already here.* And it came from inside, not from outside or from U.S. government campaigns. European Islam and American Islam can be models for each other. Muslims are working hard to promote gender equality, for example, and moderates state that inequality is not a firm tenet of Islam any longer but a mark of misguided tradition. In the U.S., a woman has led group prayers, a practice approved by an influential scholar of Islamic law.[113]

In Europe, a "liberal wave" has been building. Across Europe, new parties—socially liberal, pro-European Union, and anti-populist—are forming or re-forming to counter the far-right wave.[114] They do not label themselves as left or right, but rather as rational and effective, opposed to xenophobia and populism. They represent groups, not individuals. These have appeared in Spain, Hungary, and Poland so far, and admirers hope to see this spread to their own countries. It is noteworthy that the mayor of London is Muslim, Sadiq Khan, elected in 2016; so far he has proven to be popular.

As the number of Arabs and Muslims in the West continues to grow, Muslims will go from less than 1 percent of the population to about 2 percent in the U.S. by 2050.[115] Muslims are expected to make up about 8 percent of Europe's population by 2030, up from 6 percent in 2010.[116] But considering long-term trends and nascent goodwill, there is no need to fear a "Eurabia" there.[117]

In the United States, there is a heightened and growing interest in this region, especially since 9/11. Enrollments in Arabic language, Islamic studies, and Middle East studies have tripled and quadrupled. Students have been spending summers and their junior year in Egypt, Morocco, Tunisia, Jordan, the United Arab Emirates, and Oman (other countries are now restricted because of security concerns). Between 2001 and 2013, the number of American students studying in Arabic-speaking countries increased over sevenfold, from 890 to 6,400.[118] Because Arabic has been listed by the State Department as a critical language, there are many scholarships and programs available from government and nongovernment sources. There are more than 35,000 college and university students studying Arabic; it is the eighth most commonly studied language in the U.S.[119] This is an excellent investment in their own and their society's future.

CHAPTER 14

THE ARAB
COUNTRIES:
SIMILARITIES AND
DIFFERENCES

Generalizing about Arabs is a little like generalizing about Europeans—they have many traits in common, but regional differences are
striking. Arabs are more alike than Europeans, however, because they
share the same language and, most importantly, they believe that they
are a cultural unit, "one Arab nation comprised of numerous Arab states."
Arab nationalism has a broad appeal, despite shifting political alliances.

The national and social characteristics described here, as well as
statistical information, reveal some notable differences among various
Arab national groups. The most important single difference that affects
foreigners is the distinction between the conservatism of Saudi Arabia
(and to some extent, the rest of the Arabian Peninsula) and the more
liberal, tolerant ways of life elsewhere.

Because of wars and unrest, borders in the Levantine region (Lebanon,
Syria, and Iraq) are not stable and will eventually be readjusted to reflect
political and social realities. These countries are not really nation-states.[1]

All of the countries are challenged by the large number of young
people in their population (half or more are under age 30 in most cases),
and their increasing assertiveness. There is a notable generational shift
underway. Among the young in particular, new technology is driving

rapid changes in society and political thought. The Arab Spring series of demonstrations for democracy and freedom in 2011 may be the single most significant event in the region since the majority of Arab states became independent after World War II. It was a breath of fresh air—not just the ideas but also the positive images of Arabs in the news and on television.

It is significant that along with governmental change there appears to be a transition to attitudes that are less pro-American, and American power in the region is perceived as weakening.[2] There are also strong pro-Palestinian sympathies coming to the fore. Arabs from Morocco to the Gulf always mention the Palestine issue as one of their top concerns—it underlies all other issues with the West. Palestine is a pivotal issue in modern Arab nationalism, and the concern is as great as it ever was.

The Arab Labor Organization stated that unemployment in the Middle East was the worst worldwide. The general rate of unemployment exceeds 15 percent, which equates to over 17 million persons unemployed in the Arab region.[3] There is an urgent need for reform of education policies and training programs to deal with this.

Water resources are a looming problem. The entire Arab world is dry and the supply of water is scant, much of it depending on underground aquifers. As the population increases from its current 425 million to a projected 600 million by 2050, the amount of fresh water available per person will be cut in half, and declining resources will likely lead to political disputes.[4] Several solutions are being tried, including drip irrigation, desalinization, recycling, and, in some cases, renting fertile agricultural land in other countries.

There are also dramatic differences among the Arab countries: some are very rich, others are desperately poor. We hear that the Arabs are awash in oil, but in reality, most Arab countries have far less income than developed economies. Relative prosperity can be seen from averaged purchasing power per capita income in 2015.

National Income Per Capita 2015[5]

($US)

Yemen	2,500
Sudan	2,600
Morocco	5,500
Egypt	5,889
Jordan	6,100
Iraq	7,100
Algeria	7,500
Tunisia	9,900
Libya	11,300
Lebanon	15,800
Oman	29,800
Bahrain	29,800
United Arab Emirates	29,900
Saudi Arabia	31,300
Kuwait	42,100
Qatar	102,100

By way of comparison, the GDP per capita in the U.S. in 2015 was about $52,800.

All Arab countries have had within them a degree of unrest among their people, because of authoritarian governments, corruption, unemployment, high prices, and strained resources.

The Fragile States Index rated these four countries in 2015:[6]

Very High Alert

Yemen	111.5
Syria	110.8

High Alert

Iraq	104.7

Alert

Libya	96.4

Events move so quickly in the Middle East that we can only describe the situation at a certain date. But at least you will know what to look for, for more information.

The Arab countries discussed below are listed from west to east, north to south.

THE ARAB STATES IN AFRICA

The Maghrib

The Maghrib (Maghreb) or Al-Maghrib Al-Arabi are terms used for the entire region of North Africa (the adjective form is *Maghribi*); *Maghrib* comes from Arabic and means "the Arab West." Four countries are of concern here: Morocco, (also called Al-Maghrib) Algeria, Tunisia, and Libya.

This region has been inhabited by Berbers (a Caucasian people) for millennia, since at least 3000 B.C., and today Berber (called Tamazight, with several dialects) is the mother tongue of 14 million to 25 million people in the Maghrib, most of whom are bilingual in Arabic. Most speakers are in Morocco and Algeria, with several thousand in Libya and Tunisia, as well as Mali and Niger.[1] (Numbers are approximate, since language is usually not recorded in censuses.)

Arabians and some Arabs arrived in the seventh century, and there were several migrations after that, so that by the twelfth century, about 10 percent of the population were Arab. Many Arabic speakers came from Spain in the late fifteenth and early sixteenth centuries. Berber ethnicity is present in about 80 percent of the people in Morocco and Algeria, and about 60 percent in Tunisia and Libya. Fewer than half of them speak Berber.[2] Most Berbers live in rural villages and work the land; a few are nomadic.

Berber nationalism is growing and will be a significant social and political factor in the future, especially in Morocco and Algeria, where a Berber alphabet has been devised and introduced in schools and the language is heard on the radio. Newspapers and magazines have appeared. Berbers have used the Internet to establish themselves internationally as a distinct cultural group. Local music is influenced by Berber tradition.

Berber was recognized as one of Morocco's official languages in 2011,[3] and as a "national language" in Algeria in 2001. But Berbers in the Moroccan Rif region still feel marginalized and have frequently protested.

Regional Maghribi dialects of Arabic are distinctive and almost unintelligible to Arabs in the east; they constitute a separate dialect group called Western Arabic. The Maghrib has its own special foods, religious practices, style of art and architecture, music, and traditional clothing, with much Berber influence.

Morocco

Morocco, a monarchy, has been strongly influenced by its proximity to Europe and its colonization by France until independence in 1956. Educated Moroccans are bilingual in Arabic and French, and although a campaign of Moroccanization was been underway, French is still needed for professional and social advancement. Some Spanish is spoken in northern Morocco, and a growing number of Moroccans, particularly younger people with commercial interests, now speak English. Morocco sees itself as moderate and pro-Western, and it has a free-trade agreement with the U.S.

The royal family traces its descent from the Prophet Muhammad, which bolsters its legitimacy (the king's ancestry is inscribed on a pillar in a mosque in Casablanca for all to see). King Hassan II ruled for 38 years before his death in 1999; his son King Muhammad VI now rules, and he is making efforts toward political and social liberalization. So far, he has not faced serious political demonstrations.

This calm is jeopardized, however, because although Morocco has maintained a tradition of political moderation, large numbers of the younger generation, especially, are turning toward Islamic radicalism and are playing a bigger role in Islamist militant groups, including in Iraq.[1] There have been incidents of terrorism, mainly directed at touristic sites: bombings occurred in Casablanca in 2003 and 2007, and a Moroccan group was responsible for a bombing in Spain in 2004. The government remains vigilant, and the last incident was a bombing in Marrakesh in 2011.

In addition to cracking down, the government, among other things, instituted mainstream religious training in 2006 to counteract extremist, puritanical Islam and re-emphasize mainstream Sunni Islam. About 400 of the students in religious training are women (and female religious "guides" perform almost all the functions of a male imam, except for delivering the Friday sermon).[2] The Ministry of Islamic Affairs is making every effort to promote moderation.

Morocco has made a slow but real transformation from a traditional monarchy to constitutional monarchy, with an elected parliament. It has genuine political parties and leaders, as well as a fairly free press (the most provocative paper, *Le Journal Hebdomadaire*, was fined and finally forced to close in 2010).[3] The king has instituted a commission to examine past human-rights abuses (which occurred during his father's reign) and forged stronger economic ties with the West.[4] Because there is security and stability, it allows for reforms.

A moderate Islamist party, the Justice and Development Party (PJD) won parliamentary elections in October 2016. As of this writing, they plan to form a coalition government with two other parties.[5] They are the only one of the Islamist parties to survive in office after the Arab Spring.

Educated women in Morocco have been entering the professions for a generation, especially in the urban areas. Half of the students in universities are women; one-third of the members of the judicial body are women.[6] A growing number of women cover their hair, yet consider themselves to be modern, educated, and emancipated; they state that they are simply asserting their identity as Muslims. One problem for women is the disparity in pay as compared to men; it is about 17 percent less, according to UNICEF.[7]

Family law is intended to be compatible with both Sharia law and international conventions on human rights. The government first revised the family law code in 2004, and women may initiate divorce, obtain custody of children, and claim an equal share of goods acquired during marriage. The age for marriage was raised to 18, and polygamy severely restricted.[8] But gender equality is moving slowly; judges still allow under-age marriage and often rule against women's interests.

Women are becoming more active in official positions as their education level increases. A quota was imposed in 2011 reserving one-third of the seats in the Lower House of Parliament for women. There is one female minister in the cabinet. The mayor of Marrakesh is a woman. And there is an active feminist movement advocating for further gains.

There are three distinct social classes: the royal family and a small educated elite, a growing middle class comprised of merchants and professionals, and a lower class that includes more than half of the people. The population was estimated at 35 million in 2017, with a growth rate that is among the highest in the world. About 28 percent of the population was under age 15.[9]

The ethnography of Morocco is mixed; most people are mixed Arab and Berber (the king's mother is Berber), and a large number are of sub-Saharan African descent, especially in the southern part of the country. Berber speakers number about 8 million. Recently, the Qur'an was translated into the Berber Tamazight language, and there is a Berber research institute.[10]

There is a trend toward urbanization, which began early in the twentieth century. Cities have grown quickly, with severe housing shortages and expanding slums. Tribalism is important in rural parts of the country, and farming remains the occupation of half of the people.

About 40,000 Moroccans migrate abroad each year; the unemployment rate was 10 percent in 2017.[11] Of more immediate concern is unemployment and limited prospects among young people age 15–24 (a factor in the appeal of terrorist groups), which was 22.5 percent.[12] Currently about 2.8 million men work outside the country, mainly in France and Spain.

Education has increased greatly since Morocco's independence. The literacy rate varies by age, with a high of 96 percent for people under age 15. The overall literacy rate decreased to 32 percent (from 42 percent ten years earlier).[13] Literacy is increasing slowly because many rural children are not in school, despite attendance being free and compulsory. The government hopes to eradicate illiteracy by 2024.[14] Both French and Arabic are taught in schools, along with a few hours of Tamazight.

Although about 99 percent of the Moroccans are Muslims, other religions have always been practiced freely. Half of the Jews in the Arab world reside in Morocco, approximately 2,500 (from a high of 250,000 to 350,000 in the 1950s). King Hassan protected Jews in the days of Vichy France, and the current king has said that they are welcome to return (there are about 1 million Moroccan Jews in Israel).[15] Morocco's 25,000 Christians are of European origin; converts from Islam face severe disapproval. The practice of Islam is often mixed with local folk practices, such as the veneration of saints' tombs and their artifacts. Religious brotherhoods, mainly Sufi, are also common.

The Moroccan economy is largely dependent on agriculture, tourism, and phosphate mining (Morocco is the world's largest exporter of phosphates). Fishing is important, as well as the textile industry, which has grown enormously in the past thirty years. Economic growth is the highest in North Africa and the Middle East at 4.8 percent in 2017, up from 1.8 percent in 2016.[16]

Morocco has long been at conflict because it annexed the Western Sahara in 1975, a sparsely populated region in the south and a former Spanish colony, the Spanish Sahara. This issue is unresolved and is opposed by the local Polisario Front. After a 16-year guerrilla war, peace was brokered by the U.N. in 1991, but its status is still uncertain because no referendum on independence has been held. Its independence is recognized by Algeria and Mauritania. The border with Algeria has been closed since 1994.

Moroccans are friendly and hospitable and usually very interested in becoming acquainted with foreigners. The elite are at ease with Westerners because of their exposure to French and European cultures. There are several study abroad programs for young Americans learning Arabic in Morocco.

Algeria

Algeria is a constitutional republic with a democratically elected government, although the military is very influential. Since the early 1990s, there has been a shift from a state capitalist to a free-market economy. President Abdelaziz Bouteflika, first elected in 1999, was re-elected for his fourth term in April 2014, although he is in failing health. There are more than forty political parties (which must be approved by the Ministry of Interior). The president's role is limited, and there is a constant process of bargaining and factionalism. In June 2014, one of the largest gatherings of the Algerian opposition took place; the goal was to move Algeria from a military-based regime to a real democracy.[1]

Algeria is the world's eighth largest producer of liquefied natural gas, and the largest gas producer in Africa. Gas and oil provide 98 percent of the national income. Hydrocarbons have long been the backbone of the economy, accounting for roughly 60 percent of budget revenues, 25 percent of GDP, and over 95 percent of export earnings. Algeria has the tenth-largest reserves of natural gas in the world and is the sixth-largest gas exporter. It ranks 16th in oil reserves.[2] It also has income from mining and agriculture.

Algeria experienced a devastating civil war, starting in 1991, between the government and Islamist activists, the largest group being the Islamic Salvation Front (FIS). The war began after the government canceled elections in 1992, when FIS was projected to win. Guerrilla warfare began, and throughout the 1990s Algeria experienced a rising cycle of violent attacks, many of them random, many in villages, to the point that 300 to 400 people were killed each week. Ultimately the figure reached about 150,000.[3] This was met with severe government retaliation, and FIS was banned. The population is still polarized between secular and Islamic groups, radicals and moderates.

Algeria is immense, the largest country in Africa and the Arab world, but 85 percent of it is in the Sahara Desert region, and only 3 percent is suitable for agriculture, along the temperate northern coast. The population is 39 million, with a population growth of 1.61 percent. Ninety-one percent of the people live along the coast. Twenty-four percent of the population is under age 15, 70 percent under age 30, and there is a desperate housing shortage. Schools operate in shifts (attendance doubled between 1999 and 2015),[4] and healthcare facilities are overburdened. Education is free and compulsory to age 16, and the literacy rate is 80 percent and climbing.

Because the unemployment rate is high, about 2 million Algerians work abroad, mostly in France and Spain. Many are menial workers, but there is also a brain drain as the educated people leave.

Partly because of rapid population growth, the people remain poor; 35 percent live below the poverty line.[5] The country faces social problems such as rapid urban migration and unemployment. The unemployment rate increased to 10.50 percent in the third quarter of 2016, up from 9.90 percent in the second quarter of 2016. It averaged 14.42 percent from 1999 until 2016, reaching an all-time high of 29.50 percent in the third quarter of 2000.[6] The unemployment rate for persons age 16–25 is high—30 percent.[7]

Algeria's state of emergency, declared in 1992 after the Islamist insurgency, was lifted in February 2011. There were demonstrations and protests in early 2011 (during the Arab Spring), and the government cut taxes and lowered food prices. In April 2011, the president also promised to amend the constitution to reinforce representative democracy. Algeria began a five-year, $286 billion development program to update the infrastructure; provide jobs; and encourage manufacturing, agriculture, and other ways to reduce dependence on oil and gas.[8] This had moderate success, but then it was affected by declining oil prices. Another five-year plan is in place, 2015–2019, intended to further lessen dependence on oil and gas, lessen government control of the economy, increase the separation of powers, and promote social programs.[9] The economy has grown at a rate of 4 percent annually since 2000.[10] There is a call to "globalize," i.e., encourage foreign investment and entrepreneurship, and to lessen protectionism in trade.[11]

Arabization has been strongly emphasized, partly as a reaction to the Algerians' experience with French colonization and their long, traumatic war from 1954 to 1962. Independence was achieved in 1962, but at a terrible cost—1.5 million Algerians and 18,000 French dead.[12] Even though Arabic is the official language of the country, French is still widely used, particularly for professional purposes. Both languages are taught in the schools, but only younger Algerians are truly comfortable with Standard (written) Arabic.

Arab nationalism has been promoted through government political campaigns, the news media, and the school curriculum, although it has eased now because of fears of increasing religiosity and Islamism (although the Islamist political parties are weakening).[13] Many in the younger generation are more religious than their parents. The people are 99 percent Muslim.

A branch of Al-Qaeda operates in Algeria. "Al-Qaeda in the Islamic Maghrib" (AQIM) is competing with the Islamic State (IS) to be the primary jihadist movement.[14] The group has a history of kidnapping and violence inside and outside of the Maghrib, and it recently sent a rocket toward a gas plant in Algeria, which did no damage. It tends to target military and security forces.

Almost all Algerians are of Berber ethnic origin, but about 70 percent identify themselves as Arabs and only 30 percent as Berbers. Arabic is the native language of 80 percent of the people. Algeria's social classes consist of a small professional and technocratic elite, a growing middle class, and a large number of poor people. A growing number of educated Algerians are entering professional and technical fields. Women comprise 69 percent of university graduates.

Women make up 70 percent of Algeria's lawyers and 60 percent of its judges.[15] They also dominate medicine. They are starting to drive buses and taxis. Women make up an ever-increasing percentage of the workforce, now about 35 percent, which is more than twice what it was a generation ago. More women are wearing the hijab headscarf. Many women are delaying marriage, partly because of high unemployment for both men and women. In a poll reported by Afro Barometer, 78 percent of Algerians agreed that women should have equal rights and receive the same treatment as men.[16]

Outside the cities, family and social traditions are conservative. The government instituted a Family Code in 1984, which restricted women's rights, but the president has stated that it must be amended. Now a husband marrying another wife can be grounds for the woman to divorce. If a man divorces a woman and is judged to have abused the privilege, she may be awarded damages and support if she does not have family support.

In 2013, more than 70 percent of the population felt the country to be "going in the right direction," and 87 percent felt proud to be Algerian. 65 percent of Algerians said that they do not fear political violence or intimidation.[17] In May 2017, the ruling party, the FLN, won the majority of seats in parliamentary elections. The Islamist parties are either banned or are not acting together.

Algerians are very accommodating toward foreigners, although a bit reserved. Algeria is a lovely country, with a beautiful coastline in the north and the Sahara Desert in the south.

Tunisia

Tunisia is a small but diverse country, with a population of only 11 million. It gained its independence from France in 1956. From that time until early 2011, it was governed by one secular political party. President Habib Bourguiba, who led the country to independence, was quietly removed in 1987. His successor was Zine Al-Abedin Ben Ali, who later fled the country after prolonged political protest demonstrations, the first that occurred during the Arab Spring. Tunisians had a bloodless victory, a "Jasmine Revolution," and they are proud that theirs was the inspiration for many uprisings in the Arab world in 2011.

There was an interim government after the president fled in January, and elections for the Constituent Assembly were held in October 2011, with the freedom to vote much improved.[1] A new president was elected in December. The prime minister was from the winning political party, Annahda (formerly banned), which described itself as "moderate Islamist," and it governed in a coalition with two left-leaning parties.[2] The hardline Islamists protested, and a curfew was imposed in eight areas. Critics on the other side feared that it was a threat to secularism, and there were also protests about the possible curtailment of women's rights.

The current government is stable, but there was a long adjustment period and there has been an ongoing economic crisis, especially with the decrease of tourism. Dissatisfaction led to the assassination of an opposition anti-Islamist leader in February 2013 and another leftist leader in July. In addition, two widely publicized terrorist incidents occurred—an attack on the Bardo Museum in March 2015, and an attack on tourists in Sousse in June 2015. A state of emergency was declared and security tightened, and eighty mosques were closed, accused of spreading extremism.[3]

A new constitution was adopted in January 2014. In October 2014, another new government was elected in the first free legislative elections in Tunisia. The government is comprised of secularists, trade unionists, and liberals.[4] Beji Caid Essebsi became the fourth and current president. The group that mediated between the parties in 2013 and 2014 (the National Dialogue Quartet) won the Nobel Peace Prize.

Tunisia is now an electoral democracy,[5] the only Arab country that has achieved this status. This became possible because there is a separation of church and state (Islamist fundamentalists played no role), the army promoted peaceful change and did not seek power, and there is a strong civil service and middle class.

The Tunisian government has encouraged private enterprise, and about 60 percent of the people are middle or upper class, although fewer in the south. Tunisia is the most advanced country in the Arab world in terms of women's rights, family planning, and education, and it is considered a model of success in economic reform and family law. It has long been praised for its progressive social policies. Freedom of worship is guaranteed in the constitution, at the same time giving religion a greater role in public life than before. There have been clashes with hardline Islamists, especially in the south. 99 percent of the Tunisians are Muslim.

A seventh multi-partisan government elected in 2016 plans to impose an austerity program in 2017, with revised taxes and tighter fiscal controls. In 2016 there were strikes by teachers, doctors, and lawyers, among others. Tunisia has lost most of its tourism income (it once brought in half of the annual income and is now 11 percent), and the country depends on loan guarantees and economic partnerships with the European Union. France will help with a five-year package to help poor regions and focus on employment of young people. The U.S. will aid in improving security along the Libyan border.[6]

About a third of the people work in agriculture; olive oil and dates are significant exports. This sector is being reinvigorated by adopting some desert farming practices, such as drip irrigation. The government encourages diversification and especially light industry, which has become an important source of employment and now generates 30 percent of the national income.[7]

Although the government established agricultural cooperatives and production has been rising, people are still leaving the rural areas and moving to the cities, where they join the urban poor, living in crowded conditions. Most of the government's investment projects are in the coastal areas, and there is an effort to correct regional imbalances because unemployment and poverty are higher in the south.[8]

Because the economy is still recovering, about 1.2 million Tunisians work outside the country, more than half of them in France and others mainly in Italy and Germany. About 40,000 still work in Libya. Since 2000, migration has grown at a rate of 4 percent annually, compared with a population growth of 1 percent.[9]

The Tunisian government has signed bilateral labor agreements with several countries to manage migration and ensure workers' rights. These include France, Italy, Germany, Canada, and Qatar, among others.[10] Unemployment is 18 percent (women, 27 percent, and youth, more than 40 percent).[11]

The government allocates 6.25 percent of its operating budget to primary and secondary education, and 95 percent of eligible children are in primary schools. Literacy is high—97 percent for youth and 81 percent for adults.[12] Half of the people are under age 25.

Tunisia has been at the forefront of the Arab nations in its effort to liberalize its society. Tunisian women are among the most liberated in the Arab world; they are well educated and active in the workplace in such fields as education, social services, healthcare, office administration, and the judicial system. Laws benefiting women were enacted in the 1950s. Women have the same divorce rights as men. Polygamy is outlawed, and the minimum age for a woman's marriage is 17. Laws were made in the 1990s that further strengthened women's rights, pertaining to custody and financial support. In 2017 a law was passed outlawing violence against-women and harassment in a public place.

While most women wear Western clothing, some older or tradi-tional women wear loose outer cloaks, which they pull over to partially cover their faces when in public. Women's clothing is modest by Western standards. The hejab, once banned, is now legal, and there are no official regulations pertaining to women's dress.

The Tunisians are descended from Berber and Arabian stock, but all speak Arabic, the official language. Educated people are bilingual in Arabic and French, and many semi-educated people speak some French. French is taught in schools alongside Arabic; there has been a campaign for the Arabization of education. While more than 60 percent of the Tunisians are Berber, the language is spoken only in certain rural areas in the south.[13]

There is freedom of religion in Tunisia. Only about 1,800 native Jews remain, most of them on the southern island of Jerba. The government pays the salary of the Grand Rabbi, in addition to partially subsidizing restoration and maintenance costs of synagogues.[14] Jerba has the oldest synagogue in Africa.

Islam in Tunisia is mixed with a number of folk practices, such as the veneration of saints' tombs and periodic saints' festivals. The central city of Kairouan is a pilgrimage site because of its antiquity and importance to Islam.

Because Tunisians have always had much contact with foreigners, their society is cosmopolitan, at least in the cities, and many Tunisians are well-traveled. They are friendly and hospitable to foreign visitors.

Libya

Libya is in such a state of violence and turmoil, with competing groups trying to seize power, that it has been classified as a "failed state."* The

---

* The other failed states in the Middle East are Yemen and South Sudan.

country is entangled in a violent, nationwide power struggle. There is now a UN-installed "unity" government, set up at a heavily-guarded naval base in Tripoli in March 2016.[1] The situation is still unstable and volatile.

At the end of Muammar Qaddhafi's* rule, when he was losing control, an international coalition under NATO determined that it had to intervene in Libya to protect threatened civilians and prevent a massacre.[2] The air campaign ended with Qaddhafi's removal and death in October 2011, and the formation of a transitional government followed. Some critics say that NATO should have stayed on to assure stability; this is controversial. In any case, a humanitarian disaster was avoided, which was the original goal.

The National Transitional Council, a rebel leadership council, took over, but it did not control the many armed militias that had come into being in opposition to Qaddhafi. The NTC was secular and liberal. A General National Congress was elected in August 2012 in Tripoli, and power was handed over.[3]

Elections in June 2014 created a new parliament, located in the city of Tobruk and sponsored by the anti-Islamist group Operation Dignity, which won international recognition. There was still friction with the Tripoli group, and finally the U.N. was able to broker a "unity" government in late 2015. The prime minister is Fayez al-Sarraj, leading the Government of National Accord.[4] It, too, faces considerable opposition.

Libyan civilians have been caught in these power struggles, and international aid organizations estimate that 2.5 million people need humanitarian assistance and protection, including half a million children.[5] The number of internally displaced people has fallen from 417,000 in mid-2016 to 313,000 in early 2017.[6]

There have been numerous battles between militias, the most notable of which was in 2014 between Islamist militias and the parliament-backed security battalion, which destroyed Tripoli's main airport. Several groups have seized oil terminals, both the Tripoli and Tobruk militias, and even the Berbers, each demanding more recognition.[7] In March 2017, militias took a string of key oil ports, casting peacemaking efforts into doubt.[8]

Libya now exports less than one fifth of its earlier oil production, and the government's money is almost gone. Oil terminals were again seized

* The Library of Congress has listed twenty(!) ways to spell Qaddhafi's name. This is because most of the consonants do not have equivalents in English.

in 2017 by Islamic militants after the army retreated to avoid further damage, and the situation remains uncertain.[9] Libyan oil has always been important to Europe. Russia has recently signed a major contract to help develop Libyan oilfields, in order to enhance its role in future negotiations and decisions in Libya, assuming that President Trump would not be as likely to object as previous presidents.[10]

In December 2016, Libyan forces of the new government defeated the Islamic State and drove them from their base in Sirte with the help of American airstrikes. This was a coastal city they had occupied since early 2015, where they had access to 150 miles of Mediterranean coastline.[11] There is concern about the IS reorganizing; it is active in other parts of the country and has attracted as many as 3,000 militants.[12]

There is also an arm of Al-Qaeda that participated in the September 2012 attacks on the U.S. diplomatic mission in Benghazi.[13] It is said to be working with the Islamic State in operating training camps, some of which were attacked by U.S. warplanes in early 2017.[14]

A problematic issue is the Political Isolation Law of 2014, which disqualifies Qaddhafi-era officials from public office (similar to the law in Iraq in 2003 disqualifying former government officials). There were 1.2 million state employees in 2010.[15]

Qaddhafi's rule was authoritarian, but he did use oil money to improve the country, and Libya became a welfare state. The people (particularly the middle and lower classes) experienced a dramatic rise in their standard of living over four decades, although with shortages of some goods. There were steady improvements in health and nutrition programs, transportation, communications, and education. Nine years of education is compulsory, and 90 percent of the children were in school; literacy reached 83 percent among younger Libyans. Today, the schools are hard-hit by security problems, with many school buildings destroyed, abandoned, or used as shelters. About 180,000 are out of school because of security and transportation problems.[16]

The population of Libya is 6.4 million. Libyans are a homogeneous ethnic group; 97 percent are of mixed Berber and Arab descent, and all speak Arabic. Tribalism is an important source of identity (it accounted for much of Qaddhafi's support). Although under Qaddhafi there were theoretically no social classes because of the government's stated policy of strict egalitarianism and rule "by the people," in reality rule has been authoritarian and only a few people were part of the elite upper class.

Ethnic Berbers are about 10 percent of the population, or 600,000, and they were subjected to Qaddafi's program of Arabization. Their language and culture are not officially recognized. One group has drafted a constitution for an autonomous region in eastern Libya, the Nafusa region.[17] They see this issue as a matter of human rights.

Libya's economic viability is almost entirely dependent on oil; its soil is poor, its natural resources and water sparse. Less than 10 percent of the land is suitable for agriculture (90 percent is desert). Once, 75 percent of the country's food was imported, but this has fallen off sharply and the government subsidizes bread.[18] Large numbers of foreigners have lived and worked in Libya (approximately 1.5 million in 2010),[19] though most of them have left. Libya badly needs its own trained and skilled workers.[20]

Before Qaddafi's takeover, most people lived as pastoralists, farmers, or tribal seminomads, who were largely uneducated and lived simply. In 1951, Libya was considered one of the poorest countries in the world. When oil was discovered in 1959, its effect on the economy was immediate. By 1969, the country's revenues were twenty times greater than they had been in 1962, and now it is 86 percent urban.[21] After independence in 1951, Libya was ruled by King Idris, its only king, whose family had aided the British in Cyrenaica during World War II. He ruled from 1951 to 1969, after which he was exiled.[22]

Because of Libyan terrorism and political policies, the country was under U.S. sanctions from 1986 to 2003, and U.N. sanctions from 1992 to 2003. Sanctions by the European Union were lifted in 2004. Libya is especially notorious for shooting down a plane over Lockerbie, Scotland, in 1988.

Libya has a history of sending university students abroad, especially to the United States, the U.K., Australia, Canada, Egypt, South Africa, and Europe. In 2013, about 40,000 students were sent abroad to study at levels ranging from post-graduate to vocational training to English-language courses.[23] The number declined right after the change of government, but then improved. Problems include the country's security and the lack of money available.[24] In 2015, there were about 20,000 Libyan students studying abroad at the expense of the government. These numbers have lessened. In 2017, the U.N.-backed government stated that all Libyan students abroad must return home at the end of their studies or be prosecuted.[25]

Women are doing quite well in Libya, although not as well as during the Qaddhafi era. Women constitute 30 percent of the workforce, and they are working in all social, political, and economic activities, including as ministers, judges, doctors, and lawyers. Most have more modest jobs, as teachers, secretaries, and nurses. A few have succeeded as business entrepreneurs.[26] The majority of university graduates are women, and 77 percent of university-age women are pursuing higher education, compared with 63 percent of the men.[27] But they are not making headway in politics. The society is conservative, and some women decline working outside the home. They also fear the security situation and Islamist militias. Outside the cities, women face more obstacles (family and social disapproval, hesitance to hire women).

Libyan women were active in the uprising in opposition to Qaddhafi's government in 2011, but they feel now that they are being sidelined, particularly in high-level government jobs and decision-making positions. The Libyan Women's Forum was formed in 2011 to empower women to participate more effectively in the development of the country.[28] Their activities include education campaigns on law, the constitution, women in government, and women's rights.

The legal age for marriage for both men and women is 20 years, and the former practice of early marriage has declined sharply. Polygamy is legal but uncommon, although more practiced than under Qaddhafi.[29] Most domestic law is governed by Sharia law, with some modifications.

Libya has been overrun with African refugees on their way to Europe, mainly Italy. In 2016 alone, more than 181,000 refugees and migrants arrived, and 25,000 unaccompanied children.[30] The government does not control their living conditions, and they are exploited and abused, held in forced-labor camps and makeshift prisons. Militias make profits from trafficking, sometimes holding people for ransom. Many have died making the sea crossing in inadequate boats. Some 34 detention centers are holding between 4,000 and 7,000 detainees.

Libyans are 99 percent Muslim. Qaddhafi's government promoted Islam mixed with a strong revolutionary message to guide social change and control dissent, and it opposed Islamism. Qaddhafi's type of social controls have lessened. Patriotism and Arab nationalism are strong, and people are hopeful about the future, counting on a unity government.

❈ THE NILE VALLEY

The Arab countries in the Nile Valley include Egypt and Sudan.

Egypt

Egypt is important because it has by far the largest population of any Arab nation, approximately 94.5 million.* As in all Arab countries, the proportion of young people is high—33 percent under age 15 in 2016 (down from 40 percent in 1990).[1] The population doubled between 1947 and the early 1980s (it went from 44 million when Mubarak took power in 1981 to 80 million), but as a result of vigorous government campaigning, the population growth rate decreased to 2.5 percent in 2016. Because less than 5 percent of Egypt's land is habitable, its population density is among the highest in the world. In Egypt, 95 percent of the people live on 5 percent of the land.[2]

Egypt dominated the news while its secular Arab Spring revolution was occurring in early 2011, and with Mubarak's departure, a new government was formed. It is notable that the younger generation showed a new assertiveness and lack of fear, spurred on by easy communications and organization through social media sites. It was a watershed event after decades of enduring dictators. (As of now, Egypt is again ruled by a dictatorial system, but the people will not be as willing to tolerate it passively as in the past.)

Many people saw the military as their protector and savior, shielding them from reprisals by the regime, police, and security apparatus and preventing internal fighting and destruction.[3] This did not last, however, as the military began using excess force and mass arrests. In the new constitution of 2014, a prominent role was reserved for the military, which is unlikely ever to cede power.

After Mubarak's fall, activists continued to protest in a "second revolution," because there were still too many people in power associated with

---

* The second largest Arab population is in Sudan, with 42 million, a distant second. And many Sudanese, especially in the south, are not Arabs.

the former regime, including military officers. Among the protesters' goals were the end to the emergency law (which allowed arrests without charges, in place since 1981), freedom, justice, a non-military government, and a say in managing Egypt's resources.[4] The emergency law was lifted in May 2012.*

Elections for parliament were held in November 2011. The Islamists were more cohesive than the newer political parties, which gave them an advantage. The Muslim Brotherhood won the elections with 47 percent of the vote, and an ultraconservative party (Salafi) had 27 percent of the votes, for a total of over 70 percent.[5] These were the first genuinely free elections in Egypt since the overthrow of the monarchy in 1952. They were observed by the Carter Center based in the U.S.,[6] among others.

Presidential elections were held in June 2012. Muhammad Morsi, the Muslim Brotherhood candidate, was elected with 52 percent of the vote, the second Islamist ever to be a head of state.†

Many people soon became unhappy with Morsi's authoritarianism. He announced that the presidency was above the law and not subject to judicial review, but later this was rescinded. He announced massive tax increases, including huge raises in the prices of staple foods, and this was also rescinded. There developed crises in gas and electricity. He began to introduce Islamists into all levels of government. Sectarian differences resurfaced.

Finally, in June 2013 the people rebelled.‡ Led by Abdel-Fattah el-Sisi,§ head of the armed forces, 3 million people came into the streets to demand that Morsi be deposed. He was removed by Sisi in a military coup d'etat in July, after just one year in office. Many in the West criticized this action, because Morsi had been democratically elected. Egyptians countered that he did not follow what he was elected to do, and he was spending more effort trying to gain political control than in solving economic and social problems. He was not a moderate; he had tried to

---

* President Abdel-Fattah el-Sisi imposed a counterterrorism law in August 2015 that is even stronger. People can be detained without judicial review.

† The first was Omar al-Bashir, president of Sudan.

‡ It is important to the Egyptians to call this action a rebellion, not a revolution, which is a term more used in the West.

§ el-Sisi's name is difficult to spell and pronounce in English, so just calling him "Sisi" has become the convention in English.

take over the government for the Islamists.[7] The army was seen by many as their protector and savior; it had not interfered with demonstrations.

The Muslim Brotherhood protested against the military coup, and it was banned. There was a crackdown on Morsi's supporters; the most notorious incident occurred when pro-Morsi protesters were crushed in the notorious August 2013 Rabaa massacre, in which at least 817 civilians were massacred. In all, crackdowns on most forms of opposition resulted in tens of thousands of dissidents detained, and thousands killed.[8]

A governing council served as interim authority until elections. Morsi was tried and condemned to death; this was later revoked. Sisi positioned himself as a strong leader who was needed to restore stability. He was elected president in May 2014, with 96 percent of the vote (voter turnout was 47.5 percent).[9] His rule quickly developed into a military dictatorship, justified by the war against Islamists. When Mubarak was declared innocent in 2017, many people were so discouraged that they were apathetic. They say that their earlier hopes were naïve, and dissent is as dangerous as before.[10]

The military was able to take advantage of the liberals' lack of expertise and the Muslim Brotherhood's incompetence and take full power for itself.[11]

Egypt's long history and ancient traditions have resulted in a homogeneous and distinctive society with much about its culture that is unique. Egyptians all speak Arabic, except for some Nubians in the far south, and English is the most common second language. French is also spoken by many. Eighty-five percent are Sunni Muslim, and 15 percent Coptic Christian, an indigenous Christianity followed in Egypt and Ethiopia,* among others. There has been an upswing in religious clashes, however, and the government is cracking down hard. The vast majority of Egyptians want to continue to live in harmony, and they worry about this trend.

About 10 percent of the Egyptians are in the elite upper class, which dominates the country politically and economically. The middle class is expanding and has reached about 40 percent. At least half of the people live at the poverty level or slightly higher. They are peasant farmers or villagers, or among the many urban poor.

---

* It is Monophysite, one of the variations originating in Alexandria in the fourth to sixth century.

Egypt hosts as many as 5 million refugees and immigrants – 250,000 to 300,000 Syrian refugees and 3 million Sudanese immigrants. Many of the Sudanese have lived in Egypt for generations.[12]

Because of its long tradition of education for the upper and middle classes, Egypt has an abundance of professionally trained people. At any given time there are about 1.3 million Egyptians working abroad as teachers, doctors, accountants, and laborers.[13] Many work in the Arabian Peninsula, most in Saudi Arabia, and a large number in Kuwait.[14] About 750,000 work in Libya, although it can be dangerous, and it is not arranged through the government like other work abroad.[15] In February 2015, 21 Christian Egyptians were killed in Libya by the Islamic State.

Health has improved dramatically due to government programs instituted in the 1960s, and life expectancy is 71 for men and 74 for women. Unfortunately, education has not fared as well. Despite education being free and compulsory, the rate of literacy is only 77 percent, but growing. The 2030 Agenda for Sustainable Development has set a target that by 2030 all youth and a substantial proportion of adults, both men and women, achieve literacy and numeracy.[16]

Unemployment was 12.7 percent overall in 2016. Of the unemployed Egyptians, 90 percent are between ages 15 and 29,[17] and one of the strident demands in both recent rebellions was the creation of jobs. Unemployment for young men is 21 percent, and for young women 47 percent. One third of them have a secondary or higher education.

Egypt's primary source of income is oil and gas, which has reached 40 percent of the GDP.[18] Intensive agriculture has always been central to the Egyptian economy; it was 40 percent of the GDP in the 1960s, and is now 14 percent. Egypt's exports include cotton, textiles, medical products, cement, and steel. Services account for 46 percent of the GDP (banking, shipping through the Suez Canal, trade, tourism) and industry 39 percent.[19]

Once there was an agricultural surplus but now Egypt imports 40 percent of its food and 60 percent of its wheat.[20]

Tourism has always been important to the economy. It was thriving and growing until affected by terrorism and violent events. In 2007, it was worth almost 20 percent of the GDP; by 2016 it was about 11 percent.[21] Tourism once employed 12 percent of the Egyptian workforce, so many people have lost their employment.

A looming problem is water. More water is needed constantly. The Nile River must be shared with Ethiopia and Sudan, which are upriver, making Egypt vulnerable. This issue has been negotiated for years, and in March 2015 an agreement was signed.[22] Ethiopia plans to build the Great Ethiopian Renaissance Dam to enable it to receive its fair share of Nile waters. This continues to be a source of concern for the Egyptians.

Egypt's land is rich but is no longer flooded annually by the Nile, which deposited a layer of silt. Since the building of the Aswan Dam, water has been regulated and fertilizers must be used. The country loses 60,000 acres of its best farmland yearly to urbanization (illegally), and this has devoured between 1.5 million and 2 million acres of Egypt's most fertile lands in the past forty years.[23] The government is in turn reclaiming 200,000 acres of desert each year and using drip irrigation to conserve water, but this cannot compensate for the loss. Much of this is the result of the rapidly increasing population and the urgent need for housing. The state will have to reclaim the illegally taken agricultural land and develop urban areas in the desert (rather than trying to farm it). If this happens, it will cause major social upheaval.

Egypt receives more foreign aid from the U.S. than any other Arab country, $1.3 billion annually. The U.S. provided $6.5 billion in military assistance to Cairo between 2011 and 2015.[24] Canada gave $14.5 million, and the European Union gave 1.1 billion euros in 2016. Saudi Arabia, the UAE, and Kuwait pledged $12 billion to Egypt, and Saudi Arabia added $8 billion in investment and aid over five years.[25]

Poverty is increasing. Inflation reached 30 percent in February 2017. It was over 12 percent in April 2011 (compared with 9 to 15 percent in 2016). Prices of goods have risen about 16.5 percent in the past year.[26] Food has risen 37 percent. There is a shortage of sugar, a staple food (used in tea several times a day). The prices of sugar and cooking oil were increased twice in three months. Bread subsidies are an explosive issue in Egypt, where over 70 million people receive state rations. Protests broke out in March 2017 when subsidized bread was lessened from five loaves to three per day for each ration card.[27]

This was not helped when a general in the security services told people it was rude to complain about shortages and prices, and suggested they "go hungry" for the sake of Egypt.[28]

And then there is fuel. The government raised the price by up to 47 percent literally overnight in November 2016 (this after already raising its price abruptly in 2014).[29]

Egyptian women have always been at the forefront in women's rights, and they have been integrated into the workforce at all levels for a generation. Half the university students are women, and 35 percent of those studying science and technology. Egypt was in fact the first Arab country to admit women to its national university, in 1928, and education is entirely coed. In 1957, two women were the first to serve in an Arab parliament, and in the most recent government, 75 women were elected and 14 appointed, for a total of 89 out of 568 seats in the People's Assembly.[30] This is the highest number in Egypt's history. About 35 percent of the university professors are women, compared to 22 percent in the United States.[31,32]

The government has amended women's rights constantly, as shown, for example, in divorce laws. In 1979, the divorce law was amended but then declared unconstitutional in 1985. In 2000, the law was again amended, granting women much broader grounds for divorce, although the right to divorce is still gender-biased.[33] Although virtually no urban women covered their hair in the 1960s, a growing number (over 90 percent) have made the decision to do so.[34]

Sexual harassment and assaults have been a problem in Egypt. In 2014 a strict law was passed after joint work by twenty-five organizations.[35] Seven men were sentenced to lengthy prison terms for assault at Tahrir Square while a crowd was gathered during the Arab Spring protests. Cairo University adopted a strict sexual harassment policy, followed by Ain Shams University, and it is spreading.[36]

Egypt is vibrant with cultural energy—it is the leader of the Arab nations in such fields as filmmaking and literature. It has long been a dominant cultural influence in the Arab world. At any given time there are about 400 young Westerners studying Arabic in Egypt (some left during the rebellion and are returning), most of them at the American University in Cairo. It is common for students to want to return to Egypt, and many want to live there. Cairo, home to 14 million people, is a big, hot, crowded, polluted, poor city—still, *to know it is to love it.*

The Egyptian people are known to be especially friendly and good-humored, and they are very outgoing toward foreigners.

Sudan

Sudan is actually two nations now, Sudan and South Sudan, the south having won its independence in July 2011. Sudan is the third largest country in Africa and the second largest Arab country. It is dominated by the Nile River and its tributaries. It is tribal and diverse, with considerable sub-Saharan African influence on its social structure and ethnic composition.

Sudan split into (north) Sudan and South Sudan in July 2011. In both the north and south, the country has one of the most ethnically diverse populations in the world, with a total of over 400 languages, 19 major ethnic groups, and 597 subgroups, most of them in the non-Arab south.[1] Many people are of Nilotic ethnic origin. Sudan is one of the poorest countries in the world, with an annual per capita income in 2015 of $4,121 in north Sudan and $2,000 in South Sudan.[2] Forty-six percent of the people live below the poverty line in the north; in the south, the number of poor went from 45 percent in 2011 to 66 percent in 2015.[3,4]

Sudan has long been divided into two distinct regions, the Arab north (Muslim) and the non-Arab south (mainly Christian)*—the ten provinces in the south make up one-third of Sudan's land area. In both areas, many of the people are farmers or pastoralists who have little contact with modern life.

The two regions fought two long and brutal wars, the first from the time of Sudanese independence from Britain and Egypt in 1956 until a peace agreement in 1972. The peace lasted until 1983. In 1983, the government tried to implement Sharia law (there are almost no Muslims in the south, only 6 percent of the people) which, among other things, led to a resumption of war. It lasted until 2005, when a Comprehensive Peace Agreement was signed.[5] After prolonged negotiations, a referendum was held in 2011, in which 98.83 percent of the people in the south voted to separate.[6]

In the north the president is Omar al-Bashir, an autocratic ruler who has been in office since 1989. He took power in a coup and was elected in 2010 and 2015. He initiated a national dialogue in 2014, but some groups have not joined, and the dialogue is suppressed because there are ongoing arrests, restrictions on public gatherings, and limits on freedom of speech. Al-Bashir faces two international arrest warrants on charges of genocide, war crimes, and crimes against humanity.[7]

In April 2016, South Sudan's president, Salva Kiir, formed a Transnational Government of National Unity with the main opposition leader as vice president.[8] Heavy fighting broke out in Juba in July, however, but

---

* Animism is still practiced in some remote areas.

was stopped after three days. The goal is to draft a constitution that will lead to national elections.[9] There are 13,500 U.N. peacekeepers in South Sudan, with 4,000 more due to arrive.[10] (Darfur is considered separately.)

Unlike most urbanized Arab populations, in Sudan 60 percent of the people live in rural areas and work in agriculture, although in this large country only 7 percent of the land is arable and depends on the Nile River and its tributaries. The southern region, which is 83 percent rural, has a huge economic potential in its oil and minerals, rare timbers, and abundant water (if the conflicts ever subside!).[11]

Oil was discovered in the south in 1979. Large-scale exports began in 1999 and now make up 54 percent of (north) Sudan's export earnings and about 80 percent of earnings in South Sudan.[12,13] Southerners have resented the disproportionate share of oil money being spent in the north.[14] South Sudan is the most oil-dependent country in the world, and it is landlocked, which is a problem. It is estimated that the oil will be used up by about 2035.[15]

In Khartoum, Sudan's capital, parts are glitzy, with oil money financing big buildings and affluent neighborhoods. But these are alongside mud brick slums and camps, mainly on the outskirts of town. North Sudan has over 3 million refugees from other areas. In South Sudan, over 1.5 million people have fled the country, about 760,000 in 2016 alone. Sixty percent of them are children.[16] They are an economic burden on north Sudan, Egypt, Chad, and Ethiopia in particular, and depend on help from aid organizations.

This huge country has a population of only 42 million; 75 percent of the Sudanese live in the north. The population of Khartoum is almost 2 million. In Sudan, 40 percent are age 15 or younger.[17] The growth rate is 2.9 percent a year, and the population is forecast to increase 80 percent by 2050, placing huge pressures on education, health, and food sources. The population of South Sudan is estimated at 13 million, although uncertain because of refugees. Juba, the largest city, is the capital and has about 370,000 people.[18] South Sudan plans to build an entirely new capital city.

There is a separate conflict in the Darfur region (which is the western one-fifth of the country, population 7.6 million). This conflict has caused 300,000 deaths, and 2.5 million people have been displaced.[19] About 19,000 uniformed peacekeeping troops from the African Union are in the area, as well as 3,500 others in the UNAMID (African Union/United Nations Hybrid Operation in Darfur) program, all trying to stabilize the situation.[20]

Many parts of South Sudan are isolated; some do not even have a cash economy. The civil war in the south has been deemed one of the worst sustained conflicts, and the worst famine, since World War II.[21] In South Sudan as a whole, some 2 million people are dead and about 4 million displaced from their homes.[22] The northern government, or groups it tolerates, have been repeatedly accused of genocide, human rights abuses, and toleration of slavery.

In 1993, Sudan was placed on the U.S. list of countries that sponsor international terrorism. The U.S. imposed comprehensive sanctions in 1997 and 2007, but lifted some of them in 2017.[23] The Sudanese government has been isolated internationally, and this acceptance of separation into north and south is seen by some as a way for the president, Omar al-Bashir, to effect an end to sanctions and possibly avoid trial in the International Criminal Court for war activities. Sudan and South Sudan are considered among the world's most corrupt states.[24] The U.S. State Department considers South Sudan to be a source, transit, and destination country for persons trafficked for forced labor and sexual exploitation.[25]

The northern Sudanese are Arabs (in language, only partially in ethnicity). Tribalism is dominant in the north as well as the south, and many men are marked with identifying facial scars, as is common in sub-Saharan Africa. Arabic is the official language in the country, although only about 60 percent of the people speak it. English is also an official language. The literacy rate in the north is 76 percent, while it is only 27 percent in the south.

Because education has been available to the upper and middle classes for generations (in the north), this group is highly literate. There is a large pool of well-educated Sudanese professionals, but because of low salaries at home, about 1.2 million work abroad, mainly in the Arabian Peninsula.[26] This has caused a shortage of trained manpower in the country; at the same time, the overall unemployment rate was 20 percent in 2016.

Education for women has been steadily increasing, but only about 24 percent of Sudanese women work outside the home, mainly as teachers and social workers. Sudanese culture is extremely conservative in its view of women's rights. The birth rate is high—3.7 children per woman in the north (down from 6.5 in 1960).[27] Women rarely cover their faces, but they all wear a long cloak and voluminous scarves in public.

Since a military coup in 1983, Sudan has had the only avowed Islamist government in the Arab world (Saudi Arabia is conservative but not Islamist), with Islamic law prevailing. Women's rights had been granted after independence in 1956 (free consent to marriage and rights in divorce and custody and support of children), but when the current government came into power, strict Islamic Sharia was enforced, and many discriminatory practices were reinstated. Sudanese women now have no legal right to ownership of property or access to land and cannot manage their assets freely, nor can they obtain bank loans.[28] Except for a small number of liberated, educated women in the elite class, women are generally separated from men, even at mealtimes. There are several organizations that work for improving the rights of women.

Women in South Sudan once had much greater cultural freedom than in the north and were active in public affairs. They are seeking 30 percent representation in the new state at all levels; they constitute 60 percent of the population.[29] Women in the north have a 25 percent quota in parliament.[30]

Sudanese are known throughout the Arab world as friendly, sincere, and generous, and they are proud of this reputation.

❀ THE ARAB STATES IN ASIA

The Levant

The Levant, a French term, refers to the countries of the eastern Mediterranean: Lebanon, Syria, and Palestine, as well as Jordan and Iraq geographically; not so much ethnically. The adjective form is *Levantine*. This area has long been called "Sham" in Arabic, translated as Greater Syria or the Levant (French).*

The Levantine people in Lebanon, Syria, and Palestine are mainly from the same Semitic origin, descended from indigenous inhabitants of the region (from Neolithic times), including groups mentioned in the Bible

---

* There is much confusion about the acronyms ISIS and ISIL, the Islamic State of Iraq and Sham. It is a matter of how to translate "Sham"—Syria or Levant. Because of the confusion, many people simply call this group the Islamic State. It is "Daesh" in Arabic, an acronym for its name in Arabic.

such as Canaanites, Phoenicians, Moabites, and Jebusites. They constitute a linguistic and cultural unit and identify with each other. Jordanians, however, are of Bedouin descent, from the northern Arabian Peninsula (now Saudi Arabia). Many Iraqis are Arabian too, because Iraq was seriously depopulated and then repopulated by Bedouin tribes from Arabia (the Arabic spoken in Baghdad is a Bedouin dialect).

The borders in the Levant do not conform to geography or history; they were drawn by Britain and France after World War I, when these countries had mandates over the region. This was agreed on in the infamous Sykes-Picot agreement. Borders may well change after all; the states in the region are only about one hundred years old.

The acronym UNRWA will be referred to in this section; it stands for the United Nations Relief and Works Agency for Palestine Refugees in the Near East.

Lebanon

Lebanon is a small country, both in size and population (a little over 4 million), with a diverse geography and a long history of commercial and maritime importance. Its people are descended from a (non-Arabian) Semitic stock, mainly Phoenician and Canaanite. Religious diversity and social class have been divisive and have created barriers to social integration. All Lebanese feel an intense loyalty to their own clan and religious group. The Lebanese speak Arabic, and educated people also speak French, English, or both.

From 1975 to 1990, Lebanon experienced a disastrous civil war, during which 25 percent of the population was displaced and at least 130,000 people were killed. Religious tensions were part of the cause—the Christians (between 25 and 43 percent, estimates vary) have traditionally had more wealth and political power than the more numerous Muslims (about 60 percent), who in turn are divided between Sunnis (about 25 percent) and Shia (about 35 percent, estimates vary). Religion has become a substitute for ethnic affiliation in many cases; it is of overriding importance in defining the Lebanese population. Lebanon has by far the highest number of Christians in the Arab world, divided into many sects.

A third influential denomination is the Druze religion; they are classified as Muslims. The religion originated in Lebanon in the eleventh century and is derived from Shia Islam, and they are about 5 percent of the population. Altogether, 18 religious sects are officially recognized, and many government positions are reserved for certain religions. The social and political effects of this mix of religious groups can well be imagined; it has affected government and social stability.

During Lebanon's civil war, the factions were religion-based. The Syrian army occupied the country from 1976 to 2005, partly because of the unrest. Because Lebanon was carved out of Syrian territory by Western powers, many Syrians have had a kind of proprietary feeling toward Lebanon. Lebanon was created by the French in 1920 as a haven for Christians, who had suffered massacres by the Druze and the Turks in the 1860s. This was done through an agreement among Europe's Great Powers and Ottoman authorities.

The Syrian troops were resented by some of the Christians but welcomed by many in other religious groups. Syria (and its ally, Hezbollah)* stand accused of assassinating the (Sunni) prime minister, Rafik Hariri, in February 2005, which led to pressure for the Syrian pullout.

The Lebanese government is something of a house of cards. Offices are assigned by religion: the president is Christian, the prime minister is Sunni Muslim, and the speaker of Parliament is Shia Muslim. (This no longer reflects the numbers in each religion, and many believe it should be adjusted.) Seats in Parliament are regulated by religious quota, about half Muslim and half Christian. Some of these decisions were originally made based on the last census in 1932 (when Christians were 56 percent of the population); another census is not planned because it could upset the delicate religious balance.

Lebanon was without a president from May 2014 until October 2016 due to a political stalemate; finally, Michel Aoun, a Maronite Christian, was elected. In November 2016, he nominated Saad Hariri to form a government.[1] This was assembled in December, with the main purpose of preserving security against regional violence, especially in Syria. Parliamentary elections were scheduled for May 2018.[2]

Prior to the beginning of the civil war in 1975, the Lebanese government was pro-Western and pro-capitalist, and the country was a leader in

---

* Hezbollah is a Shia militia that has grown powerful and now controls the government. The ruling Assad family in Syria is Shia. These groups are also allied with Iran. Everything ties together eventually.

service industries such as banking, commerce, and tourism. The Lebanese once had the highest standard of living in the Arab world and the most cosmopolitan way of life, at least in Beirut. Now that the war is over, great efforts have been made to become once again the commercial center of the Middle East (actually, there is no other Arab alternative; the Gulf states are distant). Beirut is rebuilt and Lebanon is again open for business. Per-capita income was $18,240 in 2017, very high compared with other countries in the area.

Social classes are clearly defined in Lebanon, with a small upper class of about 7 percent, a sizable middle class of 30 percent, and a large lower class made up of about half of the people.[3] This is not counting refugees, who comprise at least 13 percent of the people. The lower classes are quite poor, and the majority of them live in urban areas. Agricultural production is limited by inadequate natural resources, and imports far exceed exports. Unemployment was 18 to 20 percent from 2003 to 2008, and between 7 and 11 percent in 2016.[4] The youth unemployment rate, however, is 34 percent. Many of the available jobs are low-skilled, although the education system is excellent and turns out many skilled graduates. It is difficult to get a good job without the right personal contacts, so the educated tend to leave to work abroad.

Free public education has long been available in Lebanon, and the literacy rate is 90 percent. In the mid-nineteenth century, French and American missionaries established schools and universities in Lebanon. The missionaries had a strong influence, and they trained many future leaders and intellectuals of the Arab world.

The Christians in Lebanon are no longer the majority, but they had dominated the government (this was the basis for the civil war). The Shia party Hezbollah steadily gained more power, and in January 2011, the government fell and Hezbollah's candidate was selected to head the next government.[*,5] The situation is sensitive; sectarian fighting resumed briefly in 2008 and could well break out again.[6] Lebanon went without a government for 18 months in 2007–2008.[7] There was a bomb attack in May 2011 that killed six Italian peacekeepers, and some worry that a new era of instability may be at hand.[8]

---

* For a description of Hezbollah's history, see "Hezbollah's Rise Amid Chaos," by Robert F. Worth, *New York Times*, 15 January 2011.

Lebanon is overwhelmed with a refugee crisis, having received so many refugees from neighboring countries in the past few years that it went from 69th to second largest number of refugees in 3½ years (Pakistan is first).[9] It has the highest per-capita concentration of refugees in the world.

There are about 455,000 Palestinian refugees in Lebanon, which means that they constitute over 10 percent of the population.[10] Although they arrived in 1948, or are descendants of those who did, they are considered foreigners and are denied basic rights. They are confined to twelve crowded refugee camps and cannot attend public schools, own property (this law was imposed in 2001), or make an enforceable will.[11] Palestinians engage in menial work and are not allowed to work in as many as twenty professions, including medicine and law, although restrictions were eased somewhat in 2010. Most of them must rely heavily on UNRWA for basic services such as health and education, because they do not have much access to services the Lebanese government provides. Most live in appalling conditions, which have been described as "catastrophic."[12]

The Palestinians' presence is controversial—they are almost all Sunni Muslims and, if given citizenship, would affect the religious electoral balance, so it is opposed by the Christians and Shia. Palestinians are the poorest community in Lebanon, with little hope of improving their lot.

Because of Lebanon's location, it has refugees from all the neighboring areas. It has had Iraqi refugees since 1997. Currently there are 6,000 to 10,000 Iraqis, many undocumented.[13] The overwhelming number of new refugees are from Syria, about 1.5 million.[14] Recent changes in visa requirements have made it almost impossible for more Syrians to enter without a visa or sponsor. They, too, live in deteriorating conditions, with almost no access to health and education, and poor food security; 70 percent are below the poverty line. They do not have camps; 60 percent live in substandard shelters, including garages, warehouses, unfinished buildings, and tents, with the rest in apartments.[15] They are almost entirely dependent on the U.N. and charitable organizations. Many Syrian refugee children work to help support their families.

The upper-class and middle-class Lebanese are well-traveled and sophisticated, and they are politically oriented and very patriotic. Some, mainly Christians, believe that Lebanon should be more Western than Arab and should identify with Europe; others, mainly Muslims, identify with pan-Arab sentiments and want to de-emphasize Western influence. The Lebanese have migrated abroad since the late nineteenth century (more live outside the country than inside), and the sustained contacts with these emigrants all over the world has influenced the society and economy.

Urban Lebanese women, especially Christians, are active in the professions, commerce, and social organizations. Women constitute 32 percent of the workforce, one-fourth of them in the professional sector. They generally dress in the Western manner and mix freely in society. In contrast, women in rural areas are restricted by the prevailing traditional values. The hejab headscarf has become more frequent.

Women were granted the right to vote and run in elections in 1952. The government initiated a National Action Plan to improve the status of women from 1997 to 2000 and has instituted a National Authority on Women's Affairs as well.[16]

But there is a long way to go. Four women are in the current Parliament comprised of 128 members.[17] There are active organizations seeking to place more women in leadership positions and to replace some Islamic laws with civil ones, because women are still discriminated against in laws concerning family, right to travel, and the right to work. There is a push to improve women's rights under a national Personal Status law, rather than relying on numerous different religious courts;[18] this was not addressed in the last session of the new government, however.

Beirut is exceptionally built up and modernized, situated along the Mediterranean seacoast. It is sometimes called "the Paris of the Middle East." The society in the city is the most liberal in the Arab world; it is luxurious and highly social, with an active nightlife. Many students from Europe and the U.S. have studied at the American University in Beirut, as well as several other universities. Westerners feel comfortable there. The many problems under the surface are hidden in the bustle and lively commerce of downtown.

Syria

Syria is currently in the midst of a devastating civil war that has spread throughout the country. The statistics are numbing. In 2017, there were up to 465,000 people dead; more than 11 million people have been forced from their homes; and there were over 5 million refugees, mostly in

Lebanon, Jordan, Iraq, and Turkey. About 2.5 million are children.[1] About 10 percent of Syrian refugees have sought safety in Europe.

In all, *over half* the population have been killed or forced from their homes. Inside Syria, more than 6.3 million people are displaced, and 13.5 million need humanitarian assistance. According to the Syrian Network for Human Rights, more than 65,000 Syrians have vanished since 2011, almost all of them tortured and killed in government detention centers.[2] Many die of starvation. Currently, there are an estimated 200,000 detainees.[3] This has been described as a "state policy of extermination of the civilian population, a crime against humanity" by the United Nations.[4]

The current population in Syria is 18.8 million (including refugees from elsewhere), down from 23 million in 2011, when the war started.[5] (These numbers do not quite add up; numbers are approximate in different sources.) The population is projected to be 17.4 million at the beginning of 2018; balanced against births, it will be a net loss of 1,100 persons per day.[6]

Syria has many religions and ethnic groups—90 percent are Muslims (74 percent are Sunni and the rest belong to other Islamic sects). Minority groups include Christians, 5 to 7 percent, and Druze, about 3 percent. Of the Sunni Muslims, one-tenth are Kurds. The most notable Muslim sect is that of the Alawites (a variation of Shiism), who comprise only 14 percent of the population but have controlled the government since 1970 when the current Assad regime took power. This has caused tension in a majority-Sunni country. As one observer said, "The weight of their history is so heavy."[7]

The civil war began in 2011, when pro-democracy Syrians joined other countries in protesting their government during the Arab Spring. There were peaceful demonstrations throughout the country, but the government of Bashar al-Assad (called Assad in English, pronounced AS-sad) responded with great force and brutality, and armed opposition groups began fighting back.

The standoff between pro-government forces and anti-government rebels, most notably the Free Syrian Army, continues and has brought on enormous devastation. Both sides are receiving support from other organizations and other countries. Syria is "the keystone of the Levant."[8] It has become more than just a battle between those for or against the Assad regime—so many factions and so many neighboring countries have an interest. It has been suggested that ultimately Syria should be partitioned, because this would weaken the country. None of these plans is in consultation with the Syrian people, however.

A key factor has been the intervention of regional and world powers, including Iran and Russia vs. the United States and Saudi Arabia. Outside military, financial, and political support for the government and the opposition has contributed directly to the intensification and continuation of the fighting, and this has turned Syria into a proxy battleground. And there are about 20,000 foreign fighters, one-fifth from Western nations.[9]

Because the Syrian government is Shia, it is allied with Shia Iran, the Iraqi Shia government, and Hezbollah, a Lebanese Shia militia. There are also other Iranian and Iraqi Shia militias. Russia is a major supporter and supplier of arms and airplanes, and has launched airstrikes against the opposition rebels. Russia wants to preserve its naval presence in Tartous on the Mediterranean and an airbase in Latakia, the Alawite heartland. Iran is working to become the strongest nation in the region and is using Syrian territory to funnel arms, train its military, and reinforce its presence in case the regime falls.

Opposing them are the Sunnis in Syria and Iraq. The Sunnis are supported by the U.S. in order to counter influence from Iran and Russia, and to oppose the Assad regime's human rights abuses. Saudi Arabia, a bastion of Sunni Islam, is seeking to counter the influence of its rival Iran and has been a major provider of military and financial assistance to the rebels, including those with Islamist ideologies. Turkey is a key supporter of the Syrian opposition and has also faced the burden of hosting 2.5 million refugees.

All parties are opposed to the two Sunni Jihadist groups Al-Qaeda and the Islamic State (IS). Al-Qaeda's affiliate controls large parts of the northwestern province of Idlib. As for the IS, in 2014, the Global Coalition was formed, with 68 international partners dedicated to defeating it.[10] The IS controls large swaths of northern and eastern Syria, yet it is so despised that it is battling everyone—government forces, rebel brigades, and Kurdish militias, as well as facing airstrikes by Russia and a U.S.-led multinational coalition. Turkey agreed to let the U.S.-led coalition against IS use its airbases for strikes on Syria after an IS bomb attack in July 2015. Saudi Arabia took part in the U.S.-led coalition air campaign against the IS. France and the U.K. have participated in bombing IS targets and are also providing support and training.

Antiquities have been destroyed, some receiving international publicity, such as Palmyra. Much of Syria, especially in old cities, has layers of history showing various civilizations of the past—Canaanite, Roman, Umayyad, and Ottoman. This is one of the oldest settled regions in the world, and its treasures are being lost.

The U.S. has had economic sanctions against Syria since 2004, imposed because of support for terrorism (across Iraq's border) and for pursuing missile programs.[11] In May 2011, the U.S. imposed personal sanctions against President Assad and six of his officials, on the grounds of human rights abuses—killing hundreds and arresting thousands of protesters in the months since the troubles began in January.[12] In 2017, sanctions were tightened because of Assad's use of chemical weapons in 2014 and 2015.[13]

In the past, Syria's socialist government had been secular, authoritarian, and cautious in its relations with the West. Syria gained independence from France in 1946, and from that time, there were numerous short-term governments and coups, until the Assad takeover in 1970. Hafiz Al-Assad died in 2000, and his son Bashar has been president since then. The country has been under an "emergency law" (arbitrary arrests and detentions, curtailed rights of assembly and expression) since 1964.

Syria and Iraq were the only secular governments in the Middle East. After this, it is highly doubtful that there will be secular governments in the future.

Syria is densely populated because only half of the land is habitable; the rest is drought-stricken or desert. Most people live in urban areas. Before the war, the standard of living was constantly improving; now, 85 percent of the Syrians live in poverty, two-thirds of them in extreme or abject poverty.[14] About 7 million are food-insecure. And some households spend up to a quarter of their income just on water. Education and healthcare were once widely available; many facilities are destroyed now. Syria is one of the few Arab countries that had achieved the target of universal primary education, and literacy was 84 percent. Today, 2.7 million children are out of school, and many more among refugees. Secondary and university students have been welcomed in Jordan and Turkey, but with the war lasting so long, their education may still be curtailed.[15]

Agricultural production has been an important factor in Syria's economy, as are oil, phosphates, and textiles. Land reform and the establishment of agricultural cooperatives led to improvements in the lives of small farmers. A looming crisis, however, is lack of water, which affects the entire Middle East region. A severe drought began in 1998, and scientists say it is the driest period in 900 years and the worst drought in 500 years.[16] The drought caused 75 percent of Syria's farms to fail and 85 percent of livestock to die between 2006 and 2011, according to the United Nations. The collapse in crop yields forced as many as 1.5 million Syrians to migrate to urban centers. This is expected to get worse and is related to global warming.

On top of this, Syria still has its own refugees from elsewhere. There are 450,000 Palestinian refugees in the country. This is after about 110,000 have left, about 60,000 of them going outside the Middle East region.[17] But many cannot leave because neighboring countries place barriers on their entrance. Over 95 percent of the Palestinian refugees are in critical need of sustained humanitarian assistance in order to survive.[18]

There are also about 1 million Iraqi refugees in Syria. More than 14,000 fled the fighting in Mosul in one month.[19]

And finally, on to another subject besides war. Syrian women in the upper class have been well educated for two generations and have long been working, primarily in education and medicine; they once held over 35 percent of positions in the national university system. They represent 39 percent of the workforce and about 10 percent of the positions in government.

But women do not have equality in the legal system, which is a combination of civil and Sharia law. The society is conservative. The most prominent advocate for women is the Syrian Women's Observatory, founded in 2005, which acts as an advocate for women's rights. It spreads knowledge about rights and succeeded in making the government drop a proposed "personal status law" that was severe and was judged a violation of women's rights. Women have been active in alternative media since the war started. But Islamist sentiment is present in the society, and while traditionally Syria has a good reputation for women's rights within the Arab world, the annual World Economic Forum Gender Gap Index shows that the status of women has worsened in recent years.[20]

Syria is a stunning country with much to see. It is claimed that Damascus is the oldest continually inhabited city in the world.* Syrians have always been friendly and welcoming to Westerners. At one time, there were several study-abroad programs for students learning Arabic. There were usually about 200 Western students living in Damascus, about 50 of them American. They returned home telling of how friendly and nice the Syrians were toward them. Many of them still hope they can eventually return.

Palestine

It is not possible to discuss Palestine without reference to conflict, military occupation, and daily hardships brought on by the people's situation. These factors are so overwhelming that we start there.

Palestine (the Palestinian Territories) includes three regions, the West Bank, East Jerusalem, and Gaza, which is under separate governance. The Palestine Authority governs the West Bank and East Jerusalem, and Hamas governs Gaza. Hamas (the Islamic Resistance Movement) was elected democratically in 2006 but has not been recognized by the U.S., the E.U., or Israel, because it denies Israel's right to exist. One reason Hamas was elected is because of its extensive social and charity work over the years, such as providing medical centers, food banks, summer camps, schools, and sometimes direct financial aid to families.[1] Many other facilities are run by other charities as well, in both Gaza and the West Bank. Some of these facilities are supported by supplemental money from international donors.

The total population of Palestine is a little over 4 million, 2.5 million in the West Bank and 1.8 million in Gaza, plus about 3 million refugees outside of Palestine (in camps in Lebanon, Syria, and Jordan). In total, some 6.1 million Palestinians now have refugee status and are registered with UNRWA, the United Nations Relief and Works Agency for Palestine Refugees.†[2] Palestine wants a Right of Return for these people, (a doubtful concession to expect). Other difficult issues include recognition and security for Israel, trade and travel agreements, withdrawal of Israeli forces,

---

* "Damascus has seen all that has ever occurred on earth, and still she lives." —Mark Twain

† Numbers are approximate and don't quite add up.

the demilitarization of Palestine, the status of Jerusalem, and whether there can be a "two-state solution" or the Arabs will be absorbed into a greater Israel.*

There is constant talk about making Palestine an independent state and joining the two parts into a contiguous whole, with borders yet to be determined. A "land swap" is envisioned, with Israel keeping some land in the West Bank. But there are now 400,000 settlers in some 130 separate settlements in the West Bank.[3] This is in violation of international law and was condemned 14–0 in the U.N. in 2016.[4] East Jerusalem had been traditionally Palestinian, and they envision it as their future capital. But there are 200,000 settlers in East Jerusalem, and Israel has plans to add 600 more settlement homes.[5] East Jerusalem is surrounded by 17 Jewish settlements. Arabs have been reduced to only 39 percent of the population, and they face a housing shortage.

Since the 1967 occupation, no Palestinian towns or villages have been built, nor is there any policy to allow the towns to grow, and they are becoming severely overcrowded. There is also the problem of home demolitions, an official policy of reprisal by Israel for "terrorism;" building without a permit (even if built before the Israeli occupation;) and other infractions. From 1967 to 2015, more than 46,000 demolitions took place in all areas of Palestine.[6] Palestinians went on strike in early 2017, because half a million Palestinians in Israel and East Jerusalem face displacement as a result of demolitions.[7] Demolitions often happen in strategic areas which are later allotted to settlements.† It discourages Palestinians from living in these areas and is a form of collective punishment.

The simplest step for a two-state solution would be to return to borders before the 1967 war, but that is now impossible; it is the preference of the U.S. government to use those borders at least as a starting point for negotiations, and Hamas has stated that it would approve these borders but not recognize Israel.[8] This is envisioned as part of the "peace process," which has been under discussion for decades. The U.S. has been involved

---

* There are also 1.1 million Palestinians (this includes descendants) expelled in 1967.
† Numbers are increasing. In 2015, 447 houses were demolished in the West Bank and 74 in East Jerusalem. In the first seven months of 2016, 564 houses were demolished in the West Bank and 72 in East Jerusalem, for an average of 23 and 4 per week, respectively. ("Demolitions of Palestinian homes and other structures in the West Bank." Caabu.org, 18 August 2016.)

from the beginning, but is not viewed as an "honest broker" and has lost credibility among many.*

There have been constant clashes along Palestine's borders, and both sides point to provocations. Israel has built a 450-mile steel-concrete barrier wall to separate it from nearly all the Palestinians; it intends this as a permanent border. It swallowed up 733 square kilometers of land, or 13 percent of the West Bank. The wall surrounds many Palestinian towns and in some cases separates people from their fields. It is intended to protect settlements as well, which are connected to Israel via flyover highways that require special license tags for use (Arabs use military checkpoints on the ground).

Many of the Palestinians live in great poverty, especially in the densely crowded Gaza refugee camp (1.8 million people living in an area roughly twice the size of Washington, D.C.). Gaza is the most crowded place in the world, with 4,279 individuals per square kilometer.[9] The people's movement, as well as imports and exports, have been severely restricted; Egypt opened a corridor on its border with Gaza in May 2011 to alleviate shortages, but it has often been closed. Israel controls 48 percent of Gaza's arable land, 85 percent of the maritime area promised to Gaza in the Oslo Accords, and all airspace and territorial waters.[10]

The Palestinians' grievances include Israel's confiscations of their land, the expansion of settlements, humiliating checkpoints, home demolitions, open-ended detentions, extrajudicial killings, and thousands of dead civilians.[11] Additional statistics (from September 2000 to July 2014): 1,091 Israelis and 6,890 Palestinians killed, as well as 134 Israeli children and 2,150 Palestinian children killed; 12,000 Israelis and 92,000 Palestinians injured; and 7,000 Palestinian men held prisoner, along with 70 women and 438 children.[12] In 2017, the unemployment rate was 6.4 percent in Israel, 25.7 percent in the West Bank, and 43 percent in Gaza, the highest in the world.[13] Gaza's youth unemployment is 60 percent.

And all this was before the extensive lengthy attack on Gaza for seven weeks in July and August 2014. Heavy bombing and overwhelming military presence meant that there was little safety for the people, and

---

* The image of the U.S. was improved slightly when it abstained (for the first time) at the U.N.'s vote condemning Israeli settlements in 2016. This may change. With a new presidential administration the US has withdrawn from UNESCO, which named a mosque in Hebron as a Palestinian world heritage site (Hebron is not part of the original territory granted to Israel).

many were among the 2,100 civilians killed, including 253 women and 519 children (there were also 66 Israeli soldiers and 7 Israeli civilians killed).[14] There were 20,000 homes destroyed or severely damaged, as well as medical facilities, 244 schools, and a number of U.N.-designated shelters. Soldiers raided nearly 1,300 residential, commercial, and public buildings. About 60 percent of Gaza's production capacity was destroyed.[15] After the war, nearly half a million people were living in emergency shelters or with other families because about one-fourth of the population was displaced, and remained so.

Israel has maintained a blockade on Gaza going back to the late 1990s, and it was widened in 2007, after Hamas was elected. This includes construction equipment, medical supplies, and most important, a restriction on basic food supplies. UNWRA has supplied basic food needs for over a million people. There is enough food to prevent starvation, but there is malnutrition among children and anemia is very high at all ages. Almost half of all households in Gaza suffer from moderate or severe food insecurity.[16] People's movement is also highly restricted in Gaza; they are essentially "locked in."

The Israelis have grievances in turn. They state that because of terrorism, their security is not guaranteed, so they cannot withdraw the military forces that have occupied the entire West Bank for fifty years. They state that during the last Gaza war, Hamas fired about 4,600 rockets toward Israel (most were intercepted).[17]

U.S. funding is usually through nongovernmental organizations (NGOs) for projects such as infrastructure, improved water access, healthcare, education, and vocational training.[18] The U.S. also partially funds U.N. agencies such as UNRWA. U.S. aid to Palestine was $237 million in 2016; in contrast, $3 billion is given to Israel annually. Today 80 percent of Gaza's residents and 50 percent in the West Bank are reliant on humanitarian aid.[19] The U.S. (under President Obama) sent an additional $221 million in late 2016 for this purpose.[20] Money to Israel is for military assistance, while money to Palestine is for economic support and social services.

But enough about conflict. Let's talk about the people.

Palestinians are among the most homogeneous in the Arab world, in that 98 percent are Sunni Muslim and 2 percent are Christian (down from about 8 percent in 1949). The 52,000 Christians (estimates range from

50,000 to 90,000) in the three regions of Palestine are concentrated in East Jerusalem (2.5 percent, down from 51 percent in 1947), Bethlehem, and Ramallah. They belong to many different sects. The majority of Palestinian Christians live abroad, in the Americas and in Arab countries, and they were estimated at 500,000 worldwide in 2012.[21] They have 8 percent representation in the Palestinian Legislative Council.[22]

Palestine's economy is not self-sustaining, due to lack of access to land in Israeli-controlled areas, import and export restrictions, and little private sector growth. There have been economic downturns due to political stalemate and Israeli restrictions, the separation barrier, and the Gaza war. The entire country relies heavily on international donor aid, primarily from the U.S., most nations in Western Europe, Saudi Arabia, Kuwait, and Japan. But donations have been declining; they were more than $3 billion in 2010, but between 2013 and 2014, they were approximately $1.2 billion. The total was $750 million in 2015, a drop of almost 30 percent, before Gaza was practically destroyed.[23] The West Bank economy depends on agriculture, 3.5 percent, industry, 25.2 percent, and services, 71.4 percent (as of October 2016).[24] The Gaza economy was agriculture, 3.3 percent (only 29 percent of the land is arable), industry, 21.7 percent, and services, 61.9 percent. Gaza's exports of agricultural produce are frequently disrupted and blocked and cannot be relied upon. Israeli restrictions have severely affected its economy.

The population growth rate is high, overall about 3 percent per year. In the West Bank, 37 percent of the population is under age 15, as are 45 percent in Gaza. In the West Bank, 18 percent of the people lived below the poverty line in 2011, and 40 percent in Gaza.

Education is good, although subject to disruptions and school closure because of events. Literacy is 95.2 percent for women and 98.6 percent for men, the highest in the Arab world. There are 23 colleges and universities.

Healthcare is a problem, however, because of inadequate hospitals and medical personnel, a lack of specialists, and lack of investment; spending per person is ten times in Israel compared to Palestine.[25] Some Palestinians have access to medical care in Israel, and there have been training programs for Palestinian doctors and nurses there for years. But the separation barrier has led to restricting the movement of patients, doctors, ambulances, and medications within the area.[26]

Palestinian women have many advocacy groups, and their legal status is improving. Recent legislation accords them equality before the law, but there are still discriminatory laws in effect regarding marriage, divorce, custody, and inheritance, left over from Jordanian and Egyptian law in the West Bank and Gaza, respectively. Women are marginally represented among judges and police. The Palestinian Labor Law and Social Status Law are mostly gender-sensitive. Few women own property, much of the reason being poverty. Children whose mother holds a Jerusalem residency permit have difficulty going to school there if their father is from elsewhere (marriage does not entitle a spouse to a permit from the Israelis). The third draft constitution of March 2003 states that Palestinians will not be subject to "any discrimination on the basis of race, sex, color, religion, political convictions, or disability."[27]

In the West Bank, women average 3 children each, and in Gaza, 4.7 children. Only 10 percent of the women are in the workforce, although among those with thirteen or more years' schooling, 56 percent are employed. But women reportedly earn only 65 percent of men's wages in the West Bank and 77 percent in Gaza.

A surprising number of foreign students are in the Jerusalem and West Bank area learning Arabic. They report making good friends and finding acceptance, including a welcome for Americans.

Jordan

Jordan is a relatively new nation. It was created under a British mandate at the end of World War I as a kingdom to be ruled by the Hashemites (Hashemites are originally from the Hejaz region of western Saudi Arabia, where they led the fight against the Turks in the Arab Revolt during World War I). Jordan became independent of Britain in 1946. Its borders are artificial—Jordan was essentially the leftovers when the borders of adjoining nations were determined by the British (for their own interests). Jordan ceded the West Bank (of the Jordan River, occupied by Israel since 1967) to the Palestinian Authority in 1988.

Over half of Jordan's 6.8 million people are Palestinians, most of whom arrived after the wars of 1948 and 1967. Many Palestinians are well educated and many are wealthy. Most Palestinians have been granted Jordanian citizenship and have the same political and economic rights as Jordanians do. Two million Palestinians are refugees; 370,000 live in ten refugee camps.

In the past few years, Jordan has been overwhelmed with vast numbers of refugees from Iraq and Syria.[1] There are about 500,000 Iraqi refugees, only 61,000 of whom are registered with the U.N. refugee agency. Of 1.4 million Syrians, 658,000 are registered as refugees.[2] Most Syrians live away from the main camps because there is no room. The U.N. says that two-thirds of these families live below the poverty line, while one in six lives in extreme poverty.[3] Almost half of the households have no heating, and electricity, sanitation, and medical care are lacking. Recently, the U.N. identified 10,000 families as eligible for assistance, but due to lack of funds they cannot be helped.

The Jordanian government's budget, water, electricity, and other services are seriously overtaxed by these numbers. Donors are working to provide schools and teachers, and about 50,000 new Syrian students were to be be enrolled in 2016, increasing the number to 193,000. But still, about 80,000 of the 225,000 school-aged Syrian children in Jordan were out of school last year. In addition, 25,000 Syrian children whose education has been disrupted will be enrolled in catch-up programs to enable them to enter public schools in the coming years. The lack of educational opportunities is a key reason Syrian refugees want to flee to Europe.[4]

Jordan went through a traumatic civil war in September 1970, also known in the Arab world as Black September. It was an attempt by the Palestine Liberation Organization (PLO) and the more radical Popular Front for the Liberation of Palestine (PFLP) to topple Jordanian King Hussein and seize control of the country. Up to 15,000 Palestinian militants and civilians were killed; swaths of Palestinian towns and refugee camps, where the PLO had amassed weapons, were leveled. The PLO leadership was decimated, and 50,000 to 100,000 people were left homeless.[5] The PLO was expelled from Jordan and moved its headquarters to Beirut and later to Tunis, then to the West Bank.

There is a significant distinction between Palestinians (who identify more readily with Lebanese and Syrians) *and Jordanians.* The Palestinian dialect is predominant in the urban centers, but elsewhere the Jordanians speak their own dialect, close to the Bedouin and Arabian Peninsular dialects. The Jordanian Arabic dialect (considered a bit rustic, not as sophisticated) has been encouraged and promoted in television programs. Most Jordanians speak English, but there is an effort at language planning, to strengthen the use of Arabic rather than foreign languages.[6] Jordanians (not Palestinians) hold most of the administrative posts in the country.

About 33 to 40 percent of the Jordanians are Bedouins (2.5 million), most of whom live in the *badia,* the semi-arid steppe that comprises 80 percent of Jordan's land. By now, only about 1 percent of them are nomadic. There are many tribes, the largest of which is the Bani Hasan, with about 1 million people. The Hashemite Fund for the Development of the Jordanian Badia was instituted in 2003 to help the Bedouins care for the environment and their animals and restore ecosystems in the hope that they can maintain their lifestyle. Many settled Bedouins work in the tourism industry, and there is some concern that this may affect the authenticity of their traditions in time.[7]

After the death of King Hussein in 1999, his son Abdullah assumed the throne. The Jordanian government is viewed as moderate and pro-Western. Jordan and the U.S. work together in counterterrorism and have done so for thirty years.

Most Jordanians are Sunni Muslim, but 6 percent of the population is Christian (400,000 people). Religion has not been a divisive factor in the society. King Abdullah is a leading proponent of moderate Islam and has called for the "quiet majority" of Muslims to "take back our religion from the vocal, violent, and ignorant extremists."[8] He initiated a legal and scholarly effort to undermine clerics who issue religious rulings that justify violence. The government has arrested Islamic militants and controlled radical preachers. Jordan joined an international coalition against the IS and in 2015 carried out airstrikes against IS targets.[9]

Jordan is a constitutional monarchy, with a parliament. The latest parliamentary elections were held in 2016. Women won 20 of 130 seats in the last parliamentary elections, compared with 18 out of 150 in the previous parliament.[10] The Islamic parties won 16 seats, but most of those elected were businessmen or tribal candidates who support the government.[11]

Despite the government's pro-Western policies, it still must contend with the results of a Pew Global Attitudes Project poll in April-May 2011, in which a large majority of the people viewed the U.S. unfavorably because of "a perception that the U.S. acts unilaterally, opposition to the war on terror, and fears of America as a military threat."[12] In 2015, 86 percent viewed the U.S unfavorably.[13]

When uprisings were breaking out all over the Arab world in 2011, Jordanians demonstrated too. They did not call for the downfall of the government, but were protesting government corruption, rising prices, rampant poverty, and high unemployment (13.5 percent). The king replaced appointed members in parliament, revised laws governing public organization and political activity, amended the constitution, and formed the National Dialogue Committee.[14]

Jordan has one of the smallest economies in the Arab world. It is poor in natural resources, and despite numerous economic initiatives, the nation is heavily dependent on foreign aid. There are worsening water shortages. Only 6 percent of the land is arable, and 3 percent of the population are farmers. Jordan is 84 percent urban. The economy is based on tourism, industry, agriculture, and exports such as textiles, potash, and phosphates; "services" account for 78 percent of occupations. Tourism is variable, always subject to a downturn when there is unrest in the region. Most people have experienced a decrease in income. Approximately 14 percent of the people live below the poverty line. Per-capita income was $5,500 in 2017.[15] Rapid privatization of previously state-owned industries and liberalization of the economy is spurring unprecedented growth in Jordan's urban centers such as Amman and Aqaba.

Jordan's location between Israel and Iraq is a disadvantage, and it has suffered because of both neighbors. Before the Gulf War of 1991, 75 percent of its trade was with Iraq ($1 billion per year); this was reduced to one-quarter of that amount. Some 380,000 Jordanians returned from jobs in the Arabian Gulf at the time of the first Gulf War, and unemployment rose to 30 percent. The second Gulf War caused an even greater crisis in the energy supply situation, as oil had been imported (below market cost) from Iraq; it is far more expensive now.

Jordan joined the World Trade Organization in 2000 and entered into a Jordan-U.S. Free Trade Agreement in 2001. Both exports and tourism have been hit by the impact of the conflicts in Syria and Iraq. Regional instability also depressed business and consumer confidence last year, restraining private consumption and reducing investment inflows from the Gulf countries. At the same time, the unemployment rate was higher as the labor market could not absorb the increased supply resulting from the large influx of refugees.

Jordan's literacy rate is 95.4 percent, one of the highest in the Middle East. Jordan also has an excellent nationwide health program.

Jordanian women are well educated and working in a wide array of fields; about 27 percent are in the workforce, almost entirely in the cities. Queen Rania is championing the cause of women's rights. Sharia law, combined with civil law, is used in the country.

Jordanians are very personable, warm, and welcoming. They enjoy friendships with foreigners. More and more Western students are going to Jordan to study Arabic; language programs and schools are popping up all over. Foreigners are unanimous in their praise of the country and people.

Iraq

Iraq has a proud history and was the home of five magnificent ancient civilizations.* But time after time, Iraq was beset by invasions and conquests. Iraq (Mesopotamia) is underpopulated, considering its antiquity and fertility; this is the consequence of repeated wars and devastation. Iraq's location has always made it a strategic battlefield for the region.

Only 75 percent of the Iraqis are Arabs, and 20 percent are Kurds, who are bilingual in Kurdish and Arabic. (Note: Kurds are not Arabs or Semitic; they are ethnically Aryan, related to the Persians.) The remainder are small ethnic groups, such as Turkomans, Assyrians, and Armenians. Arabic is the official language, and English is widely spoken.

In Iraq, 97 percent of the people are Muslim, of whom 60 percent are Shia, and 3 percent are Christians and other minorities, such as Mandeans and Chaldeans. Iraq has been strongly influenced by its Islamic heritage because several sites sacred to Shia Muslims are located there and have long been the object of religious pilgrimages. Iraqis feel a special affinity to Jordanians because both are predominantly Arabian (not Levantine).

Iraq's revolutionary socialist government was established after the Hashemite monarchy (imposed by the British) was overthrown in 1958, and there were four coups after that. The Ba'ath political party took power in 1968, and Saddam Hussein was president from 1979 to 2003.

Iraq has been hard-hit by two wars, ten years apart (not to mention an eight-year war with Iran prior to these two). The first phase was Gulf

* Sumerian, Akkadian, Babylonian, Assyrian, neo-Babylonian. This region is often called "the cradle of civilization."

War I, after Iraq's invasion of Kuwait in 1990.* This was followed by an international embargo on trade and financial transactions (except for medicine and food) imposed in 1991—these are referred to by Iraqis and other Arabs as "the American sanctions." In ten years the sale of oil went from generating 95 percent of the foreign earnings to 10 percent. Social services declined drastically, and money that was intended for food and medicine in the oil-for-food program was mostly diverted to government loyalists. By 2001, an estimated 800,000 to 1.2 million people had died because of the embargo, half a million of them children under the age of five.[2] Because of scarcities, the Iraqis became more dependent on the government for necessities, including drinking water.

Then came Gulf War II, the American invasion of March 2003.† The chaotic results are well known, resulting in 1 million dead. Even as 8 million Iraqis voted and exuberantly demonstrated their love of freedom and democracy in the elections of January 2005, at the same time 92 percent of them wanted the Americans out. Sanctions ended, with a gradual transfer of governance to U.S./U.K. authorities in Iraq.

Strong sectarian/ethnic tensions are present; the U.S. dismantled the state when it intervened and used sectarian divisions to consolidate its power. Ministers and military officers were fired, and the U.S. worked to privatize state-owned enterprises without Iraqi input.[4] This drove many Sunnis into rebel and Islamist groups. The current government is Shia and it is shaky because it has not included Sunnis. Iraq needs a period of calm to build up its institutions and economy, but it is doubtful that this will occur.‡ The 2005 power-sharing constitution was never implemented. Iraq may in fact be a "failed state," and perhaps it is best partitioned.[6]

---

* The territory of Kuwait was once Iraq's Nineteenth Province, until the British took it away and bestowed Kuwait on the current ruling family. One version of events is: "British imperialism gave us Kuwait and in the view of the American imperialism made sure we still have Kuwait, in the face of Iraqi attempts to undo British conniving."[1]

† All over the world 36 million people took part in almost 3,000 protests against the Iraq war, the largest anti-war protest in history.[3]

‡ Iraq was created in 1918 from three separate Ottoman provinces, Sunni, Shia, and Kurdish, by the British when they had a mandate over the region. The boundaries were based on "consultation with the tribes, consideration of Britain's need for oil, and her own idiosyncratic geopolitical beliefs."[5] In 1921, the British imported and crowned a

Iraq is comprised of three parts: the Sunni northwest, the Shia south, and the Kurdish northeast. The Kurds have been brutalized by the former Iraqi regime and current Syrian regime, and oppressed in Turkey. They have set up a region which they refer to as Kurdistan, and they aspire to its independence when final adjustments are made in the region. The Kurds had secured most of the land in Iraq to which they laid claim, but the Iraqi army invaded and reclaimed oil fields and a military base. But the Kurds are not going to give up. They have been promised an independent state for one hundred years and in September 2017, 93 percent of them voted for independence (they are the largest distinct ethnic group in the region to lack a state of their own). If they create Kurdistan from Iraqi land, they still have to deal with Syria, Turkey, and Iran to have a complete country. Most of the Western nations oppose Kurdish independence because it will upset the fragile political situation, although Israel is in favor.[7] The Kurds have been ardent allies in the fight against the IS.

The population of Iraq is 32 million (down from 34 million), and 39 percent of the people are under age 15. Here are some statistics of which most Westerners are unaware: As a result of the Gulf Wars, in 2003 about 25 percent of the children were malnourished, which is up 73 percent from 1991. Infant mortality more than doubled between the late 1980s and early 2000s; by 2001 it was about 133 per thousand births (as compared with 4 to 5 in Western Europe and 6.7 in the U.S.).[8] A United Nations report stated, "The country's fall on the UNDP Human Development Index from 96 to 127 reflects one of the most rapid declines in human welfare in recent history."[9] A UNICEF report stated that in mid-2005, 4,000 children under the age of five died every day.[10]

About 7 percent of the children were reported as malnourished in 2009; in 2017, it was 7.8 percent.[11] There are severe problems with water, sewage, and electricity, which affects the standard of living. A World Health Organization survey found that 17 percent of Iraqis over 18 suffer from mental disorders such as depression, phobias, post-traumatic stress disorder, and anxiety.[12] 3 million to 4 million people are internally displaced.[13] There are currently 11 million to 13 million people (one-third of

---

Hashemite king, Faisal (a Sunni), who ruled until a bloody military coup in 1958. The British denied independence to the Kurds.

the population) in dire need of humanitarian assistance, including over 5 million children.[14] Even in 2017, 23 percent of the population was living on less than $2 per day. Much of this distress is blamed on institutional problems, economic turmoil, corruption, terrorism, and foreign meddling.[15]

The flight of over 250,000 refugees, many of whom were doctors, lawyers, academics, and engineers, stripped the society of the services these people provide.[16]

Women and children are the most affected by food and medical shortages. Immunization programs are behind, and there was a cholera outbreak in late 2015, finally contained.[17]

Nutrition was improved by a law to fortify flour with micronutrients, lacking especially among women and children, in 2006. But because of war and unrest, the mills practicing fortification decreased from 95 percent in early 2013 to 65 percent by the end of that year.[18] Since then, the percentage has fallen continuously.

In 2017, the city of Mosul fell as the last outpost of the IS in Iraq; 750,000 people were trapped there. Several groups are cooperating in fighting the IS, but past experience indicates that old rivalries will reappear in the post-IS period. There has been no agreement on issues such as distribution of power, land, money, and oil. Former president Obama stated that trust must be built on compromise, the "no victor, no vanquished" principle, with no side taking a maximalist position.[19] The Shia government squandered an opportunity to share power with the Sunnis and the Kurds, and the IS is filling the vacuum.[20]

Considerable damage against civilians was done by the American barrage of missiles in Mosul in March 2017, but no lasting damage to structures was achieved. More than 200 were killed, mostly women and children, in the single most deadly incident in the war against the IS.[21] In fact, the death toll has decreased precipitously under the Trump administration.

Education has been hard hit. Enrollment in primary schools dropped from 100 percent in 1980 to 85 percent in 1996, and 76 percent in 2003. It was 85 percent in 2007, and the target was 100 percent enrollment by 2015.[22] The 2014 UNICEF enrollment figures were 90 percent, falling far short of the 100 percent target. Fewer than half of children who enroll in primary education actually finish school. Once, 92 percent of the population was literate; in 2011, the rate was 74 percent. It was better in 2017, up to 81 percent.

Only 12 percent of Iraq's land is cultivated, and efforts have long been underway to reclaim more (it was irrigated and fertile in ancient times). Today, Iraq is 70 percent urban.

Iraqi women had always been among the most liberated in the Middle East and were thoroughly integrated into the workface, many as professionals. Within a span of twenty years, thousands of women became lawyers, physicians, professors, engineers, scientists, and writers. In 1959, Iraq became the first country in the Middle East to have a female minister and four female judges. The 1959 Code of Personal Status gave women equal political and economic rights and extensive legal protections, so they were full participants in society.[23] The ruling Ba'ath party was secular and promulgated laws specifically aimed at improving women's status. It set up the General Federation of Iraqi Women, which coordinated more than 250 urban and rural centers for job training, education, and social programs. Women were granted equal opportunities in the civil service sector, as well as maternity leave and freedom from harassment in the workplace.[24]

In an example of the law of unintended consequences, the impressive progress toward women's rights was completely wiped out by the two Gulf Wars. After the first Gulf War, Saddam decided to embrace Islamic and tribal traditions as a political tool in order to consolidate power. Many steps toward women's advancement were reversed—there were changes to the personal status laws and the legal code.[25] As the economy grew worse under the sanctions, women were pushed out of the labor force to ensure employment for men. All state ministries were required to enforce restrictions on women working. Freedom to travel abroad was restricted, and coeducational secondary schools were changed to single-sex only.

In 2005, a new constitution was voted in, with a return to Sharia law in its most conservative interpretation. Women lost ground—it reinstates ancient punishments, forced marriage, and one-sided divorce. Women are discouraged from driving, and most now spend their time at home, some fearing attacks or kidnapping. Shia predominate in the National Assembly. A quota of seats on the Supreme Court, which will weigh the constitutionality of all laws, was set aside for Muslim clerics, but this was suspended because of opposition from women's groups.[26] Women have 25 percent of the seats in the parliament (they lobbied for 40 percent). More women are wearing the hejab or covering entirely, whereas the Ba'ath regime had strict laws against Islamization and the role of religion in society.[27] One woman summarized, "We are suffering right now. The war took all our rights. We're not free because of terrorism."[28]

Women went from being visibly active in the Iraqi workforce in the 1980s—including the marketing and professional services sectors—to being nearly nonexistent by 2013. The streets of Baghdad were once full of women driving, women could walk around in public at all times of the day without worry, and university campuses were once filled with women who did not wear headscarves. One political analyst said in 2010, "Iraq is formally advanced, with many female M.P.'s and ministers. But this is only a false bright image. In reality, Iraq is left behind other countries."[29]

There are between 750,000 and 1 million widows in Iraq,* and a survey found that three-fourths of them are not receiving pensions. Some widows are reduced to begging. There are no government agencies assigned to help widows. Even non-governmental organizations have few programs related to widowed women.[30]

There are about 800,000 children who have lost one or both parents. Children without extended family to take them in now comprise an entire generation. Many are in "safe houses," where some have been for ten or more years. The number of orphans is still growing.

Government welfare legislation is held up by sectarian disagreements.[31] There are no child protection laws and human trafficking occurs. Child labor has increased, with over half a million children under the age of 14 now working.[32]

Until recently, most Iraqis were determinedly secular. There was little sectarian tension; in fact, people frequently married across Sunni-Shia lines. Now it is doubtful that Iraq will ever again have a secular government. Most Westerners would prefer to see a system that separates church and state. Unfortunately, this has become difficult for Americans to promote when the current trend in the U.S. appears to be mixing faith and government.

---

* Some UN agencies estimate 3 million.

Baghdad is still a beautiful city, with its parks and its broad boulevards, illuminated against the Tigris River at night. It was designed in the eighth century, had a million inhabitants by the tenth century, and was the very heart of Islamic civilization during its Golden Age from the eighth to the thirteenth centuries. There are still traces of the inner city's circular, geometric plan.

Iraq once had one of the highest living standards in the Middle East. It had advantages: an educated populace, a relatively small population, and plenty of money. Iraq was filled with universities, museums, libraries, and art galleries. It was a cosmopolitan center of culture, art, and intellect. No longer. Never again?

❀ THE ARABIAN PENINSULA

The Arabian Peninsula is the homeland of the Semitic Arabian people, in the true ethnic sense. This region has had the least contact with foreigners and is the most conservative in its traditions. In the Peninsula (often called Al-Jazeera), by law the men wear the long robe and head cloth ("the national dress") on official occasions and at work. Women wear long dresses and add a covering cloak when in public. Veiling (full face cover) is common in this region, but it is not universal. Veiling is required by law only in Saudi Arabia.

The Peninsula can be divided into three distinct regions: Saudi Arabia, Yemen, and the Arabian Gulf states (also commonly called the Persian Gulf). Saudi Arabia is rich (although less so than before), Yemen is poor, and the Arabian Gulf states are fabulously rich, their societies changing very quickly. Most foreigners particularly love the Gulf states—the people are friendly and hospitable, the cities are flamboyantly sleek and modern, with every convenience—yet there is a desert-Arab charm and simplicity of values that permeates everything. Many foreigners who first come to the Gulf for work are soon trying to extend their stay as long as possible.

Saudi Arabia

Saudi Arabia has always been prominent in the news because of its wealth, its size, its political prominence in the region, and its promotion of conservative Islam. It is a relatively new nation, is mostly desert, and has a population of 31 million (up from 6 million in 1970). The population growth rate was 1.5 percent per year in 2014 (down from 6 percent in 1980),[1] and 30 percent of the people are under age 15.

Prior to unification in 1935 by King Abdel-Aziz Ibn Saud, the region that is now Saudi Arabia was loosely governed and inhabited by numerous Bedouin tribes. The Hashemites controlled the west coast region (Hejaz), with its port of Jeddah and its holy cities, Mecca and Medina. Ibn Saud conquered the region in 1924 (as well as other areas in the 1920s), and his descendants still rule. Also included in the new nation are the central highlands (the Najd) and the Eastern Province, on the oil coast. Saudi Arabia has evolved into a viable nation since its official founding in 1932, and most of the people say they have a Saudi identity.

Two important elements influence Saudi society: the fact that Arabia was the birthplace of Islam, and the discovery of oil in 1938, which led to sudden wealth. Religiosity, conservatism, wealth, and foreign workers—all of these factors are present in Saudi Arabia and result in ever-changing attitudes and social policies.

Muslim pilgrimages to the holy cities of Mecca and Medina occur throughout the year and especially at the annual Hajj pilgrimage season. This is a significant source of income and prestige for the nation; one of the king's titles is "Keeper of the Two Holy Mosques." During the Hajj, in the twelfth Islamic month every year, the entire country is filled with pilgrims, 2 million from all over the world. There are special airports, camping areas, and health facilities. Saudi Arabia is often referred to as the Holy Land; its Islamic history is central to its identity.

Saudi Arabia is the world's leading producer and exporter of oil, which accounts for 90 percent of its export earnings. Although oil was first produced in 1938, the real effects of wealth were not felt until the 1960s and 1970s. The Saudis' immense wealth and their religious activities have made them influential in the Muslim world and particularly in the Arabian Peninsula region (in competition with Iran). The proposals of modernizers inside Saudi Arabia are constantly balanced by demands from the religious authorities with whom the government is allied and whose support it needs.

Until the 1960s, most of the population was nomadic or seminomadic. Because of rapid economic and urban growth, more than 95 percent of the population is now settled, and the people are 83 percent urban. Some cities and oases have densities of more than 1,000 people per square kilo-meter. Arable land is scarce. Saudi Arabia tapped aquifers and became self-sufficient in wheat in the 1980s, even exporting some. But they are phasing out the program because it uses too much water.[2] Saudi Arabia has started searching for farmland in Africa, South America, Southeast Asia, and in the American Southwest, with the goal of growing crops to be shipped home.[3]

The king governs with a Consultative Council (Shura) and decisions are made by consensus, a native model of governing. The ruler also meets citizens in an open session, a *majlis*, and the people have a voice on matters national or personal, which maintains Saudi authenticity. "For the West, the stability and security of Saudi Arabia is the single most important factor in the region . . . . Saudi Arabia continues to be the key to global economic stability. The kingdom has staunchly opposed communism, radical Arab nationalism, radical Khomeini Shi'ism, and the extremes of Al-Qaeda and the IS."[4]

In 2016, there were 10.4 million foreign workers in the kingdom.[5] This compares with a Saudi workforce of 7.3 million.[6] In 2010, a new law was passed to require foreign workers to wait two years before transferring sponsorship to a new employer; this was done to stabilize the job market.[7] The country's goal is to reduce the number of foreigners to less than 20 percent of the population; it was 35 percent in 2016.[8] But it will not happen quickly at the professional level, in that much of the youth population lacks the education and technical skills needed by the private sector. The plan is to replace foreigners with Saudis, especially in management positions.

Young university graduates, who were once assured of good positions, are finding that jobs and upward mobility are far less certain. National income has fallen since the heyday of the 1970s, and there is financial pressure from low oil prices (less than half what they were in 2014) and the expensive war in Yemen. Unemployment was 6 percent in 2016 (29 percent for ages 16 to 29 and 33 percent for women).[9] Three hundred thousand people enter the Saudi workforce every year. Per-capita income in 2017 was a relatively modest $21,000.

The government continues to pursue economic reform and especially diversification of sources of income. King Salman, who assumed the throne in January 2015, has continued spending on job training and educa-tion as part of his reform program. In 2009, the previous king, Abdullah, opened the King Abdullah University of Science and Technology, Saudi Arabia's first coeducational university; all religious and ethnic groups are welcome.[10] It is being built and administered by the Aramco (Arabian-American) oil company, not by the Ministry of Education.*

An important figure in economic reform is Prince Mohammed bin Salman, King Salman's son, who was named Deputy Crown Prince at age 29. He envisions a "sweeping overhaul," which is called "Saudi Vision 2030." His aim is more diversity, more foreign capital, less bureaucracy, and more productive work for Saudis, including women.[11] Part of the plan is to promote four "economic cities," announced in 2006, which will have specialized industries, such as seaport services, agribusiness, minerals, and energy. The hope is to triple non-oil revenue by the year 2020.[12] Since 2015, non-oil revenue increased from $30 billion to $53 billion. "Saudi Vision 2030" has the royal cabinet's backing and aims for $160 billion by 2020 and $267 billion by 2030.[13] The prince has staked his reputation on remaking Saudi Arabia's economy.

King Abdullah initiated an inter-faith dialogue in 2008 to encourage religious tolerance on a global level, "the spread of moderation that embodies the Islamic concept of tolerance."[14] In February 2009, he reshuffled the cabinet to increase the number of moderates holding ministerial and judicial positions, and also appointed the first woman to the cabinet.[15] Saudi Arabia's top religious leadership, the Council of Senior Ulema, issued *fatwas* in 2010 and 2014 denouncing terrorism *and those who finance it* (much private Saudi money has gone to terrorist groups). They stated, "Terrorism has nothing to do with Islam . . . it is nothing more than corruption and criminality rejected by Islamic Sharia law and common sense."[16]

Health and education facilities are both excellent, and have been supported lavishly. Life expectancy was age 40 in 1955; it was age 75 in 2015. The entire country is well provided with schools and universities, as well as hospitals and primary care centers. About 70 percent of the doctors and 50 percent of the nurses are foreign. Literacy is 94 percent (compared with less than 3 percent in the early 1960s). In universities, 50 to 60 percent

---

* Religious police are not allowed on campus.

of the students are women. There is a record number of Saudi students studying in the U.S., about 60,000 in 2015.[17]

Saudi Arabia has been a welfare state. The government subsidized food, water, electricity, and other consumer products, and still provides interest-free loans. But hard times are coming; the country had a deficit of nearly $100 billion in 2016.[18] Subsidies have been cut, and indirect taxes are being considered, such as a value-added tax.[19] The Saudi *riyal* may be devalued. Other costs have recently been increased, such as visas and traffic violations. In the future, there may be taxes on foreign salaries and remittances.[20] In September 2016, salaries, overtime, and vacation time were cut. Top salaries, including ministers, were cut by 20 percent, and ordinary workers lost 11 days' pay when the government moved to the Gregorian calendar.[21] As one Saudi put it, "Life as usual and business as usual can no longer continue."[22]

In this austere Sunni Wahhabi country, there are 2 million to 3 million Shia, who make up 40 to 50 percent of the population of the Eastern Province, and 5 percent of the total population.[23] (This is a highly sensitive issue, and a census has never been taken.) The Shia have limited employment opportunities; they are rarely accepted into national security positions, such as the military and the Ministry of Interior.[24] The number of Shia admitted to universities is also restricted, as are the construction of Shia mosques and schools (the building of Shia mosques was banned for thirty years). No Shia elite has developed.

Many of the skilled and semi-skilled Saudi employees working in the oil industry are Shia, because the oil wealth is in the Eastern Province. In 1979, the Shia rioted, demanding a more equitable share of the money, and there were protests in 2011–12, as well as outrage when a Shia cleric was executed in January 2016. More infrastructure is being built in this region, and in 2003, the government initiated an internal "national dialogue" to give a hearing to minority religious groups; although it is ongoing, not much has changed.[25]

There is no freedom of religion in Saudi Arabia. The government prohibits public practice of non-Muslim religions, and there are no non-Muslim places of worship. (Christians usually meet in private homes.) Saudi Arabia is absolutely unique in the Muslim world in this respect. *Unfortunately, thousands of foreigners have worked in Saudi Arabia, and*

Westerners often see its society and laws as representative of all Arab and Muslim governments. When you read accounts of events, attitudes toward non-Muslims, treatment of women and the like, keep in mind if they occurred in Saudi Arabia; it is very different.

Alcohol, pork products, "pornography" (pictures of nude paintings or statues, photos of women wearing little clothing, non-Muslim religious pictures), and religious artifacts such as Bibles, crosses, or statues of Buddha are all forbidden. Print materials from abroad are subject to censorship. Even Muslims from other countries need time to adjust to the harsh social control.

Saudi Arabia has by far the most severe restrictions on women in the Middle East, if not the world.* It is the only country that has rejected modifications of Islamic law to conform more closely to modern times. Saudi women are fully veiled in public, in a long black cloak (an *abaya*). They could not travel alone or leave the country without permission from male relatives until mid-2017, when the law was finally changed.[26] Due to protests and international criticism, the ban on driving was lifted and will take effect in June 2018. In December 2001, women were issued separate identification cards, so now they have a fully legal identity.[27] In 2008, a government decree was issued, allowing women to stay in a hotel or rent an apartment alone.[28] Women voted for the first time in 2015 in municipal elections.

Few women work outside the home (about 17 percent), although they are over half of the university graduates.[29] Many women are entering the workforce as professionals—scientists, medical personnel, teachers and professors, and working in "women's banks" (ordinarily, Saudis do not work in menial jobs). Usually women do not work side by side with men, and if in the same office or building, there is a separation, with the exception of banks and some hospitals. Some have been granted law licenses.[30] There are women-only shops and businesses.

The government plans to promote women's employment to replace some foreign workers. When they diversify away from oil, it makes little sense to have half of their population staying at home instead of working

---

* The Taliban in Afghanistan would institute even more restrictions on women if they took control.

and contributing. There is a newly emerging class of Saudi professional women. The woman in the king's cabinet said, "The king and the political system are saying that the time has come. There are small steps now. There are giant steps coming."[31] A woman who heads the women's department at the Institute of Public Administration added, "You have to prove that participating in public affairs and taking leadership positions doesn't jeopardize Islamic values and Saudi identity."[32] Many women own their own businesses, often computing companies and retail stores.

During the uprisings in Arab countries in early 2011, there were modest incidents in some cities, predominantly staged by Shia demonstrators. Other rather minor demonstrations focused on labor and infrastructure complaints. These were met with a strong police presence and some arrests, but nobody was killed. It is noteworthy that groups of women also appeared, calling for release of their imprisoned relatives.[33]

On the international scene, Saudi Arabia has come under strong criticism, accused of fostering terrorism, including 9/11, as well as carrying on a war in Yemen against Shia rebels in which many civilians have been killed by aerial and drone attacks. There was a large demonstration in Sana (Yemen) in October 2016, after 140 people were killed and 525 wounded in a single attack.[34] The European Union has imposed an arms embargo on Saudi Arabia, and other European nations have pulled out of agreements.[35] A bill was passed in the U.S. Congress allowing relatives of 9/11 victims to sue the Saudi government. The government cut off funding of terrorist groups some time ago and views terrorism as a threat to the country's stability.[36]

Presumably, Saudi Arabia will buy $110 billion in arms in 2017 from President Donald Trump. President Obama, who had sold them more than $115 billion worth of arms in his eight years in the White House, had refused to sell more.[37] This issue is controversial.

Saudi Arabia (and other nations) is now engaged in a dispute with Qatar, accusing it of supporting terrorist groups and being too close to Iran (Saudi Arabia's rival in the Gulf for potential political power). It has cut diplomatic relations. This is an ongoing issue.

The image of Saudi Arabia to a visitor is one of modern cities with high-rise buildings, huge freeways, luxury shopping malls thronged with people, and fast-food shops, mixed with vistas of the desert, tents, and camels. Saudis like Western consumer goods, and their life continues to change quickly. They are reserved, not quick to welcome foreigners into their private lives, but are very generous and hospitable.

Yemen

Yemen, long isolated from outside contact and influences, is one of the most colorful and tradition-oriented countries in the Arab world. It was called "Arabia Felix" by the Romans and was known as the main source of incense.

Social practices in Yemen have changed relatively slowly since modernization programs were introduced in the late 1960s. Much of the country is rugged and mountainous, and outside of the cities it is a land of tribes and guns. Many of Yemen's 27 million people live in some 150,000 remote villages;[1] only 34 percent of the people are in urban areas. Yemen's architecture is traditional and distinctive, mainly fired-brick high-rise buildings decorated with white geometric designs.* It is the poorest country in the Arab world, but it is spectacularly beautiful, with its mountains, valleys, and terraced hillsides. Unlike the rest of the Peninsula, Yemen has a temperate climate and much of it is green.

For 300 years Yemen was divided into two separate nations, North Yemen and South Yemen (formerly Aden). The king of North Yemen was deposed in 1962; the current regime has been in power since 1976. Aden became independent of Britain in 1967 and was ruled by pro-Soviet Marxists beginning in 1971. In 1990 the two countries united under a broadly socialist government, with the capital in Sanaa. Since the union, numerous clashes have occurred, including a civil war in mid-1994, when the south tried to break away from the dominant north. Another region is the arid Hadramaut, the long coast along the southern rim of the Arabian Peninsula. It still produces incense.

In the north, the most notable division is between Sunni Muslims and the Zaidi (Shia) sect, which dates to the thirteenth century; each group has well-defined geographic boundaries. Yemen is a majority-Sunni country—about 56 percent. The Shia are 44 percent, located mainly in the south and southeast, where the central government has had the least control. Sharia is the basis of law. Islam is taught in public schools, but

---

* The Old City of Sanaa has been inhabited for more than 2,500 years and is a UNESCO world heritage site.

because the government is concerned that unlicensed religious schools deviate from formal educational requirements and promote a militant ideology, it closed more than 4,500 of these institutions and deported foreign students studying there.[2] The government has also monitored mosques for sermons that incite violence.

Yemenis speak Arabic, including some unusual, isolated dialects in remote areas, and educated Yemenis speak English. Yemeni men wear distinctive dress, a sarong-like skirt and a wide belt in which they place the traditional dagger (*jambiyya*). The women wear brightly-colored clothing but in public are completely covered in a black cloak.

In 1993, Yemen conducted the only fully free elections ever held in the Arabian Peninsula. President Ali Abdullah Saleh (a Shia) was elected for a term of seven years. During the "Yemeni Revolution" in 2011, at the time of the Arab Spring, people complained of corruption and nepotism. Saleh stood down, ending his 33-year rule, and in 2012 his vice president, Abd Rabbuh Mansur Hadi, was elected president unopposed. Under Hadi, who was charged with leading a transition to democracy, they created a multiparty national unity government that represented a wide range of political forces from across the country. A constitution was drawn up and a referendum scheduled.

That referendum, which would have ushered in a new era of rule of law for Yemen, never took place. Yemen fell apart in regional, religious, tribal, and political conflicts. In September 2014, militias from the Houthi (Shia) political movement, allied with troops loyal to the deposed Saleh regime and supported and financed by Iran, occupied the capital of Sanaa and placed the president of the transitional government under house arrest (he later fled the country and has set up his government in Aden).[3] The Houthi-Saleh forces then moved across the country, occupying various towns and cities and taking over local governments.

The Houthi-Saleh coup is responsible for the war and destruction in Yemen.[4] It undermined the rights and freedoms Yemenis enjoyed during the transitional period. The forces of the counterrevolution shut down newspapers, satellite channels, and radio stations. The coup leaders banned political parties, human rights organizations, and civic groups. Thousands have been detained, tortured, or killed.

Yemenis who supported the transitional government rose in opposition, and war began in 2014. In response, a coalition of nine Arab and African states, led by Saudi Arabia and supported by the U.S., France, and Britain,* launched a military campaign in 2015 to defeat the Houthi-Saleh forces (who are seen as a proxy for Iran) and to restore Yemen's government.[5] The Saudi coalition has engaged in air campaigns, including controversial drone strikes which killed civilians. The U.N. investigated ten coalition airstrikes between March and October 2016 that killed at least 292 civilians, including some 100 women and children, and the panel found no evidence that the airstrikes had targeted legitimate military objectives.[6]

Antiquities have been ravaged, some structures going back to the sixth century B.C. Much of the destruction is because of battles. There is no money or manpower to monitor this.

In addition to local forces, both Al-Qaeda and the Islamic State have a strong and expanding presence, especially in the southern and eastern areas. Al-Qaeda† and the IS (both Sunni groups) are fighting the Houthi forces (on the same side as the Saudi coalition and Western allies, but they also target each other). The IS has launched suicide attacks that target Shia mosques and civilians.[7]

The general situation in Yemen indicates that the phenomenon of al-Qaeda or Islamic State-style jihadism is likely to expand, whether in its current shape or in new forms and under new names.[8] Saudi Arabia's support of rebels fighting Houthis ironically strengthens Al-Qaeda and the IS; some rebels fight alongside them, since they have the same Houthi enemy.[9]

Extremism is basically impossible to control in Yemen—there are 1,900 miles of unpatrolled coast, and another thousand miles of wide-open frontier.[10] One notable event was the bombing of the *U.S.S. Cole* in 2000. In early 2017, Houthi rebels attacked a Saudi warship, killing two sailors. Afterward, the *U.S.S. Cole* was again sent to patrol the area to increase U.S. presence.[11]

Al-Qaeda's attempt to create its own emirate failed when, in 2015, it took control of Al-Mukalla, a seaport in oil-rich Hadramaut. Pro-government troops, supported by UAE troops, recaptured the city in April 2016. There have been efforts at ceasefire talks to end the war, but in January 2017, President Hadi refused to meet to discuss terms.

---

* Included in the coalition are Bahrain, Kuwait, the United Arab Emirates, Egypt, Jordan, Morocco, and Sudan. Qatar recently withdrew.

† Al-Qaeda is also referred to as AQAP (Al-Qaeda in the Arabian Peninsula).

The death toll of civilians stood at 100,000 in 2017. Far more severe, however, is the humanitarian disaster that has developed throughout Yemen. Prior to the 2014 war, Yemen had numerous problems that are now exacerbated by the conflict—high population growth, food and water scarcity, female illiteracy, widespread poverty, and economic stagnation. About half of Yemen's people live in areas affected by the conflict. As of 2017, an estimated 3 million people were internally displaced. The U.N. estimated in early 2017 that *over two-thirds of the population were in urgent need of aid,* and reported that *"an astounding 10.3 million Yemenis . . . require immediate assistance to save or sustain their lives [and] at least two million people need emergency food assistance to survive."*[12]

About 14 million people cannot access healthcare services due to drug shortages and conflict-related destruction, and there was a cholera outbreak in late 2016. It had affected over 1 million people in late-2017 and was called the worst cholera outbreak in the world. In the city of Taiz, more than 350,000 people are in urgent need of medical care.[13] The port of Hodeida, which handles 60 percent of Yemen's commercial traffic, is under a Saudi naval blockade; it supplies the capital city of Sanaa (population almost 2 million). Food, medical supplies, and fuel are all affected. Houthi rebels are using Hodeida to import munitions, and much of the infrastructure of the port is destroyed. n late 2017, Saudi Arabia closed off Yemen by air, sea, and land.*

Yemen's health facilities are among the least developed in the Arab world. Infant mortality is still very high (55 per 1,000 births) and life expectancy is only age 64. In general, sanitation is poor and awareness of general health practices low. Healthcare is also hampered by a severe shortage of qualified practitioners, particularly in rural areas. Nearly 2.2 million Yemeni children need urgent aid, as malnutrition is at an "all-time high," a UNICEF report claims.[15] The figures represent a 200 percent increase from 2014, with severe acute malnutrition affecting 462,000 children.

An estimated 200,000 Somali refugees are living in several Yemeni cities; more than 26,000 have returned to Somalia.[16]

---

* A cultural note: Poetry is being effectively used as part of the resistance to the government. Poetry is used at conflict mediations, weddings, funerals, and other social gatherings. It spreads messages and increases influence.[14]

The adult male literacy rate reached 70 percent in 2015, compared with 54 percent in 2004. Now 3 million children are out of school, almost 2 million since the start of the conflict. At the beginning of 2016, 1,600 schools remained closed due to insecurity, physical damage, or use as shelters.[17]

Yemen's economy has contracted sharply. About 54 percent of the population was below the poverty line in early 2017, and the unemployment rate was 27 percent. Production of oil fell by 77 percent in 2015.[18] Per capita income fell from $3,900 in 2014 to $2,500 in 2016, and inflation in 2015 reached 30 percent.[19] Public investment has come to a complete stop.

The climate of Yemen has always made intensive agriculture possible, much of it on terraced land, but only 2.9 percent of the land is arable. Cotton and coffee are sources of revenue (the first coffee in Europe was imported from Yemen, probably through the port of Mocha). Traditional skills include construction and stonemasonry, carpentry, and metalworking.

The former South Yemen has a semi-arid climate, and the people have traditionally been fishermen and merchants (in the coastal area), as well as farmers and herders. The south's geographical location has been advantageous for commerce with countries of the Indian Ocean.

Yemen's great hope for the future was once oil, first exported in 1993. In 2000, oil constituted nearly 97 percent of total exports; in 2011, the percentage dropped to 70 percent. Before the conflict in 2014, oil was 65 percent of government revenue. Oil resources are declining, and two major fields will be drained in ten years.[20] The government began a program to diversify the economy in 2006. In 2009, Yemen exported its first liquefied natural gas as part of this diversification effort, and it has grown to become a major export. However, since the second quarter of 2015, oil and gas exports have stopped.

About 2 million Yemenis work abroad, more than half of them in Saudi Arabia, and in 2013 they sent home $2 billion.[21] Remittances constitute an important part of Yemen's economy, second only to oil and gas. Yemen also depends on foreign aid.

Yemen faces a looming problem of inadequate water; indeed, it is on the verge of drying out. This water crisis is long-standing; as tension over water resources reached a fever pitch, Yemen began to fracture along sectarian and regional lines, which finally contributed to the conflict in 2014, the first to be called a "climate-driven war."[22] The capital city of Sanaa, which has depended on nearly-depleted aquifers, may run dry within a decade or sooner. Water is transported by truck, and the price keeps going up; only 40 percent of the houses are connected to the municipal water supply. Groundwater is dwindling, and the rural economy could disappear within a generation.[23]

Yemen's water is 99 percent from illegal wells, and what water there is, is seriously mismanaged. Yemen cannot afford desalinization, and other methods have not been successful. Rainwater is not being collected. An estimated 60 percent of water is lost through leaks in antiquated equipment.[24] Lack of access to fresh water is a major factor leading to illness and malnutrition.

Productivity and prosperity are also affected by the social custom (mostly among men) of chewing a leaf called *qat*, which produces a feeling of mild euphoria. Qat is chewed every day, beginning in the early afternoon. Unfortunately, much fertile land is devoted to growing this plant, and it consumes more than half of Yemen's scarce water.[25] It is widely grown as a cash crop, instead of food. Yemen now imports 90 percent of its food.

Yemen faces a severe problem in its population growth. It was estimated at 2.34 percent per year in 2017, and the fertility rate is 3.77 children per woman.[26] The population tripled since 1980, and will triple again by 2060. Fully 43 percent of the people are under age 15.

Women in north Yemen are fully veiled in public and many are uneducated. Only 7 percent overall work outside the home for pay; of those, 21 percent of the working women have secondary degrees and 48 percent have a university degree.[27] Younger women, especially if unmarried, are interested in pursuing a career and want equality with men. In former South Yemen, women were granted equal status under the then-Marxist government (the only communist government in the Middle East) and were recruited into many work fields. Women in southern Yemen are more integrated into society than in any other Arabian Peninsula country.

But Yemeni women have a long way to go. The large majority of women over 25 or 30 are illiterate, and the female-to-male income ratio is 30:100.[28] Many women do not have identification cards or voter status. Currently, there are no women in parliament.

Ravaged by war, climate change, water shortage, depletion of oil, and government mismanagement, Yemen is already in many ways a failed state. It faces economic collapse and will require immense assistance just to provide for its people's basic needs in years to come. One political analyst has asserted that Yemen is not a nation-state at all, and never was. He states, "Yemen has functioned for three millennia as a fluid equilibrium between central authority, tribal autonomy, and differing cultural and religious allegiances. Identity and political loyalty have nothing to do with shared institutional nationalism, but rather reflect responsibility to family, clan, and tribe."[29] Another analyst writes, "One should look at Yemen as a geographic place that is always in a state of civil war; it is merely a question of intensity . . . . The Yemenis are never going to solve their differences, but from time to time, they live with them. The West and the Gulf just need to make certain that those differences stay in Yemen and are not exploited by outsiders."[30]

The outlook is not encouraging.

The Arabian Gulf States

The five Arabian Gulf states—Kuwait, Bahrain, Qatar, the United Arab Emirates (UAE,) and Oman—are situated along the eastern coast of the Arabian Peninsula. Kuwait became independent of England in 1961, and the rest were under British administration until 1971.

These countries, as well as Saudi Arabia, are joined in the Gulf Cooperative Council (GCC), which promotes economic integration in the region. Income is high and population is low but rapidly increasing. Citizens pay no income taxes or import taxes, and for citizens, corporate taxes are non-existent or very low. Most countries can afford to generously subsidize many of the people's living costs. This is a stark difference from other Arab countries, most of which are poor.

It is a dramatic change from the poverty of the past. The traditional sources of income had been trade, herding, fishing, pearling, and piracy. Everything has been turned upside down in the last fifty or sixty years since the discovery of oil and natural gas.

For the Gulf states, there have been frightening political developments, and all at once: the street revolutions of 2011; the rise of Muslim Brotherhood parties; the turmoil in some countries that has spawned jihadist groups and militias; the growing influence of Iran; and concerns that the U.S. is trying to disengage itself from the Middle East.[1]

Although this is the most conservative region of the Arab world (along with Saudi Arabia), a few women serve in parliament and as ministers in the governments. Women's rights are receiving much publicity.

Many American and British universities are opening branches in the Gulf states: Qatar, Abu Dhabi, Dubai, Sharjah and Ras Al-Khaymah (UAE), and Oman.

Kuwait

Although Kuwait is small, it is an important country, mostly because of its vast oil wealth, the basis of its economic and political influence among the Arab states. It gained its independence from Britain in 1961 and has since been ruled by the Al Sabah royal family. Kuwait has had a National Assembly and parliamentary elections off and on since 1962, most recently in 2016. Fifty delegates are elected, and 15 appointed by the emir. Power lies in the hands of the ruler, the emir, who has suspended the Assembly numerous times over the years.

The opposition (Islamist, nationalist, and liberal) won almost half of the 50 seats in the National Assembly in November 2016. Although 15 women ran for election, only one woman was elected.[*,1] Political parties are illegal.

There are about 3 million people in Kuwait, of whom the majority are non-Kuwaitis (about 450,000 were Palestinian until the first Gulf War in 1991, when they were expelled; there were less than 40,000 living there in 2012).[†] Many expatriates are from the U.S., Britain, and South Asia. The government has prioritized replacing foreign workers with Kuwaitis in professional and managerial jobs.

In many ways, Kuwaiti society is like other Gulf states and Saudi Arabia—it is tribal, religious, and conservative. About 65 percent of the Kuwaitis are Sunni, and 35 percent are Shia. Their practice of Islam is not as austere as that in Saudi Arabia.

The dominant fact of life in Kuwait is the government's enormous oil-based wealth. Production of oil began in 1946, and within 15 years,

---

* In 2006, women were granted the right to run for office, but none won in 2006 or 2008. Finally, in May 2009, four women were elected. In 2012, no women won seats.
† The Ministry of Education announced in early 2017 that it would end this restriction and hire hundreds of Palestinians to teach mathematics and science in its schools.[2]

poverty was virtually eradicated.[3] Like Saudi Arabia, Kuwait is a welfare state.

Oil sales had long been 95 percent of government income. Due to lowered oil prices, Kuwait's oil revenue dropped by 45 percent in the first eleven months of 2015.[4] Kuwait has the reputation of being the shrewdest and most sophisticated of the major Arab overseas investors, and per-capita income is still one of the highest in the world. But with a fall in oil prices the government is considering cutting government spending, raising the cost of public services, and introducing taxes for the first time.[5] Government spending declined 17 percent in 2015, and was held at that rate in 2016. The subsidy in electricity is being cut, and a 10 percent corporate tax is considered for 2019.[6] The deficit in 2016 was 13 percent, the first deficit in 16 years; there was a $45 billion surplus in 2014.

Another factor that will dominate Kuwaiti affairs for many years is the Iraqi invasion of 1990, followed by the first Gulf War. Although the economic effects have largely been overcome, the psychological consequences will be felt for a generation.

Kuwait cooperated with the U.S. in the second Gulf War, and when it invaded Iraq in 2003, Kuwait was the main staging area for military preparations. At one point in early 2005, there were 30,000 American military personnel in the country. The Kuwaitis are the most pro-American in the Arab world; they still feel gratitude for their liberation. Even they have been shaken by recent events, however (Palestine, Iraq, Afghanistan), and many are beginning to reconsider their unqualified political support.

Progress in health, education, infrastructure, and economic development has completely changed the Kuwaiti way of life in the past sixty years. Kuwait City is modern and filled with malls, high-rises, and expensive compounds. The people are 98 percent urbanized. The literacy rate is now 95 percent (Kuwait had something of a head start in development, compared with the other Gulf states). Healthcare is superb. Kuwaitis have everything money can buy.

Virtually all water comes from seawater desalinization plants, an expenditure impossible for governments with less money and more people. The government encourages large families, and the birth rate is 2.6 children per woman; 26 percent of the population is under age 14.

Women in Kuwait are the most emancipated in the Gulf region.[7]

They are generally veiled in public, although this is easing up. Many are active in education and commerce, and even in the police force. They are not prohibited from working in the same environment as men. Women currently receive two-thirds of the bachelor's degrees granted each year. About half of them work.

Kuwaiti women can travel, drive, or work without male permission, and they can hold senior government positions. They may work at night (which was previously forbidden).[8] They attained the right to vote in 2005. They are, however, restrained by Islamic law, although some issues are governed by civil or administrative courts.

Kuwaitis are cordial to foreigners, although they prefer private and family social circles.

Bahrain

Bahrain, which is an island in the Arabian Gulf, is the most modernized of the Gulf states. It was the first to produce oil; its production and refining bring in about 86 percent of the nation's income, but this is decreasing. Endowed with smaller oil resources than its neighbors, the government has diversified to dry-dock ship services, aluminum production, and light engineering. It has turned to petroleum processing and refining and has transformed itself into an international banking center, so now Bahrain has one of the most advanced and diversified economies in the Gulf region. Bahrain entered into a Free Trade Agreement with the U.S. in 2006.[1] It is the headquarters of the U.S. Navy's Fifth Fleet.

But Bahrain is the one country in the Gulf that has serious internal opposition and subsequently, a damaged human rights record. It is 70 percent Shia, ruled by a Sunni emir; it is the only Peninsular country with a Shia majority. Bahrain became the center of the news during the Arab Spring demonstrations in early 2011. There was a Shia uprising, demanding a new constitution, release of Shia prisoners, and an end to discrimination by the emir's government. The uprising was put down by force, with the assistance of the Saudi Arabian military. The state of emergency was lifted in June 2011, and foreign troops withdrew.[2]

With the events in early 2011, Bahrain lost some of its luster as a modern center for promoting arts and culture. International image is important to Bahrain's economy, and it was damaged. The Shia Islamist Al-Wefaq opposition party was dissolved by the government, accused of creating "an environment for terrorism, extremism, and violence."[3] It is essentially outside the political system, and social tensions are exacerbated. The Shia community is subject to policing because the government suspects Iranian connections.*[4] Bahrain is becoming increasingly dependent on Saudi Arabia. Promised investigation into acts by security officials never took place. Many opposition leaders are in jail, and there is a crackdown on dissent.

Bahrain's population is 1.4 million, and it is 89 percent urbanized, making it one of the most densely populated countries in the Middle East. The primary religious groups are Muslim (70 percent), Christian (15 percent), and Hindu (10 percent). About 90 percent of the people live in two principal cities. In 2014, the number of foreigners was greater than the number of citizens, 52 percent. This has brought calls for limiting the influx of foreigners, who are mostly from South and East Asia, as well as from the U.S. and Britain.[6] Unemployment is officially 3.7 percent, but among the young it is closer to 5.6 percent and expected to rise. It is also higher among the Shia.

Bahrain was a British protectorate from 1861 until its independence in 1971. It was ruled by an emir, and its first elected parliament was in 1973. In 1975, the National Assembly dramatically attempted to legislate the end of the Al-Khalifa family's rule and also to expel the U.S. Navy. In reaction, the emir dissolved the National Assembly, and in 1992 he appointed a consultative council (Shura), which has 40 members, to balance the elected 40-member Chamber of Deputies. There have been many incidents since the 1990s stemming from the disaffection of the Shia majority. There is also concern about the rise of Iranian influence and arms among the Shia.

The current ruler since March 1999, Shaikh Hamad bin Isa Al-Khalifa, pronounced in February 2002 that Bahrain had become a constitutional

---

* The connection with Iran was reinforced in April 2017 when a bomb factory and arsenal were seized at a villa; it is a type of threat that has occurred sporadically over three years. A threat of heavily armed, militant cells is emerging, and the U.S. is more willing to overlook repressive behavior in the service of maintaining a strong defensive shield against future Iranian aggression.[5] To Iran, Bahrain represents a loss of Persian influence in the Gulf.

monarchy (rather than a heredity emirate) and changed his status from emir to king. The first elections in nearly thirty years were held at that time, with women being allowed to vote and run for office. Parliamentary elections were held in 2006, with the Shia opposition attaining 40 percent of the vote, and 2010, when the Shia opposition party attained almost half of the seats.*,8 In 2014, when a coalition of opposition parties boycotted the election, a political impasse ensued, with neither side able to compromise. In the election, the Sunni electorate participated strongly.[9] Elections are next slated for 2018.

Bahrain's small size and population have contributed to its rapid modernization. Life expectancy is age 78. Literacy is 91 percent. Per-capita annual income is $50,300. Bahrain is working to establish itself as a center for higher education and has two universities.

Bahrain imports almost all its food; agriculture represents less than 1 percent of its income. The land is almost entirely desert, and the people traditionally had made their living from the sea. The economy of the country has been affected by lower oil prices. Bahrain entered 2017 without an adopted budget. One official stated, "Beautiful days are over, Bahrain is to witness lean years."[10]

Despite Bahrain's lack of money, it purchased arms from the U.S. in 2015 when the Obama administration lifted restrictions relating to human rights (for which it was criticized). The Trump administration went further, with an $8 billion sale of military and industrial deals, with no conditions, after which the Bahraini government moved to dissolve a moderate, secular opposition party; restore the power of a domestic intelligence agency to make arrests, and authorize military trials of civilians.[11] Some have said that these purchases will help silence U.S. criticism. An overall problem is that if Bahrain becomes destabilized, it could trigger a sectarian conflict that Iran could exploit.

The city of Manama is pretty and prosperous. Bahraini men generally wear a traditional robe. For women, the dress code is more relaxed than elsewhere. They may wear a head cover and a black cloak, but it is common to see foreign as well as local women wearing modern (but modest) clothing as well.

---

* They later resigned their seats in protest because of government repression of demonstrations.[7] A special by-election had to be held.

Bahraini women, many of whom are well educated, constitute about 29 percent of the workforce, up from 17 percent in 1991.

Bahrain is a favorite tourist destination in the Gulf. It is connected to the mainland by a causeway to Saudi Arabia. It is very liberal and has an active nightlife.

Qatar

Qatar (pronounced KA-tar) is a small peninsula, fabulously rich in both oil and gas; it is one of the richest countries in the world. The population is 96 percent urbanized, and 80 percent of the people live in the capital city, Doha. Since the discovery of oil in 1949, Qatar's population has exploded: 100,000 in 1970; 350,000 in 1991; 840,000 in 2011; and 2.3 million in 2017. But these numbers are high because 85 percent of the residents are foreigners, including white-collar professionals, construction workers, and service personnel. Because of the huge influx of male laborers, women constitute just 28 percent of the population.[1] There are about 300,000 native Qatari citizens.

Until the discovery of oil, the Qatari people were engaged in fishing, pearling, and trading, many living in dire poverty. The ruling family signed a treaty with Britain in 1868, and it was a British protectorate from 1916 until it gained independence in 1971. The emir transferred power to his son, Tamim bin Hamad Al-Thani, in June 1995. The constitution was overwhelmingly approved by referendum in 2003. The constitution created a legislative body, the Consultative Council, to be two-thirds elected by universal suffrage, and one-third appointed by the emir. The first general elections for the Consultative Assembly were scheduled to be held in Qatar for the second half of 2013 but were postponed in June 2013 and again in June 2016. The emir has extended the influential Advisory Council's term for another three years, effectively postponing legislative elections until at least 2019.[2]

There is a municipal council election in which citizens vote. It was started in 1999, and in 2015 the fifth election was held. Women won two of the twenty-nine seats.[3]

Oil, gas, and derivative products bring in 90 percent of export earnings, and in 2016 Qatar had the world's highest GDP per capita ($129,726). Qatar always had a high annual economic growth rate (an all-time high of 32.90 percent in the first quarter of 2010, 14 percent in 2011,) but with the drop in oil prices, the rate in 2016 was 2.6 percent, and in 2017 it was estimated at 3.4 percent.[4] Although only a little over 1 percent of the land is arable, Qatar produces half of the vegetables it consumes. Many people maintain large herds of goats, sheep, camels, and cattle in the desert, and fishing is still a mainstay.

Health programs are numerous and lavishly funded, and life expectancy is now age 79. Qatar had a phenomenal population growth rate of over 6 percent annually between 1990 and 1998, and the government encourages large families. The national growth rate is now down to 1.7 percent, with 21 percent of the people under age 15.[5] The average is 1.9 children per woman.

A social problem is the condition of migrant workers, who face travel restrictions, passport retention, and lack of freedom to change jobs.

Qatar is pushing education strongly. Through the Qatar Foundation, an initiative sponsored by the ruler's wife, Qatar created Education City, which hosts several American and European universities and many training institutes, so that fewer of its students have to study abroad. Literacy is 97 percent. Unemployment is only 0.3 percent.

The population of Qatar is 77.5 percent Muslim, 8.5 percent Christian, and 14 percent "other." Of the Muslims, 80 percent are Sunni and 20 percent Shia. There has been no sectarian tension, and over 80 nationalities live in Qatar.

Qatar is comparatively liberal, certainly in comparison with Saudi Arabia. Women can drive, and many are well educated. They are about 51 percent of the workforce (they do not work because of need), which is the highest percentage in the Gulf.[6] The social status laws are still discriminatory toward women in relation to marriage, divorce, inheritance, child custody, and nationality.[7] Women usually cover in a black cloak when in public, but they are free to dress otherwise. Women first voted in 1999 and can run for elective office. There is a strong emphasis on equality and human rights, and there is a National Human Rights Committee. (This does not pertain to third-world laborers, however, who have little protection and poor living conditions.)

Qatar has influence far beyond its size and population. It has been energetic in attracting foreign institutions, and its most prominent attribute is its influential satellite television station Al-Jazeera, which is seen throughout the Middle East. The ruler increased freedom of the press in 1998, ending censorship, and has generously funded Al-Jazeera. The government does not regulate its content and it has been critical of several Arab regimes. Qatar is slated to host the soccer World Cup in 2022.

Here is a good summary about Qatar:

> For years, the tiny, energy-rich country of Qatar has carved out a niche in the Arab world by trying to be everything to everyone. It houses an American military base and floods the region's airwaves with its influential media, all while keeping close ties to Iran and a wide selection of Islamist movements.[8]

Qatar is the location of the U.S. Central Command's Forward Headquarters, at the Al Udeid Air Base, the largest U.S. base in the Middle East.

Qatar suddenly dominated the news when, in June 2017, seven countries broke off diplomatic relations; these included Saudi Arabia, the UAE, Bahrain, Egypt, Yemen, the Maldives, and the government in eastern Libya. Qatar has been criticized for years for its support of the Muslim Brotherhood and Hamas, and other allied Islamist groups, as well as back-channel relations with Iran. Al-Jazeera has also been an irritant.

In 2014, Saudi Arabia, Bahrain, the UAE, and Egypt withdrew their ambassadors in protest, citing Islamists as "terrorists."[9] Qatar persisted in supporting these groups, even as it attempted to strengthen its relationship with the U.S. and its Gulf Cooperation Council neighbors.

It was Saudi Arabia that initiated the break, cutting off land, air, and sea travel to Qatar. This was shortly after a visit to Saudi Arabia from President Trump, and it is possible that the Saudis felt emboldened by his remarks. Trump's support of the Saudis has created a problem for U.S. efforts to build broader coalitions in the region and for stability needed for military operations against IS (it is alleged that Trump did not know what he was unleashing).[10] Rather than having "united the entire Muslim world in a way that it really hasn't been in many years," as he claimed, Trump precipitated a regional crisis. The Saudis and others now anticipate "no pushback" from the U.S. on human rights and the war in Yemen.

Further adding to the tension was Qatar's payment of $1 billion in ransom to Islamist groups for 26 Qataris, including members of the royal family, taken hostage while hunting in Iraq and held for 16 months.[11] In April 2017, Qatar paid a group of Iraqi militia that was said to have ties with Iran. Also exacerbating the situation was the hacking of a news site misquoting the Qatari emir.

It appears that Qatar is settling in for a long standoff, and shows no signs of conceding. They have airlifted food and even herds of dairy cattle. Qatar has received support from Europe, Turkey, and also U.S. Secretary of State Rex Tillerson.[12]

Israel has made overtures toward some of the Gulf states, including Qatar, in order to undercut Iranian influence in the Middle East. The Gulf states are unlikely to recognize Israel's right to exist, but countering Iranian influence through informal economic and security cooperation, including military action, is likely to continue. (In Saudi Arabia in 2015, 53 percent of the Saudis viewed Iran as Saudi Arabia's biggest enemy, while 18 percent named Israel.)[13] Qatar severed relations after Israel's attack on Gaza, but is considering restoring them.[14] It aspires to become a neutral world power.

The social organization in Qatar is still tribal and strongly family-centered; many people live in compounds that hold several related families. Qataris are friendly to foreigners, who enjoy the country and the society.

United Arab Emirates (UAE)

The United Arab Emirates is a federation of small territories that was created as an independent nation in 1971–1972 by uniting seven of the Trucial States (so called by the British, to replace the infamous name "Pirate Coast"). The combined population is 9.6 million. UAE citizens comprise about 20 percent of the population (the rest are foreign workers), and 40 percent of them live in Abu Dhabi. Dubai is the largest city in the Emirates, with a population of 2.7 million. The country is 86 percent urban, and nearly 85 percent of the population lives in three emirates, Abu Dhabi, Dubai, and Sharjah.

Abu Dhabi is by far the largest of the former territories, comprising 87 percent of the UAE's total area. Abu Dhabi is the capital city, and Dubai is the main port and has become a prosperous commercial center for the whole Gulf region. Dubai created the Dubai International Financial Centre in 1994, intended to become a regional center on a par with New York and London.[1] It has indeed become a regional financial hub and is a free zone and headquarters for international financial firms, and it sits on a 110-acre campus. It has its own legal system, and it is also known for some whimsical expenditures, such as an indoor ski slope, the tall Burj Al-Arab tower, and the creation of residential islands,[2] which are highly successful. In 2016, its occupancy rate was 98 percent.

The UAE was ranked at the top spot in the Middle East in the 2017 Index of Economic Freedom, and eighth globally.[3]

Abu Dhabi began oil production in 1962, Dubai in 1969, and Shar-jah in 1973. Life has been transformed—former fishing villages are now modern cities filled with high-rise buildings and superhighways. The other four small emirates (Ajman, Umm Al-Quwain, Ras Al-Khaimah, and Fujairah), each with a small population, have no oil and are changing more slowly. The entire country has been transformed.

Per-capita income is the second highest in the Gulf (after Qatar), at $67,167 in 2016.[4] The UAE has the most diversified economy in the GCC. Oil and natural gas once accounted for more than 85 percent of the government's revenues, but with diversification of the economy into construction, manufacturing (metals and textiles), and a large services sector, oil exports contributed only 37 percent of the GDP in 2015. Service industries contributed 52 percent.[5]

Previously, people made their living from fishing, pearling, oasis-farming, and animal herding. Despite the prosperity, nearly 20 percent of the citizens were below the poverty line in 2011 (latest figures).[6] Tourism contributed $64 billion to the UAE's economy in 2016, and this figure is set to almost double over the next 10 years. All the emirates earn income through the sale of exotic postage stamps.

Ambitious programs have been established in education, health, and agricultural production. The UAE wants to preserve the environment and achieve a balance between economic and social development.[7] Vision 2021 focuses on quality of air, water, and clean energy. It also aims for superb infrastructure, telecommunication, and suitable housing for eligible UAE nationals.

Literacy is 94 percent, and life expectancy 77.5 years. The population growth rate is 2.5 percent; there is an average of 2.3 children per woman.[8]

Women in the UAE are veiled in public and most participate little in public life, but this will change with the next generation because women's education through university is strongly encouraged by the government. More women than men are enrolled in universities. The number of women in the workforce has grown to 33 percent, compared with 2.2 percent in

1975.[9] They constitute 75 percent of the positions in the education and health sectors. Forty-seven percent of working women are professionals, and 12.6 percent are senior managers. There are eight female ministers in the government.[10]

The UAE has three women ambassadors, to Finland, Denmark, and Latvia.[11] Women have joined the armed forces, the police, and the customs agency. There are businesswomen's councils in Abu Dhabi and Dubai, with more than 12,000 members. There is also a Gender Balance Council and a Dubai Women's Establishment.

The UAE has a Federal National Council, with 20 members appointed by the rulers and 20 indirectly elected by an electoral college. In 2006, a limited number of citizens were eligible to vote, including women. In the 2015 election, the number of voters was expanded; 35 percent of eligible voters turned out to vote, and 19 men and one woman were elected.[12] The UAE is expanding to universal suffrage gradually, with the intention of including women.

Women remain subject to discrimination in law and in practice, notably in matters of marriage and divorce, inheritance, and child custody. They are inadequately protected against violence within the family. Sharia law applies in family affairs.

The average length of schooling in the UAE is 13 years, higher than elsewhere in the Arab world. There are 16 foreign universities in the UAE, including American and British institutions; it seems that everyone is getting on the bandwagon. A controversial issue at present is how to balance teaching in Arabic and English; Arabic is the heritage, but 30 percent of the university's budget is used for remedial English courses—English is essential for technical subjects. Some UAE students are not adequately skilled in written Standard Arabic, and some even have problems speaking the local dialect.[13]

The UAE is known for tolerance; there are more than 200 nationalities and 40 churches, as well as Hindu and Sikh temples. The constitution guarantees equal rights, and many Hindus and Sikhs have moved there to escape persecution elsewhere.[14] The country is 80 percent Sunni Muslim, 16 percent Shia, and 4 percent Christian and Hindu.

There was a petition in March 2011 (at the time of the Arab Spring) by about 100 Emirati activists and intellectuals calling for political reform, including establishing a parliament and expanding the electorate. In April, four activists were arrested for these criticisms of the government. All seven emirates are ruled autocratically.

During the world economic downturn of 2009–2010, Dubai was hard hit by depressed real estate prices and lacked sufficient cash to meet debt obligations. In December 2009, Dubai received a $10 billion loan from Abu Dhabi, and by now the economy has rebounded.[15] Recently, however, low oil prices have prompted the UAE to take steps to reduce its social spending, including eliminating fuel subsidies in August 2015.[16]

The UAE depends heavily on foreign workers, who comprise 88 percent of the workforce, two thirds of them from south Asia.[17] After a walkout staged by thousands of laborers in Dubai in 2006, the government has regulated midday breaks (because of the heat), and improved health benefits and living conditions. The Labor Ministry even paid back wages when companies did not. The government is working to upgrade labor standards in order to better protect foreign workers.[18] Three new labor rules issued by the Ministry of Labour include ministry-approved contracts, conditions for terminating employees, and labor permits to work for new employers.

The UAE's strategic plan for the next few years focuses on economic diversification and creating more job opportunities for nationals through improved education and increased private sector employment (they are unwilling to do manual work). Currently, the unemployment rate is 3.7 percent, but 12 percent among youth.[19]

The UAE has been a major contributor of emergency relief to regions in need, especially in Africa. Established in 1971, the Abu Dhabi Fund for Development has financed 442 development projects in 76 countries around the world since its inception.[20]

Western foreigners enjoy living in the UAE, and many have been there for many years. In a poll, young Arabs have said that if they leave their country, the UAE is their first choice as a destination.

Oman

Oman is situated in the southeast corner of the Arabian Peninsula, in a strategic location at the entrance to the Arabian Gulf. It is larger than the other Gulf countries, but not as rich. Oman is ruled by a sultan and is a monarchy.

Oman's population is about 3.6 million, of whom about 1 million are foreigners (over half of them from southern India). Thirty-one percent of the population is under age 15, 66 percent is age 15 to 64, and only 3 percent is over age 65.[1] The Omani citizens are 85 percent Arabians, and the rest are of Zanzibari, Baluchi, or south Asian and African origin. Seventy percent of the Omanis are citizens. The people are 75 percent Ibadhi Muslim (a sect that is neither Sunni nor Shia), and 25 percent other Muslim or Hindu.[2] Almost everyone speaks Arabic; some non-Arabic Semitic languages are still spoken in the far south. Tribalism is still the main source of identity for the Omani people.

Oman then has had ties with Britain since 1891 (although it was not formally a protectorate); the British came in because of piracy and remained a strong presence until 1971.

The discovery of oil in 1967 exacerbated impatience with the old sultan, who was reactionary and oppressive: he sanctioned slavery, and the Omani people were beset with poverty, disease, illiteracy, and social restrictions (for example, a prohibition against smoking and travel inside the country). All this had caused 600,000 people to go into exile. In 1970, the sultan was deposed by his British-educated son Qaboos, who still rules and is popular. He began the extensive modernization of the country.

Oman saw dramatic changes in health, education, and commercial development. Electricity, telephones, radio, television, public education, roads, hospitals, public health programs—all are new since 1970. The U.N. Development Program (UNDP) listed Oman as the most-improved nation over the last 40 years from among 135 countries worldwide.[3]

Oman does not have extensive oil reserves like its Gulf neighbors, and supplies are dwindling—oil accounted for 46 percent of export earnings in 2015.[4] Oman has actively pursued a development plan that focuses on diversification, industrialization, and privatization, with the objective of reducing the oil sector's contribution to GDP to 9 percent by 2020. Unlike elsewhere in the Gulf, Oman is only 77 percent urbanized. About 30 percent of the people work in oasis agriculture and in fishing. Although Oman has a considerable amount of potentially arable land, it lacks manpower and water. In some remote interior areas, the people have little contact with the rest of the country. Agriculture accounts for only 1 percent of the country's exports.

The sultan has instituted a development plan called "Vision 2020," which calls for diversification of the economy by the year 2020, because the oil is estimated to run out in five to fifteen years.[5] There is much ongoing domestic and foreign investment in the non-oil sector, primarily gas-based industries and tourism. Oman entered a free-trade agreement with the U.S. in January 2009. Per-capita income was $43,700 in 2016.[6]

The government has given high priority to education, to develop a domestic workforce, essential for Oman's economic and social progress. Sultan Qaboos University was opened in 1996, and there are many colleges of technology, science, finance, and nursing. Scholarships are awarded for study abroad. In 2017, there was a ratio of 1.23 women for every man enrolled in higher education; even in engineering, 52 percent are female.[7] Thirty-two percent of the women are in the workforce. Literacy is 94 percent (up from 18 percent in 1970), and the expected length of schooling is 12 years. Unemployment was 7.2 percent in 2014.

Because of improved healthcare, Oman's growth rate has been truly amazing. The population tripled between 1965 and 1990. The growth rate is now about 2 percent per year (down from 3.5 percent). Thirty percent of the population is under age 14. The average is 2.8 children per woman (down from 6). Life expectancy is 74 years. Healthcare is free.

The sultan rules alone, with an elected advisory body, the 84-member Consultative Council, and an appointed Council of State. There are no political parties. The sultan also serves as prime minister, defense minister, finance minister, foreign affairs minister, and chair of the central bank. Legislation is in the form of royal decree issued by the sultan. Seven women were elected to the Consultative Council in 2016.[8] Members of the Council of State are appointed by the sultan from the government, the military, the private sector, tribal leaders, and regional interests (including nine women).[9] Oman was the first GCC state to grant women voting rights; the sultan established universal suffrage in 2003.[10] The country has three female ministers and two women ambassadors (to the Netherlands and the U.S.).

Oman has often gone its own way politically—it has not directly intervened in regional conflicts such as in Yemen or Syria. It did not downgrade its relationship with Iran as the other GCC states did during the

Saudi-Iran dispute, which arose after Saudi Arabia executed a prominent Shia cleric. The Omani government has stated that it is better to maintain relations and reach agreements with Iran than to maintain an adversarial relationship, and Oman has served as a broker between the U.S. and Iran. Oman is active in international efforts to counter terrorism and was the first Gulf state to allow U.S. bases, and it has close military ties to Britain.

Omani men wear a white robe and either a pillbox hat or a turban, often elaborately decorated. This is an influence from Iran and the East. Women wear a black robe and a decorated, diaphanous veil.

During the uprisings across the Arab world in early 2011, some Omanis also demonstrated, and there was a monthlong sit-in on the Globe Roundabout, which was finally cleared by force. They were demanding economic benefits, an end to corruption, and greater political rights. The sultan pledged to create more government jobs and implement economic and political reforms.[11] There are activists who want a rule of law, freedom of speech, and political institutions such as a functioning legislature.[12]

Oman is a delightful country for foreigners, diverse and interesting, and the people are warm and welcoming. Tourism is sure to do well.

✦ ✦ ✦ ✦ ✦ ✦ ✦ ✦ ✦ ✦ ✦ ✦ ✦ ✦ ✦ ✦ ✦ ✦

CONCLUSION

The more you socialize and interact with Arabs, the sooner you will abandon your stereotyped impressions of them. Individuals behave differently, but patterns emerge if you look for them. Soon you will be able to understand and even predict actions and reactions, some of which may be different from what you expected. Your task is to become aware of how and why things happen in order to feel comfortable with new social patterns as soon as possible.

Arab culture is complex but not unfathomable or totally exotic; many people find it similar to life in the Mediterranean area and Latin America.* Arabs are demonstrative, emotional, and full of zest for life, while at the same time bound by stringent rules and social expectations. Westerners need not feel obliged to imitate Arabs in order to be accepted. All that is necessary for harmonious relations is to be nonjudgmental and to avoid any actions that are insulting or shocking. Westerners, especially Americans, are accustomed to being open and up front with beliefs and feelings. This forthrightness needs to be tempered when operating in the tradition-bound culture of the Middle East.

Arabs are accustomed to dealing with foreigners and expect them to behave and dress differently and to have different ideas from themselves. Foreigners are forgiven a great deal; even conservative people make allowances, particularly when they trust your motives. The essential thing is to

---

*This is due, in part, to the fact that the Arabs ruled Spain for the seven centuries preceding the discovery of the New World.

make a sincere, well-meaning effort to adapt and understand. This attitude is readily apparent and will go a long way in helping you form comfortable work relations and friendships. Perhaps you will find yourself on good enough terms with an Arab friend to ask for constructive criticism from time to time. If you do, tactful hints will be offered—listen for them.

Most Arabs are genuinely interested in foreigners and enjoy talking to and developing friendships with them. But their attitude toward Westerners is a mixture of awe, goodwill, and puzzled wariness. They admire Westerners' education and expertise, and most of them have heard favorable reports from others who have visited Western countries. Many Arabs express the hope that they can visit or study in the West, and in some countries, travel and immigration to Western countries are popular.

At the same time Arabs feel that Western societies are too liberal in many ways and that Westerners are not careful enough about their personal and social appearance. Arabs have a great deal of pride and are easily hurt; thus, they are sensitive to any display of arrogance by Westerners and to implied criticisms. They also disapprove of and resent Western political policies in the Arab world.

Moving to an Arab country or interacting with Arabs need not be a source of anxiety. If you use common sense, make an effort to be considerate, and apply your knowledge of Arab customs and traditions, it will be easy to conduct yourself in a way that reflects creditably on your background and home country. At the same time, you will have a rich and rewarding experience.

THE ARABIC LANGUAGE

Learning Arabic is indispensable for gaining a real insight into Arab society and culture. If you intend to study Arabic, you should choose the type that suits your own needs best.

Arabs associate foreign learners of Arabic with scholars, who (in the past) have tended to concentrate on Standard Arabic, so if you ask an Arab to give you lessons in Arabic, he or she will usually want to start with the alphabet and emphasize reading. If your interest is mainly in learning spoken Arabic, you will have to make that clear from the outset.

When you speak Arabic, you will find that your use of even the simplest phrases, no matter how poorly pronounced, will produce an immediate smile and comment of appreciation. I have had literally hundreds of occasions on which my willingness to converse in Arabic led to a delightful experience. A typical example occurred once when I was shopping in a small town in Lebanon and spent about half an hour chatting with the owner of one of the shops. When I was about to leave, he insisted on giving me a small brass camel, "because you speak Arabic."

Arabs are flattered by your efforts to learn their language (although they are convinced that no foreigner can ever master it), and they will do everything to encourage you. Even just a little Arabic is a useful tool for forming friendships and demonstrating goodwill.

❊ COLLOQUIAL ARABIC DIALECTS

The Arabic dialects fall into five geographical categories:

Category	Dialects	Native or Other Language Influence
1. North African (Western Arabic)	Moroccan Algerian Tunisian Libyan Mauritanian	Berber
2. Egyptian/Sudanese	Egyptian Sudanese	Turkish, Coptic, Nilotic
3. Levantine	Lebanese Syrian Palestinian	Local Semitic languages (Aramaic, Phoenician, Canaanite)
4. Arabian Peninsular	Jordanian Saudi Yemeni Kuwaiti Bahraini Qatari Emirates (Emirati) Omani	Farsi (in the Gulf states), Bedouin dialects, South Arabian languages
5. Iraqi*	Iraqi	Local Semitic languages (Assyrian, Chaldean) Farsi, Turkish

*Iraqi is essentially a non-urban dialect, with three distinct varieties, similar to both Jordanian and Kuwaiti Arabic.

Speakers of dialects in two of the categories—Egyptian/Sudanese and Levantine—have relatively little difficulty being understood. The North African, Iraqi, and Arabian Peninsular dialects, however, are relatively difficult for other Arabs to understand.

The most noticeable differences among dialects occur in the vocabulary, although there are grammatical discrepancies too. These variations should be taken into account when you are choosing a dialect to study, since it is almost useless to study a dialect different from the one spoken in the country to which you are going.

Simple words and phrases, such as greetings, vary widely, while technical and erudite words are usually the same. Educated Arabs get around this problem by using classical words, but a foreigner is more likely to experience each dialect as a different language. The following are examples of differences among dialects.

SLIGHTLY DIFFERENT

	Egyptian	**Saudi**	**Moroccan**
paper	*wara'a*	*waraga*	*werqa*

	Jordanian	**Moroccan**	**Egyptian**
beautiful	*jameela*	*jmila*	*gameela*

	Saudi	**Tunisian**	**Lebanese**
heavy	*tageel*	*thaqeel*	*ti'eel*

COMPLETELY DIFFERENT

	Lebanese	**Egyptian**	**Iraqi**	**Tunisian**
How are you?	*keefak?*	*izzayyak?*	*shlownak?*	*shniyya hwalik?*

	Moroccan	**Egyptian**	**Jordanian**	**Saudi**
now	*daba*	*dilwa'ti*	*halla'*	*daheen*

	Lebanese	**Kuwaiti**	**Moroccan**	**Egyptian**
good	*mneeh*	*zayn*	*mezyan*	*kwayyis*

Attitudes toward Dialects

Arabs tend to regard their own dialect as the purest and the closest to Classical Arabic; I have heard this claim vigorously defended from Morocco to Iraq. In fact, though, where one dialect is closer to the Classical with respect to one feature, another dialect is closer with respect to another. No dialect can be successfully defended as pure except possibly the Najdi dialect spoken in central Arabia, which has been the most isolated from non-Arabic influences.

Arabs view the Bedouin dialects as semi-Classical and therefore admirable, although a bit archaic. Most Arabs find the Egyptian dialect to be the most pleasing to listen to because the pronunciation is "light." Eastern

Arabs tend to look down on western Arabic (North African) because of their difficulty in understanding the dialect (which they attribute, wrongly, to Berber usages). Most of the differences between western and eastern Arabic stem from changes in pronunciation and word stress.

Because all Arabs view their local dialect as the best, they are quick to advise a foreigner that theirs is the most useful, but usefulness depends entirely on where you are in the Arab world.

❋ THE STRUCTURE OF ARABIC

The structure of Arabic is like that of all Semitic languages. Its most striking feature is the way words are formed, which is called the "root and pattern" system. A root is a set of three consonants that carry the meaning of the word. The vowels in a word form patterns and, depending on how they are intermixed with the consonants, determine the part of speech of a word. The consonants and vowels have different functions in a word, and together their combinations yield a rich vocabulary. Here are some examples from Classical Arabic, distinguishing roots and patterns (patterns may contain affixes—additional syllables added at the beginning, in the middle, or at the end of words).

		Meaning
Roots:	k-t-b	writing
	r-k-b	riding
Patterns:	-a-(a)-a (i)	(completed action, past tense)
	-aa-i-	agent (one who does an action)
	ma—a-	place (where the action is done)
Words:	kataba	he wrote
	rakiba	he rode
	kaatib	writer, clerk
	raakib	rider
	maktab	(place for writing) office, desk
	markab	(place for riding) boat
	markaba	vehicle

As you learn vocabulary, you will notice that words that have the same core meaning come in varying patterns, but almost all can be reduced to a three-consonant base. For example, other words that share the consonants *k-t-b* are

kitaab	book
kitaaba	writing
maktaba	library, bookstore
maktuub	letter, something written, fate

Personal names in Arabic usually have a meaning. Below is a group of names from the same three-consonant base, *h-m-d*, which means "to praise":

Muhammad	Hamdy
Mahmoud	Hammady
Hameed	Hamoud
Hamed	Ahmed

You can see why foreigners find Arabic names confusing.

Arabic pronunciation makes use of many sounds that do not occur in English, mostly consonants produced far back in the mouth and throat. Some of these consonants show up in the English spelling of words, such as *gh* (Baghdad), *kh* (Khartoum), *q* (Qatar), and *dh* (Riyadh). In Classical Arabic there are twenty-eight consonants, three long vowels, and three short vowels. In the Arabic dialects, some consonants have been dropped or merged with others, and some consonants and vowels have been added—features that distinguish one dialect from another.

❖ TRANSCRIPTION

There are varying spellings for Arabic words, because some of the sounds do not exist in English, and because words can be transcribed according to different phonetic systems. There is technically a correct way to spell every word, but complete accuracy often makes the words hard to read. Conventions have grown up around spelling common Arabic words.

Any of these spellings is acceptable. The column marked Accurate is the closest to actual Arabic pronunciation.

Note: North African words, especially names, are written according to the French system, so they do not look like words transcribed into English.

English	French	Accurate	Other
Mohammad		Muhammad	Mohamed
			Mohammed
Hussein	Hocine	Husayn	Hussain
			Huseen
Al-Hussein	Lahoussine	Al-Husayn	El-Hussain
Shukry	Choucri	Shukri	
Sharif	Cherif	Shariif	Shareef
Koran	Coran	Qur'aan	Qur'an
Abdel-Hakim	Abdelhakime	Abd al-Hakiim	Abdul-Hakim
Abdel-Rahman	Abderahmane	Abd ar-Rahmaan	Abdul-Rahman
Saladin		Salaah ad-diin	Salahedin
Ayesha	Aicha	'Aa'isha	Aisha, Aysha
Suleiman	Slimane	Sulaymaan	Sulayman
Gamal, Jamal		Gamaal, Jamaal	
Said		Sa'iid	Saeed, Sayeed
Qaddhafi		Al-Qadhdhaafi	Qaddafi
			Qaddafy
			Gaddafy

The consonant sounds are quite consistent (except for dialect variation, as in the example *Gamal, Jamal*). The short (single) vowels (not the
long doubled vowels) have great variation and usually do not affect the
meaning of the word, so they have many spellings. The more common a
word is, the more variations you are likely to see.

❋ ARABIC WRITING

The Arabic alphabet has twenty-eight letters and is written from right
to left. Numerals, however, are written from left to right. Most letters

connect with the preceding and following letters in the same word. Some-times two or three sounds are written using the same letter; in this case they are differentiated from each other by the arrangement of dots, for example:

b	ب	r	ر	s	س
t	ت	z	ز	sh	ش
th	ث				

Because consonants carry the meaning of words, the Arabic alphabet (like all Semitic alphabets) includes only the consonants and the long vowels (for example, *aa*, which is a different vowel from *a* and is held longer when pronounced). The short vowels do not appear in the alphabet, but the Arab reader knows what they are and can pronounce the words correctly because these vowels come in predictable patterns. Additional signs (diacritical marks) mark short vowels, doubled consonants, and the like, but these are used only in texts for beginners—and are always included in the text of the Qur'an in order to assure correct reading.

The numerals in Arabic are very easy to learn. We refer to our own numbers as "Arabic numerals" because the system of using one symbol for 0 through 9 and adding new place values for tens, hundreds, and so forth, was borrowed from the Arabs to replace the Roman numeral system. Nevertheless, although their numerals are used the same way as ours, they are not alike (note especially their numbers 5 and 6, which look like our 0 and 7).

0	•	6	٦
1	١	7	٧
2	٢	8	٨
3	٣	9	٩
4	٤	10	١٠
5	٥		

79	790	100	345	1963
٧٩	٧٩٠	١٠٠	٣٤٥	١٩٦٣

There are several styles of handwriting, and in each the shapes of the individual letters are slightly different. The difference between North

African or western script, for instance, and eastern script is especially noticeable.

❀ CALLIGRAPHY AS AN ART FORM

Decorative calligraphy, as you might guess, is one of the highest artistic expressions of Arab culture. Most letters of the alphabet are full of flowing curves, so an artist can easily form them into elaborate designs. Calligraphy usually depicts Qur'anic quotations or favorite proverbs, and the patterns are often beautifully balanced and intricate. Calligraphic designs are widely used to decorate mosques, monuments, books, and household items such as brass trays.

Calligraphy and arabesque geometric designs have developed because of the Islamic injunction against paintings and statues in places of worship. This emphasis is very evident in Islamic architecture.

❀ SOCIAL GREETINGS

Arabs use many beautiful, elaborate greetings and blessings—and in every type of situation. Most of these expressions are predictable—each situation calls for its own statements and responses. Situational expressions exist in English, but they are few, such as "How are you?"/"Fine," "Thank you"/"You're welcome," and "Have a nice day." In Arabic there are at least thirty situations that call for predetermined expressions. Although these are burdensome for a student of Arabic to memorize, it is comforting to know that you can feel secure about what to say in almost every social context.

There are formulas for greetings in the morning and evening, for meeting after a long absence, for meeting for the first time, and for welcoming someone who has returned from a trip. There are formulas for acknowledging accomplishments, purchases, marriage, or death and for expressing good wishes when someone is engaged in a task, or has just had a haircut! All of these situations have required responses, and they are beautiful in delivery and usually religious in content. Some examples follow.

English (Statement/Response)	Arabic Translation (Statement/Response)
Good morning./Good morning.	Morning of goodness./Morning of light.
Good-bye./Good-bye.	[Go] with safety./May God make you safe.
Happy to see you back./Thanks.	Thank God for your safety./May God make you safe.
(Said when someone is working)	God give you strength./ God strengthen you.
(Said when discussing future plans)	May our Lord make it easy.
Good night./Good night.	May you reach morning in goodness./And may you be of the same group.
I'm taking a trip. What can I bring you?/What would you like?	Your safety.
I have news. Guess what I heard.	[May it be] good, God willing.

Conversational ritual expressions are much used in Arabic. Sometimes a ritual exchange of formalities can last several minutes, particularly among older and more traditional people.

The Arabs have the charming custom of addressing strangers with kinship terms, which connotes respect and goodwill at the same time. Here is an example of the use of these terms with strangers in Yemeni society (they are as widely used elsewhere).

"Brother, how can I help you?"

"Take this taxi, my sisters, I'll find another."

"My mother, it's the best that I can do."

"You're right, uncle."

Ritualistic statements are required by etiquette in many situations. Meeting someone's small child calls for praise carefully mixed with blessings; for example, "May God keep him" or "[This is] what God wills." Such statements reassure the parents that you are not envious (you certainly would not add, "I wish I had a child like this!"). Blessings should also be used when seeing something of value, such as a new car or a new house. When someone purchases something, even a rather small item, the usual word is *Mabrook*, which is translated "Congratulations" but literally means "Blessed." Some of the most common phrases are given here.

English	**Arabic**
Hello./Hello.	*Marhaba./Marhabtayn.*
Good morning./Good morning.	*Sabah alkhayr./Sabah annoor.*
Peace be upon you./ And upon you peace.	*Assalamu 'alaykum./Wa 'alaykum assalam.*
Good-bye./Good-bye. ([Go] with safety./May God make you safe.)	*Ma'a ssalama./Allah yisallimak.*
Thank you./You're welcome.	*Shukran./'Afwan.*
Congratulations./Thank you. (Blessed./May God bless you.)	*Mabrook./Allah yibarik feek.*
Welcome./Thanks. (Welcome./ Welcome to you.)	*Ahlan wa sahlan./Ahlan beek.*
If God wills.	*Inshallah.* (Said when speaking of a future event)
What God wills.	*Mashallah.* (Said when seeing a child or complimenting someone's health)
Thanks be to God.	*Alhamdu lillah.*
Thanks be to God for your safety.	*Hamdillah 'ala ssalama.* (Said when someone returns from a trip or recovers from an illness)

Some Arabic expressions sound much too elaborate to be used comfortably in English. There is no need to use them exactly in translation if you are speaking English, as long as you express good wishes.

NOTES

Preface

1. David Fromkin, *A Peace to End All Peace* (New York: Henry Holt, 1989), 306.
2. Charles Krauthammer, "'Munich,' the Travesty," *Washington Post*, 13 January 2006.
3. Felipe Umana, "Arab Spring Turns to Winter in Much of the Middle East, North Africa," Fragile States Index, 17 June 2015.
4. "Offensive on Iraq's Mosul may produce a million migrants: Turkey," *World News*, Reuters, 4 October 2016.
5. Drew DeSilver and David Masci, "World's Muslim population more widespread than you might think," Pew Research Center, 31 January 2017.
6. Raphael Patai, *The Arab Mind* (1973; reprint) (Long Island: Hatherleigh Press, 2002).
7. Ralph Peters, "When Devils Walk the Earth," in *Beyond Terror: Strategy in a Changing World* (Mechanicsburg, PA: Stackpole Books, 2002), 22–65.

Introduction: Patterns of Change

1. Nadim Kawatch, "Arab World needs to rise to the literacy challenge," Emirates 24/7 News, 28 July 2010.
2. "Adult and Youth Literacy," UNESCO Institute for Statistics, Fact Sheet, 26 September 2013.
3. "Field Listing: Literacy." The World Factbook, Central Intelligence Agency, 2015.
4. "School Enrollment, Tertiary, Country Ranking," *Index Mundi*, 2014.
5. Elizabeth Fernea, "Islamic Feminism Finds a Different Voice," *Foreign Service Journal* 30 (May 2000).
6. Maha El-Swais, "Despite high education levels, Arab women still don't have jobs," *Voices and Views: Middle East and North Africa*, World Bank, 9 March 2016.
7. "Life Expectancy for Countries," Infoplease, 2015.
8. Ibn Warraq, "Demographics: Why Islamic Societies are Dying," *New English Review* (UK), April 2016.

9. Kate Moran, "Leveraging the Youth Bulge to Transform the Arab World," Center for Private Enterprise, CIPE Development Blog, 2 February 2016.
10. Ahmed Driouchi, *Knowledge-Based Economic Policy Development in the Arab World* (Forum Euromediterraneen des Instituts de Sciences Economiques, 2014), 273–291.
11. "Urbanization." The World Factbook, Central Intelligence Agency, 2017.
12. Judith Miller, "Displaced in the Gulf War: 5 Million Refugees," *New York Times*, 16 June 1991.
13. "Arabic Speaking Internet Users Statistics," Internet World Stats, 6 March 2017.
14. "United States Internet Users," Internet Live Stats, 2016. "Top 20 Countries with Highest Number of Internet Users," Internet World Stats, 2017.
15. Colum Lynch, "Report Urges Arab Governments to Share Power," *Washington Post*, 5 April 2005.
16. David K. Willis, "The Impact of Islam," *Christian Science Monitor* weekly international edition, 18–24 August 1984.
17. John O. Voll, Foreword to *The Gulf and the Struggle for Hegemony* (Middle East Institute: Washington, D.C., 2016).
18. Ahmad S. Mousalli, *Modern and Radical Islamic Fundamentalism* (Gainesville: University of Florida Press, 1999), 181–186.
19. Benazir Bhutto, "Politics and the Modern Woman," in *Liberal Islam: A Sourcebook*, ed. Charles Kurzman (New York: Oxford University Press, 1998), 107.
20. Muhammad Sayyid Qutb, "The Role of Religion in Education," In *Aims and Objectives of Islamic Education*, ed. S. N. Al-Attas (Jeddah: King Abdulaziz University, 1979), 60.
21. Osman Bakar, *The History and Philosophy of Islamic Science* (Cambridge, England: Islamic Texts Society, 1999), 214.

Chapter 1

1. "Population Density per Square Mile of Countries," Infoplease, 2009.
2. "Background Note: Egypt," U.S. Department of State Bureau of Near Eastern Affairs, 10 November 2010.
3. Desmond Stuart, *The Arab World* (New York: Time Life Books, 1972), 9–10.
4. Halim Barakat, *The Arab World: Society, Culture, and the State* (Berkeley: University of California Press, 1993), 21.
5. "Unmarried Childbearing," Centers for Disease Control and Prevention, 2008.

Chapter 2

1. Recorded December 2004 in Doha, Qatar.
2. David Shipler, *Arab and Jew: Wounded Spirits in a Promised Land* (New York: Penguin Books, 1986), 387.
3. Ghada Karmi, *In Search of Fatima: A Palestinian Story* (London: Verso, 2002), 181.

Chapter 3

1. George N. Atiyeh, *Arab and American Cultures* (Washington, D.C.: American Enterprise Institute for Public Policy Research, 1977), 179.
2. T. E. Lawrence, *The Seven Pillars of Wisdom* (New York: Doubleday, 1926), 24.

Chapter 4

1. Edward T. Hall, *The Hidden Dimension* (New York: Doubleday, 1966), 15.
2. "Hussein trial court to be disbanded," *Washington Post*, 5 May 2011.

Chapter 5

1. Nicholas D. Kristof, "Islam, Virgins, and Grapes," *New York Times*, 23 April 2009.
2. Neil MacFarquhar, "New Translation Prompts Debate on Islamic Verse," *New York Times*, 23 March 2007.
3. "Poll: Islamic women liked as leaders," United Press International, 30 March 2006.
4. Aida F. Akl, "Will Women Benefit from Middle East Revolution?" News.com, 29 March 2011.
5. "Timeline of Women's Right to Vote Around the World," *Gulf News*, 12 December 2015.
6. "Women in National Parliaments," Inter-Parliamentary Union (Geneva), 1 May 2017. "Proportion of seats held by women in national parliaments," World Bank, 2016.
7. "New IPU and UN Women Map shows women's representation in politics stagnates," Inter-Parliamentary Union, 15 March 2017.
8. "Al Azhar confirms hijab is not a part of the religion," World Muslim Congress, 23 May 2012.
9. Thomas Omstad, "The Casbah Connection," *U.S. News and World Report*, 9 May 2005.
10. Lesley Hazelton, *After the Prophet* (New York: Anchor Books, 2009), 108.
11. Karen Armstrong, *Muhammad: A Biography of the Prophet* (San Francisco: HarperSanFrancisco, 1992), 198.
12. *Ibid.*, 199.
13. "Tolerance and Tension," Pew poll, 2013.
14. Bernard Lewis, "Targeted by a History of Hatred: The United States is now the unquestioned leader of the free world, also known as infidels," *Washington Post*, 10 September 2002.
15. Barakat, *The Arab World: Society, Culture and State*, 113.
16. Donna Lee Bowen and Evelyn A. Early, eds., *Everyday Life in the Muslim Middle East* (Bloomington: Indiana University Press, 1993,) 77.
17. "Quotation of the Day," *New York Times*, 13 April 2005.

Chapter 6

1. Kathy Lally, "Egypt Calls," *Washington Post*, 1 May 2011.
2. Aida Hasan, "Arab Culture and Identity: Arab Food and Hospitality," Suite University Online, 1999. www.suite101.com.

Chapter 7

Chapter 8

1. Alean Al-Krenawi and John R. Graham, "Principles of Social Work Practice in the Muslim Arab World," *Arab Studies Quarterly* 25, no. 4 (Fall 2003): 85.
2. "Fatima Urges Protection of Arab Family," *UAE Interact*, Ministry of Information and Culture, 1999.
3. Hanan Hamamy, "Consanguineous Marriages in the Arab World," National Centre for Diabetes, Endocrinology and Genetics (Amman), July 2003.
4. *Ibid.*
5. David Brown, "Global Study Examines Toll of Genetic Defects," *Washington Post*, 30 January 2006.

Chapter 9

1. Robin Wright, "Islam's Soft Revolution," *Time*, 30 March 2009, 38.
2. Tom Heneghan, "Turkey 'not reforming Islam, but itself' with Hadith review," Reuters, *Faith World*, 29 February 2008.
3. Mustafa Akyol, "Sexism Deleted in Turkey," *Washington Post*, 16 July 2006.
4. Michelle Boorstein, "For critics of Islam, 'Sharia' is a loaded word," *Washington Post*, 27 August 2010.
5. *Ibid.*
6. *Ibid.*
7. "Text Analytics Program Proves Quran Less Violent Than the Bible," *The Muslim Post*, 6 February 2016.

Chapter 10

1. Mounir Al-Ba'albaki, *Al-Mawrid: A Modern English-Arabic Dictionary* (Beirut: Dar El-Ilm lil-Malayen, 2004), 101–12.
2. Ghazi Algosaibi, "The crisis of modern Arabic poetry," in *Arabian Essays* (Routledge and Kegan: UK, 1982), 101.
3. Andrew Hammond, *Popular Culture in the Arab World* (Cairo: American University in Cairo Press, 2007), 56.
4. Leslie J. McLoughlin, *Colloquial Arabic (Levantine)* (London: Routledge and Kegan Paul, 1982), 2–3.

5. Helen Altman Klein and Gilbert Kuperman, "Through an Arab Cultural Lens," *The Military Review*, May-June 2008, 103.

Chapter 11

1. Daniel Pipes, *Militant Islam Reaches America* (New York: W. W. Norton & Co. 2003), 247–8.
2. Mark Clayton, "How Are Mosques Fighting Terror?" *Christian Science Monitor*, 12 August 2004.
3. Steve Emerson, *American Jihad: The Terrorists Living Among Us* (New York: Free Press, 2002), 41.
4. Eric Bochlert, "Terrorists under the Bed," *Salon.com*, 5 March 2002.
5. Mark Potok, "Hate Rises," *Washington Post*, 9 March 2008.
6. "Hate Groups, State Totals," Southern Poverty Law Center, 2017.
7. Abigail Hauslohner, "Southern Poverty Law Center says American hate groups are on the rise," *Washington Post*, 15 February 2017.
8. *Ibid.*
9. Robert A. Pape, *Dying to Win: The Strategic Logic of Suicide Terrorism* (New York: Random House, 2005), 23.
10. *Ibid.*, 104.
11. Sarah Kershaw, "The Terrorist Mind: An Update," *New York Times*, 10 January 2010.
12. Alon Ben-Meir, "Killing in the Name of God," *Huffington Post*, 17 July 2013.
13. Mary Habeck, *Knowing the Enemy: Jihadist Ideology and the War on Terror* (Yale University Press, 2006), 109.
14. R. Stephen Humphreys, *Between Memory and Desire: The Middle East in a Troubled Age* (Berkeley: University of California Press, 1999), 174.
15. Guy Raz, "The War on the Word 'Jihad,'" *All Things Considered*, National Public Radio, 31 October 2006.
16. Abdul Wahab Bashir, "Scholars Define Terrorism, Call for Joint Action to Defend Islam," *Arab News* (Saudi Arabia), 12 January 2002.
17. Karen Armstrong, *Muhammad: A Biography of the Prophet* (San Francisco: HarperSanFrancisco, 1992), 168.
18. Riad Saloojee, "The Nature of Islam," *Globe and Mail* (Canada), 16 January 2000.
19. Waleed Ziad, "Jihad's Fresh Face," *New York Times*, 16 September 2005.
20. Habeck, *op. cit.*
21. Katherine Zoepf, "Deprogramming Jihadists," *New York Times*, 9 November 2008.
22. 2015 Sees Dramatic Spike in Islamic Extremism Arrests," Anti-Defamation League, 21 March 2016.
23. Adam Deen, "Why are converts to Islam specifically vulnerable to becoming extremists?" *The Independent* (UK), 24 March 2017.
    Beenish Ahmed, "Why Converts to Islam Are So Susceptible to Becoming Terrorists," ThinkProgress, 3 February 2016.
24. Amanda Ripley, "Reverse Radicalism," *Time*, 24 March 2008.

25. Cottee, *op. cit.*

26. Michael Scheuer, *Imperial Hubris: Why the West Is Losing the War on Terror* (Washington D.C.: Brassey's Inc., 2004), 17.

27. Frederick Kunkle, "Are good works good politics?" *Washington Post*, 9 April 2011.

28. Erica Simmons, "A Passion for Justice," *New Internationalist* (UK), No. 210, August 1990, 9.

29. Robin Wright, "Inside the Mind of Hezbollah," *Washington Post*, 16 July 2006.

30. "Worldwide Suicide Rates," Suicide and Mental Health Association International, February 2005.

31. Alaa Al-Aswani, *On the State of Egypt* (New York: Vintage Books, 2011), 88.

32. Jackie Spinner, "An Attack Burns Anguish into Kurdish Region," *Washington Post*, 6 February 2005.

33. "Islam, Jihad, and Terrorism," Institute of Islamic Information and Education, 14 October 2004.

34. Jonathan Steele, "Terrorism Is Not an Enemy State that Can Be Defeated," *The Guardian* (UK), 23 November 2003.

35. Abdeslam Maghraoui, "American Foreign Policy and Islamic Renewal," United States Institute of Peace Special Report, July 2006.

36. *Ibid.*

37. Tariq Ramadan, "Islam's role in an ethical society," *The Guardian* (UK), 23 February 2010.

38. Jonathan Laurence, "The Prophet of Moderation: Tariq Ramadan's Quest to Reclaim Islam," *New York Times*, 18 June 2007.

39. Arwa Ibrahim, "Arab world's top televangelist goes on 'novel' trajectory," *Middle East Eye* (UK), 8 January 2015.

40. Samantha M. Shapiro, "Ministering to the Upwardly Mobile Muslim," *New York Times Magazine*, 30 April 2006.

41. Laurence, *op. cit.*

42. Robert F. Worth, "Preaching Moderate Islam and Becoming a TV Star," *New York Times*, 3 January 2009.

43. Kevin Sullivan, "Younger Muslims Tune in to Upbeat Religious Message," *Washington Post*, 2 December 2007.

44. Jeffrey Fleishman, "Egypt's provocative voice of moderate Islam," *Los Angeles Times*, 6 August 2010.

45. Garrett Nada, "New Islamic TV Expands Across Mideast," Wilson Center, 5 November 2012.

46. "About Free Muslims Coalition," Free Muslims Coalition, 30 May 2011.

47. "Report Instances of Extremism or Support of Terrorism," Free Muslims Coalition, 2005.

Chapter 12

1. "Main Findings of the 2016 Arab Opinion Index Available Now," Arab Center for Research and Policy Studies (Doha), 13 March 2017.

2. Richard Wike, Bruce Stokes, and Jacob Poushter, "America's Global Image," Pew Research Center, 28 June 2017.

3. "Arab Attitudes 2011," *Arab America*, 2012.

4. Jennifer Rubin, "Trump's un-American speech in Saudi Arabia," *Washington Post*, 21 May 2017.

5. Jon Dean and Sophie Evans, "ISIS reveals 6 reasons why they despise Westerners as terrorist's sister claims he wanted revenge for US airstrikes in Syria," *The Mirror* (UK), 26 May 2017.

6. "Transcript of bin Ladin's speech," *Al-Jazeera*, 30 October 2004.

7. Emily Badger, "Why Are the World's Muslims So Mad at America?" *Pacific Standard*, 19 May 2011.

8. Zoltan Grossman, "From Wounded Knee to Syria: A Century of U.S. Military Interventions," Evergreen State College, 2014.

9. Joe Lauria, "Why We're Never Told Why We're Attacked," Consortiumnews.com, 3 April 2016.

10. Grossman, *op cit.*
    "Poll Data: Arabs Doubt U.S.," Layalina Productions, Inc., 13–26 April 2007.

11. John L. Esposito and Dalia Mogahed, "Muslim True/False," *Los Angeles Times*, 2 April 2008.

12. Sheldon Richman, "Another Frankenstein's Monster," *Commentaries*, Future of Freedom Foundation, 27 December 2002.

13. Mahdi Darius Nazemroava, "Plans for Redrawing the Middle East: The Project for a 'New Middle East,'" Global Research, 6 March 2017.

14. Max Blumenthal, "The Manchester Bombing is Blowback from the West's Disastrous Interventions and Covert Proxy Wars," *AlterNet*, 25 May 2017.

15. Robert Fisk, "What Theresa May Won't Talk About When She Talks About Terrorism," *Counterpunch*, 7 June 2017.

16. *Ibid.*, quoting Condaleezza Rice, Mark Levine, and Michael Ledeen.

17. F. William Engdahl, "The Greater Middle East Project," Katehon Think Tank, 20 January 2017.

18. Alexander Kuznetsov, "United States Must Answer for War Crimes in the Middle East," Strategic Culture Foundation (Russia), 15 October 2016.

19. Jonathan Cook, "Here's What Will Probably Happen if Assad Falls in Syria (Hint: The Opposite of Peace and Democracy)," *AlterNet*, 10 May 2017.

20. Mohamed El-Bendary, *The "Ugly American" in the Arab Mind* (Potomac Books, Washington, D.C., 2011), 41

21. *Ibid.*, 36

22. E. W. Said, "A Stupid War," *Al Hayat* (Beirut), 15 April 2003.

23. Richard Stengel, "One Thing We Need to Do," *Time*, 11 September 2006.

24. "President Bush Addresses the Nation," *Washington Post*, 20 September 2001.

25. Alana Goodman, "If It's Freedom We Hate, Why Didn't We Attack Sweden?" *Commentary*, 23 December 2010.

26. "Why Do They Hate Us? The Forbidden Answer," *News and Politics*, 2 November 2010.

27. Glenn Beck, "Remember Why We Were Attacked on September 11," Fox News, 11 September 2009.

28. Franklin Lamb, "Giuliani Plays the Islamic Terror Card," *Counterpunch*, 26 April 2007.

29. Roger Simon, "Giuliani warns of 'new 9/11' if Dems win," *Politico*, 24 April 2007.
30. Paul Goodman, "Islamists don't hate us for what we do. They hate us for who we are," *Conservative Home*, 8 January 2015.
31. "Why is America the Target of Militant Islam?" *Frontline*, PBS, October 2001.
32. "U.S. Public Diplomacy in the Middle East on a New Course," Layalina Productions, Inc., 18 December 2009.
33. Saul Hudson, "U.S. Halts Arabic Magazine Meant to Boost U.S. Image," Reuters, 22 December 2005.
34. Joe Conason, "Why Nobody Watches Our Arab TV Channel," *Salon*, 12 May 2010.
35. Tiffany Gabbay, "Why Do They Hate Us? It's a Pretty Long List," *The Blaze*, 21 September 2012.
36. Armstrong Williams, "No Excuse for Anti-Americanism," *Townhall*, 1 June 2004.
37. Barry Rubin, "The Real Roots of Arab Anti-Americanism," *Foreign Affairs*, November-December 2002.
38. Bernard Lewis, "The Roots of Muslim Rage," *The Atlantic Monthly*, September 1990.
39. Bernard Lewis, "Targeted by a History of Hatred: The United States is now the unquestioned leader of the free world, also known as infidels," *Washington Post*, 10 September 2002.
40. Samuel P. Huntington, "The Clash of Civilizations," *Foreign Affairs* 72, no. 3 (Summer 1993).
41. Samuel P. Huntington, *The Clash of Civilizations and the Remaking of World Order* (New York: Simon and Schuster, 1996), 211.
42. Zainab Salbi, "What people in the Middle East say in private about the West," *New York Times*, 26 May 2015.
43. C. J. Werleman, "Starbucks, McDonalds, and Anti-Americanism in the Middle East," *Middle East Eye* (UK), 8 January 2015.
44. Khaled Dawood, "Arab Opinions," *Al-Ahram Weekly*, 30 July 2004.
45. "The 2015 Arab Opinion Index: Arab Public Attitudes Toward Democracy," Arab Center, Washington, D.C., 7 March 2016.
46. Rami Khouri, "For Arabs, A Cruel Echo of History," *Daily Star* (Beirut), 21 March 2003.
47. "Arab dawn: Arab youth and the demographic dividend they will bring," Brookings, 28 December 2015.
48. "Most Americans Want Democracy in the Middle East," *International Iran Times*, No date.
49. Charles Krauthammer, "Why It Deserves the Hype," *Time*, 14 February 2005.
50. Fouad Ajami, "Bush Country," *Daily Star* (Beirut), 23 May 2005.
51. Fouad Ajami, "The Meaning of Lebanon," The Foundation for the Defense of Democracy, 1 May 2005.
52. Charles Krauthammer, "Syria and the New Axis of Evil," *Washington Post*, 1 April 2005.
53. "President Obama Talks to Thomas L. Friedman About Iraq, Putin, and Israel," *New York Times*, 8 August 2014.

54. Rami Khoury, "Unprecedented Opportunity," interview by staff of the Center for Public Integrity, 16 March 2005.

55. Huntington, "The Clash of Civilizations," *op. cit.*

56. Nicholas Kristof, "Bigotry in Islam and Here," *New York Times*, 9 July 2002.

57. Franklin Graham, "My View of Islam," *Covenant News*, 9 December 2001.

58. "Islam is Violent," Jesus-is-Lord, 29 November 2008.

59. Robert Kraychik, "Ayaan Hirsi Ali: 'Anti-Semitism is Back ... Because of Islam," *The Daily Wire*, 8 May 2017.

60. Alan Cooperman, "A Timely Subject—and a Sore One," *Washington Post*, 7 August 2002.

61. Nassir M. Al-Ajmi, "Heart-to-Heart Talk—A Friend to Friend Discussion," The Ladah Foundation, 23 October 2003.

62. Kristof, *op. cit.*

63. Rodrique Ngawi, "Rwanda Turns to Islam after Genocide," *Times Daily*, 7 November 2002.

Chapter 13

1. "Demographics," Arab American Institute, Islam Online, 18 February 2014.

2. *Ibid.*

3. Kathleen Marker, "Professional Life," in *Daily Life of Arab Americans in the 21st Century*, ed. Anan Ameri and Holly Arida (Westport, CT: Greenwood, ABC-CLIO, LLC, 2012), 155.

4. Samia El-Badry, "Arab Americans Well-Educated, Diverse, Affluent and Highly Entrepreneurial," Allied Media Corp, no date.

5. "Healing the Nation: Arab American Response to September 11 Attacks," Arab American Institute, 2001.

6. Daniel Williams, "Unveiling Islam: Author Challenges Orthodox Precepts," *Washington Post*, 7 March 2005.

7. Alan Cooperman and Mary Beth Sheridan, "Muslims to Provide Food on Sept. 11," *Washington Post*, 9 September 2005.

8. "Muslim Charity Provides Disaster Relief to Hurricane Sandy Victims," *Washington Report on Middle East Affairs*, March 2013.

9. Cody Switzer, "Responses from Charities to the Japan Earthquake and Pacific Tsunami," *The Chronicle of Philanthropy*, 18 March 2011.

10. "Muslim veterans vow to protect Jewish cemeteries amid anti-Semitic threats," Fox News, 2 March 2017.

11. Jonah Bennett, "Islam Set to Become the Second-Largest Religion in America by 2040," *The Daily Caller News Foundation*, 8 January 2016.

12. "Muslims in America—A Statistical Portrait," Embassy of the United States, Baghdad, 28 September 2016.

13. "Distribution of Mosques in USA 2015," *Islam Threat*, April 2015.

14. "Muslim Demographics in Canada," *Islam Threat*, 25 March 2015.
    Abdul Malik Mujahid, "Profile of Muslims in Canada," Sound Vision, 8 October 2016.

15. M. D. and Erasmus, "Why Canadian Muslims seem happier than British ones," *The Economist*, 22 July 2016.
16. "Mosques and Islamic Centers in Canada," Islamic Supreme Council, 20 January 2010, www.islamicsupremecouncil.com/canada.htm.
17. "Muslims in America," *op. cit.*
18. Dalia Mogahed and Fouad Pervez, "American Muslim Poll," Institute for Social Policy and Understanding, March 2016.
19. Miriam Khan, "More than 5,000 Muslims Serving in U.S. Military, Pentagon Says," ABC News, 8 December 2015.
20. "Muslims in America," *op. cit.*
21. John Zogby, "American Muslim Poll, November-December 2001," Zogby International, 2001, www.amperspective.com.
22. Virginia Culver, "Many American Muslims Well-Off, College Educated, Poll Shows," *Denver Post*, 18 January 2001.
    Michael Lipka, "Muslims and Islam: Key findings in the U.S. and around the world," Pew Research Center, 22 July 2016.
23. Zogby, *op. cit.*
24. "Muslim Americans: Middle Class and Mostly Mainstream," Pew Research Center, 22 May 2007.
    Carol Morello, "In Poll, Muslim Largely Upbeat about Life in U.S.," *Washington Post*, 30 August 2011.
25. "Muslims and Latinos much more prominent in TV crime news than in real-life crime," *Science Daily*, 7 January 2015.
    Karla Dieseldorff, "FBI Says 94% of Terrorist Attacks in the U.S. since 1980 Are by Non-Muslims," *Morocco World News*, 18 December 2015.
26. *Ibid.*
27. V. V. B., "Why America does not take in more Syrian refugees," *The Economist*, 18 October 2015.
28. *Ibid.*
29. *Ibid.*
30. "Iraq Emergency," UNHCR.org, 15 September 2017.
31. Editorial Board, America, "America has accepted 10,000 Syrian refugees. That's still too few," *Washington Post*, 2 September 2016.
32. Phillip Connor, "U.S. admits record number of Muslim refugees in 2016," Pew Research Center, 5 October 2016.
33. "America has accepted," *op. cit.*
34. Conrad Hackett, "5 facts about the Muslim population in Europe," Pew Research Center, 19 July 2016.
35. "Number of Muslims in Western Europe," Pew Research Center, 15 September 2010.
    "Islam: European Muslim Population," Jewish Virtual Library, February 2016.
36. Brianne Tolj, "Muslim population in Australia soars to 600,000 as religion becomes the nation's second-biggest—a 77% jump in the past decade, according to Census," *Daily Mail* (Australia), 26 June 2017.
37. "Islam: European Muslim Population," *op. cit.*
38. Molly Moore, "In a Europe Torn over Mosques, A City Offers Accommodation," *Washington Post*, 9 December 2007.

39. Soeren Kern, "Europe's Mosque Wars," *Pundicity*, 18 August 2010.
40. *Ibid.*
41. *Ibid.*
42. *Ibid.*
43. Adrian Michaels, "The EU is facing an era of vast social change, reports Adrian Michaels, and few politicians are taking notice," *The Telegraph* (UK), 8 August 2009.
44. *Ibid.*
45. Rafiq Tschannen, "List of cities in the European Union by Muslim population," *Muslim Times*, 6 October 2013.
46. Jeff Jacoby, "Why there are Muslim ghettos in Belgium, but not in the U.S.," *Boston Globe*, 27 May 2016.
47. *Ibid.*
48. Omer Taspinar, "Europe's Muslim Street," *Foreign Policy* 135 (March-April 2003): 77.
49. Martin Walker, "The World's New Numbers," *Wilson Quarterly* (Spring 2009): 26.
50. *Ibid.*
51. "EU Opens Debate on Economic Migration," EurActiv, 14 January 2005.
52. Scott Timberg, "Middle East through Western Eyes," *Los Angeles Times*, 7 September 2007.
53. "Islamophobia: Understanding Anti-Muslim Sentiment in the West," Gallup, Inc., 2011.
54. Shelley Slade, "The Image of the Arab in America: Analysis of a Poll of American Attitudes," *Middle East Journal* 35, no. 2 (Spring 1981): 143.
55. Brian Whitaker, "Why the Rules of Racism Are Different for Arabs," *The Guardian* (UK), 18 August 2000.
56. William Booth, "Cast of Villains," *Washington Post*, 23 June 2007.
57. Kerstin Grimsley, "More Arabs, Muslims Allege Bias on the Job," *Washington Post*, 12 February 2001.
58. Michelle Boorstein and Felicia Sonmez, "Familiar sparring in hearing on civil rights of Muslims," *Washington Post*, 30 March 2011.
59. Alan Cooperman, "September 11 Backlash Murders and the State of Hate," *Washington Post*, 20 January 2002.
60. "The Truth about American Muslims," *New York Times*, 1 April 2011.
61. Josh Harkinson, "Anti-Muslim Hate Groups Have Tripled with the Rise of Trump," *Mother Jones*, 15 February 2017.
62. Juan Cole, "How Americans Hate: 8-fold Increase in Islamophobic Crime Since 2000," *AlterNet*, 15 April 2016.
63. Lipka, op. cit.
64. Mohamed Younis, "Perceptions of Muslims in the United States: A Review," Gallup, Inc., 11 December 2015.
    Claudia Deane and Darryl Fears, "Negative Perception of Islam Increasing," *Washington Post*, 9 March 2006.
65. Stephen Piggott, "3 Men Arrested in Plot to Bomb Kansas Mosque," *AlterNet*, 17 October 2016.

66. Zachary A. Goldfarb, "Va. Lawmaker's Remarks on Muslims Criticized," *Washington Post*, 21 December 2006.
67. Paul Farhi, "Talk Show Host Graham Fired by WMAL Over Islam Remarks," *Washington Post*, 23 August 2005.
68. Ernesto Londono, "Teacher Charged After Uproar Over Arabic," *Washington Post*, 13 September 2006.
69. Jon Hurdle, "Arabic flashcards land student in U.S. detention," Reuters, 10 February 2010.
70. Ralph Ellis and Darius Johnson, "Muslim family seeks apology after being forced off United flight," CNN, 2 April 2016.
71. Carma Hassan and Catherine Shoichet, "Arabic-speaking student kicked off Southwest flight," CNN, 18 April 2016.
72. Robin Shulman, "In New York, a Word Starts a Fire," *Washington Post*, 24 August 2007.
73. *Ibid.*
74. Laila Al-Marayati and Basil Abdelkarim, "The Crime of Being a Muslim Charity," *Washington Post*, 11 March 2006.
75. Mary Beth Sheridan, "U.S. Muslim Groups Cleared," *Washington Post*, 18 November 2005.
76. Margot Adler, "Developer: Plans for N.Y. Mosque Moving Forward," *All Things Considered*, National Public Radio, 5 May 2011.
77. Annie Gowen, "Nowhere near Ground Zero, but no more welcome," *Washington Post*, 23 August 2010.
78. "Intolerance," *New Yorker*, 20 September 2010, 47.
79. "The Truth about American Muslims," *op. cit.*
80. "Muslim Charities and the War on Terror," The Charity & Security Network (CSN), December 2011.
81. "Islamophobia in the 2016 Presidential Election," Council on American-Islamic Relations, 29 September 2016.
82. Edward E. Curtis IV, "5 Myths about mosques in America," *Washington Post*, 29 August 2010.
83. "Paper or Plastic? A More Perfect Union Project," Virginia Interfaith Center, 6 April 2010.
84. "The Truth about American Muslims," *op. cit.*
85. Carol Hymowitz, "The Rise of Muslim-Friendly Workplaces in Corporate America," *Bloomberg News*, 19 July 2016.
86. Jacqueline Trescott, "Kennedy Center Plans Festival as Olive Branch to Arab Culture," *Washington Post*, 28 April 2006.
87. Yasser Louati, "Islamodiversion: How Sarkozy and France's Political Class Outdo Trump, Exploiting Islamophobia to Distract from Economic Problems," *AlterNet*, 11 October 2016.
88. Glenn Greenwald, "Large number of Americans favor violent attacks against civilians," *Salon*, 23 May 2007.
89. Jason Burke and Ian Traynor, "Fears of an Islamic revolt in Europe begin to fade," *The Guardian* (UK), 25 July 2009.

90. Walker, *op. cit.*

91. Doug Bandew, "Maybe Europe Isn't Lost to Islamic Terrorism," Cato @ Liberty, Cato Institute, 26 July 2009.

92. Dean Obeidallah, "Are All Terrorists Muslims? It's Not Even Close," *Daily Beast*, 14 January 2015.

93. Ruth Wodak, *The Politics of Fear: What Right-Wing Populist Discourses Mean* (Sage Publications: New York, 2015).

94. Alice Foster, "Where in the world are the burka and niqab banned?" *Daily Express* (U.K.), 23 September 2016.

95. "The Islamic veil across Europe," BBC News, 1 July 2014.

96. *Ibid.*

97. "Muslim women wearing veil 'refused bus ride' in London," BBC News, 23 July 2010.

98. Harriet Agerholm, "Muslim face veil ban for workers is not discriminatory, Austrian court rules," *The Independent* (UK), 11 July 2016.

99. Mona Eltahawy, "Rending the veil—with little help," *Washington Post*, 18 July 2010.

100. Seamus Milne, "This tide of anti-Muslim hatred is a threat to us all," *The Guardian* (UK), 25 February 2010.

101. Hackett, *op. cit.*

102. "Europe's Rising Far Right: A Guide to the Most Prominent Political Parties," *New York Times*, 13 June 2016.
    Samuel Osborne, "The most far-right countries in Europe, mapped," *The Independent* (U.K.), 23 May 2016.

103. Philip Oltermann, "Austria rejects far-right candidate Norbert Hofer in presidential election," *The Guardian* (UK), 4 December 2016.

104. Tyler Durden, "Dutch General Election Results: Prime Minister Rutte Wins, Wilders' Freedom Party Slides," Zero Hedge, 15 March 2017.

105. The Data Team, "The rise of the far right in Europe," *The Economist*, 24 May 2016.

106. Yvonne Yazbeck Haddad and Michael J. Balz, "Taming the Imams: European Governments and Islamic Preachers since 9/11," *Islam and Christian-Muslim Relations* 19, no. 2 (April 2008): 215.

107. "Denmark Imposes Restrictions on Imams," Islam Online, 18 February 2004.

108. Edward Cody, "Tensions grow for Muslims as French debate national identity," *Washington Post*, 19 December 2009.

109. Laurie Goodstein, "Poll Finds U.S. Muslims Thriving, but Not Content," *New York Times*, 2 March 2009.

110. "Perceptions of Muslims," *op. cit.*

111. "Muslim Migration into Europe: Eurabia Come True?" *FrontPage Magazine*, 11 December 2015.

112. Sarah Wildman, "Third Way Speaks to Europe's Young Muslims," *International Reporting Project*, Johns Hopkins School of Advanced International Studies, Spring 2003.

113. Tariq Ramadan, *Western Muslims and the Future of Islam* (Oxford: Oxford University Press, 2004), 6.

114. Martin A. Lee, "Not a Prayer," *Harper's*, June 2004, 79.
115. Besheer Mohamed, "A new estimate of the U.S. Muslim population," Pew Research Center, 6 January 2016.
116. Laurie Goodstein, "Forecast Sees Muslim Population Leveling Off," *New York Times*, 27 January 2011.
117. Hackett, op. cit.
118. Goodstein, op. cit.
119. Vicki Valosik, "Arabic is Blooming," *International Educator*, January-February 2017.
120. "Defying prejudice, more Americans learn Arabic," *Al-Jazeera*, 18 December 2015.

Chapter 14

1. Roby C. Barrett, *The Gulf and the Struggle for Hegemony* (Washington, D.C.: Middle East Institute, 2016).
2. Tom Mills and Gilbert Achcar, "Is U.S. Control over the Middle East Weakening?" *South African Civil Society Information Service*, 9 June 2015.
3. Editorial, "Unemployment is a source of Instability in MENA [Middle East North Africa]," *Arab Weekly* (UK), 29 January 2016.
4. Lisdey Espinosa Pedraza and Marcus Heinrich, "Water Scarcity: Cooperation or Conflict in the Middle East and North Africa?" *Foreign Policy Journal*, 2 September 2016.
5. "GDP per Capita," *Index Mundi*, 2015.
6. J. J. Messner, ed., "Fragile States Index 2016," Fund for Peace, 27 June 2016.

The Arab States in Africa

The Maghrib

1. Irene Thompson, "Berber Branch," AWL [About World Languages], 27 December 2016.
2. Ursula Lindsey, "The Berber Language: Officially Recognized, Unofficially Marginalized?" Al-Fanar Media (UK), 27 July 2015.
3. "The Amazigh (Berber)," Phoenician International Research Center, 2011.

MOROCCO

1. Tania Ildefonso Ocampos, "Morocco reaches critical stage on road to reform," *Middle East Eye* (UK), 3 March 2016.
2. Emma Batha, "Morocco's Islamic women preachers lead social revolution," *World News*, Reuters, 19 May 2015.
3. Jane Kramer, "The Crusader," *New Yorker*, 16 October 2006.
4. Ahmad Charai and Joseph Braude, "All Hail the (Democratic) King," *New York Times*, 11 July 2011.
5. Aziz Yaakoubi and Patrick Markey, "Moderate Moroccan Islamists win election, coalition talks seen tough," *World News*, Reuters, 8 October 2016.

6. Mohamed Alauoi, "Moroccan women judges strive for equal rights," *Arab Weekly* (UK), 25 September 2016.
7. Chaima Lahsini, "Gender Wage Gap: Moroccan Women Make 17% Less Than Men," *Morocco World News*, 11 March 2017.
8. Stephanie Willman Bordat and Saida Kouzzi, "The Challenge of Implementing Morocco's New Personal Status Law," Carnegie Endowment for International Peace, 20 August 2008.
9. "Morocco Population," Country Meters, 2017.
10. Emma Schwartz, "Giving Voice to a Long-Repressed People," *U.S. News and World Report*, 24–31 March 2008, 29.
    Ursula Lindsey, "The Berber Language: Officially Recognized, Unofficially Marginalized?" Al-Fanar Media (UK), 27 July 2015.
11. Safa Othmani, "Morocco's Unemployment Rate to Exceed 10% in 2017, Warns IMF [International Monetary Fund]," *Morocco World News*, 12 October 2016.
12. "Morocco Youth Unemployment Rate 1999–2017," *Trading Economics*, February 2017.
13. The Borgen Project, "Education in Morocco: Literacy Rates Continue to Make Strides," The Blog, Borgen Project, October 2016.
14. *Ibid.*
15. Harun Yahya, "Peaceful Coexistence in Morocco between Jews and Muslims," *Morocco World News*, 9 May 2016.
16. Othmani, op. cit.

Algeria

1. Anna Jacobs, "Politics in Algeria is about More than Who's President," *Muftah*, 12 November 2014.
2. "Country Analysis Brief: Algeria," U.S. Energy Information Administration, 11 March 2016.
   "Algerian Economy 2016." The World Factbook, Central Intelligence Agency, 2016.
3. Craig Smith, "Voices of the Dead Echo Across Algeria," *New York Times*, 18 April 2004.
4. "Education in Algeria: Past Successes, Challenges and Goals," The Borgen Project, January 2017.
5. "14 million under poverty line in Algeria, group says," *Middle East Monitor*, 17 October 2015.
6. "Algeria Unemployment Rate," *Trading Economics*, 2017.
7. *Ibid.*
8. Kamel Abdallah, "Algeria's constitution amended," *Al-Ahram Weekly*, 20–26 December 2012.
9. Djamila Ould Khettab, "Algeria set to approve new constitution," *Al-Jazeera*, 2 February 2016.
10. "Algeria GDP Growth Rate 2001–2017," *Trading Economics*, 2017.
11. Aida Alami, "Two Algerias: Country gripped by economic debate," *Al-Jazeera*, 2 March 2015.

12. Nabila Ramdani, "Fifty years after Algeria's independence, France is still in denial," *The Guardian* (UK), 5 July 2012.
    "The Algerian War," Indiana University, 7 April 2008.
13. Dalia Ghanem-Yazbeck, "The Decline of Islamist Parties in Algeria," Carnegie Endowment for International Peace," 13 February 2014.
14. Emily Estelle and Brenna Snyder, "AQIM [Al-Qaeda in the Islamic Maghrib] and ISIS in Algeria: Competing Campaigns," *Critical Threats*, 2 June 2016.
15. Michael Slackman, "A Quiet Revolution in Algeria: Gains by Women," *New York Times*, 26 May 2007.
16. "Algeria 5 years after the Arab Uprisings," Algeria, Afro Barometer, 15 April 2013.
17. *Ibid.*

TUNISIA

1. "Tunisia Constituent Assembly Elections," International Republican Institute, 23 October 2011, 3.
2. Karina Piser, "How Tunisia's Islamists Embraced Democracy," *Foreign Policy*, 31 March 2016.
3. "Tunisia beach attack: State of emergency declared," BBC News, 4 July 2015.
4. Mischa Benoit-Lavelle, "Tunisia's Celebrated Labor Union is Holding the Country Back," *Foreign Policy*, 20 July 2016.
5. "Tunisia country profile," BBC News, 17 January 2017.
6. Eileen Burne, "Runoff presidential election completes Tunisia's transition to full democracy," *The Guardian* (UK), 21 December 2014.
7. Hisham Aidi, "Tunisia's long road ahead," *Al-Jazeera*, 28 January 2016.
8. Fatim-Zohra El Malki, "Challenges Facing the New Tunisian Government," Atlantic Council, MENA [Middle East North Africa] Source, 2 September 2016.
9. Anouar Boukhars, "The Reckoning: Tunisia's Perilous Path to Democratic Stability," Carnegie Endowment for International Peace, 2 April 2015.
10. "Tunisia—Economy," Global Security, 20 January 2017.
11. Ivan Martin, Mohamed Kriaa, and Mohamed Alaa Demnati, "Migrant Support Measures from an Employment and Skills Perspective (MISMES), Tunisia," European Training Foundation, April 2015.
12. Katharina Natter, "Revolution and Political Transition in Tunisia: A Migration Game Changer?" Migration Policy Institute, 28 May 2015.
13. "Tunisia—Socio-Economic Indicators," UNESCO Institute for Statistics, 2014.
14. "Tunisian Berber: Maintenance and Revitalization," Graduate Center, City University of New York, 2015.
15. "Tunisia 2015 International Religious Freedom Report," United States Department of State, Bureau of Democracy, Human Rights, and Labor, 2015.

LIBYA

1. "Libya Country Profile," BBC News, 1 March 2017.
2. Shadi Hamid, "Everyone says the Libya intervention was a failure. They're wrong," Brookings, 12 April 2016.

3. "Libya Country Profile," *op. cit.*

4. Mattia Toaldo, "Political Actors," European Council on Foreign Relations, 15 June 2016.

5. Gaert Cappelaere, "More than half a million children in Libya need humanitarian assistance," UNICEF, 10 August 2017.

6. "Libya Situation Report #12, 7 March 2017," World Food Program, 2017.

7. Andrew McGregor, "Berbers Seize Libyan Oil Terminal to Press Demand for Recognition," Aberfoyle International Security (Canada), 14 November 2013.

8. Chris Stephen, "Libyan militias capture key oil ports and refinery," *The Guardian* (UK), 4 March 2017.

9. Rami Musa, "Libyan militias seize control of major oil terminals," *Washington Times*, 3 March 2017.

10. Steven Cook, "Vladimir Putin Has a Plan to Upend the Political Order of the Middle East. Spoiler Alert: It's Working," *From the Potomac to the Euphrates*, Council on Foreign Relations, 6 March 2017.

11. Patrick Wintour, "ISIS loses control of Libyan city of Sirte," *The Guardian* (UK), 5 December 2016.

12. Eric Schmitt, "ISIS Remains Threat in Libya Despite Defeat in Surt, U.S. Officials Say," *New York Times*, 8 December 2016.

13. Mary Fitzgerald, "Jihadists," European Council on Foreign Relations, 15 June 2016.

14. Eric Schmitt and Michael Gordonjan, "U.S. Bombs ISIS Camps in Libya," *New York Times*, 19 January 2017.

15. Ian Black, "Libya's descent into violence—the Guardian briefing," *The Guardian* (UK), 16 February 2015.

16. Mustafa Fetouri, "In Libya, the education system suffers more than most," *The National* (UAE), 15 November 2016.

17. Karlos Zurutuza, "Libyans fear ethnic conflict," *Al-Jazeera*, 6 January 2015.

18. Jonathan Saul and Ulf Laessing, "Libya food imports fall as turmoil disrupts delivery," Reuters, 31 July 2015.

19. David Goodman, "United States and Other Nations Step Up Libyan Evacuations," *New York Times*, 23 February 2011.

20. "Background Note: Libya," Bureau of Near Eastern Affairs, U.S. Department of State, 17 November 2010.

21. J. A. Allen, *Libya, The Experience of Oil* (Boulder, CO: Westview Press, 1981), 22.

22. "Libya's Forgotten King," *Al-Jazeera World*, 19 November 2015.

23. Sara Custer, "Libya scholarships to send 40,000 abroad," *PIE News*, Professionals in International Education, 13 May 2013.

24. Abdel Moneim Alaghima and John Dyer, "Libya's Foreign Scholarship Program Is Crumbling," *Al-Fanar Media* (UK), 9 July 2015.

25. Olfa Andolsi, "UN-backed government orders Libyan students abroad to return home after finishing studies," *Libya Herald*, 5 June 2017.

26. Sami Zaptia, "Hundreds of Libyan women receive entrepreneurship training—project expanded to all Libya and into 2017," *Libya Herald*, 30 January 2017.

27. Jessica Sarhan, "Libyan women struggle to join the workforce," *Al-Jazeera*, 26 November 2014.

28. "Empowering Women for a Better Libya," Libyan Women Forum, 2015.

29. Stein, op. cit.
30. Karen McVeigh, "Refugee women and children 'beaten, raped and starved in Libyan hellholes,'" *The Guardian* (UK), 2 March 2017.

EGYPT

1. "Egypt Demographics Profile 2016," *Index Mundi*, 2016.
2. Maggie Fick and Shadi Bushr, "More people, less water means rising food imports for Egypt," Reuters, 9 July 2014.
3. Tarek Heggy, "Egypt's Revolution: What Happened?" Gatestone Institute, 1 June 2011.
4. CNN Wire Staff, "Egypt lifts unpopular emergency law," CNN, 2 June 2012.
5. David Kirkpatrick, "Islamists win 70% of Seats in the Egyptian Parliament," *New York Times*, 21 January 2012.
6. "Final Report of the Carter Center Mission to Witness the 2011–12 Parliamentary Elections in Egypt," Carter Center, 2012.
7. Ian Black, "Egypt's overthrow of Morsi creates uncertainty for Islamists everywhere," *The Guardian* (UK), 12 July 2013.
8. "What's become of Egypt's Mohammed Morsi?" BBC News, 22 November 2016.
9. Patrick Kingsley, "Abdel Fatah al-Sisi won 96.1% of vote in Egypt presidential election, say officials," *The Guardian* (UK), 3 June 2014.
10. Jihad Abaza, "'Our blood is cheap': Mubarak acquittal leaves Egyptians numb," *Middle East Eye* (UK), 8 March 2017.
11. Amanda Taub, "The unsexy truth about why the Arab Spring failed," *Vox*, 27 January 2016.
12. Omer Karasapan, "Who are the 5 million refugees and immigrants in Egypt?" Brookings, 4 October 2016.
13. "More Egyptians Migrate for Work Abroad in 2015," *Egyptian Streets* (Egypt), 30 August 2016.
14. Rabie Passant, "Discordant friends: Egyptian workers in Saudi Arabia," *Mada Masr* (Egypt), 22 April 2016.
15. Nadia Ahmed, "Why Egyptians are risking their lives to work in Libya," *The Guardian* (UK), 20 February 2015.
16. Nourhan Fahmy, "Egypt has fourth highest illiteracy rate among 13 Arab states," *Aswat Masriya* (Egypt), 8 September 2016.
17. Hossam Mounir, "Unemployment rate reaches 12.7% in Q1 of 2016," *Egypt Daily News*, 15 May 2016.
18. Amr Adly, "Egypt's Oil and Political Discontent," Carnegie Middle East Center, 2 August 2016.
19. "Egypt GDP—composition by sector," *Index Mundi*, 8 October 2016.
20. Nader Noureddin, "Egypt is suffering from an acute food deficit, estimated at around 60 percent of its strategic food needs." *Al-Ahram Weekly*, 21 Oct 17
21. "Egypt—Travel & Tourism Total Contribution to GDP," *World Data Atlas*, Knoema, 2015.
22. "Egypt, Ethiopia and Sudan sign deal to end Nile dispute," BBC News, 23 March 2015.

23. Ahmed El-Sayed Al-Naggar, "Urban encroachment, lost development, and Egypt's next president," *Ahram Online*, 12 April 2014.
24. Julian Pecquet, "What Happened to the Billions the U.S. Gave to Egypt?" *Al-Monitor*, 13 May 2016.
25. "Canada's development assistance in Egypt," *Global Affairs Canada*, 16 December 2016.
    "Egypt and the E.U.," European Union External Action, 5 November 2016.
    Omar Mawi, "Saudi Arabia Comes to the Rescue of the Egyptian Economy," *Geopolitical Monitor* (Canada), 25 April 2016.
26. "Egypt Inflation Rate 2010–2017," *Trading Economics*, 17 February 2017.
27. MEE Staff, "Egypt bread riots: Government says 'fight against corruption' behind cuts," *Middle East Eye* (UK), 8 March 2017.
28. MEE Staff, "'Go hungry': Egyptian general tells millions to stop complaining about crisis," *Middle East Eye* (UK), 13 March 2017.
29. "Egypt to raise fuel prices by up to 47 percent at midnight," *Mada Masr* (Egypt), 3 November 2016.
30. Hend El-Behary, "Women's representation in new parliament highest in Egypt's history," *Egypt Independent*, 13 March 2017.
31. "Gender Equality in the Egyptian Higher Education System," Freie Universitat Berlin, 2012.
32. Jack Grove, "Proportion of female professors up, but still below a quarter," World University Rankings, 28 February 2015.
33. Cynthia Okoroafor, "International Women's Month: 15 years after a no-fault divorce law was passed, Egyptian women still suffer in the courts," Ventures Africa (Nigeria), 10 March 2016.
34. "Haughty about the hijab," *The Economist*, 27 August 2015.
35. Sarah Lynch, "Cairo University's New Sexual Harassment Policy a Novelty in the Region," *Al-Fanar Media* (UK), 21 July 2014.
36. "Egyptian university seeks to combat sexual harassment on campus," *New Arab* (UK), 13 April 2016.

SUDAN
1. "Ethnic Groups of Sudan," *World Atlas*, 10 November 2016.
2. "Sudan: GDP per capita PPP," *The Global Economy.com*, Council on Foreign Relations, 2017.
   "South Sudan GDP per capita (PPP)," *Index Mundi*, 2016.
3. "Sudan, Population below poverty line," *Index Mundi*, 2014.
4. "About South Sudan," UN Development Program, 2015.
5. Mike Congrove, "What are the three major reasons why Sudan split into two in 2011?" *Quora*, 25 April 2016.
6. Josh Korn, "Sudan Leader to Accept Secession of South," *New York Times*, 7 February 2011.
7. "Sudan profile—long overview," BBC News, 7 December 2015.
8. Clayton Hazvinei Vhumbunu, "Conflict Resurgence and the Agreement on the Resolution of the Conflict in the Republic of South Sudan," *Relief Web*, 19 October 2016.

9. *Ibid.*
10. "UN Peacekeepers to Stay in South Sudan through 2017," VOA News, 16 December 2016.
11. "About South Sudan," *op. cit.*
12. "Sudan Exports by Category," *Trading Economics*, December 2016.
13. "About South Sudan," *op. cit.*
14. "Population and Failing States: Sudan," Population Institute, 2009.
15. "South Sudan Economic Overview," World Bank, 20 October 2016.
16. "UN: Refugees from South Sudan cross 1.5 million mark," *Al-Jazeera*, 10 February 2017.
    Catherine Wachiaya, "Number of refugees fleeing South Sudan tops 1.5 million," UNHCR [United Nations High Commissioner for Refugees], 10 February 2017.
17. "Sudan age structure," *Index Mundi*, 8 October 2016.
18. "South Sudan population," Worldometers, 2017.
19. "Sudan: Blame traded over civilian deaths in Darfur," *Al-Jazeera*, 3 January 2017.
20. "African Union/United Nations Hybrid Operation in Darfur (UNAMID)," United Nations Peacekeeping, 2017.
21. Patrick Martin, "UN officials warn of worst famine crisis since World War II," World Socialist Web Site, 13 March 2017.
22. "Darfur Genocide," WorldWithoutGenocide.org, 2015.
23. "US lifts 20-year economic embargo on Sudan," *Al-Jazeera*, 14 January 2017.
24. "Sudan Corruption Report," GAN Business Anti-Corruption Portal, May 2016.
    Karin Zeitvotel and Nabeel Biajo, "South Sudan Seen as One of the World's Most Corrupt Nations," VOA, 3 December 2014.
25. "South Sudan: 2016 Trafficking in Persons Report," U.S. Department of State, Office to Monitor and Combat Trafficking in Persons, 2016.
26. "Sudan Migration Country Profile," Secretariat for Sudanese Working Abroad, *Zunia*, 27 February 2011.
27. "Sudan Total Fertility Rate," *Index Mundi*, 2016.
28. "Good Girls Don't Protest," Human Rights Watch, 23 March 2016.
29. "Sudan: Women in parliament," The Global Economy.com, 2015.
30. Liv Tønnessen, "Beyond numbers? Women's 25% parliamentary quota in post-conflict Sudan," *Journal of Peace, Conflict and Development* 17 (2011): 43–62.

The Arab States in Asia

LEBANON

1. "Lebanon country profile," BBC News, 6 November 2016.
2. "New government announced under PM Saad al-Hariri," *Al-Jazeera*, 18 December 2016.
3. "Lebanese Social Classes," *Reddit*, 15 January 2014.
4. Nadine Mazloum, "Crippling the youth: Unemployment in Lebanon at an all-time high," *Newsroom Nomad* (Lebanon), 19 August 2016.
5. Tom Charles, "The Unknown Hell of Palestinian Refugees in Lebanon," *Jadaliyya*, Arab Studies Institute, 12 December 2011.

6. "Lebanon: Syria Crisis," ECHO [European Commission on Humanitarian Aid and Civil Protection] Factsheet, European Commission, March 2017.

7. *Ibid.*

8. Liz Sly, "Six Italian U.N. peacekeepers injured in bomb attack in southern Lebanon," *Washington Post*, 28 May 2011.

9. "Lebanon hosts second largest refugee population," *Daily Star* (Beirut), 7 January 2015.

10. "Where We Work," UNRWA [United Nations Relief and Works Agency], 2014.

11. Meghan Monahan, "Treatment of Palestinian refugees in Lebanon," *Human Rights Brief*, 2 February 2015.

12. Charles, op. cit.

13. Chris Herlinger, "Syrian and Iraqi refugees wait in Lebanon for safety, new life," Global Sisters Report, *National Catholic Reporter*, 17 March 2016.

14. "Lebanon: Syria Crisis," *op. cit.*

15. Herlinger, op. cit.

16. "The Lebanese National Action Plan," *Women Watch*, United Nations, 2008.

17. Mona Alami, "Parliamentary presence sticking point for Lebanon's women," Syria Pulse, *Al-Monitor*, 19 March 2015.

18. "Unequal and Unprotected," Human Rights Watch, 19 January 2015.

SYRIA

1. "Quick facts: What you need to know about the Syria crisis," Mercy Corps, 9 March 2017.

2. "After the 'Arab Spring': Country by country," Amnesty International, 2016.

3. "The Disappeared of Syria," *Al-Jazeera*, 13 November 2016.

4. "Syria Population," *Country Meters*, 1 January 2017.

5. "Syria Population," *World Meters*, 1 July 2017.

6. "UN report: Syrian government actions amount to 'extermination,'" *The Guardian* (UK), 8 February 2016.

7. Thomas L. Friedman, "In the Arab World, It's the Past vs. the Future," *New York Times*, 26 September 2011.

8. *Ibid.*

9. Gene Thorp and Swati Sharma, "Foreign fighters flow to Syria," *Washington Post*, 17 January 2015.

10. "UK action to combat Daesh," UK Government, no date.

11. "Obama Renews Syria Sanctions," Agence France-Presse, 3 May 2010.

12. Matthew Lee and Martin Crutsinger, "U.S. slaps sanctions on Syria's Assad for abuses," Associated Press, 18 May 2011.

13. Gregory Korte, "U.S. sanctions Syria for use of chemical weapons," *USA Today*, 12 January 2017.

14. "Why is there a war in Syria?" BBC News, 13 March 2017.

15. Anna Patton, "Getting Syria's college students back into class," *Devex*, 6 July 2016. Layla Azzeh, "Jordanian universities open to receiving Syrian students, need funds," *Jordan Times*, 25 June 2015.

16. Brian Kahn, "Syria's drought 'has likely been its worst in 900 years,'" Guardian Environmental Network, *The Guardian* (UK), 2 March 2016.

Elaisha Stokes, "The Drought that Preceded Syria's Civil War Was Likely the Worst in 900 Years," VICE News, VICE Media, 3 March 2016.

17. "Palestinian Syrians: Twice Refugees," Al-Jazeera, 23 March 2016.

18. "Syria Crisis," UNRWA [United Nations Relief and Works Agency], February 2017.

19. Osama Bin Javald, "Thousands of Iraqi fleeing Mosul cross into Syria," Al-Jazeera, 18 November 2016.

20. "The Global Gender Gap Report 2016," World Economic Forum, 2016.

PALESTINE

1. Kim Murphy, "Hamas Victory is Built on Social Work," *Los Angeles Times*, 2 March 2006.

2. "On World Refugee Day: Palestinian refugees remain deprived of international protection," Badil Resource Center for Palestinian Residency and Refugee Rights (Palestine), 20 June 2016.

3. Greg Myre and Larry Kaplow, "7 Things to Know about Israeli Settlements," National Public Radio, 29 December 2016.
"On World Refugee Day," *op. cit.*

4. "7 Things to Know," *op. cit.*

5. Peter Beaumont, "Israel reveals plans for nearly 600 settlement homes in East Jerusalem," *The Guardian* (UK), 22 January 2017.

6. "Resisting Occupation, Constructing Peace," Israeli Committee Against House Demolitions, 2015.

7. Zena Tahhan, "Palestinians in Israel strike over home demolitions," *Al-Jazeera*, 11 January 2017.

8. "Hamas moves to approve '1967 borders'—but not recognize Israel," The Great Middle East.com (Russia), 9 March 2017.

9. "Population Density," Palestinian Central Bureau of Statistics, Palestine National Authority, 12 May 2011.

10. "Debunking Israel's 11 Main Myths about Gaza, Hamas, and War Crimes," *Huffington Post*, 28 July 2014.

11. Mousa Abu Marzook, "What Hamas is Seeking," *Washington Post*, 31 January 2006.

12. "Deaths in the Conflict, 1987–2014," ProCon.org, 2 September 2014.
"The Impact of the Conflict on Children," If Americans Knew.org, 31 December 2016.
"Israelis and Palestinians Injured in the Current Violence," If Americans Knew.org, 11 March 2017.
"Statistics," Addameer Prisoner Support and Human Rights Association (Palestine), January 2017.

13. "Gaza's Unemployment Rate Highest in World, World Bank Says," *Haaretz* (Israel), 3 April 2015.

14. "Assessing the Damage and Destruction in Gaza," *New York Times*, 15 August 2014.

15. "Sixty-ninth Session, 23rd Meeting," UN Fourth Committee, 6 November 2014.
"Gaza Crisis: Toll of Operations in Gaza," BBC, 1 September 2014.

"Our Work," U.S. Agency for International Development, 17 March 2017.
16. "The Gaza Strip: The Humanitarian Impact of the Blockade," U.N. Office for the Coordination of Humanitarian Assistance, 14 November 2016.
17. Rachel Banning-Lover, "US Aid in Palestine: 'It's not about solving the world's problems but people's daily ones,'" *The Guardian* (UK), 3 October 2016.
18. *Ibid.*
19. "OCHA: One in two Palestinians to need humanitarian assistance in 2017," U.N. Office for the Coordination of Humanitarian Assistance, Alternative Information Center, 2017.
20. Matthew Lee and Richard Lardner, "U.S. sent $221 million to Palestinians in Obama's last hours," *Salon*, 24 January 2017.
21. Elizabeth Blade, "Modern Day Exodus: the Palestinian Christians," *Israel Today*, 28 June 2012.
22. "Palestine Update: Muslim-Christian Solidarity in Palestine," Global Ministries, 21 February 2014.
23. "West Bank." The World Factbook, Central Intelligence Agency, 3 May 2011. Adnan Abu Amer, "Why donor countries are giving less to the Palestinians," *Al-Monitor*, 24 February 2016.
24. "Gaza Strip Population below poverty line," *Index Mundi*, 8 October 2016.
25. Ido Efrati, "Huge Disparities between Israeli, Palestinian Health-care Systems, Says Rights Group," *Haaretz* (Israel), 11 January 2015.
26. Yair Amikam, "The Palestinian Medical Crisis: An Exchange," *New York Review of Books*, 14 June 2007.
27. "Women's Rights in the Middle East and North Africa: Citizenship and Justice, Palestine (Palestinian Authority and Israeli-Occupied Territories)," Freedom House, 2011.

JORDAN

1. Dale Gavlak, "People have stopped paying attention to Iraqi refugees in Jordan, and it's getting 'critical and dangerous,'" *America*, Catholic News Service, 3 February 2017.
2. "Syria Regional Refugee Response," UNHCR [United Nations High Commissioner for Refugees], 5 April 2017.
3. "Syria refugees: UN warns of extreme poverty in Jordan," BBC News, 14 January 2015.
4. "Education for Syrian Refugee Children: What Donors and Host Countries Should Do," Human Rights Watch, 16 September 2016.
5. Pierre Tristam, "Black September: The Jordanian-PLO Civil War of 1970," ThoughtCo.com, 30 March 2017.
6. Fawwaz Al-Abed Al-Haq, "Islam and language planning in the Arab world: A case study in Jordan," *Iranian Journal of Language Studies* 3, no. 3 (2009): 267–302.
7. "Transforming Jordan's Badia Deserts into 'Ecosystems of Opportunity,'" World Bank, 21 March 2016.
8. Alan Cooperman, "Jordan's King Abdullah Pushes for Moderation," *Washington Post*, 14 September 2005.

9. "Jordan: Extremism and Counter-Extremism," Counter-Extremism Project, 2017.
10. Olivia Cuthbert, "Women gain ground in Jordan election despite yawning gender gap," *The Guardian* (UK), 22 September 2016.
11. Areej Abuqudairi, "Can Jordan's new parliament spearhead political change?" *Al-Jazeera*, 26 September 2016.
12. Imtiaz Muqbil, "Ten Years after 9/11, Pew Poll Shows U.S.-Muslim Schism as Wide as Ever," *Travel Impact Newswire*, 18 May 2011.
13. "Global Publics Back U.S. on Fighting ISIS, but are Critical of Post-9/11 Torture," Pew Research Center, 22 September 2015.
14. "Jordan: Overview," National Democratic Institute, 2016.
15. "Jordan Economy 2017." The World Factbook, Central Intelligence Agency, 2017.

IRAQ
1. Andrew Hammond, *Popular Culture in the Arab World* (Cairo: American University in Cairo Press, 2007), 8.
2. "Half Million Child Deaths 1991–1998," Global Policy Forum, United Nations, 2000.
3. Rainer Bohme, ed., "The Economics of Information Security and Privacy," Springer Science & Business Media, 29 November 2013.
4. Vijay Prashad, "The Rehabilitation of George W. Bush, War Criminal," *AlterNet*, 7 March 2017.
5. Ellen Knickmeyer, "Ghosts of Iraq's Birth," *Washington Post National Weekly Edition*, 13–19 March 2006.
6. David L. Phillips, "It is Time to Recognize Iraq as a Failed State," *Huffington Post*, 24 February 2017.
7. Noah Millman, "Kurdistan, and the problem of an endless parade of new nation states," *The Week*, 29 September 2017.
8. "Health Situation in Iraq," World Health Organization, United Nations, 2003.
9. "Iraq: Briefing on Health," U.N. Office for Coordination of Humanitarian Affairs, 18 May 2002.
10. John Pilger, "Squeezed to Death," *The Guardian* (UK), 4 March 2005.
11. "Prevalence of Child Malnutrition (Percentage Underweight under Age Five), 2000–2009," Global Health Facts, Kaiser Foundation, 2009.
12. Alissa J. Rubin, "Iraqi Surveys Start to Unveil the Mental Scars of War, Especially among Women," *New York Times*, 7 March 2009.
13. Sophia Akram, "Regional conflicts overshadow Iraqi mental health," *New Internationalist*, 5 April 2016.
14. "UNICEF Iraq Monthly Humanitarian Situation Report, January 2017," *Relief Web*, 6 March 2017.
15. Nazli Tarzi, "A not-so-historical deal: Iraq's post-IS vision runs into trouble," *Middle East Eye* (UK), 27 January 2017.
16. Chantal Berman and Omar Dewatchi, "Costs of War: Iraqi Refugees," Watson Institute for International Studies, December 2016.
17. "Iraq Humanitarian Response Plan," World Health Organization, 2016.
18. Lena Kampehl, "Fighting widespread malnutrition in Iraq," World-Grain.com, 27 September 2016.

19. Thomas Friedman, "President Obama Talks to Thomas L. Friedman about Iraq, Putin, and Israel," *New York Times*, 8 August 2014.
20. *Ibid.*
21. Jon Queally, "With 200+ Iraqi Civilians Feared Dead, Carnage Surging Under Trump," *Common Dreams*, 26 March 2017.
22. "Iraq." The World Factbook, Central Intelligence Agency, 12 January 2011.
23. "Iraqi Women and Children's Liberation Act of 2004, S 2519," *The Orator*, U.S. Congress, 15 June 2004.
24. "Background on Women's Status in Iraq Prior to the Fall of the Saddam Hussein Government," *Human Rights Watch Briefing Paper*, Human Rights Watch, November 2003.
25. Tina Susman, "Iraqis divided by treatment of women in constitution," *Los Angeles Times*, 9 October 2007.
26. John Leland and Riyadh Mohammed, "Iraqi Women Are Seeking Greater Political Influence," *New York Times*, 17 February 2010.
27. Adnan Abu Zeed, "Iraqi women don more conservative dress," *Al-Monitor*, 23 December 2014.
28. Ben Hubbard, "Saudi Arabia Agrees to Let Women Drive," *New York Times*, 26 September 2017.
29. Nancy Trejos, "Women Lose Ground in the New Iraq," *Washington Post*, 16 December 2006.
30. Nermeen Mufti, "Iraq's widows, abandoned and ignored, turn to begging," *Arab Weekly* (UK), 15 May 2015.
31. Caroline Hawley, "Iraq conflict: Crisis of an orphaned generation," BBC News, 28 November 2012.
32. Maher Nazeh and Saif Hameed, "Child labor doubles in Iraq as violence, displacement hit incomes," Reuters, 10 July 2016.

SAUDI ARABIA
1. "Saudi Arabia." The World Factbook, Central Intelligence Agency, 28 September 2016.
2. Andrew Martin, "Mideast Facing Choice between Crops and Water," *New York Times*, 21 July 2008.
3. Ana Swanson, "An incredible image shows how powerful countries are buying up much of the world's land," *Washington Post*, 21 May 2015.
4. Roby C. Barrett, *The Gulf and the Struggle for Hegemony* (Washington, D.C.: Middle East Institute, 2016), 26.
5. "KSA population 21.1 Saudis, 10.4 million expats," *Arab News* (Saudi Arabia), 4 February 2016.
6. Florence Foster, "New Rules for Foreign Workers in Saudi Arabia," Move One, Inc., 22 April 2010.
7. "Saudi Arabia, 2016," *op. cit.*
8. Heather Murdock, "Saudi Arabia Seeks to Shed Dependency on Foreign Labor," VOA News, 25 January 2016.
9. "Egypt's youth unemployment problem has erupted—but what about Britain's?" *Money Week* (UK), 31 January 2011.

10. "Saudi Arabia looks to the future, opens coed university," *Al-Arabiyya News*, 2 November 2010.
11. "Can Mohamed bin Salman transform Saudi Arabia?" *Washington Post*, 20 June 2016.
12. David Ignatius, "A 30-year-old Saudi prince could jump-start the kingdom—or drive it off a cliff," *Washington Post*, 13 June 2016.
13. Samuel Oakford, "Saudi Arabia Reveals How It Will End Its Oil 'Addiction' by 2020," VICE News, 25 April 2016.
14. David Ignatius, "A Saudi fatwa for moderation," *Washington Post*, 13 June 2010.
15. "Are women on their way at last?" *The Economist*, 1 May 2010.
16. Ian Black, "Saudi clerics declare ISIS terrorism a 'heinous crime' under Sharia law," *The Guardian* (UK), 17 September 2014.
17. Ivana Kottasova, "Saudi Arabia cuts funding for students abroad," CNN Money, 9 February 2016.
18. "Saudi Arabia slashes ministers' pay, cuts public sector bonuses," CNBC (Canada), 27 September 2016.
19. Margharita Stancati, "Oil Income Falling, Saudi Raises Government Fees and Fines," *Wall Street Journal*, 9 August 2016.
20. *Ibid.*
21. Tim Daiss, "'We're Doomed for Bankruptcy' Unless Changes Made, Says Saudi Official," *Forbes*, 23 October 2016.
22. Nicholas Kulish, "Saudi Arabia, Where Even Milk Depends on Oil, Struggles to Remake Its Economy," *New York Times*, 14 October 2016.
23. Anya Clarkson, "Saudi Arabia: Anti-Shia Discrimination in Employment and the Work Place," The Centre for Academic Shii'a Studies (UK), July 2014.
24. Scott Wilson, "Shiites See an Opening in Saudi Arabia," *Washington Post*, 28 February 2005.
25. "Saudi Arabia: King's Reform Agenda Unfulfilled," Human Rights Watch, 23 January 2015.
26. Mazin Sidahmed, "Thousands of Saudis sign petition to end male guardianship of women," *The Guardian* (UK), 26 September 2016.
27. Ben Hubbard, "Saudi Arabia Agrees to Let Women Drive," *New York Times*, 26 September 2017.
28. Faiza Saleh Ambah, "Saudi Women See a Brighter Road on Rights," *Washington Post*, 31 January 2008.
29. Kelly McEvers, "Saudis slow to accept working women," *Marketplace*, 23 April 2008.
30. Juliane von Mittelstaedt and Samiha Shafy, "How Working Women are Remaking Saudi Arabia," *Spiegel Online* (Germany), 23 June 2015.
31. "Women are taking over Saudi Arabia's workforce," *Fortune*, 10 August 2015.
32. Andrew Lee Butters, "Saudi's Small Steps," *Time*, 19 October 2009.
33. *Ibid.*
34. Mike Giglio, "Saudi's Surprise Renegades," *Newsweek*, 9 May 2011.
35. Ahmad Al-Haj, "Thousands March in Yemen to Protest Saudi-Led Airstrike That Killed 140," *Time*, 9 October 2016.
36. Sarah Lazare, "Conference Examines the U.S. 'Special Relationship' with Human Rights Abuser Saudi Arabia," *AlterNet*, 16 March 2016.

37. Scott Shane, "Saudis and Extremism: 'Both the Arsonists and the Firefighters,'"
    New York Times, 26 August 2016.
38. Chris Enloe, "Top Obama official Samantha Power gets brutal lesson in self-
    awareness after criticizing Trump's Saudi arms deal," *The Blaze*, 21 May
    2017.

YEMEN

1. Max Rodenbeck, "Yemen, Al-Qaeda, and the U.S." *New York Review of Books*, 30
   September 2010, 39.
2. "Yemen: International Religious Freedom Report 2010," U.S. Department of State,
   17 November 2010.
3. "Yemen's Hadi declares Sanaa 'occupied capital,'" *Middle East Monitor*, 1 March
   2015.
4. Tawakkol Karman, "Yes, Yemen's revolution was worth it—despite everything
   that came next," *Washington Post*, 24 February 2017.
5. Michelle Nichols, "U.N. experts warn Saudi-led coalition allies over war crimes
   in Yemen," *Reuters World News*, 29 January 2017.
6. *Ibid.*
7. Farea Al-Muslimi, "As Yemen's civil war continues, extremist groups are thriving
   in the chaos," Carnegie Middle East Center, 7 September 2015.
8. *Ibid.*
9. Naser Arrabyee, "Rising Extremism in Yemen," Carnegie Endowment for International Peace, 19 February 2016.
10. Karl Vick, "Yemen Walks Tightrope in Terrorism Stance," *Washington Post*, 29
    September 2001.
11. "U.S. Navy destroyer is sent to patrol off coast of Yemen after Iranian-backed
    militia's suicide attack on Saudi warship," *Daily Mail* (UK), 3 February 2017.
12. Les Roopanarine, Patrick Wintour, Saeed Kemali Dehghan, and Ahmad Algo-
    hbary, "Yemen at 'point of no return' as conflict leaves almost 7 million close to
    famine," *The Guardian*, 24 March 2017.
13. "UN delivers medicine to Yemen's besieged Taiz city," *Al-Jazeera*, 4 March 2017.
14. Mariam Elba, "How Poetry Became a Political Medium in Yemen," *Muftah*, 27
    September 2017.
15. "Child malnutrition at 'all-time high' in Yemen: UN agency," *Reuters World News*,
    12 December 2016.
16. Mohamed Al-Azaki, "Somali refugees live in alarming conditions in Yemen,"
    Wardheer News (Somalia), 16 December 2016.
17. "Yemen: Overview," World Bank, 1 October 2016.
18. "Oil Sector Recovery in Yemen Urgently Needed," *Yemen Socio-Economic Update*
    no. 14, Ministry of Planning and International Cooperation, *Relief Web*, May
    2016.
19. "Yemen's Economic Outlook—Spring 2016," World Bank, 2016.
20. Christopher Boucek and David Donadio, "A Nation on the Brink," *The Atlantic*,
    April 2010, 53.
21. "Saudi deports thousands of Yemenis, remittances to suffer—official," *Reuters
    World News*, 1 April 2013.

22. Michael Cruikshank, "Yemen is on the verge of running out of water," Think-Progress, 13 March 2017.
23. Christopher Ward, "Water Crisis in Yemen" (Lecture, St. Anthony's College, Oxford, 4 June 2015).
24. Frederika Whitehead, "Water scarcity in Yemen: the country's forgotten conflict," *The Guardian* (UK), 2 April 2015.
25. Nicole Glass, "The Water Crisis in Yemen: Causes, Consequences and Solutions," *Global Majority E-Journal*, June 2010.
26. "Yemen People 2017," Theodora.com, 2017.
27. "Young and unmarried Yemeni women more likely to pursue career and financial independence," Institute for Women's Policy Research, 1 December 2010.
28. "Yemen: Worst Place to Live as a Woman," Borgen Project, November 2013.
29. Roby Barrett, *"The Gulf and the Struggle for Hegemony"* (Washington, D.C.: Middle East Institute, 2016), 456.
30. Stasa Salacanin, "Yemen's road to perdition," *BQ Magazine* (Qatar), May 2015.

The Arabian Gulf States

1. Rami Khouri, "The Saudis are worried, and not just about kings," Press Reader, *The Guardian Weekly* (UK), 9 October 2015.

Kuwait

1. "Kuwait poll: Opposition wins nearly half of parliament," *Al-Jazeera*, 27 November 2016.
2. Habib Toumi, "Kuwait lifts decades-long ban on Palestinian workers," *Gulf News* (Dubai), 6 February 2017.
3. Peter Mansfield, *The New Arabians* (New York: Doubleday, 1981), 112.
4. Ahmed Feteha and Mohammed Sergie, "Kuwait Mulls Income, Sales Taxes as Oil Hits 12-Year low," *The National* (Canada), 21 January 2016.
5. *Ibid.*
6. Hiba Koraytem and Nemr Kanafani, "Public finance Kuwait: New budget keeps spending unchanged; deficit likely at 13% of GDP," NBK Economic Research, 2 August 2016.
7. Ali Z. Alzuabi, "Sociopolitical Participation of Kuwaiti Women in the Development Process: Current State and Challenges Ahead," *Journal of Social Service Research*, 42, no. 5 (2016): 689–702.
8. "Kuwait: New labor law grants women the right—and flexibility—to work late," *Los Angeles Times*, 5 June 2010.

Bahrain

1. "U.S.-Bahrain Free Trade Agreement," Council on Foreign Relations, 11 January 2006.
2. Joby Warrick, "Bahrain ends state of emergency, vows talks on political reform," *Washington Post*, 1 June 2011.

3. Kristin Smith Diwan and Michael Esfahani, "Bahrain's New Order," Arab Gulf States Institute in Washington, 19 August 2016.
4. Elizabeth Dickinson, "Bahrain's Elections and the Opposition," Middle East Institute, 23 December 2014.
5. Souad Mekhennet and Joby Warrick, "In Bahrain's militant cells, U.S. sees Iran," *Washington Post*, 2 April 2017.
6. "GCC: Total population and percentage of nationals and non-nationals in GCC countries," Gulf Labor Markets and Migration, Gulf Research Center, 31 March 2015.
7. "Bahrain's by-elections," BBC News, 23 September 2011.
8. Dickinson, *op. cit.*
   "Boycotted elections underline Bahrain's polarized politics," *The Economist*, 24 November 2014.
9. Dickinson, *op. cit.*
10. "Bahrain to Enter First Third of Year without Adopted Budget. MPs: Beautiful Days are Over," *Bahrain Mirror*, 19 February 2017.
11. Editorial Board, "Trump is letting human rights deteriorate, and Bahrain is Exhibit A," *Washington Post*, 13 March 2017.

QATAR

1. "Qatar Population 2017," *World Population Review*, 20 November 2016.
2. Emiri Diwan, "Legislative elections in Qatar postponed until at least 2019," *Doha News*, 17 June 2016.
3. "Qatari women win 2 out of 29 seats in municipal council vote," *NewsOK*, 14 May 2015.
4. "Qatar GDP and Economic Data, Country Report 2017," *Global Finance*, 2016.
5. "Qatar Population," *Country Meters*, 5 January 2017.
6. Lesley Walker, "Qatar home to highest proportion of employed women in the Gulf," *Doha News*, 15 March 2016.
7. "Qatar 2016/2017," Amnesty International annual report, February 2017.
8. Anne Barnard and David D. Kirkpatrick, "5 Arab Nations Move to Isolate Qatar, Putting the U.S. in a Bind," *New York Times*, 5 June 2017.
9. "How the Middle East has gone cool towards Qatar," BBC News, 10 March 2014.
10. *Ibid.*
11. Barnard and Kirkpatrick, *op. cit.*
12. Jared Malsin, "Qatar settles in for a long standoff," *Time*, 7 August 2017.
13. Samuel Ramani, "Israel Is Strengthening Its Ties with the Gulf Monarchies," *Huffington Post*, 12 September 2016.
14. "Qatari diplomat admits to 'excellent' relations with Israeli officials," *New Arab* (U.K.), 13 February 2017.

UNITED ARAB EMIRATES (UAE)

1. "Financial Management: United Arab Emirates," POGAR [Programme on Governance of the Arab Region], U.N. Development Programme, 2004.

2. "DIFC [Dubai International Finance Center] posts robust 2016 figures," *Khaleej Times* (Dubai), 2 March 2015.
3. "UAE tops economic freedom index in Mideast," Trade Arabia News Service (Bahrain), 16 February 2017.
4. Issac John, "UAE's per capita income remains high," *Khaleej Times* (Dubai), 16 June 2016.
5. *Ibid.*
6. "United Arab Emirates 2017." The World Factbook, Central Intelligence Agency, 22 February 2017.
7. "UAE committee on sustainable development goals announced," *The National* (Canada), 14 February 2017.
8. "United Arab Emirates 2017," *op. cit.*
9. Haseeb Haider, "Emirati women grads outnumber men in UAE workforce," *Khaleej Times* (Dubai), 27 August 2016.
10. Sherouk Zakaria, "UAE intensifies efforts for women's empowerment," *Khaleej Times* (Dubai), 6 February 2017.
11. Roberta Pennington, "Special report: Arabic 'at risk of becoming foreign language in UAE,'" *The National* (Canada), 2 March 2015.
12. "United Arab Emirates 2017," *op. cit.*
13. Pennington, *op. cit.*
14. Samir Salama, "How the UAE Actively Promotes Religious Tolerance, Peaceful Coexistence," *Gulf News* (Dubai), 15 September 2016.
15. Isaac John, "UAE business conditions rebound," *Khaleej Times* (Dubai), 5 April 2015.
16. "United Arab Emirates 2017," *op. cit.*
17. *Ibid.*
18. Anwar Ahmad and Thamer Al Subaihi, "Workers and employers praise UAE labour law reforms," *The National* (Canada), 30 September 2015.
19. "United Arab Emirates," Index of Economic Freedom 2017. "Youth Unemployment Rate for the United Arab Emirates," FRED Economic Data, Economic Research (Federal Reserve Bank of St. Louis), 1 May 2017.
20. "76 countries benefit from Abu Dhabi funds," *Khaleej Times* (Dubai), 26 July 2015.

OMAN

1. "Oman Population," *Country Meters*, 4 May 2017.
2. *Ibid.*
3. Tavia Grant, "Oman most-improved nation in last 40 years, UN index says," *Globe and Mail* (Canada), 4 November 2010.
4. "Oman Economy 2017." The World Factbook, Central Intelligence Agency, 12 January 2017.
5. Saleh Al Shaibany, "In post-oil economy, Oman turns sleepy fishing port to bustling trading hub," *The National* (Canada), 7 February 2017.
6. "Oman Economy 2017," *op. cit.*
7. Gautam Viswanathan, "Gender parity in education a positive sign," *Pressreader: Times of Oman*, 19 March 2017.

8. "Seven women elected to Oman municipal councils," *Al-Arabiya—English*, 25 December 2016.
9. Kenneth Katzman, "Oman: Reform, Security, and U.S. Policy," Congressional Research Service, 26 April 2016.
10. Linda Pappas Funsch, *Oman Reborn: Balancing Tradition and Modernization* (Palgrave Macmillan: New York, 2015).
11. Katzman, *op. cit.*
12. *Ibid.*

BIBLIOGRAPHY

Abaza, Jihad. "'Our blood is cheap': Mubarak acquittal leaves Egyptians numb." *Middle East Eye* (UK), 8 March 2017.

Abdullah, Kamel. "Algeria's constitution amended." *Al-Ahram Weekly*, 20–26 December 2012.

"About Free Muslims Coalition." Free Muslims Coalition, 30 May 2011.

"About South Sudan." UN Development Program, 2015.

Abu Amer, Adnan. "Why donor countries are giving less to the Palestinians." *Al-Monitor*, 24 February 2016.

Abu Marzook, Mousa. "What Hamas is Seeking." *Washington Post*, 31 January 2006.

Abu Zeed, Adnan. "Iraqi women don more conservative dress." *Al-Monitor*, 23 December 2014.

Abuqudairi, Aareej. "Can Jordan's new parliament spearhead political change?" *Al-Jazeera*, 26 September 2016.

Adler, Margot. "Developer: Plans for N.Y. Mosque Moving Forward." *All Things Considered*. National Public Radio, 5 May 2011.

Adly, Amr. "Egypt's Oil Dependency and Political Discontent." Carnegie Middle East Center, 2 August 2016.

"Adult and Youth Literacy." UNESCO Institute for Statistics, Fact Sheet 26, September 2013.

"African Union–United Nations Hybrid Operation in Darfur (UNAMID)." United Nations Peacekeeping, 2017.

"After the 'Arab Spring': Country by country." Amnesty International, 2016.

Agerholm, Harriet. "Muslim face veil ban for workers is not discriminatory, Austrian court rules." *The Independent* (UK), 11 July 2016.

Ahmad, Anwar, and Thamer Al Subaihi. "Workers and employers praise UAE labour law reforms." *The National* (Canada), 30 September 2015.

Ahmed, Beenish. "Why Converts to Islam Are So Susceptible to Becoming Terrorists." ThinkProgress, 3 February 2016.

Ahmed, Nadia. "Why Egyptians are risking their lives to work in Libya." *The Guardian* (UK), 20 February 2015.

Aidi, Hisham. "Tunisia's long road ahead." *Al-Jazeera*, 28 January 2016.

Ajami, Fouad. "Bush Country." *Daily Star* (Beirut), 23 May 2005.

Ajami, Fouad. "The Meaning of Lebanon." Foundation for the Defense of Democracy, 1 May 2005.

Akl, Aida F. "Will Women Benefit from the Middle East Revolution?" News.com, 29 March 2011.

Akram, Sophia. "Regional conflicts overshadow Iraqi mental health." *New Internationalist,* 5 April 2016.

Akyol, Mustafa. "Sexism Deleted in Turkey." *Washington Post,* 16 July 2006.

Alaghima, Abdel Moneim, and John Dyer. "Libya's Foreign Scholarship Program is Crumbling." *Al-Fanar Media* (UK), 9 July 2015.

Al-Ajmi, Nassir M. "Heart-to-Heart Talk—A Friend to Friend Discussion." Ladah Foundation, 23 October 2003.

Alami, Aida. "Two Algerias: Country gripped by economic debate." *Al-Jazeera,* 2 March 2015.

Alami, Mona. "Parliamentary presence sticking point for Lebanon's women." Syria Pulse, *Al-Monitor,* 19 March 2015.

Al-Aswani, Alaa. *On the State of Egypt.* New York: Vintage Books, 2011.

Alauoi, Mohamed. "Moroccan women judges strive for equal rights." *The Arab Weekly* (UK), 25 September 2016.

Al-Azaki, Mohamed. "Somali refugees live in alarming conditions in Yemen." Wardheer News (Somalia), 16 December 2016.

"Al Azhar confirms hijab is not part of the religion." World Muslim Congress, 23 May 2012.

Al-Ba'albaki, Mounir. *Al-Mawrid: A Modern English-Arabic Dictionary.* Beirut: Dar El-Ilm lil-Malayen, 2004.

"Algeria." Afro Barometer, 2013.

"Algeria 5 years after the Arab uprisings." Afro Barometer, 15 April 2013.

"Algeria GDP Growth Rate 2001–2017." *Trading Economics,* 2017.

"Algeria Unemployment Rate." *Trading Economics,* 2017.

"Algerian Economy 2016." The World Factbook, Central Intelligence Agency, 2016.

"The Algerian War." (No author), Indiana University, 7 April 2008.

Algosaibi, Ghazi. "The Crisis of Modern Arabic Poetry." In *Arabian Essays,* 101. UK: Routledge and Kegan, 1982, 98–111.

Al-Haj, Ahmad. "Thousands March in Yemen to Protest Saudi-Led Airstrike that Killed 140." *Time,* 9 October 2016.

Al-Haq, Fawwaz Al-Abed. "Islam and language planning in the Arab world: A case study in Jordan." *Iranian Journal of Language Studies* 3, no. 3 (2009): 267–302.

Al-Krenawi, Alean, and John R. Graham. "Principles of Social Work Practice in the Muslim Arab World." *Arab Studies Quarterly* 25, no. 4 (Fall 2003): 85.

Allen, J. A. *Libya, The Experience of Oil.* Boulder, CO: Westview Press, 1981.

Al-Marayati, Laila, and Basil Abdelkarim. "The Crime of Being a Muslim Charity." *Washington Post,* 11 March 2006.

Al-Muslimi, Farea. "As Yemen's civil war continues, extremist groups are thriving in the chaos." Carnegie Middle East Center, 7 September 2015.

Al-Naggar, Ahmed El-Sayed. "Urban encroachment, lost development, and Egypt's next president." *Ahram Online,* 12 April 2014.

Al Shaibany, Saleh. "In post-oil economy, Oman turns sleepy fishing port to bustling trading hub." *The National* (Canada), 7 February 2017.

Alzuabi, Ali Z. "Sociopolitical Participation of Kuwaiti Women in the Development Process: Current State and Challenges Ahead." *Journal of Social Science Research* 42, no. 5 (2016): 689–702.

"The Amazigh (Berber)." Phoenician International Research Center, 2011.

Ambah, Faiza Saleh. "Saudi Women See a Brighter Road on Rights." *Washington Post*, 31 January 2008.

Amikan, Yair. "The Palestinian Medical Crisis: An Exchange." *New York Review of Books*, 14 June 2007.

"An Iraq Fit for Children: Building Iraq's Future." *Quarterly Newsletter*, United Nations Children's Fund, no. 02 (2010).

Andolsi, Olfa. "UN-backed government orders Libyan students abroad to return home after finishing studies." *Libyan Herald*, 5 June 2017.

"Arab Attitudes 2011." *Arab America*, 2012.

"Arab dawn: Arab youth and the demographic dividend they will bring." Brookings, 28 December 2015.

"Arabic Speaking Internet Users Statistics." Internet World Stats, 6 March 2017.

"Are women on their way at last?" *The Economist*, 1 May 2010.

Armstrong, Karen. *Muhammad: A Biography of the Prophet*. San Francisco: HarperSanFrancisco, 1992.

Arrabyee, Naser. "Rising Extremism in Yemen." Carnegie Endowment for International Peace, 19 February 2016.

"Assessing the Damage and Destruction in Gaza." *New York Times*, 15 August 2014.

Atiyeh, George N. *Arab and American Cultures*. Washington, D.C.: American Enterprise Institute for Public Policy Research, 1977.

Azzeh, Layla. "Jordanian universities open to receiving Syrian students, need funds." *Jordan Times*, 25 June 2015.

B., V. v. "Why America does not take in more Syrian refugees." *The Economist*, 18 October 2015.

"Background Note: Egypt." Bureau of Near Eastern Affairs, U.S. Department of State, 10 November 2010.

"Background Note: Libya." Bureau of Near Eastern Affairs, U.S. Department of State, 17 November 2010.

"Background on Women's Status in Iraq Prior to the Fall of the Saddam Hussein Government." *Human Rights Watch Briefing Paper*, Human Rights Watch, November 2003.

Badger, Emily. "Why Are the World's Muslims So Mad at America?" *Pacific Standard*, 19 May 2011.

"Bahrain to Enter First Third of Year without Adopted Budget. MPs: Beautiful Days are Over." *Bahrain Mirror*, 19 February 2017.

"Bahrain's by-elections." BBC News, 23 September 2011.

Bakar, Osman. *The History and Philosophy of Islamic Science*. Cambridge: Islamic Texts Society, 1999.

Bandew, Doug. "Maybe Europe Isn't Lost to Islamic Terrorism." Cato @ Liberty, Cato Institute, 26 July 2009.

Banning-Lover, Rachel. "US Aid in Palestine: 'It's not about solving the world's problems but people's daily ones.'" *The Guardian* (UK), 3 October 2016.

Barakat, Halim. *The Arab World: Society, Culture and State.* Berkeley: University of California Press, 1993.

Barnard, Anne, and David D. Kirkpatrick. "5 Arab Nations Move to Isolate Qatar, Putting the U.S. in a Bind." *New York Times,* 5 June 2017.

Barrett, Roby C. *The Gulf and the Struggle for Hegemony.* Washington, D.C.: Middle East Institute, 2016.

Bashir, Abdul Wahab. "Scholars Define Terrorism, Call for Joint Action to Defend Islam." *Arab News* (Saudi Arabia), 12 January 2002.

Batha, Emma. "Morocco's Islamic women preachers lead social revolution." *World News,* Reuters, 19 May 2015.

Beaumont, Peter. "Israel reveals plans for nearly 600 settlement homes in East Jerusalem." *The Guardian* (UK), 22 January 2017.

Beck, Glenn. "Remember Why We Were Attacked on September 11." Fox News, 11 September 2009.

Ben-Meir, Alon, "Killing in the Name of God." *Huffington Post,* 17 July 2013.

Bennett, Jonah. "Islam Set to Become the Second-Largest Religion in America by 2040." *Daily Caller News Foundation,* 8 January 2016.

Benoit-Lavalle, Mischa. "Tunisia's Celebrated Labor Union is Holding the Country Back." *Foreign Policy,* 20 July 2016.

Berman, Chantal, and Omar Dewatchi. "Costs of War: Iraqi Refugees." Watson Institute for International Studies, December 2016.

Bhutto, Benazir. "Politics and the Modern Woman." In *Liberal Islam: A Sourcebook,* edited by Charles Kurzman, 107–111. New York: Oxford University Press, 1998.

Bin Javald, Osama. "Thousands of Iraqis fleeing Mosul cross into Syria." *Al-Jazeera,* 18 November 2016.

Black, Ian. "Egypt's overthrow of Morsi creates uncertainty for Islamists everywhere." *The Guardian* (UK), 12 July 2013.

Black, Ian. "Libya's descent into violence—the Guardian briefing." *The Guardian* (UK), 16 February 2015.

Black, Ian. "Saudi clerics declare ISIS terrorism a 'heinous crime' under Sharia law." *The Guardian* (UK), 17 September 2014.

Blade, Elizabeth. "Modern Day Exodus: the Palestinian Christians." *Israel Today,* 28 June 2012.

Blumenthal, Max. "The Manchester Bombing is Blowback from the West's Disastrous Interventions and Covert Proxy Wars." AlterNet, 25 May 2017.

Bochlert, Eric. "Terrorists under the Bed." *Salon.com,* 5 March 2002.

Bohne, Ranier, ed. "The Economy of Security and Policy." Springer Science and Business Media, 150, 29 November 2013.

Book Talk, Penguin Random House, 7 November 2006.

Boorstein, Michelle. "For critics of Islam, 'Sharia' is a loaded word." *Washington Post,* 27 August 2010.

Boorstein, Michelle, and Felicia Sonmez. "Familiar sparring in hearing on civil rights of Muslims." *Washington Post,* 30 March 2011.

Booth, William. "Cast of Villains." *Washington Post,* 23 June 2007.

Bordat, Stephanie Willman, and Saida Kouzzi. "The Challenge of Implementing Morocco's New Personal Status Law." Carnegie Endowment for International Peace, 20
August 2008.

Boucek, Christopher, and David Donadio. "A Nation on the Brink." *The Atlantic*, April
2010.

Boukhars, Anouar. "The Reckoning: Tunisia's Perilous Path to Democratic Stability."
Carnegie Endowment for International Peace, 2 April 2015.

Bowen, Donna Lee, and Evelyn A. Early, eds., *Everyday Life in the Muslim Middle East*.
Bloomington: Indiana University Press, 1993.

"Boycotted elections underline Bahrain's polarized politics." *The Economist*, 24 November 2014.

Brown, David. "Global Study Examines Toll of Genetic Defects." *Washington Post*, 30
January 2006.

Burke, Jason, and Ian Traynor. "Fears of an Islamic revolt in Europe begin to fade." *The
Guardian* (UK), 25 July 2009.

Burne, Eileen. "Runoff presidential election completes Tunisia's transition to full democracy." *The Guardian* (UK), 21 December 2014.

Butters, Andrew Lee. "Saudi's Small Steps." *Time*, 19 October 2009.

"Can Mohamed bin Salman transform Saudi Arabia?" *Washington Post*, 20 June 2016.

"Canada's development assistance in Egypt." *Global Affairs Canada*, 16 December,
2016.

Charai, Ahmad, and Joseph Braude. "All Hail the (Democratic) King." *New York Times*,
11 July 2011.

Charles, Tom. "The Unknown Hell of Palestinian Refugees in Lebanon." *Jadaliyya*, Arab
Studies Institute, 12 December 2011.

"Child malnutrition at 'all-time high' in Yemen: UN agency." *Reuters World News*, 12
December 2016.

Clarkson, Anya. "Saudi Arabia: Anti-Shia Discrimination in Employment and the Work
Place." Centre for Academic Shii'a Studies (UK), July 2014.

Clayton, Mark. "How Are Mosques Fighting Terror?" *Christian Science Monitor*, 12
August 2004.

CNN Wire Staff. "Egypt lifts unpopular emergency law." CNN, 2 June 2012.

Cody, Edward. "Tensions grow for Muslims as French debate national identity." *Washington Post*, 19 December 2009.

Cole, Juan. "How Americans Hate: 8-fold Increase in Islamophobic Crime since 2000."
AlterNet, 15 April 2016.

Conason, Joe. "Why Nobody Watches Our Arab TV Channel." *Salon*, 12 May 2010.

"Conflict in the Republic of South Sudan." *ReliefWeb*, 19 October 2016.

"Conflict in the Republic of South Sudan." *Relief Web*, 19 October 2016.

Congrove, Mike. "What are the three major reasons why Sudan split into two in 2011?"
Quora, 25 April 2016.

Connor, Philip. "U.S. admits record number of Muslim refugees in 2016." Pew Research
Center, 5 October 2016.

Cook, Jonathan. "Here's What Will Probably Happen If Assad Falls in Syria (Hint: The
Opposite of Peace and Democracy)." *AlterNet*, 10 May 2017.

Cook, Steven. "Vladimir Putin Has a Plan to Upend the Political Order of the Middle East. Spoiler Alert: It's Working." *From the Potomac to the Euphrates*, Council on Foreign Relations, 6 March 2017.

Cooperman, Alan. "A Timely Subject—and a Sore One." *Washington Post*, 7 August 2002.

Cooperman, Alan. "Jordan's King Abdullah Pushes for Moderation." *Washington Post*, 14 September 2005.

Cooperman, Alan. "September 11 Backlash Murders and the State of Hate." *Washington Post*, 20 January 2002.

Cooperman, Alan, and Mary Beth Sheridan. "Muslims to Provide Food on Sept. 11." *Washington Post*, 9 September 2005.

"Country Analysis Brief: Algeria." U.S. Energy Information Administration, 11 March 2016.

Cruikshank, Michael. "Yemen is on the verge of running out of water." ThinkProgress, 13 March 2017.

Culver, Virginia. "Many American Muslims Well-Off, College Educated, Poll Shows." *Denver Post*, 18 January 2001.

Curtis, Edward E. IV. "5 Myths about Mosques in America." *Washington Post*, 29 August 2010.

Custer, Sara. "Libya scholarships to send 40,000 abroad." *PIE News*, Professionals in International Education, 13 May 2013.

Cuthbert, Olivia. "Women gain ground in Jordanian election despite yawning gender gap." *The Guardian* (UK), 22 September 2016.

D., M., and Erasmus. "Why Canadian Muslims seem happier than British ones." *The Economist*, 22 July 2016.

Daiss, Tim. "'We're Doomed for Bankruptcy' Unless Changes Made, Says Saudi Official." *Forbes*, 23 October 2016.

"Darfur Genocide." World Without Genocide.org, 2015.

The Data Team. "The rise of the far right in Europe." *The Economist*, 24 May 2016.

Dawood, Khaled. "Arab Opinions." *Al-Ahram Weekly*, 30 July 2004.

Dean, John, and Sophie Evans. "ISIS reveals 6 reasons why they despise Westerners as terrorist's sister claims he wanted revenge for US airstrikes in Syria." *The Mirror* (UK), 26 May 2017.

Deane, Claudia, and Darryl Fears. "Negative Perception of Islam Increasing." *Washington Post*, 9 March 2006.

"Deaths in the Conflict, 1987–2014." ProCon.org, 2 September 2014.

"Debunking Israel's 11 Main Myths About Gaza, Hamas, and War Crimes." *Huffington Post*, 28 July 2014.

Deen, Adam. "Why are converts to Islam specifically vulnerable to becoming extremists?" *The Independent* (UK), 24 March 2017.

"Defying Prejudice, more Americans learn Arabic." *Al-Jazeera*, 18 December 2015.

"Demographics." Arab American Institute, Islam Online, 18 February 2014.

"Denmark Imposes Restrictions on Imams." Islam Online, 18 February 2004.

DeSilver, Drew, and David Masci. "World's Muslim population more widespread than you might think." Pew Research Center, 31 January 2017.

Dickinson, Elizabeth. "Bahrain's Elections and the Opposition." Middle East Institute, 23 December 2014.

Dieseldorff, Karla. "FBI Says 94% of Terrorist Attacks in the U.S. since 1980 Are by Non-Muslims." *Morocco World News*, 18 December 2015.

"DIFC [Dubai International Financial Centre] posts robust 2016 figures." *Khaleej Times* (Dubai), 30 April 2017.

"The Disappeared of Syria." *Al-Jazeera*, 13 November 2016.

"Distribution of Mosques in USA 2015." *Islam Threat*, 25 March 2015.

Diwan, Emiri. "Legislative elections in Qatar postponed until at least 2019." *Doha News*, 17 June 2016.

Diwan, Kristin, and Michael Esfahani. "Bahrain's New Order." Arab Gulf States Institute in Washington, 19 August 2016.

Driouchi, Ahmed. *"Knowledge-Based Economic Policy Development in the Arab World."* Forum Euromediterraneen des Instituts de Sciences Economiques (FEMISE), 2014.

Durden, Tyler. "Dutch General Election Results: Prime Minister Rutte Wins, Wilders' Freedom Party Slides." Zero Hedge, 15 March 2017.

Editorial Board. "America has accepted 10,000 Syrian refugees. That's still too few." *Washington Post*, 2 September 2016.

Editorial Board. "Trump is letting human rights deteriorate, and Bahrain is Exhibit A." *Washington Post*, 13 March 2017.

"Education for Syrian Refugee Children: What Donors and Host Countries Should Do." Human Rights Watch, 16 September 2016.

"Education in Algeria: Past Successes, Challenges and Goals." Borgen Project, January 2017.

"Education in Morocco: Literacy Rates Continue to Make Strides." Blog, Borgen Project, October 2016.

Efrati, Ido. "Huge Disparities between Israeli, Palestinian Health-care Systems, Says Rights Group." *Haaretz* (Israel), 11 January 2015.

"Egypt and the EU." European Union External Action, 5 November 2016.

"Egypt Demographics Profile 2016." *Index Mundi*, 2016.

"Egypt, Ethiopia and Sudan sign deal to end Nile dispute." BBC News, 23 March 2015.

"Egypt GDP—composition by sector." *Index Mundi*, 8 October 2016.

"Egypt Inflation Rate 2010–2017." *Trading Economics*, 17 February 2017.

"Egypt to raise fuel prices by up to 47 percent at midnight." *Mada Masr* (Egypt), 3 November 2016.

"Egypt—Travel and Tourism Total Contribution to GDP." *World Data Atlas*, Knoema, 2015.

"Egyptian university seeks to combat sexual harassment on campus." *New Arab* (UK), 13 April 2016.

"Egypt's youth unemployment problem has erupted—but what about Britain's?" *Money Week* (UK), 31 January 2011.

Elba, Mariam. "How Poetry Became a Political Medium in Yemen." *Muftah*, 27 September 2017.

El-Badry, Samia. "Arab Americans Well-Educated, Diverse, Affluent and Highly Entrepreneurial." Allied Media Corp., no date.

El-Behary, Hend. "Women's representation in new parliament highest in Egypt's history." *Egypt Independent*, 13 March 2017.

El-Bendary, Mohamed. *The "Ugly American" in the Arab Mind*. Washington, D.C: Potomac Books, 2011.

Ellis, Ralph, and Darius Johnson. "Muslim family seeks apology after being forced off United flight." CNN, 2 April 2016.

El Malki, Fatim-Zohra. "Challenges Facing the New Tunisian Government." Atlantic Council, MENA [Middle East North Africa] Source, 2 September 2016.

El-Swais, Maha. "Despite high education levels, Arab women still don't have jobs." *Voices and Views: Middle East and North Africa*, World Bank, 9 March 2016.

Eltahawy, Mona. "Rending the veil—with little help." *Washington Post*, 18 July 2010.

Emerson, Steve. *American Jihad: The Terrorists Living among Us*. New York: Free Press, 2002.

"Empowering Women for a Better Libya." Libyan Women Forum, 2015.

Engdahl, F. William. "The Greater Middle East Project." Katehon Think Tank, 20 January 2017.

Enloe, Chris. "Top Obama official Samantha Power gets brutal lesson in self-awareness after criticizing Trump's Saudi arms deal." *The Blaze*, 21 May 2017.

Esposito, John L., and Dalia Mogahed. "Muslim True/False." *Los Angeles Times*, 2 April 2008.

Estelle, Emily, and Brenna Snyder. "AQIM [Al-Qaeda in the Islamic Maghrib] and ISIS in Algeria: Competing Campaigns." Critical Threats.org, 2 June 2016.

"Ethnic Groups of Sudan." *World Atlas*, 10 November 2016.

"EU Opens Debate on Economic Migration." EurActiv, 14 January 2005.

"Europe's Rising Far Right: A Guide to the Most Prominent Political Parties." *New York Times*, 13 June 2016.

Fahmy, Nourhan. "Egypt has fourth highest illiteracy rate among 13 Arab states." *Aswat Masriya* (Egypt), 8 September 2016.

Farhi, Paul. "Talk Show Host Graham Fired by WMAL over Islam Remarks." *Washington Post*, 23 August 2005.

"Fatima Urges Protection of Arab Family." *UAE Interact*, Ministry of Information and Culture, 1999.

Fernea, Elizabeth. "Islamic Feminism Finds a Different Voice." *Foreign Service Journal*, 30 May 2000.

Feteha, Ahmed, and Mohammed Sergie. "Kuwait Mulls Income, Sales Taxes as Oil Hits 12-Year Low." *The National* (Canada), 21 January 2016.

Fetouri, Mustafa. "In Libya, the education system suffers more than most." *The National* (Canada), 15 November 2016.

Fick, Maggie, and Shadi Bushr. "More people, less water means rising food imports for Egypt." Reuters, 9 July 2014.

"Field Listing: Literacy." The World Factbook, Central Intelligence Agency, 2015.

"Final Report of the Carter Center Mission to Witness the 2011–12 Parliamentary Elections in Egypt." Carter Center, 2012.

"Financial Management: United Arab Emirates." POGAR (Programme on Governance of the Arab Region), U.N. Development Programme, 2004.

Fisk, Robert. "What Theresa May Won't Talk about When She Talks about Terrorism." *Counterpunch*, 7 June 2017.

Fitzgerald, Mary. "Jihadists." European Council on Foreign Relations, 15 June 2016.

Fleischman, Jeffrey. "Egypt's provocative voice of moderate Islam." *Los Angeles Times*, 6 August 2010.

"For critics of Islam, 'Sharia' is a loaded word." *Washington Post*, 27 August 2010.

Foster, Alice. "Where in the world are the burka and niqab banned?" *Daily Express* (UK), 23 September 2016.

Foster, Florence. "New Rules for Foreign Workers in Saudi Arabia." Move One, Inc., 22 April 2010.

"14 million under poverty line in Algeria, group says." *Middle East Monitor*, 17 October 2015.

Friedman, Thomas L. "In the Arab World, It's the Past vs. the Future." *New York Times*, 26 September 2011.

Friedman, Thomas L. "President Obama Talks to Thomas L. Friedman about Iraq, Putin, and Israel." *New York Times*, 8 August 2014.

Fromkin, David. *A Peace to End All Peace*. New York: Henry Holt, 1989.

Funsch, Linda Pappas. *Oman Reborn: Balancing Tradition and Modernization*. New York: Palgrave Macmillan, 2015.

Gabbay, Tiffany. "Why Do They Hate Us? It's a Pretty Long List." *The Blaze*, 21 September 2012.

Garrett, Nada. "New Islamic TV Expands Across Mideast." Wilson Center, 5 November 2012.

Gavlak, Dale. "People have stopped paying attention to Iraqi refugees in Jordan, and it's getting 'critical and dangerous.'" *America*, Catholic News Service, 3 February 2017.

"Gaza Crisis: Toll of Operations in Gaza." BBC, 1 September 2014.

"Gaza Strip Population below poverty line." *Index Mundi*, 8 October 2016.

"The Gaza Strip: The Humanitarian Impact of the Blockade." Office for the Coordination of Humanitarian Assistance, UN, 14 November 2016.

"Gaza's Unemployment Rate Highest in World, World Bank Says." *Haaretz* (Israel), 3 April 2015.

"GCC: Total population and percentage of nationals and non-nationals in GCC countries." Gulf Labor Markets and Migration, Gulf Research Center, 31 March 2015.

"GDP per Capita." *Index Mundi*, 2015.

"Gender Equality in Egyptian Higher Education System." Freie Universitat Berlin, 2012.

Ghanem-Yazbeck, Dalia. "The Decline of Islamist Parties in Algeria." Carnegie Endowment for International Peace, 13 February 2014.

Ghazal, Mohammad. "Population stands at around 9.5 million, including 2.9 million guests." *Jordan Times*, 30 January 2016.

Giglio, Mike. "Saudi's Surprise Renegades." *Newsweek*, 9 May 2011.

Glass, Nicole. "The Water Crisis in Yemen: Causes, Consequences and Solutions." *Global Majority E-Journal*, June 2010.

"The Global Gender Gap Report 2016." World Economic Forum, 2016.

"Global Publics Back U.S. on Fighting ISIS, but are Critical of Post-9/11 Torture." Pew Research Center, 22 September 2015.

Goldfarb, Zachary A. "Va. Lawmaker's Remarks on Muslims Criticized." *Washington Post*, 21 December 2006.

"Good Girls Don't Protest." Human Rights Watch, 23 March 2016.

Goodman, Alana. "If It's Freedom We Hate, Why Didn't We Attack Sweden?" *Commentary*, 23 December 2010.

Goodman, David. "United States and Other Nations Step Up Libyan Evacuations." *New York Times*, 23 February 2011.

Goodman, Paul. "Islamists don't hate us for what we do. They hate us for who we are." *Conservative Home*, 8 January 2015.

Goodstein, Laurie. "Forecast Sees Muslim Population Leveling Off." *New York Times*, 27 January 2011.

Goodstein, Laurie. "Poll Finds U.S. Muslims Thriving, but Not Content." *New York Times*, 2 March 2009.

Gowen, Annie. "Nowhere near Ground Zero, but no more welcome." *Washington Post*, 23 August 2010.

Graham, Franklin. "My View of Islam." *Covenant News*, 9 December 2001.

Grant, Tavia. "Oman most-improved nation in last 40 years, UN index says." *Globe and Mail* (Canada), 4 November 2010.

Greenwald, Glenn. "Large number of Americans favor violent attacks against civilians." *Salon*, 23 May 2007.

Grimsley, Kerstin. "More Arabs, Muslims Allege Bias on the Job." *Washington Post*, 12 February 2001.

Grossman, Zoltan. "From Wounded Knee to Syria: A Century of U.S. Military Interventions." Evergreen State College, 2014.

Grove, Jack. "Proportion of female professors up, but still below a quarter." World University Rankings, 28 February 2015.

Habeck, Mary. *Knowing the Enemy: Jihadist Ideology and the War on Terror.* Yale University Press, 2006, 109.

Hackett, Conrad. "5 facts about the Muslim population in Europe." Pew Research Center, 19 July 2016.

Haddad, Yvonne Yazbeck, and Michael J. Balz. "Taming the Imams: European Governments and Islamic Preachers since 9/11." *Islam and Christian-Muslim Relations* 19, no. 2 (April 2008): 215–235.

Haider, Haseeb. "Emirati women grads outnumber men in UAE workforce." *Khaleej Times* (Dubai), 27 August 2016.

"Half Million Child Deaths 1991–1998." Global Policy Forum, UN, 2000.

Hall, Edward T. *The Hidden Dimension.* New York: Doubleday, 1966.

Hamamy, Hanan. "Consanguineous Marriages in the Arab World." National Centre for Diabetes, Endocrinology and Genetics (Amman), July 2003.

"Hamas moves to approve '1967 borders'—but not recognize Israel." The Great Middle East.com (Russia), 9 March 2017.

Hamid, Shadi. "Everyone says the Libyan intervention was a failure. They're wrong." Brookings, 12 April 2016.

Hamilton, Lee H. "Why Do They Hate Us?" *Huffington Post*, 3 February 2015.

Hammond, Andrew. *Popular Culture in the Arab World*. Cairo: American University in Cairo Press, 2007.

Harkinson, Josh. "Anti-Muslim Hate Groups Have Tripled with the Rise of Trump." *Mother Jones*, 15 February 2017.

Hasan, Aida. "Arab Culture and Identity: Arab Food and Hospitality." Suite University Online, 1999.

Hassan, Carma, and Catherine Shoichet. "Arabic-speaking student kicked off Southwest flight." CNN, 2 April 2016.

"Hate Groups, State Totals." Southern Poverty Law Center, 2017.

"Haughty about the hijab." *The Economist*, 27 August 2015.

Hauslohner, Abigail. "Southern Poverty Law Center says American hate groups are on the rise." *Washington Post*, 15 February 2017.

Hawley, Caroline. "Iraq conflict: Crisis of an orphaned generation." BBC News, 28 November 2012.

Hazelton, Lesley. *After the Prophet*. New York: Anchor Books, 2009.

"Healing the Nation: Arab-American Response to September 11 Attacks." Arab American Institute, 2001.

"Health Situation in Iraq." World Health Organization, UN, 2003.

Heggy, Tarek. "Egypt's Revolution: What Happened?" Gatestone Institute, 1 June 2011.

Heneghan, Tom. "Turkey 'not reforming Islam, but itself' with Hadith review." Reuters, *Faith World*, 29 February 2008.

Herlinger, Chris. "Syrian and Iraqi refugees wait in Lebanon for safety, new life." Global Sisters Report, *National Catholic Reporter*, 17 March 2016.

"How the Middle East has gone cool towards Qatar." BBC News, 10 March 2014.

Hubbard, Ben. "Saudi Arabia Agrees to Let Women Drive." *New York Times*, 26 September 2017.

Hudson, Saul. "U.S. Halts Arabic Magazine Meant to Boost U.S. Image." Reuters, 22 December 2005.

Humphreys, R. Stephen. *Between Memory and Desire: The Middle East in a Troubled Age*. Berkeley: University of California Press, 1999.

Huntington, Samuel P. "The Clash of Civilizations." *Foreign Affairs* 72, no. 3 (Summer 1993).

Huntington, Samuel P. *The Clash of Civilizations and the Remaking of World Order*. New York: Simon and Schuster, 1996.

Hurdle, Jon. "Arabic flashcards land student in U.S. detention." Reuters, 10 February 2010.

"Hussein trial court to be disbanded." *Washington Post*, 5 May 2011.

Hymowitz, Carol. "The Rise of Muslim-Friendly Workplaces in Corporate America." *Bloomberg News*, 19 July 2016.

Ibn Warraq. "Demographics: Why Islamic Societies are Dying." *New English Review* (UK), April 2016.

Ibrahim, Arwa. "Arab world's top evangelist goes on 'novel' trajectory." *Middle East Eye* (UK), 8 January 2015.

Ignatius, David. "A Saudi fatwa for moderation." *Washington Post*, 13 June 2010.

Ignatius, David. "A 30-year-old Saudi prince could jump-start the kingdom—or drive it off a cliff." *Washington Post*, 13 June 2016.

"The Impact of the Conflict on Children." If America Knew, ifamericaknew.org, 31 December 2016.

"Intolerance." *New Yorker*, 20 September 2010.

"Iraq: Briefing on Health." Office for the Coordination of Humanitarian Affairs, UN, 18 May 2002.

"Iraq Emergency." UNHCR.org, 5 September 2017.

"Iraq Humanitarian Response Plan." World Health Organization, 2016.

"Iraq." The World Factbook, Central Intelligence Agency, 21 January 2011.

"Iraqi Women and Children's Liberation Act of 2004, S 2519." *The Orator*, U.S. Congress, 15 June 2004.

"Islam: European Muslim Population." Jewish Virtual Library, February 2016.

"Islam is Violent." Jesus-is-Lord, 29 November 2008.

"Islam, Jihad, and Terrorism." Institute of Islamic Information and Education, 14 October 2004.

"The Islamic Veil across Europe." BBC News, 1 July 2014.

"Islamophobia in the 2016 Presidential Election." Council on American-Islamic Relations, 29 September 2016.

"Islamophobia: Understanding Anti-Muslim Sentiment in the West." Gallup, Inc., 2011.

"Israelis and Palestinians Injured in Current Violence." If Americans Knew.org, 11 March 2017.

Jacobs, Anna. "Politics in Algeria is about More than Who's President." *Muftah*, 12 November 2014.

Jacoby, Jeff. "Why there are Muslim ghettos in Belgium, but not in the U.S." *Boston Globe*, 27 May 2016.

John, Isaac. "UAE business conditions rebound." *Khaleej Times* (Dubai), 5 April 2015.

John, Isaac. "UAE's per capita income remains high." *Khaleej Times* (Dubai), 16 June 2016.

"Jordan Economy 2017." The World Factbook, Central Intelligence Agency, 2017.

"Jordan: Extremism and Counter-Extremism." Counter-Extremism Project, 2017.

"Jordan: Overview." National Democratic Institute, 2016.

Kahn, Brian. "Syria's drought 'has likely been its worst in 900 years.'" Climate Central, Guardian Environmental Network, *The Guardian* (UK), 2 March 2016.

Kampehl, Lena. "Fighting widespread malnutrition in Iraq." World-Grain.com, 27 September 2016.

Karasapan, Omer. "Who are the 5 million refugees and immigrants in Egypt?" Brookings, 4 October 2016.

Karman, Tawakkol. "Yes, Yemen's revolution was worth it—despite everything that came next." *Washington Post*, 24 February 2017.

Karmi, Ghada. *In Search of Fatima: A Palestinian Story*. London: Verso, 2002.

Katzman, Kenneth. "Oman: Reform, Security, and U.S. Policy." Congressional Research Service, 26 April 2016.

Kawatch, Nadim. "Arab World needs to rise to the literacy challenge." Emirates 24/7 News, 28 July 2010.

Kern, Soeren. "Europe's Mosque Wars." *Pundicity*, 18 August 2010.

Kershaw, Sarah. "The Terrorist Mind: An Update." *New York Times*, 10 January 2010.

Khan, Miriam. "More than 5,000 Muslims Serving in U.S. Military, Pentagon Says." ABC News, 8 December 2015.

Khouri, Rami. "For Arabs, A Cruel Echo of History." *Daily Star* (Beirut), 21 March 2003.

Khouri, Rami. "The Saudis are worried, and not just about kings." *Press Reader, The Guardian Weekly* (UK), 9 October 2015.

Khouri, Rami. "Unprecedented Opportunity." Interview by staff of the Center for Public Integrity, 16 March 2005.

Kingsley, Patrick. "AbdelFatah al-Sisi won 96.1% of vote in Egyptian presidential election, say officials." *The Guardian* (UK), 3 June 2014.

Kirkpatrick, David. "Islamists Win 70% of Seats in the Egyptian Parliament." *New York Times*, 21 January 2012.

Klein, Helen Altman, and Gilbert Kuperman. "Through an Arab Cultural Lens." *Military Review* (May-June 2008).

Knickmeyer, Ellen. "Ghosts of Iraq's Birth." *Washington Post National Weekly Edition*, 13–19 March 2006.

Koraytem, Hiba, and Nemr Kanafani. "Public finance Kuwait: New budget keeps spending unchanged; deficit likely at 13% of GDP." NBK Economic Research, 2 August 2016.

Korn, Josh. "Sudan Leader to Accept Secession of South." *New York Times*, 7 February 2011.

Korte, Gregory. "U.S. sanctions Syria for use of chemical weapons." *USA Today*, 12 January 2017.

Kottasova, Ivana. "Saudi Arabia cut funding for students abroad." CNN Money, 9 February 2016.

Kramer, Jane. "The Crusader." *New Yorker*, 16 October 2006.

Krauthammer, Charles. "'Munich,' the Travesty," *Washington Post*, 13 January 2006.

Krauthammer, Charles. "Syria and the New Axis of Evil." *Washington Post*, 1 April 2005.

Krauthammer, Charles. "Why It Deserves the Hype." *Time*, 14 February 2005.

Kraychik, Robert. "Ayaan Hirsi Ali: 'Anti-Semitism is Back ... Because of Islam.'" *Daily Wire*, 8 May 2017.

Kristof, Nicholas. "Bigotry in Islam and Here." *New York Times*, 9 July 2002.

Kristof, Nicholas. "Islam, Virgins, and Grapes." *New York Times*, 23 April 2009.

"KSA population 21.1 Saudis, 10.4 million expats." *Arab News* (Saudi Arabia), 4 February.

Kulish, Nicholas. "Saudi Arabia, Where Even Milk Depends on Oil, Struggles to Remake Its Economy." *New York Times*, 14 October 2016.

Kunkle, Frederick. "Are good works good politics?" *Washington Post*, 9 April 2011.

"Kuwait: New labor law grants women the right—and flexibility—to work late." *Los Angeles Times*, 5 June 2010.

"Kuwait poll: Opposition wins nearly half of parliament." *Al-Jazeera*, 27 November 2016.

Kuznetsov, Alexander. "United States Must Answer for War Crimes in the Middle East." Strategic Culture Foundation (Russia), 15 October 2016.

Lahsini, Chaima. "Gender Wage Gap: Moroccan Women Make 17% Less than Men." *Morocco World News*, 11 March 2017.

Lally, Kathy. "Egypt Calls." *Washington Post*, 1 May 2011.

Lamb, Franklin. "Giuliani Plays the Islamic Terror Card." *Counterpunch*, 26 April 2007.

Laurence, Jonathan. "The Prophet of Moderation: Tariq Ramadan's Quest to Reclaim Islam." *New York Times*, 18 June 2007.

Lauria, Joe. "Why We're Never Told Why We're Attacked." *Consortiumnews.com*, 9 April 2016.

Lawrence, T. E. *The Seven Pillars of Wisdom*. New York: Doubleday, 1926.

Lazare, Sarah. "Conference Examines the U.S. 'Special Relationship' with Human Rights Abuser Saudi Arabia." *AlterNet*, 16 March 2016.

"The Lebanese National Action Plan." *Women Watch*, United Nations, 2008.

"Lebanese Social Classes." *Reddit*, 15 January 2014.

"Lebanon Country Profile." BBC News, 6 November 2016.

"Lebanon hosts second largest refugee population." *Daily Star* (Beirut), 7 January 2015.

"Lebanon: Syria Crisis." ECHO [European Commission on Humanitarian Aid and Civil Protection] Factsheet, European Commission, March 2017.

Lee, Martin A. "Not a Prayer." *Harper's*, June 2004.

Lee, Matthew, and Martin Crutsinger. "U.S. slaps sanctions on Syria's Assad for abuses." Associated Press, 18 May 2011.

Lee, Matthew, and Richard Lardner. "U.S. sent $221 million to Palestinians in Obama's last hours." *Salon*, 24 January 2017.

Leland, John, and Riyadh Mohammed. "Iraqi Women are Seeking Greater Political Influence." *New York Times*, 17 February 2010.

Lewis, Bernard. "The Roots of Muslim Rage." *The Atlantic*, September 1990.

Lewis, Bernard. "Targeted by a History of Hatred: The U.S. is now the unquestioned leader of the free world, also known as infidels." *Washington Post*, 10 September 2002.

Laurence, Jonathan. "Prophet of Moderation: Tariq Ramadan's Quest to Reclaim Islam." *New York Times*, 18 June 2007.

"Libya Country Profile." BBC News, 1 March 2017.

"Libya Situation Report #12, 7 March 2017." World Food Program, 2017.

"Libya's Forgotten King." *Al-Jazeera World*, 19 November 2015.

"Life Expectancy for Countries." Infoplease, 2015.

Lindsey, Ursula. "The Berber Language: Officially Recognized, Unofficially Marginalized?" Al-Fanar Media (UK), 27 July 2015.

Lipka, Michael. "Muslims and Islam: Key findings in the U.S. and around the world." Pew Research Center, 22 July 2016.

Londono, Ernesto. "Teacher Charged After Uproar over Arabic." *Washington Post*, 13 September 2006.

Louati, Yaser. "Islamodiversion: How Sarkozy and France's Political Class Outdo Trump, Exploiting Islamophobia to Distract from Economic Problems." *AlterNet*, 11 October 2016.

Lynch, Colum. "Report Urges Arab Governments to Share Power." *Washington Post*, 5 April 2005.

MacFarquhar, Neil. "New Translation Prompts Debate on Islamic Verse." *New York Times*, 23 March 2007.

Maghraoui, Abdeslam. *American Foreign Policy and Islamic Renewal*. United States Institute of Peace, Special Report, July 2006.

"Main Findings of the 2016 Arab Opinion Index Available Now." Arab Center for Research and Policy Studies (Doha), 13 March 2017.

Malsin, Jared. "Qatar settles in for a long standoff." *Time*, 7 August 2017.

Mansfield, Peter. *The New Arabians*. New York: Doubleday, 1981.

Marker, Kathleen. "Professional Life." In *Daily Life of Arab Americans in the 21st Century*, edited by Anan Ameri and Holly Arida, 137–162. Westport, CT: Greenwood, ABC-CLIO, LLC, 2012.

Martin, Andrew. "Mideast Facing Choice between Crops and Water." *New York Times*, 21 July 2008.

Martin, Ivan, Mohamed Kriaa, and Mohamed Alaa Demnati. "Migrant Support Measures from an Employment and Skills Perspective (MISMES), Tunisia." Migration Policy Centre, April 2015.

Martin, Patrick. "UN officials warn of worst famine crisis since World War II." World Socialist Web Site, 13 March 2017.

Mawi, Omar. "Saudi Arabia Comes to the Rescue of the Egyptian Economy." *Geopolitical Monitor* (Canada), 25 April 2016.

Mazloum, Nadine. "Crippling the youth: Unemployment in Lebanon at an all-time high." *Newsroom Nomad* (Lebanon), 19 August 2016.

McEvers, Kelly. "Saudis slow to accept working women." *Marketplace*, 23 April 2008.

McGregor, Andrew. "Berbers Seize Libyan Oil Terminal to Press Demand for Recognition." Aberfoyle International Security (Canada), 14 November 2013.

McLoughlin, Leslie J. *Colloquial Arabic (Levantine)*. London: Routledge and Kegan Paul, 1982.

McVeigh, Karen. "Refugee women and children beaten, raped and starved in Libyan hellholes." *The Guardian* (UK), 2 March 2017.

MEE Staff. "Egypt bread riots: Government says 'fight against corruption' behind cuts." *Middle East Eye* (UK), 8 March 2017.

MEE Staff. "'Go hungry': Egyptian general tells millions to stop complaining about crisis." *Middle East Eye* (UK), 13 March 2017.

Mekhennet, Souad, and Joby Warrick. "In Bahrain's militant cells, U.S. sees Iran." *Washington Post*, 2 April 2017.

Messner, J. J., ed. "Fragile States Index 2016." Fund for Peace, 27 June 2016.

Michaels, Adrian. "The EU is facing an era of vast social change, reports Adrian Michaels, and few politicians are taking notice." *The Telegraph* (UK), 8 August 2009.

Miller, Judith. "Displaced in the Gulf War: 5 Million Refugees." *New York Times*, 16 June 1991.

Millman, Noah. "Kurdistan, and the problem of an endless parade of new nation states." *The Week*, 29 September 2017.

Mills, Tom, and Gilbert Achcar. "Is U.S. Control over the Middle East Weakening?" South African Civil Society Information Service, 9 June 2015.

Milne, Seamus. "This tide of anti-Muslim hatred is a threat to us all." *The Guardian* (UK), 25 February 2010.

Mogahed, Dalia, and Fouad Pervez. "American Muslim Poll." Institute for Social Policy and Understanding, March 2016.

Mohamed, Besheer. "A new estimate of the U.S. Muslim population." Pew Research Center, 6 January 2016.

Monahan, Meghan. "Treatment of Palestinian refugees in Lebanon." *Human Rights Brief*, 2 February 2015.

Moore, Molly. "In a Europe Torn over Mosques, a City Offers Accommodation." *Washington Post*, 9 December 2007.

Moran, Kate. "Leveraging the Youth Bulge to Transform the Arab World." Center for Private Enterprise, CIPE Development Blog, 2 February 2016.

"More Egyptians Migrate for Work Abroad in 2015." *Egyptian Streets* (Egypt), 30 August 2015.

Morello, Carol. "In Poll, Muslims Largely Upbeat about Life in U.S." *Washington Post*, 30 August 2011.

"Moroccan Women and Gender Inequality in the Workplace." European Professional Women's Network, 27 April 2010.

"Morocco Population." Country Meters, 2017.

"Morocco Youth Unemployment Rate 1999–2017." *Trading Economics*, February 2017.

"Mosques and Islamic Centers in Canada." Islamic Supreme Council, 20 January 2010.

"Most Americans Want Democracy in the Middle East." *International Iran Times*, no date.

Mounir, Hossam. "Unemployment rate reaches 12.7% in Q1 of 2016." *Egypt Daily News*, 15 May 2016.

Mousalli, Ahmad S. *Modern and Radical Islamic Fundamentalism*. Gainesville: University of Florida Press, 1999.

Mufti, Nermeen. "Iraq's widows, abandoned and ignored, turn to begging." *Arab Weekly* (UK), 15 May 2015.

Mujahid, Abdul Malik. "Profile of Muslims in Canada." Sound Vision, 8 October 2016.

Muqbil, Imtiaz. "Ten Years after 9/11, Pew Poll Shows U.S.-Muslim Schism as Wide as Ever." *Travel Impact Newswire*, 18 May 2011.

Murdock, Heather. "Saudi Arabia Seeks to Shed Dependency on Foreign Labor." VOA News, 25 January 2016.

Murphy, Kim. "Hamas Victory is Built on Social Work." *Los Angeles Times*, 2 March 2006.

Musa, Rami. "Libyan militias seize control of major oil terminals." *Washington Times*, 3 March 2017.

"Muslim Americans: Middle Class and Mostly Mainstream." Pew Research Center, 22 May 2007.

"Muslim Charities and the War on Terror." Charity & Security Network (CSN), December 2011.

"Muslim Charity Provides Disaster Relief to Hurricane Sandy Victims." *Washington Report on Middle East Affairs*, March 2013.

"Muslim Demographics in Canada." *Islam Threat*, 25 March 2015.

"Muslim Migration into Europe: Eurabia Come True?" *FrontPage Magazine*, 11 December 2015.

"Muslim veterans vow to protect Jewish cemeteries amid anti-Semitic threats." Fox News, 2 March 2017.

"Muslim women wearing veil 'refused bus ride' in London." BBC News, 23 July 2010.

"Muslims and Latinos much more prominent in TV crime news than in real-life crime." *Science Daily*, 7 January 2015.

"Muslims in America—A Statistical Portrait." Embassy of the United States, Baghdad, 28 September 2016.

Myre, Greg, and Larry Kaplow. "7 Things to Know about Israeli Settlements." National Public Radio, 29 December 2016.

Nada, Garrett. "New Islamic TV Expands across Mideast." Wilson Center, 5 November 2012.

Natter, Katharina. "Revolution and Political Transition in Tunisia: A Migration Game Changer?" Migration Policy Institute, 28 May 2015.

Nazeh, Maher, and Saif Hameed. "Child labor doubles in Iraq as violence, displacement hit incomes." Reuters, 10 July 2016.

"New government announced under PM Saad al-Hariri." *Al-Jazeera*, 18 December 2016.

"New IPU and UN Women Map shows women's representation in politics stagnates." Inter-Parliamentary Union, 15 March 2017.

Ngawi, Rodrique. "Rwanda Turns to Islam after Genocide." *Times Daily*, 7 November 2002.

Nichols, Michelle. "U.N. experts warn Saudi-led coalition allies over war crimes in Yemen." *Reuters World News*, 29 January 2017.

Noureddin, Nadir. "Egypt is suffering an acute food deficit, estimated at around 60 percent of its strategic food needs." *Al-Ahram Weekly*, 21 October 2017.

"Number of Muslims in Western Europe." Pew Research Center, 15 September 2010.

Oakford, Samuel. "Saudi Arabia Reveals How It Will End Its Oil 'Addiction' by 2020." VICE News, 25 April 2016.

"Obama Renews Syria Sanctions." Agence France-Presse, 3 May 2010.

Obeidallah, Dean. "Are All Terrorists Muslims? It's Not Even Close." *Daily Beast*, 14 January 2015.

Ocampos, Tania Ildefonso. "Morocco reaches critical stage on road to reform." *Middle East Eye* (UK), 3 March 2016.

"OCHA: One in two Palestinians to need humanitarian assistance in 2017." Office for the Coordination of Humanitarian Assistance, UN, Alternative Information Center, 2017.

"Offensive on Iraq's Mosul may produce a million migrants: Turkey." Reuters, 4 October 2016.

"Oil Sector Recovery in Yemen Urgently Needed." *Yemen Socio-Economic Update*, no. 14 (May 2016).http://reliefweb.int/sites/reliefweb.int/files/resources/yseu14_english_final_1.pdf.

Okoroafor, Cynthia. "International Women's Month: 15 years after a no-fault divorce law was passed, Egyptian women still suffer in the courts." Ventures Africa (Nigeria), 10 March 2016.

Oltermann, Philip. "Austria rejects far-right candidate Norbert Hofer in presidential election." *The Guardian* (UK), 4 December 2016.

"Oman Economy 2017." The World Factbook, Central Intelligence Agency, 12 January 2017.

"Oman Population." *Country Meters*, 4 May 2017.

Omstad, Thomas. "The Casbah Connection." *U.S. News and World Report*, 9 May 2005.

"On World Refugee Day: Palestinian refugees remain deprived of international protection." Badil Resource Center for Palestinian Residency and Refugee Rights (Palestine), 20 June 2016.

Osborne, Samuel. "The most far-right countries in Europe, mapped." *The Independent* (UK), 23 May 2016.

Othmani, Safa. "Morocco's Unemployment Rate to Exceed 10% in 2017, Warns IMF [International Monetary Fund]." *Morocco World News*, 12 October 2016.

Ould Khettab, Djamila. "Algeria set to approve new constitution." *Al-Jazeera*, 2 February 2016.

"Our Work." U.S. Agency for International Development, 17 March 2017.

"Palestine Update: Muslim-Christian Solidarity in Palestine." Global Ministries, 21 February 2014.

"Palestinian Syrians: Twice Refugees." *Al-Jazeera*, 23 March 2016.

Pape, Robert A. *Dying to Win: The Strategic Logic of Suicide Terrorism*. New York: Random House, 2005.

"Paper or Plastic?—A More Perfect Union Project." Virginia Interfaith Center, 6 April 2010.

Patai, Raphael. *The Arab Mind* (1973; reprint). Long Island: Hatherleigh Press, 2002.

Patton, Anna. "Getting Syria's college students back into class." Devex, 6 July 2016.

Pecquet, Julian. "What Happened to the Billions the U.S. Gave Egypt?" *Al-Monitor*, 13 May 2016.

Pedraza, Lisdey Espinosa, and Marcus Heinrich. "Water Scarcity: Cooperation or Conflict in the Middle East and North Africa?" *Foreign Policy Journal*, 2 September 2016.

Pennington, Roberta. "Special report: Arabic 'at risk of becoming foreign language in UAE.'" *The National* (Canada), 2 March 2015.

Peters, Ralph. "When Devils Walk the Earth," in *Beyond Terror: Strategy in a Changing World*. Mechanicsburg, PA: Stackpole Books, 2002, 22–65.

Phillips, David L. "It is Time to Recognize Iraq as a Failed State." *Huffington Post*, 24 February 2017.

Piggott, Stephen. "3 Men Arrested in Plot to Bomb Kansas Mosque." *AlterNet*, 17 October 2016.

Pilger, John. "Squeezed to Death." *The Guardian* (UK), 4 March 2005.

Pipes, Daniel. *Militant Islam Reaches America*. New York: W. W. Norton & Co., 2003.

Piser, Karina. "How Tunisia's Islamists Embraced Democracy." *Foreign Policy*, 31 March 2016.

"Poll Data: Arabs Doubt U.S." Layalina Productions, Inc., 13–26 April 2007.

"Poll: Islamic women liked as leaders." United Press International, 30 March 2006.

"Population and Failing States: Sudan." Population Institute, 2009.

"Population Density." Palestinian Central Bureau of Statistics, Palestine National Authority, 12 May 2011.

"Population Density per Square Mile of Countries." Infoplease, 2009.

Potok, Mark. "Hate Rises." *Washington Post*, 9 March 2008.

Prashad, Vijay. "The Rehabilitation of George W. Bush, War Criminal." *AlterNet*, March 2017.

"President Bush Addresses the Nation." *Washington Post*, 20 September 2001.

"President Obama Talks to Thomas L. Friedman about Iraq, Putin, and Israel." *New York Times*, 8 August 2014.

"Prevalence of Child Malnutrition (Percentage Underweight under Age Five), 2000–2009." Global Health Facts, Kaiser Foundation, 2009.

"Proportion of seats held by women in national parliaments." World Bank, 2016.

"Qatar Population 2017." *Country Meters*, 5 January 2017.

"Qatar Population 2017." *World Population Review*, 20 November 2016.

"Qatar 2016/2017." Amnesty International annual report, February 2017.

"Qatar GDP and Economic Data, Country Report 2017." *Global Finance*, 2016.

"Qatari diplomat admits to 'excellent' relations with Israeli officials." *New Arab* (UK), 13 February 2017.

"Qatari women win 2 out of 29 seats in municipal council vote." *NewsOK*, 14 May 2015.

Queally, Jon. "With 200+ Iraqi Civilians Feared Dead, Carnage Surging under Trump." *Common Dreams*, 26 March 2017.

"Quick facts: What you need to know about the Syria crisis." Mercy Corps, 9 March 2017.

"Quotation of the Day." *New York Times*, 13 April 2005, 13A.

Qutb, Muhammad Sayyid. "The Role of Religion in Education." In *Aims and Objectives of Islamic Education*, edited by S. N. Al-Attas. Jeddah: King Abdulaziz University, 1979, 48–62.

Ramadan, Tariq. "Islam's role in an ethical society." *The Guardian* (UK), 23 February 2010.

Ramadan, Tariq. *Western Muslims and the Future of Islam*. Oxford: Oxford University Press, 2004.

Ramani, Samuel. "Israel is Strengthening its Ties with the Gulf Monarchies." *Huffington Post*, 12 September 2016.

Ramdani, Nabila. "Fifty years after Algeria's independence, France is still in denial." *The Guardian* (UK), 5 July 2012.

Raz, Guy. "The War on the Word 'Jihad.'" *All Things Considered*, National Public Radio, 31 October 2006.

"Report Instances of Extremism or Support of Terrorism." Free Muslims Coalition, 2005.

"Resisting Occupation, Constructing Peace." Israel Committee Against House Demolitions, 2015.

Richman, Sheldon. "Another Frankenstein's Monster." *Commentaries*, Future of Freedom Foundation, 27 December 2002.

Ripley, Amanda. "Reverse Radicalism." *Time*, 24 March 2008.

Rodenbeck, Max. "Yemen, Al-Qaeda, and the U.S." *New York Review of Books*, 30 September 2010.

Roopanarine, Les, Patrick Wintour, Saeed Kemali Dehghan, and Ahmad Algohbary. "Yemen at 'point of no return' as conflict leaves almost 7 million close to famine." *The Guardian* (UK), 24 March 2017.

Rubin, Alissa J. "Iraqi Surveys Start to Unveil the Mental Scars of War, Especially among Women." *New York Times*, 7 March 2009.

Rubin, Barry. "The Real Roots of Arab Anti-Americanism." *Foreign Affairs*, November-December 2002.

Rubin, Jennifer. "Trump's un-American speech in Saudi Arabia." *Washington Post*, 21 May 2017.

Said, E. A. "A Stupid War." *Al-Hayat* (Beirut), 15 April 2003.

Salacanin, Stasa. "Yemen's road to perdition." *BQ Magazine* (Qatar), May 2015.

Salama, Samir. "How the UAE Actively Promotes Religious Tolerance, Peaceful Coexistence." *Gulf News*, 15 September 2016.

Salbi, Zainab. "What people in the Middle East say in private about the West." *New York Times*, 26 May 2015.

Saloojie, Riad. "The Nature of Islam." *Globe and Mail* (Canada), 16 January 2000.

Sarhan, Jessica. "Libyan women struggle to join the workforce." *Al-Jazeera*, 26 November 2014.

"Saudi Arabia: King's Reform Agenda Unfulfilled." Human Rights Watch, 23 January 2015.

"Saudi Arabia looks to the future, opens coed university." *Al-Arabiyya News* (Saudi Arabia), 2 November 2010.

"Saudi Arabia slashes ministers' pay, cuts public sector bonuses." CNBC (Canada), 27 September 2016.

"Saudi Arabia." The World Factbook, Central Intelligence Agency, 28 September 2016.

"Saudi deports thousands of Yemenis, remittances to suffer—official." *Reuters World News*, 1 April 2013.

Saul, Jonathan, and Ulf Lessing. "Libya food imports fall as turmoil disrupts delivery." Reuters, 31 July 2015.

Scheuer, Michael. *Imperial Hubris: Why the West Is Losing the War on Terror.* Washington, D.C.: Brassey's Inc., 2004.

Schmitt, Eric. "ISIS Remains Threat in Libya Despite Defeat in Surt, U.S. Officials Say." *New York Times*, 8 December 2016.

Schmitt, Eric, and Michael Gordonjan. "U.S. Bombs ISIS Camps in Libya." *New York Times*, 19 January 2017.

"School Enrollment, Tertiary, Country Ranking." *Index Mundi*, 2014.

Schwartz, Emma. "Giving Voice to a Long-Repressed People." *U.S. News and World Report*, 24–31 March 2008.

"Seven women elected to Oman municipal councils." *Al-Arabiyya—English*, 25 December 2016.

"76 countries benefit from Abu Dhabi funds." *Khaleej Times* (Dubai), 26 July 2015.

"Sexism Deleted in Turkey." *Washington Post*, 16 July 2006.

Shane, Scott. "Saudis and Extremism: 'Both the Arsonists and the Firefighters.'" *New York Times*, 26 August 2016.

Shapiro, Samantha M. "Ministering to the Upwardly Mobile Muslim." *New York Times Magazine*, 30 April 2006.

Sheridan, Mary Beth. "U.S. Muslim Groups Cleared." *Washington Post*, 18 November 2005.

Shipler, David. *Arab and Jew, Wounded Spirits in a Promised Land.* New York: Penguin Books, 1986.

Sidahmed, Mazin. "Thousands of Saudis sign petition to end male guardianship of women." *The Guardian* (UK), 26 September 2016.

Shulman, Robin. "In New York, a Word Starts a Fire." *Washington Post*, 24 August 2007.

Simmons, Erica. "A Passion for Justice." *New Internationalist* (UK), No. 210, August 1990, 9.

Simon, Roger. "Giuliani warns of 'new 9/11' if Dems win." *Politico*, 24 April 2007.

"Sixty-ninth Session, 23rd Meeting." UN Fourth Committee, 6 November 2014.

Slackman, Michael. "A Quiet Revolution in Algeria: Gains by Women." *New York Times*, 26 May 2007.

Slade, Shelley. "The Image of the Arab in America: Analysis of a Poll of American Attitudes." *Middle East Journal* 35, no. 2 (Spring 1981): 143–162.

Sly, Liz. "Six Italian U.N. peacekeepers injured in bomb attack in southern Lebanon." *Washington Post*, 28 May 2011.

Smith, Craig. "Voices of the Dead Echo across Algeria." *New York Times*, 18 April 2004.

"South Sudan Economic Overview." World Bank, 20 October 2016.

"South Sudan GDP per capita (PPP)." *Index Mundi*, 2016.

"South Sudan population." Worldometers, 2017.

"South Sudan: 2016 Trafficking in Persons Report." U.S Department of State, Office to Monitor and Combat Trafficking in Persons, 2016.

Spinner, Jackie. "An Attack Burns Anguish into Kurdish Region." *Washington Post*, 6 February 2005.

Stancati, Margharita. "Oil Income Falling, Saudi Raises Government Fees and Fines." *Wall Street Journal*, 9 August 2016.

"Statistics." Addameer Prisoner Support and Human Rights Association (Palestine), January 2017.

Steele, Jonathan. "Terrorism Is Not an Enemy State that Can Be Defeated." *The Guardian* (UK), 23 November 2003.

Stengel, Richard. "One Thing We Need to Do." *Time*, 11 September 2006.

Stephen, Chris. "Libyan militias capture key oil ports and refinery." *The Guardian* (UK), 4 March 2017.

Stokes, Elaisha. "The Drought That Preceded Syria's Civil War Was Likely the Worst in 900 Years." VICE News, VICE Media, 3 March 2016.

Stuart, Desmond. *The Arab World*. New York: Time Life Books, 1972.

"Sudan age structure." *Index Mundi*, 8 October 2016."

"Sudan: Blame traded over civilian deaths in Darfur." *Al-Jazeera*, 3 January 2017.

"Sudan Corruption Report." GAN Business Anti-Corruption Portal, May 2016.

"Sudan Exports by Category." *Trading Economics*, December 2016.

"Sudan: GDP per capita (PPP)." The Global Economy.com, Council on Foreign Relations, 2017.

"Sudan Migration Country Profile." Secretariat for Sudanese Working Abroad, *Zunia*, 27 February 2011.

"Sudan, Population below poverty line." *Index Mundi*, 2014.

"Sudan profile—long overview." BBC News, 7 December 2015.

"Sudan Total Fertility Rate." *Index Mundi*, 2016.

"Sudan: Women in parliament." The Global Economy.com, 2015.

Sullivan, Kevin. "Younger Muslims Tune in to Upbeat Religious Message." *Washington Post*, 2 December 2007.

Susman, Tina. "Iraqis divided by treatment of women in constitution." *Los Angeles Times*, 9 October 2007.

Swanson, Ana. "An incredible image shows how powerful countries are buying up much of the world's land." *Washington Post*, 21 May 2015.

Switzer, Cody. "Responses from Charities to the Japan Earthquake and Pacific Tsunami." *Chronicle of Philanthropy*, 18 March 2011.

"Syria Crisis." UNRWA [United Nations Relief and Works Agency], February 2017.

"Syria Population." *Country Meters*, 1 January 2017.

"Syria Population." *World Meters*, 1 July 2017.

"Syria refugees: UN warns of extreme poverty in Jordan." BBC News, 14 January 2015.

"Syria Regional Refugee Response." UNHCR [United Nations High Commissioner for Refugees], 5 April 2017.

Tahhan, Zena. "Palestinians in Israel strike over home demolitions." *Al-Jazeera*, 11 January 2017.

Tarzi, Nazli. "A not-so-historical deal: Iraq's post-IS vision runs into trouble." *Middle East Eye* (UK), 27 January 2017.

Taspinar, Omer. "Europe's Muslim Street." *Foreign Policy* 135 (March-April 2003): 76–7.

Taub, Amanda. "The unsexy truth about why the Arab Spring failed." *Vox*, 27 January 2016.

"Text Analytics Program Proves Quran Less Violent than the Bible." *Muslim Post*, 6 February 2016.

Thompson, Irene. "Berber Branch." AWL, About World Languages, 27 December 2016.

Thorp, Gene, and Swati Sharma. "Foreign fighters flow to Syria." *Washington Post*, 17 January 2015.

Timberg, Scott. "Middle East through Western Eyes." *Los Angeles Times*, 7 September 2007.

"Timeline of Women's Right to Vote Around the World." *Gulf News* (Dubai), 12 December 2015.

Toaldo, Mattia. "Political Actors." European Council on Foreign Relations, 15 June 2016.

"Tolerance and Tension." Pew poll, 2013.

Tolj, Brianne. "Muslim population in Australia soars to 600,000 as religion becomes the nation's second-biggest—a 77% jump in the past decade, according to Census." *Daily Mail* (Australia), 26 June 2017.

Tonnessen, Liv. "Beyond numbers? Women's 25% parliamentary quota in post-conflict Sudan." *Journal of Peace, Conflict and Development* 17 (2011): 43–62.

"Top 20 Countries with Highest Number of Internet Users." Internet World Stats, 2017.

Toumi, Habib. "Kuwait lifts decades-long ban on Palestinian workers." *Gulf News* (Dubai), 6 February 2017.

"Transcript of bin Ladin's speech." *Al-Jazeera*, 30 October 2004.

"Transforming Jordan's Badia Deserts into 'Ecosystems of Opportunity.'" World Bank, 21 March 2016.

Trejos, Nancy. "Women Lose Ground in the New Iraq." *Washington Post*, 16 December 2006.

Trescott, Jacqueline. "Kennedy Center Plans Festival as Olive Branch to Arab Culture." *Washington Post*, 28 April 2006.

Tristam, Pierre. "Black September: The Jordanian-PLO Civil War of 1970." ThoughtCo.com, 30 March 2017.

"The Truth about American Muslims." *New York Times*, 1 April 2011.

Tschannen, Rafiq. "List of cities in the European Union by Muslim population." *Muslim Times* (UK), 6 October 2013.

"Tunisia beach attack: State of emergency declared." BBC News, 4 July 2015.

"Tunisia Constituent Assembly Elections." International Republican Institute, 23 October 2011.

"Tunisia country profile." BBC News, 17 January 2017.

"Tunisia—Economy." Global Security, 20 January 2017.

"Tunisia—Socio-Economic Indicators." UNESCO Institute for Statistics, 2014.

"Tunisia 2015 International Religious Freedom Report." United States Department of State, Bureau of Democracy, Human Rights, and Labor, 2015.

"Tunisian Berber: Maintenance and Revitalization." Graduate Center, City University of New York, 2015.

"Tunisian women free to marry non-Muslims." BBC News, 15 September 2017.

"2015 Sees Dramatic Spike in Islamic Extremism Arrests." Anti-Defamation League, 21 March 2016.

"The 2015 Arab Opinion Index: Arab Public Attitudes Toward Democracy." Arab Center, Washington, D.C., 7 March 2016.

"UAE committee on sustainable development goals announced." *The National* (Canada), 14 February 2017.

"UAE tops economic freedom index in Mideast." Trade Arabia News Service (Bahrain), 16 February 2017.

"UK action to combat Daesh." UK Government, no date.

Umana, Felipe. "Arab Spring Turns to Winter in Much of the Middle East, North Africa." Fragile States Index, 17 June 2015.

"UN delivers medicine to Yemen's besieged Taiz city." *Al-Jazeera*, 4 March 2017.

"UN Peacekeepers to Stay in South Sudan through 2017." VOA News, 16 December 2016.

"UN: Refugees from South Sudan cross 1.5 million mark." *Al-Jazeera*, 10 February 2017.

"UN report: Syrian government actions amount to 'extermination.'" *The Guardian* (UK), 8 February 2016.

"Unequal and Unprotected." Human Rights Watch, 19 January 2015.

"Unemployment is a source of instability in MENA [Middle East North Africa]." *The Arab Weekly* (UK), 29 January 2016.

"UNICEF Iraq Monthly Humanitarian Situation Report, January 2017." Relief Web, 6 March 2017.

"United Arab Emirates." Index of Economic Freedom, 2017.

"United Arab Emirates 2017." The World Factbook, Central Intelligence Agency, 22 February 2017.

"United States Internet Users." Internet Live Stats, 2016.

"Unmarried Childbearing." Centers for Disease Control and Intervention, 2008.

"Urbanization." The World Factbook, Central Intelligence Agency, 2017.

"U.S.-Bahrain Free Trade Agreement." Council on Foreign Relations, 11 January 2006.

"US lifts 20-year economic embargo on Sudan." *Al-Jazeera*, 14 January 2017.

"U.S. Navy destroyer is sent to patrol off coast of Yemen after Iranian-backed militia's suicide attack on Saudi warship." *Daily Mail* (UK), 3 February 2017.

"U.S. Public Diplomacy in the Middle East on New Course." Layalina Productions, Inc., December 2009.

Valosik, Vicki. "Arabic is Blooming." *International Educator*, January-February 2017.

Vick, Karl. "Yemen Walks Tightrope in Terrorism Stance." *Washington Post*, 29 September 2001.

Viswanathan, Gautam. "Gender parity in education a positive sign." *Pressreader, Times of Oman*, 19 March 2017.

Voll, John O., Foreword to *The Gulf and the Struggle for Hegemony*. Washington, D.C.: Middle East Institute, 2016.

Von Mittelstaedt, Juliane, and Samiha Shafy. "How Working Women are Remaking Saudi Arabia." *Spiegel Online* (Germany), 23 June 2015.

Wachiaya, Catherine. "Number of refugees fleeing South Sudan tops 1.5 million." UNHCR [United Nations High Commissioner for Refugees], 10 February 2017.

Walker, Lesley. "Qatar home to highest proportion of employed women in the Gulf." *Doha News*, 15 March 2016.

Walker, Martin. "The World's New Numbers." *Wilson Quarterly*, Spring 2009.

Ward, Christopher. "Water Crisis in Yemen." Lecture, St. Anthony's College, Oxford, 4 June 2015.

Warrick, Joby. "Bahrain ends state of emergency, vows talks on political reform." *Washington Post*, 1 June 2011.

Werleman, C. J. "Starbucks, McDonalds, and Anti-Americanism in the Middle East." *Middle East Eye* (UK), 8 January 2015.

"West Bank." The World Factbook, Central Intelligence Agency, 3 May 2011.

"What's become of Egypt's Mohammed Morsi?" BBC News, 22 November 2016.

"Where We Work." UNRWA [United Nations Relief and Works Agency], 2014.

Whitaker, Brian. "Why the Rules of Racism Are Different for Arabs." *The Guardian* (UK), 18 August 2000.

Whitehead, Frederika. "Water scarcity in Yemen: the country's forgotten conflict." *The Guardian* (UK), 2 April 2015.

"Why Do They Hate Us? The Forbidden Answer." *News and Politics*, 2 November 2010.

"Why is America the Target of Militant Islam?" *Frontline*, PBS (Public Broadcasting Service), October 2001.

"Why is there a war in Syria?" BBCNews, 13 March 2017.

Wike, Richard, Bruce Stokes, and Jacob Poushter. "America's Global Image." Pew Research Center, 23 June 2015.

Wildman, Sarah. "Third Way Speaks to Europe's Young Muslims." *International Reporting Project*, Johns Hopkins School of Advanced International Studies, Spring 2003.

Williams, Armstrong. "No Excuse for Anti-Americanism." *Townhall*, 1 June 2004.

Williams, Daniel. "Unveiling Islam: Author Challenges Orthodox Precepts." *Washington Post*, 7 March 2005.

Wilson, Scott. "Shiites See an Opening in Saudi Arabia." *Washington Post*, 28 February 2005.

Willis, David K. "The Impact of Islam." *Christian Science Monitor* weekly international edition, 18–24 August 1984.

Wintour, Patrick. "ISIS loses control of Libyan city of Sirte." *The Guardian* (UK), 5 December 2016.

Wodak, Ruth. *The Politics of Fear: What Right-Wing Populist Discourses Mean*. New York: Sage Publications, 2015.

"Women are taking over Saudi Arabia's workforce." *Fortune*, 10 August 2015.

"Women in National Parliaments." Inter-Parliamentary Union (Geneva), 1 May 2017.

"Women's Rights in the Middle East and North Africa: Citizenship and Justice (Palestinian Authority and Israeli-Occupied Territories)." Freedom House, 2011.

"Worldwide Suicide Rates." Suicide and Mental Health Association International, February 2005.

Worth, Robert F. "Preaching Moderate Islam and Becoming a TV Star." *New York Times*, 3 January 2009.

Wright, Robin. "Inside the Mind of Hezbollah." *Washington Post*, 16 July 2006.

Wright, Robin. "Islam's Soft Revolution." *Time*, 30 March 2009.

Yaakoubi, Aziz, and Patrick Markey. "Moderate Moroccan Islamists win election, coalition talks seen tough." *World News*, Reuters, 8 October 2016.

Yahya, Harun. "Peaceful Coexistence in Morocco between Jews and Muslims." *Morocco World News*, 9 May 2016.

"Yemen: International Religious Freedom Report 2010." U.S. Department of State, 17 November 2010.

"Yemen: Overview." World Bank, 1 October 2016.

"Yemen People 2017." Theodora.com, 2017.

"Yemen: Worst Place to Live as a Woman." Borgen Project, November 2013.

"Yemen's Economic Outlook—Spring 2016." World Bank, 2016.

"Yemen's Hadi declares Sanaa 'occupied capital.'" *Middle East Monitor* (UK), 1 March 2015.

"Young and unmarried Yemeni women more likely to pursue career and financial independence." Institute for Women's Policy Research, 1 December 2010.

Younis, Mohamed. "Perceptions of Muslims in the United States: A Review." Gallup, Inc., 11 December 2015.

"Youth Unemployment Rate for the United Arab Emirates." FRED Economic Data, Economic Research (Federal Reserve Bank of St. Louis), 1 May 2017.

Zakaria, Sherouk. "UAE intensifies efforts for women's empowerment." *Khaleej Times* (Dubai), 6 February 2017.

Zaptia, Sami. "Hundreds of Libyan women receive entrepreneurship training—project extended to all Libya and into 2017." *Libya Herald*, 30 January 2017.

Zeitvotel, Karin, and Nabeel Biajo. "South Sudan Seen as One of the World's Most Corrupt Nations." VOA, 3 December 2014.

Ziad, Waleed. "Jihad's Fresh Face." *New York Times*, 16 September 2005.

Zoepf, Katherine. "Deprogramming Jihadists." *New York Times*, 9 November 2008.

Zogby, John. "American Muslim Poll, November-December 2001." Zogby International, 2001.

Zurutuza, Karlos. "Libyans fear ethnic conflict." *Al-Jazeera*, 6 January 2015.

INDEX

eloquence of speech, 87–89
embracing, 26
emotion, 17–22
employees
    criticism of, 12–13
    intermediaries, 13
Esposito, John, 111
etiquette in Arab culture, 55–57
euphemisms, 91–92
Europe
    image of Arabs in, 138–142
    Muslims in, 129–133
    training programs for imams, 141
evil eye, 91, 93
extended family, xxxvi, 8, 25, 29, 63, 65,
    196
extremism, xiii, 96, 106, 109, 128, 156,
    206

F
face veil, 41
family
    child-rearing practices, 68–70
    children as reflection of, 69–70
    divorce, 67–68
    emotional dependence in, 65
    father's role in, 65–66
    loyalty to, 63–64
    marriage arrangement, 66–67
    mother's role in, 65–66
    obligations to, 63–64
    privacy in, 49
    relations among members of, 65–66
    role of, 65–73
    sharing of information about, 8
    status in, 65
    talking about, 70–71
    women power in, 40
Family Code, 155
family honor, 33, 64
fatalism, 18
fate, 1
father, 65–66
fatwa, 200
female genital mutilation (FGM), xxxiv
Festival of Arab Culture, 138
"Five Pillars" of Islam, 73–76

food, 52–54, 56
France, 121, 130–133, 139–141, 149, 151,
    153, 155, 157, 173, 179–180, 206
Free Muslims Coalition Against
    Terrorism, 106
Free Syrian Army, 178
friendships
    business, 10–11
    concepts of, 5
    expectations of, 5
    introductions, 7–8
    loyalty in, 7
    office relations, 11–12
    reciprocal favors, 5–7
    requests in, 5–7
    visiting patterns, 8–10
fundamentalism, 95, 121. *See also* Islamic
    fundamentalism
fundamentalists, xxxiv, 78, 96–97, 122,
    156

G
Gabbay, Tiffany, 116
Gaza, 41, 182, 184–187, 219
gender roles, 44–45
Gendy, Khaled al, 105
General Union of Syrian Women, 37
generation gap, xxxiii
Germany, 130–132, 140, 157
Ghoneim, Wael, xii
gifts, 53, 56
girls, 69
Giuliani, Rudolph, 115
Goode Jr., Virgil, 135
Goodman, Paul, 115
goodwill, 7, 89–91, 143, 228–229
Graham, Franklin, 121
"Greater Middle East" or "New Middle
    East" proposal, 112–114
greeting
    description of, 11
    of guests, 47
    kissing as form of, 26
    social, 236–238
guests
    generosity to, 47
    good-byes to, 55–56

women *(Cont.)*
  leadership roles, 37–38
  in Lebanon, 177
  men and, interactions between, 33–35
  in Morocco, 36, 150
  names of, 31
  in Palestine, 186–187
  power in the family, 40
  in Qatar, 217
  right to vote, 38
  rights of, 36
  in Saudi Arabia, 202–203
  in slavery, 36
  status of, 35–38
  in Sudan, 172
  in Syria, 181
  in Tunisia, 36, 157–158
  in United Arab Emirates (UAE), 220–221
  wearing of the hijab, 40–43
  well-educated, 46
  Western, 45–46
  in Yemen, 209
words
  proverbs, 93–94
  used in speech, 91
  written, 92–93
workforce, women in, xxix, 37–39, 155, 162, 168, 177, 181, 187, 191, 196, 202, 216

workplace discrimination, 134–135
written words, 92–93

Y
Yemen, xxxi, 107, 204–210
  climate of, 208
  economy, 208
  ethnic groups in, 204
  extremism in, 206–207
  fertility rate, 209
  health facilities, 207
  Houthi-Saleh coup, 205–206
  literacy rate, 208
  new era rule of law, 205
  north and south of, 204
  phenomenon of al-Qaeda or Islamic State-style jihadism, 206
  poverty in, 208
  Sanaa city, 204–205, 207–208
  Sharia law, 204–205
  social practices in, 204
  Somali refugees in, 207
  status of women, 209
  water crisis in, 208–209
  Yemeni Revolution (2011), 205

Z
Zakat, 75
Zayd, Dr. Abu, 36
Zionism, xi, 71
Zogby, James, 135

✿ ✿ ✿ ✿ ✿ ✿ ✿ ✿ ✿ ✿ ✿ ✿ ✿ ✿ ✿ ✿ ✿

About the Author

Margaret K. Nydell, PhD, is a scholar of Standard Arabic and Arabic regional dialects. She travelled to all of the Arab countries in her work for the U.S. State Department, administering Arabic tests at U.S. embassies and consulates, while she was directing the Arabic-language institute in Tunis. She is a specialist in Arabic dialectology, and consulted widely for government agencies and private organizations on the topics of Arab culture and society.

She obtained a M.S. and PhD from Georgetown University and taught there after leaving the government. Dr. Nydell has lived and worked in Egypt, Tunisia, and Saudi Arabia. Her other books deal with Arabic linguistics and descriptions of six dialects.